Surfside 6

Surfside 6

Behind the Scenes in Miami Beach
Authorized by Daphne Dutton

BY

MICHAEL GREGG MICHAUD

2022

Surfside 6
Behind the Scenes in Miami Beach

Authorized by Daphne Dutton

© **Copyright 2022 by Michael Gregg Michaud**

Published in the United States of America by:

BearManor Media
1317 Edgewater Dr #110
Orlando FL 32804
bearmanormedia.com

Printed in the United States.

Typesetting and layout by DataSmith Solutions

Cover by DataSmith Solutions

ISBN — 978-1-62933-862-0

Production of the one-hour crime series, *Surfside 6*, began in May, 1960, on stages 20 and 24 at Warner Bros. Studios in Burbank, California. The premiere episode aired on October 3, 1960 at 8:30 pm on ABC-TV. The premiere episode of *Cheyenne* preceded the show, and the premiere of *Adventures in Paradise* followed at 9:30 pm. The network heavily promoted *Surfside 6* in the weeks leading up to the premiere. The television audience tuned in, but the critics tuned out. John P. Shanley wrote a withering review of the show for the *New York Times* on October 4th. "The cast of *Surfside 6* a weekly, hour-long TV crime series, is composed principally of muscular young men and supple young women. They seem to be desperately in need of acting lessons. But the sour performances are only part of the trouble. Some of the more cryptic dialogue almost required subtitles. The opening episode was clearly fashioned along lines similar to *Hawaiian Eye*. The heroes in *Surfside 6* (the title refers to a telephone number) are three boyish-looking private investigators living on a houseboat at Miami Beach. There is also a girl singer. The billing for her act read: 'Cha Cha O'Brien and Her Boom Boom Boys.' Cha Cha sang one song on the program, but her boys never showed. Lucky chaps."

Despite blisteringly bad reviews, television audiences loved the show. The handsome young men and women in bathing suits made the show very watchable. Seventy-four one-hour episodes of *Surfside 6* were completed. The series ended with its final broadcast on June 25, 1962.

Table of Contents

Margarita Sierra, Troy Donahue, Lee Patterson, Diane McBain, Van Williams.

WLOF-TV

MID-FLORIDA TV FAVORITE!

"SURFSIDE 6"

Monday—8:30 P.M.

Detective-action in glittering, glamorours, and exciting Miami Beach.

CHANNEL 9

Season 1

Surfside 6 board game.

Season 2

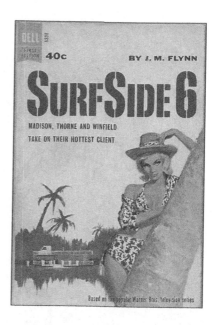

SURFSIDE 6

From the Warner Bros.
TV Show
"SURFSIDE 6"

Words and Music by
MACK DAVID and JERRY LIVINGSTON

TROY DONAHUE, LEE PATTERSON AND VAN WILLIAMS

PRICE 75¢ IN U.S.A.

M. WITMARK & SONS · NEW YORK, N. Y.

SURFSIDE 6

from the Warner Bros. T.V. Show
"SURFSIDE 6"

Tune Ukulele
G C E A

Words and Music by
MACK DAVID and
A.S.C.A.P.
JERRY LIVINGSTON
A.S.C.A.P.

*Symbols for Guitar and Banjo, Frames for Ukulele

Meet the Crew

The Producers

William T. Orr was born on September 27, 1917 in New York City. His birth name was William Ferdinand Quinn, Jr. His father was a businessman. His mother was actress Gladys Turner. Orr's parents divorced in 1923. Gladys married Morrison Orr the day after her divorce was finalized. When he was a youngster, Orr took his stepfather's last name, and the middle initial "T" in honor of his mother's maiden name. He attended Phillips Exeter Academy in Exeter, New Hampshire. Gladys' second marriage ended in 1936. When Orr was 18 years old, he moved to Los Angeles with his mother and younger sister.

William T. Orr.

His handsome good-looks earned him modeling jobs, and he began taking acting lessons. He appeared in the long-running, Los Angeles musical-comedy stage revue, *Meet the People*, hosted by Hollywood gossip columnist Louella Parsons. The show featured numerous variety acts, political satire, and songs. Orr made his mark in the show doing comic impersonations. In 1938, he signed a $300 per-week acting contract with Warner Bros. Studios.

Until 1945, he appeared in more than 20 short and feature films including *The Hardy's Ride High, The Mortal Storm, My Love Came Back, Honeymoon for Three, Thieves Fall Out, Three Sons o' Guns, Navy Blues, Unholy Partners, The Gay Sisters, The Big Street,* and *He Hired the Boss.* During World War II, he served as an officer in the Army Air Force's First Motion Picture Unit, producing and appearing in training films at the Hal Roach Studios in Culver

City. During that time, he worked with other film actors, and become lifelong friends with Ronald Reagan, William Holden, and Alan Ladd.

In 1945, Orr married actress Joy Page, Jack Warner's stepdaughter. Jack Warner hired him to be his personal assistant in 1946. Hollywood columnists heralded the news with the headline, "The Son-in-Law Also Rises." But Orr quickly proved to his critics that he was deserving of the job. He had an eye for talent, and worked closely with the studio Casting Department on the lookout for new artists. He brought James Dean, Paul Newman, and Marlon Brando, among many others, to the studio, and even secured a few small film roles for his mother. Orr began his producing career in 1955 with the series, *Warner Bros. Presents*, produced for ABC-TV broadcast. The program presented three rotating productions based on Warner film classics, *Casablanca*, *King's Row*, and *Cheyenne*, a forgotten 1929 silent film. Of the three "chapters," *Cheyenne* became an audience favorite. Orr developed and produced *Cheyenne*, the Western-themed drama that starred Clint Walker, from 1955 until 1962. The show was the first hour-long Western, and the first hour-long drama with recurring characters that lasted more than one year. He also produced the series, *Conflict* (1956-57), and the 1958 feature film-noir, *Girl on the Run*.

Ron Simon, curator of television at the Museum of Television and Radio in New York City, said, "It took a year or so to get down the budget and organization to adapt Warner Bros. film techniques to television, and Orr was pivotal in doing that. Orr was pivotal in finding new stars for television. His career signaled how important television would become in the studio system. Television began as a step-child, but because of Orr, it became equal with film in creating revenue and jobs for the studio."

Orr became the first head of the Warner Bros. Television Division. His career as a television Executive Producer is unequaled, and the stuff of Hollywood legend. His producer credits at Warner Bros. include: *The Alaskans* (1959-60), *Colt .45* (1957-60), *Bourbon Street Beat* (1959-60), *Sugarfoot* (1957-61), *The Roaring 20's* (1960-62), *Maverick* (1957-62), *Bronco* (1958-62), *Lawman* (1958-62), *Surfside 6* (1960-62), *Room for One More* (1962), *The Gallant Men* (1955-63), *Hawaiian Eye* (1959-63), *The Dakotas* (1962-63), *77 Sunset Strip* (1958-63), *Temple Houston* (1963-64), *No Time for Sergeants* (1964-65), *Wendy and Me* (1964-65), *F Troop* (1965-66), *Hank* (1965-66), and *Mister Roberts* (1965-66). In 1959, Orr won a Golden Globe Award for Television Achievement.

Most actors found Orr easy to work with, and enjoyed his professional loyalty. But in the late 1950s, he worked closely with Jack Warner to create unfair contracts, and entered into crippling wage and royalty disputes with some of the studio's biggest stars including Clint Walker and James Garner, causing both to walk off their respective series. Orr had a reputation for running his programs on restrictively tight budgets, and sometimes compromised the integrity of his series by recycling scripts from one program to another by simply switching character names and locales.

Orr ended his working relationship with Warner Bros. in 1965 to pursue independent production. For a short time, he worked with Frank Sinatra's Essex Productions. In 1970, he and his wife divorced. His only post-Warner production credit is the 1973 feature film *Wicked, Wicked.* "I liked Bill very much," Diane McBain said. "He was very good to me. And loyal. I met him when I had my first acting role in *Maverick.* In the early 1960s, he also supervised the studio feature film productions. He wanted me to be in the movie *Sex and the Single Girl,* mostly to keep me working at Warner, but it wasn't for me. That's when I left the studio. Years later, he offered me a role in *Wicked, Wicked.* It was an awful movie, and I did it because I needed the money. And I appreciated his offer. But, it was so bad, it was his last producing credit, and it was another step to end my film career, too."

William T. Orr died of natural causes at his Los Angeles home on December 25, 2002. Despite their divorce, Orr and his former wife remained close, and lived together for the last few years of his life. Orr was 85 years old. He was survived by his ex-wife, his sister, a daughter, and his son, producer Gregory Orr.

Howard "Howie" Horwitz was born in New York City on May 22, 1918. In 1942, he married Harriett Feinberg, and the couple eventually had four children. He moved his family to California, and in the early 1950s, he worked at Paramount Pictures in Hollywood as an assistant to producer George Stevens on several of his films including *A Place in the Sun* (1951), and *Shane* (1953). In 1956, Horwitz moved to Universal where he produced several films including *Appointment with a Shadow* (1957), *Slim Carter* (1957), and *Money, Women and Guns* (1958).

Howie Horwitz.

Beginning in 1958, Horwitz found his greatest success in television production when he moved to Warner Bros. Studios. Working closely with William Orr, his producing credits include *77 Sunset Strip* (1958-63), *Maverick* (1961), *Surfside 6* (1961-62), and *Hawaiian Eye* (1961-63). His later production credits include several television series including *The Immortal* (1970-71), and *Banacek* (1972-74). Horwitz produced numerous made-for-television movies including *Evil Roy Slade*, *The Questor Tapes*, *The California Kid*, *A Cry for Help*, and *Stranded*. His most memorable production credit is the classic, camp/comedy series, *Batman*. He produced all 118 episodes originally broadcast from 1966 until 1968.

"I liked Howie," Diane said. "He was funny, and had a great sense of humor. I did two two-part *Batman* episodes at his offering. He's probably best remembered for producing *Batman*, and I'm probably best remembered by many for playing the role of Pinky Pinkston on the show."

Horwitz was nominated for two Emmy Awards for producing *Batman* (Outstanding Comedy Series, 1966), and *Baretta* (Outstanding Drama Series, 1976). Horwitz died on June 25, 1976 from injuries suffered in a fall while on holiday with his family in June Lake, California. He was survived by his wife of 34 years, four children, his niece actress/singer Leslie Gore, and his nephew composer Michael Gore. Howie Horwitz was 58 years old.

Jerome "Jerry" Davis was born on September 26, 1917 in New York City. His first screen writing credit was the 1950 feature film, *Duchess of Idaho*. His other film-writing credits include *Pagan Love Song*, *King Lady*, *The Devil Makes Three*, *Apache War Smoke*, *A Slight Case of Larceny*, *Cult of the Cobra*, *The Girl Rush*, and *Pardners*. Davis transitioned into writing for television in 1954. He wrote multiple episodes of *Climax!*, *The Donna Reed Show*, *Maverick*, *Bachelor Father*, *77 Sunset Strip*, *The Farmer's Daughter*, and *Harper Valley, P.T.A.*,

Jerry Davis.

among others. Davis began working with Orr in television production at Warner Bros. Studios in 1960. His numerous production credits include *Hawaiian Eye* (1960), *Bourbon Street Beat* (1960), *77 Sunset Strip* (1960), *The Roaring 20's* (1961), and *Surfside 6* (1960-61). Davis' post-Warner television production credits include *Bewitched* (1964-66), *That Girl* (1966-67), *The Ugliest Girl in Town* (1968-69), *The Good Guys* (1969-70), *Funny Face* (1971), *The Odd Couple* (1970-73), and *Throb* (1987-88), among others.

In 1954, Davis married singer/actress Marilyn Maxwell. The couple had one son. During their difficult divorce in 1960, Maxwell accused Davis in court of marrying her for her money. Davis retaliated by saying his wife had continued her long-time affair with Bob Hope well after their marriage.

Davis was nominated for an Emmy Award in 1964 for Outstanding Writing Achievement in Comedy for *The Farmer's Daughter*, and four Emmy Awards for producing Outstanding Comedy Series for *Bewitched* in 1966, *The Odd Couple* in 1971 and again in 1972, and Outstanding New Series for *The Odd Couple* in 1971.

Jerry Davis died at Cedars-Sinai Medical Center in Los Angeles on April 11, 1991, after suffering a stroke. The Beverly Hills resident was survived by four sons; Joshua, Anthony, television writer Jeffrey, and musician Matthew, and two grandchildren. Davis was 73 years old.

The Music Men

Jerry Livingston was born on March 25, 1909 in Denver, Colorado. He completed his first musical score while he was studying piano and music theory at the University of Arizona. In 1932, he moved to New York City where he found work as a pianist for dance orchestras. In 1940, he formed his own orchestra, and in 1941 established his own music publishing business. His music – composed with lyricist Mack David – was featured in the 1943 Broadway revue, *Bright Lights of 1944*. Mack David became his frequent writing partner. Livingston moved to Hollywood in 1949. He scored dozens of films. A few of his better known songs include "Mairzy Doats," "Under a Blanket of Blue," "She Broke My Heart in Three Places," and "It's the Talk of

Mack David, Al Hoffman, and Jerry Livingston.

the Town." Livingston and David wrote the musical score for the 1950 classic Disney animated film, *Cinderella*. The film featured many memorable songs including "A Dream Is a Wish Your Heart Makes," and the Academy Award-nominated song, "Bibbidi-Bobbidi-Boo." Livingston was nominated for an Academy Award a second time for writing the title song for the 1959 film, *The Hanging Tree*.

Television work dominated his creative efforts in the early 1960s. Livingston wrote the memorable theme songs for the Warner television productions: *Bronco, 77 Sunset Strip, Hawaiian Eye, Lawman, Bourbon Street*

Beat, and *Surfside 6.* He and Mack David also wrote the theme song, "This Is It," for *The Bugs Bunny Show.*

On Wednesday, February 17, 1965, Jerry Livingston's family grabbed front page news. For years, Livingston and his wife had struggled with their mentally ill son, Gary. The night before, Gary had tried to commit suicide. On Wednesday, Livingston went to his son's room at 1 p.m. to rouse him out of bed. Gary went berserk, grabbed a gun and fired at his father, shooting him in the arm. Livingston's wife, Ruth, ran upstairs when she heard the commotion and was shot in the chest by her son when she tried to enter his room. His parents escaped, and Gary barricaded himself in his bedroom. Ruth ran downstairs and out into the backyard where she collapsed under a tree. The police were called to the home at 626 North Rodeo Drive in Beverly Hills. Gary refused to come out of his room until several rounds of teargas were fired in through his bedroom window. When he finally exited the house in his pajamas, he told the police that he was seeing a psychiatrist. He said he resented his parents, and was mad because they were "bugging him to get out of bed." He had a 12-gauge shotgun, a .22 caliber revolver, and a .22 caliber rifle in his room. Gary was taken to the prison ward of Los Angeles Country Hospital. His parents recovered.

Livingston's final movie song-writing collaboration with Mack David earned the pair another Academy Award nomination for Best Song for "The Ballad of Cat Ballou" from the 1965 film *Cat Ballou.* The composing pair also wrote the music for the 1973 Broadway show, *Molly.*

Perhaps Livingston's best known pop song is "The Twelfth of Never," a hit for Johnny Mathis. Livingston was a former president of the Songwriters Guild of America, and was inducted into the Songwriters Hall of Fame in 1981.

On July 1, 1987, Jerry Livingston suffered a fatal heart attack at his Beverly Hills home at the age of 78. He was survived by his wife, Ruth, his son Dennis, and two grandchildren.

Mack David was born on July 5, 1912 in New York City. He attended Cornell University and St. John's University Law School in pursuit of a law degree before he developed an interest in music. David joined ASCAP in 1934 when he began writing songs for films. He also wrote music for New York's Tin Pan Alley. In the early 1940s, David moved to Hollywood to work in the film industry. He composed hundreds of songs, and was nominated for eight Academy Awards throughout his decade's long career. His nominations for songs include "Bibbidi-Bobbidi-Boo" (1950), "The Hanging Tree" (1959), "Bachelor in Paradise" (1961), "Hush, Hush, Sweet Charlotte" (1964), "The Ballad of Cat Ballou" (1965), and "My Wishing Doll" (1966). His many collaborators include Jerry Livingston, Alex Kramer, Joan Whitney, Frankie Carle, Count Basie, Burt Bacharach, Ernest Gold, Elmer Bernstein, Frank De Vol, and Henry Mancini.

Working with Jerry Livingston, David composed the theme songs for numerous television series including *Casper the Friendly Ghost, 77 Sunset Strip, Hawaiian Eye, Bourbon Street Beat, Surfside 6,* and *The Bugs Bunny Show.* He shared writing credits with Livingston for the Broadway productions *Bright Lights of 1944,* and *Molly.* He was the featured lyricist for the 1966 Broadway concert show, *Gilbert Becaud on Broadway,* and his song, "I'm Just a Lucky So-and-So," was featured in the 1981 Broadway hit revue, *Sophisticated Ladies.*

David's many popular songs include "I Don't Care if The Sun Don't Shine," "Baby It's You," "It Must Be Him," "Candy," "Lili Marlene," "So This Is Love," "The Willow," "Take Me," "Just a Kid Named Joe," "Cherry Pink and Apple Blossom White," "Born to Be Blue," and "La Vie en Rose." He was inducted into the Songwriters Hall of Fame in 1975. That same year, he patented an electronic system for composing songs from fractional recordings. The system included playback units which stored records of lyrics and melodies. The operator could select words and music that fit together, and record the combination.

Mack David suffered a heart attack and died in Rancho Mirage on December 30, 1993 at the age of 81. He was survived by his wife of many years, a son and a daughter, two grandchildren, and his younger brother, composer and lyricist Hal David.

The Make-up Man

Gordon Bau was born in Minnesota on July 1, 1907. In the late 1930s, Bau, and his older brother George, worked at a California company called Rubbercraft. The company specialized in creating rubber parts for industrial purposes. While there, the brothers created rubber eye prosthetics designed to make American Hollywood actors look Asian. In time, they perfected the use and application of foam rubber for film make-up. George created a light weight, porous rubber that moved and wrinkled like human skin. The first of Gordon's more than 300 film and television make-up credits was the 1937 film, *The Life of Emile Zola.* The brothers created the ground-breaking makeup for Charles Laughton in the 1939 film, *The Hunchback of Notre Dame.*

Gordon Bau, and friend.

During World War II, Gordon created the earliest prosthetics for soldiers injured and disfigured in battle.

In the late 1940s, Gordon became the make-up supervisor at Warner Bros. Studios. George supervised the prosthetics laboratory at the studio. Gordon's film credits include *Auntie Mame, Rio Bravo, Yellowstone Kelly, Sergeant Rutledge, Susan Slade, The Days of Wine and Roses, Kisses for My President, Who's Afraid of Virginia Woolf?, Dirty Harry,* and *The All American Boy,* among many others.

In 1953, Gordon told Lydia Lane, writing for the *Los Angeles Times,* "The Hollywood make-up men have had a far-reaching influence which can be traced with interest. The trend in make-up today is toward naturalness and I think this started with Technicolor. With color films it is necessary to use a base which is very light in comparison to the heavy corrective make-up we use for black and white."

His television credits at Warner Bros. include *Conflict, Cheyenne, Maverick, Sugarfoot, Colt .45, Bronco, 77 Sunset Strip, Lawman, The Alaskans, Bourbon Street Beat, Hawaiian Eye, The Roaring 20's, Surfside 6, The Gallant Men, The Dakotas, Wendy and Me,* and *F Troop.*

"Gordy supervised my make-up for all my films at Warner," Diane recalled," and all the *Surfside* shows. He was a great story-teller, and he had such an unbelievable history working in Hollywood for so many years. Sometimes he talked under his breath about certain stars. He always made me laugh when he talked about Bette Davis. They fought over her choice of lipstick and how she over-applied it to her lips. He was very funny. And he did a wonderful job. He had a lot of standard rules he used. I remember he said, 'Rouge should never be obvious. If you notice it, you're wearing too much.' Words to live by."

In 1969, Gordon Bau entered into a short-lived marriage. He retired in 1973, and died in Los Angeles on July 21, 1975 at the age of 68.

Meet the Cast

Troy Donahue, Margarita Sierra, Lee Patterson, Diane McBain, Van Williams.

Troy Donahue

Troy Donahue played the role of Sandy Winfield II, the first of the three private detectives. He was born Merle Johnson, Jr. on January 27, 1936 in New York City. His father, Frederick Merle Johnson, was a former newsreel editor for Paramount, and later became an advertising executive at General Motors, producing the company's promotional motion pictures. His mother, Edith Frederickson, was a former New York stage actress. She was nineteen years old when she gave birth to Troy. He had one sister, Eve Johnson, eight years his junior.

Troy Donahue.

His mother missed performing, and took him to see many Broadway shows from an early age. "I guess that's where it all started, this acting bug," Troy said. "My parents both loved show business and everything about it. Me, I loved everything about *New York*."

When Troy was six, his father bought a five-acre estate with a sprawling sixteen-room house in Bayport, Long Island. "My father commuted sixty miles each way to work every day," Troy recalled.

Troy and his father spent a lot of time sailing in their family boat in Great South Bay, and fishing in the nearby creek. "My dad was my best friend. My mother read romance novels to me all the time," he said. "I think it affected me emotionally. I've been in love with *someone* ever since I can remember."

When Troy was eleven years old, his father was diagnosed with Lou Gehrig's disease. Mr. Johnson suffered terribly, and physically disintegrated for three years. During that time, Troy became the "man of the house," responsible for watching over his little sister, comforting his mother, and helping her at home. "My dad lost his ability to speak," Troy recalled. "He spent the last eight months of his life at St. Alban's Hospital in New York." Frederick Johnson died on December 5, 1950.

Troy was fourteen and a sophomore at Bayport High when his father died. He was deeply affected by his father's death, but put on a brave face for his mother and little sister. Troy was never a good student. Trying to cope with the sad situation at home, his grades plummeted. "My father's death left me the man of the house, but I wasn't up to the responsibility. I was impatient to be grown up, and it just made me wild. I needed a strong hand to smack me down, but it wasn't there any longer."

He began to hang around with a wild bunch of kids. "I didn't seem to care about anything," he said. He and his friends began drinking, and things got out of hand.

Fearful that her son would get himself into serious trouble, Edith decided to send him to New York Military Academy when he was sixteen. Surprisingly, the idea made sense to Troy. "I could see myself going right down the drain in Bayport," he said. "I was lazy, wild, spoiled and off the track. I knew I needed straightening out with formal discipline."

New York Military Academy is a top-rated military prep school in Cornwall-on-Hudson. He liked military life so well that he considered attending West Point and making the Army his career.

Troy's grades did not improve, but his sense of discipline did. He made cadet lieutenant, and excelled at sports. He played on the academy basketball and football teams, and set school records with his high jumping on the track team.

One day, a fellow cadet put a brick in the jumping pit as a prank. Troy landed on it with one knee. His knee was knocked out of joint, and the cartilage was seriously torn. He wore a leg cast for many weeks. Unable to participate in sports, he knew he couldn't attend West Point with his poor grades alone. Later, he was ruled "4-F" when he tried to enlist for military service.

Days before his scheduled graduation in June, 1954, Troy was informed that he had failed one too many classes, and had not earned enough credits to graduate. "I could hang around for a few days," Troy recalled, "and go through the graduation ceremonies and get a blank diploma. But, no thanks."

For a short time, Troy worked on a road crew in the area, but soon moved to New York City where he got a job as a bicycle messenger at Sound Masters, Inc. a film company has father had founded. With his meager salary, he stayed in cheap hotel rooms and flop houses. "Walk-ups. Walk-ins, walk-arounds, cold waters, cold-floors – everything," he recalled. "Six times I got kicked out for not paying my rent." He enrolled in the Theater Wing Workshop taught by Ezra Stone, an old family friend. At night, he took extension courses in journalism at Columbia University. He had small roles in summer stock productions at the Bucks County Playhouse and the Sayville Playhouse.

"Somehow, I learned to carry a tune in a tub and got a job singing one summer with a dance band at a resort. Next, I started the summer theater bit. You work like a dog at anything they throw your way. In the winter, I grabbed jobs waiting on tables in Manhattan so I could eat something, and go back to Ezra Stone's acting classes."

His mother sold the family estate in Bayport. She and Troy's little sister moved into a fashionable apartment on Riverside Drive in Manhattan. He never moved in with them, although his mother coaxed him to come home. "I was living on my own," he said, "if you call that living, but I needed to make it on my own." He did drop in whenever he could to get a good meal, though. "I used to get up in the morning, walk to the corner and buy a ten-cent hot-dog. Ever eat a hot dog with mustard for breakfast? It makes you so sick you don't want to see food the rest of the day!"

Troy was basically shy, and not confident with his acting abilities. At the workshop, he was surrounded by more serious and accomplished young actors in class. "They were all in a little too deep for me," he recalled. "I felt like an outsider."

His mother offered to pay for him to go to college full time, but he began to think about Hollywood. "I'd seen James Dean in *East of Eden*," he recalled, "and I decided that I could do what he did."

Troy wrote a letter to Darrell Brady, an old friend and working associate of his father, who managed a commercial film company in Los Angeles. Brady wrote back and offered him a job with his company. Brady also invited him to stay at his home until he found a proper place to live.

In February, 1956, Troy and his sister piled into a Chevy Bel Air convertible and struck out on the cross-country drive to California. Their mother, Edith, would join them after concluding her affairs in New York. Troy and Eve moved into the Brady's house in Calabasas in the San Fernando Valley. Malibu beach was a short distance away to the west by way of scenic Malibu Canyon Road. Troy went to work cutting film, and spent his free time surfing in Malibu. Edith arrived in a short time, and rented a comfortable house in Malibu for herself and Eve. Troy rented a nearby garage apartment. He bought a used MG to drive back and forth to work. "I didn't have any real plan," Troy recalled. "I didn't really know what to do, so on the weekends I'd hang around the studio district. I guess I wanted to be discovered."

One evening, Troy sat alone at the bar in The Golden Pheasant restaurant in the San Fernando Valley. It was considered an "industry watering hole," and he often had a few drinks there in the evenings after work. He wore levis, and a worn leather jacket over a white T-shirt. He was suntanned, and his sun-bleached hair was unkempt. "I could have been a beach bum or a truck driver having a beer," he recalled. "Turned out I was rigged perfectly for a young actor."

James Sheldon, a television director who had worked a couple of times with James Dean, and William Asher, a producer at Columbia Studios, were seated at a nearby table. Sheldon was gay, and Troy reminded him of Dean. "He was a cute, nineteen-year old blonde boy," Sheldon recalled. He and Asher approached Troy at the bar, and asked if he was an actor. Troy said he wanted to act, and lied about doing theater work in New York City. Sheldon retrieved a television script he had in his car and gave it to Troy. He told him to learn some lines and read for him and Asher the next day at Columbia Studios in Hollywood. "I knew James Sheldon worked with James Dean," Troy said. "I was impressed. And nervous."

Troy worked on the lines all night, and read for the two men the next morning, but it was a disaster. "I was terrible," Troy recalled. Sheldon said, "Troy wasn't very bright. And he didn't have enough ability to last. I told him to study with Sandy Meisner, but he wasn't interested." Nevertheless, Asher introduced him to Benno Schneider, Columbia's resident drama coach. Schneider spent a few hours with him, and set up a screen test for the following Monday morning.

He intended to spend the weekend working on his screen test lines, but a buddy who had just passed the bar exam wanted to go out and celebrate. Troy didn't need much encouragement to hit a bar, so they spent the evening drinking at The Golden Pheasant. Around one in the morning, they stumbled out of the bar. Troy climbed behind the wheel of the car, and they started off for his place near the beach. However, he lost control of the light weight MG, and skidded off Malibu Canyon Road. Fortunately, his friend was thrown clear of the car before it skidded off a steep ledge. The car plummeted forty feet down into the canyon before smashing into a tree. "They say my face was just two blue eyes staring out of a bucket of red paint," Troy said.

Troy suffered two cracked knee caps, a serious concussion, a bruised spinal cord, a crushed kidney, and severe shock. He lost a tooth in the crash, and needed forty stitches in his scalp, and ten in his nose. When Troy finally regained consciousness, the doctor told him he was lucky to be alive. His mother spent a month with him in the hospital. What he was most concerned about, however, was missing his scheduled screen test at Columbia.

After recovering from his injuries, a mutual friend introduced Troy to a young actress named Fran Bennett. Fran was represented by the infamously predatory gay agent, Henry Willson. She was certain Willson could help her new friend. "I knew what Henry could do with Troy," Fran recalled. "He was just Henry's cup of tea."

One day Fran frantically called Troy. "Run like hell to Henry Willson's office and meet me there. Hurry, he's leaving for Hawaii right now." Troy

arrived as Willson was leaving his office. They spoke for a few minutes. Willson said, "Go out to Universal. Say I sent you."

Troy *did* get a screen test at Universal-International. When Willson returned from Hawaii, he called Troy and told him that the studio offered him a contract, and he wanted to represent the young actor. Troy escorted Willson to many "important" Hollywood parties, where the agent introduced his new client to show business insiders. Like he had for all of this clients, Willson actually changed Troy's name – he was until then known by his real name, Merle Johnson. Willson christened him "Troy Donahue."

Troy recalled, "My mother and sister loved my new name from the start, and never call me anything but Troy."

He explained, "I didn't sign with Henry until I had gotten my own contract with Universal. Henry was still very well connected in Hollywood, but I didn't want to be indebted to him. He has this reputation." Willson urged Troy to be "single" for publicity purposes, and introduced him to his social circle which included many gay producers, directors, and actors including Tab Hunter and Rock Hudson. Whatever his personal relationship with Willson entailed, Troy's involvement with the agent haunted him for the rest of his life, and caused people to speculate about his sexuality.

With his new $125 weekly salary at Universal-International, Troy bought himself a red Porsche. After a few uncredited roles in U-I productions, Troy's first credited role was in the 1957 film, *The Tarnished Angels*. During the next eighteen months, he appeared in many forgettable films. "In most of those early films I did for Universal," Troy said, "if you went out for popcorn, you missed me."

He worked steadily, actually appearing in sixteen feature films at U-I. But he partied as hard as he worked. He spent more money than he earned, drank heavily with his friends, and drove around Hollywood like a madman. He collected four speeding tickets in quick succession, and spent two weeks in Los Angeles County jail. "Frankly," he said, "it scared the living daylights out of me. It's just a sample of what can happen to someone like me, all souped up and no place to go. Keep me busy and I work hard. Idle me down and I have the instincts of a beachcomber."

During the 1950s, the popularity of television undercut movie theater revenues. In 1959, unsatisfied with his performance, Universal dropped Troy. He guest-starred in a couple of television shows, but it wasn't enough for him to survive. He slept in his car many nights. "When you're hungry," he said, "you don't muff the next chance."

Producer Ross Hunter, a friend of Rock Hudson and Henry Willson, offered Troy a small but memorable role in a feature film called, *Imitation of Life*. The movie was based on Fannie Hurst's controversial novel about race, class, and gender. The film was a hit and finally gave Troy the attention he needed.

Willson immediately submitted Troy for the male lead in a film at Warner Bros. titled *A Summer Place*. Delmer Daves, the screenwriter and director, recalled, "There were eight other good actors after that job. But the sensitive, groping boy we were after was Troy Donahue, right out of life. He didn't have to act."

Troy's leading lady was Sandra Dee. "The hardest thing about *A Summer Place*," he recalled, "was believing it was happening to me. At U-I, I'd never got anywhere near Sandra Dee."

The story, considered shocking at the time, concerned the ill-fated love of a teenage boy and girl on summer holiday in Maine, that produces an unwanted pregnancy.

"When I found out I was going to do *A Summer Place*, and that Sandra was going to do it, too, I was very excited. I met her for the first time outside of makeup. Sandra and I loved working together. She was professional. But for me, I was full of myself at that time. I thought I was indestructible. I had this glorious career that would never end. And I would do all the films that Redford and Beatty did. I had several girlfriends. I was smoking and doping and drinking in front of the camera, off the camera, wherever. It enabled me to function. I was fearful. I lacked confidence."

The studio was impressed with Troy's potential appeal and signed him to a long-term contract at $1,000 per week. He was busied with television assignments. Warner Bros. had a production/distribution deal with ABC-TV, and produced dozens of television series. He played guest-roles on *Bronco*, *Maverick*, *Sugarfoot*, *Colt .45*, *77 Sunset Strip*, *The Alaskans*, and *Lawman*, and he was seventh billed in his first U-I contract motion picture,

The Crowded Sky, a disaster film about a Navy jet and a commercial airliner headed for a mid-air collision.

Released in November, 1959, *A Summer Place* was a soap operatic-romantic box-office smash. The trajectory of his career changed dramatically. He became a movie idol overnight. Fan clubs sprang up everywhere. He received thousands of fan letters at the studio. Delmer Daves recalled, "It was cataclysmic! The film was held over for five, six, seven weeks wherever it played!"

Troy won the 1960 Golden Globe Award for Most Promising Newcomer – Male, for his performance in *A Summer Place*. At last he felt some level of security with his career. He rented a small house near a spacious apartment he had helped secure for his mother and sister. He was twenty-three years old.

He starred in his next feature film, *Parrish*, with Claudette Colbert, Dean Jagger, Connie Stevens and Diane McBain. "I first met Troy when we were working on *Parrish* in the spring of 1960," Diane remembered. "That was my second film. It was shot at the studio, and we were on location in Connecticut. I celebrated my nineteenth birthday there. He was so handsome, and a very sweet, soft-spoken guy."

Troy and Diane McBain in *Parrish*.

During the making of *Parrish*, Troy and Diane McBain – both under contract to Warner Brothers – were told they would next star in a detective series produced by Warner Brothers for ABC-TV. Troy was cast in the role of the charming, directionless rich heir, Sandy Winfield II. Despite his misgivings, but with Henry Willson's urging, Troy began work on *Surfside 6* in May 1960. Troy recalled, "Henry tried to spin it. He told me *Surfside 6* was a good idea! TV is where it's at! I knew he didn't believe it."

Diane McBain said, "We both thought it was a step backwards, but we weren't *asked* to do the series, we were *told*. The studio reasoned that together, Troy and I were the star power driving the show."

Troy's rise in Hollywood was meteoric. Fran Bennett said that Troy was unaffected by his sudden success and celebrity. "He hasn't changed in any respect," she recalled. "There's no one I am more at ease with. I can't believe it."

"I still have my faults," Troy said. "I'm a financial idiot. I'm disorganized. I put things off. Basically I'm lazy. I drive too fast. I like sports too much, fun too much, nice things too much. But I think some of the rough edges are rubbed off at last. I've matured in several ways. I'm serious about my work and luckily I love it. To me, the whole thing is a big, wonderful ball. I can't wait for each day. I might be a fair enough actor someday, but I've got a long way to go."

His serial dating reputation was fodder for the gossip columnists. He was linked to dozens of starlets. The young secretaries at the studio considered Troy's charm to be his greatest asset. They nicknamed him, "The Blond Cobra."

"Whoever knows when love really hits you," Troy said. "I've always found I needed a girl to help me. When I was young, it was my mother. Then it was my kid sister, Evy. When I came to California there was Judi Meredith. I've sort of gone steady many times. I even asked Nan Morris to marry me. We're kind of still seeing each other. But, somehow, I just can't make the marriage scene."

Delmer Daves knew him like a father knows a son. "Troy has no self-protective devices whatever," he said. "He has no guard up, no guile. He is embarrassingly honest. He almost offers you his heart. People can get hurt this way. He has the unmistakable stamp of a well and expensively brought up boy. He has manners. He dresses well, swims, sails, rides, plays tennis – all the way upper-middle class boys with advantages do."

Lee Patterson, Troy's friend and co-star on *Surfside 6*, said, "You meet Troy and his manner seems to say, 'Hello – come on in!' So you do."

Troy's public love affairs ran hot and cold. "I've simmered down," he joked, but several fellow girlfriends had complaints about the way they were treated.

Judi Meredith once lived in an apartment above Troy. "I was the first girl Troy ever dated in this town," she recalled. She was "officially" engaged to him for a short time, but broke up with him because, she said, "he was too rough and too possessive. One night, he stormed into my place when I was about to go to bed, made a jealous scene, and pushed my face into a glass covered picture. That was it for me and Troy."

A couple of years after their romance cooled, Judi and Troy established a friendship. "I consider myself much more a friend to Troy than a romantic interest," she said, "and besides, he's a better friend than a boyfriend."

Nan Morris had a rocky romance with Troy that was ultimately sabotaged by his chronic infidelity. "I could only keep up with who else he was dating while we were together by reading the gossip columns," she said.

"Girls get what they ask for from Troy," Fran Bennett said. "And in one way or another, most of them ask. Troy doesn't have to chase them. It's usually vice-versa. But don't think Troy's not perfectly aware of his charm. He uses it to get what he wants. He has turned it on plenty to get over rough spots – especially back when he was broke, and the girl had a steady job."

One "rough spot" threatened to end his career. In 1956, Troy had met a young actress named Lili Kardell at a Halloween party at the home of the infamous astrologer to the Hollywood stars, Carroll Righter. Fate reunited Troy and Lili a few years later in August, 1960. Troy was at home one rainy night and noticed someone sitting alone in a parked car under the adjacent apartment complex carport. He dashed out in the pouring rain to see if the person was in distress, and was shocked to discover Lili sitting behind the wheel. She explained that she was waiting for a friend to get home who was running late. Troy invited her into his house to warm up. They talked until dawn. Lili said their romance began that stormy night.

The couple spent much time together, and even traveled together a few times. Lili recalled their first Christmas holiday as a couple. They shared an extravagant Beverly Hills shopping spree on Rodeo Drive. Troy shopped for his mother, sister, and grandmother. "Troy goes mad in stores," Lili said. "He's like a child. He wants to buy everything. When he went shopping, I'd tag along to keep him from going wild!"

Their courtship was fodder for gossip columns and movie magazines. After a few months, and despite the fact that Troy was seeing other women, he asked Lili to marry him in January, 1961. They got engaged at the eighteenth hole of the El Dorado golf course in Palm Springs.

Lili thought they were dating exclusively. She told a reporter, "Troy has his faults. He has to learn the hard way: you can't tell him anything. He has a temper that flares up, and fizzles out as fast. We've had our fights. If something about you bothers him though, he lets you know right away. *He'll* never get ulcers. He has a fine mind, but he isn't using it *fully*. There are a lot of things he can do if he ever buckles down to do them. With women, Troy likes to be the boss. Sometimes he's thoughtless, but he's sympathetic and kind, too. Troy needs a little of everything in a woman – sister, mother, sweetheart. He's possessive. At the same time, he doesn't like to be possessed. But Troy wants a deep relationship with a woman, and he's found he can't have that with several at a time. I think he'll make a wonderful husband if he isn't forced."

At the time, Troy said, "An engagement is a time in which two people who think they want to get married go through a period of finding out whether they're actually ready for such a move. It is a period of great fondness, closeness and mutual understanding. If this period doesn't continue, then they become just friends. A year ago I wasn't mature enough."

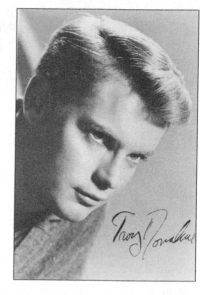

Troy's idea of what an engagement meant did not dissuade Lili. "Why did I fall in love with Troy?" she said to a journalist. "Well, on that rainy night when we first talked together, I suddenly realized this person whom I'd considered just another handsome boy-around-town was really warm, understanding, and had a really sharp mind and keen wit. I know Troy well. I know his moods, his short-fused temper, his little-boy quality that sometimes makes him do and say things he doesn't mean. In fact, it's this very combination of strong, grown-up man and charming boyishness that is so appealing about him. I love Troy and I understand him."

Lili may have thought she knew Troy well, but she didn't know that he carried on with several women even after they were engaged. "We dated for a short time in late 1960 during the first season of *Surfside*," Diane McBain recalled. "One night we tumbled into bed together, but nothing really happened. I think we both realized we were friends and not lovers. I'd heard rumors about his sexuality for years. Even back then people were talking. I don't know if he was ever with men, but his association with Henry Willson didn't help. I know he was linked with many starlets at Warner, but that was just for the movie magazines. I don't recall a serious girlfriend. He never mentioned anything like that to me. He was devoted to his mother and sister. The gay rumors dogged him all his life, but I don't know."

"Ahhh, these Lili, she is one locky girl!" *Surfside Six* co-star Margarita Sierra said upon learning of Troy's engagement. "Thees boy, he knows the nice theengs when he sees them! Nice clothes, nice cars, nice furnitures, good foods! I theenk he knows the nice girl, too, when he pick Lili! Is much compliment to her, to be picked by Troy! That one likes the good life! His wife, she should have it – how you say? – but soft!"

Troy and Margarita.

In August, 1961, Troy and Lili made front page news, but for the wrong reason. His philandering caught up with him. Lili went to Troy's house to pick up her dog, which she had left with him that morning. They had made plans for the evening, but Troy cancelled, telling her he had to work late at the studio. She decided to swing by and pick up her pet. She had a key, and let herself into Troy's house and caught him in the shower with another woman. He went on the defense, and according to Lili, he stormed out of the bathroom, and charged at her, yelling. She slapped him, and they got into a fistfight. She claimed he punched her in the face, shoved her backwards toward the door, and knocked her to the floor. He was charged with assault, and Lili filed suit against him seeking $60,450 in damages. The studio publicity department did everything it could to squelch the story.

Troy's mother told reporters, "Troy is not a violent boy, but he can be driven to violence by nagging and taunting."

"I don't know if a person can be completely nonviolent because then there would be no emotion at all," Troy said. "But the violence I have been associated with, or accused of, is something I would have avoided and do not like in any way. I am a God-fearing person. I feel that to do wrong and not learn from it is sinful.

"I like to do the right thing because if I don't, it frightens me. And I have to think about what I do. Even running a red light could be dangerous. If a judge decided to make an example of me because I was a young punk actor and let me cool off in jail, Warner Brothers could lose hundreds of thousands of dollars. I have a responsibility to myself, to my mother, to my sister, to my fans and to Warner Brothers – everybody. That sounds exaggerated, but I'm in an exaggerated position."

Studio boss, Jack Warner, trying to protect his valuable "property," quickly settled the case out of court for an undisclosed amount of money. Troy's career continued. Lili Kardell all but disappeared.

Nan Morris said, "Troy is the type of person who cannot be possessed, and just about every woman he has dated has a tendency to possess him because he's too easy-going. I could never understand what it was between Lili and Troy. I think he really didn't want to get involved. Lili never wore a ring. She was terribly possessive of Troy, so much so sometimes she wouldn't let him speak to anyone. That's against his nature because he likes everyone. Actually, I saw Troy all along during his engagement to Lili. Troy is always inviting people on the set. He'd invite me, and Lili would come and stomp around. She made everyone uneasy."

Troy did his best to avoid talking about the embarrassing Kardell incident. It was difficult to not talk about the many, many ex-girlfriends in his recent past. He told one journalist, "I was always making a big mistake in love. I tried to put on a laughing face when I fumbled. But I didn't fool anybody, least of all myself. I used to want to love desperately. I still do. But now I know the wrong kind of love would make me miserable again. I used to get terribly upset, be awfully jealous and explode when I had doubts about whether the girl I was dating actually cared for *me*."

Troy on location in Miami Beach for *Surfside 6*.

The television audience seemed oblivious to any negative publicity that trickled through the press. The studio publicity department worked overtime arranging magazine photographs and stories featuring the stars of *Surfside 6*. In a short time, the series drew a large viewing demographic. In theory, Troy alternated with Van and Lee as the lead on each episode of *Surfside 6*, but he "starred" in only ten of the first thirty-four episodes of the first season. During the production of *Surfside* in 1960, he was also filming his third feature film for the studio. *Susan Slade* was written and directed by Delmer Daves, and co-starred another Warner contract player, Connie Stevens.

Troy was able to complete eight episodes of *Surfside* in 1961 before he left for Italy to film his fourth and final feature film for Delmer Daves, *Rome Adventure.*

One of the problems that dogged Troy was his inexperience with television work. His mentor, Daves, allowed him many takes on a movie set, but actors did not have that luxury on a TV set. A one-hour television script could be filmed in one week providing the actors were comfortable working under pressure. Not one to mince words, Daves completely dismissed Troy's television acting. "It's not worth watching," he said. "He's one of those wonderful, rare, open, youthful personalities – but not on the first take. You need eleven takes to get to him, and on the twelfth he finally comes out with it. In films, you can afford to be patient with him. Television directors just don't have that kind of time."

Diane McBain explained, "The shooting schedule for television is so fast. There's just no time to do take after take. That was hard for Troy. It did take him a while to warm up. He was very insecure about that, and blamed it on the revolving door of different directors. It was easier for some of us, or maybe we cared less about it, I don't know. But it was hard on him."

"Troy Donahue is going to be one of our very big stars," Delmer Daves said. He directed Troy in his first four films. "He is the ideal – he looks like Young America wants to look." The millions of young girls who idolized him certainly agreed. On a visit to Manhattan to publicize *Parrish*, a mob of 4,000 girls broke a restaurant plate-glass window straining to catch a glimpse of him eating. "It is frightening," he said. "You feel honored. You feel panicked."

His *Rome Adventure* leading lady, Suzanne Pleshette – who would marry Troy in 1964 – had a more restrained opinion of him in public. "I was not predisposed to like him," she recalled. "At first, he seemed like all the other fellows. But he is not. Troy is a very unusual boy – gracious and considerate."

When gossip about the couple bubbled up in Hollywood, Troy told columnist Marilyn Beck, "I'm not going to be tied down to anyone. There's too much I want to do, and I want to do it alone. I'm not ready for marriage. I want to date. I'm ready for a fling. I know a lot of people have accused me of being on the brink of marriage many times. It's not true. I've only been engaged once, and that was to Lili Kardell. Even then, I was wrong. I wasn't ready for marriage with her, or anyone else. It was better that it happened the way it did. We were lucky to find out early. I can say that it happened for the best."

The more Troy's popularity grew the more conscious he became of his public position. His co-workers watched a gradual change in his behavior. "He's getting kind of wrapped up in his publicity and that's beginning to come out on the show," one said. "He's very demanding now. At first, he was a very humble and appreciative kid. Now, he shows up late for work, and he's cost a lot of directors a lot of scenes. I guess it happens to them all."

His growing temperament on the set had more to do with his own insecurity than it did with his ego, however. He fought back against the show's numerous directors by essentially directing himself. He also made the mistake of trying to direct the directors. Any problems with him stumbling over lines or freezing on camera he blamed on inept direction. He told a friend who was about to be interviewed by a reporter for *TV Guide*, "Be sure to tell him how lousy this director is and all the trouble we're having." Such behavior did not endear him to the crew.

Many guest actors on the show were less patient when Troy required more time than anyone else to complete an acceptable "take." Some found his inexperience exasperating as he blew scene after scene, dragging an already long work day into the night.

Daves said, "This boy is still learning his craft." Troy's agent, Henry Willson, said, "I think he can act, but I don't think that has anything to do with it. We all know some very great movie stars who will never be actors."

The final episode of *Surfside 6*, "Midnight for Prince Charming," was broadcast on June 25, 1962. The episode featured Van Williams and Diane McBain. Troy did not appear in the season finale.

Troy and Diane were happy to be rid of the show. Both were working on film careers at the studio. Lee and Van did not have further career obligations to Warner Brothers. Lee considered going back to England to make films. Van was happy to attend to his family business. Margarita Sierra returned to the nightclub stage.

The series had sputtered to an end, but the studio wanted to capitalize on Troy's stardom. He was receiving more than 5,000 fan letters a week, and movie exhibitors voted him the 20th most popular star in the United States.

Troy was used to being recognized in public, but television stardom emboldened fans to be aggressive and even predatory. A few months before the end of *Surfside 6*, Troy reluctantly gave up the house he had rented for three years, and moved to a more secluded house behind gates in Beverly Hills.

Troy said, "When I'm home I think I deserve and am entitled to a little privacy. Having people peer through the windows of my house and hide behind corners to stare at me – well, I can't feel kindly about that. The house I lived in was right off Sunset Strip, and perhaps it was too convenient. Believe me, the new one is not. It's way up on the side of hill with a large iron fence around it so that no one will be able to enter."

Wasting no time, Troy was shoved into another Warner/ABC-TV series, *Hawaiian Eye*. He played the role of hotel detective Philip Barton on the show's fourth, and final season. Much of the show was filmed on location in

Honolulu. Troy and his co-star Connie Stevens spoke with *TV Guide* journalist Edith Efron in a grievance-laced, prickly interview. Troy's chronic tardiness and struggles remembering lines had taken a toll on the cast and crew of the show. Connie, in particular, had long lost her patience with him.

Connie and Troy were Warner Brothers' most popular stars at the time. Efron wrote, "Their joint 'image' is the conventional stereotype of the ideal, young romantic couple: blonde, slender, vulnerable, infantile." In reality, the young actors were not only not romantic together, they barely tolerated each other on the set.

When asked to describe each other, Troy said, "Connie is intelligent. She is spirited. She is beautiful." About Troy, Connie said, "He is the kind of person who, no matter how mad you get at him, is always the first to be friendly and congenial."

"Yes, she gets mad at me," Troy added. "The other day, we were shooting a scene that has to go snap-snap. I felt I flubbed a line. I committed the cardinal sin. I stopped in the middle."

"Just when he stopped," Connie snapped, "I felt something *good* coming out of it!"

The two stars shared an impatience with the studio management of their careers, too. "I'm fighting the problem of mediocrity," Troy said. "It's hard for the people we work for to break the mediocre pattern which has been successful. We're *suffocating* from lack of good scripts. Too many business considerations mixed in with the art and craft."

Critics never embraced Connie or Troy. They were dismissed for being "pretty," and Troy was labeled a "terrible actor."

Connie said, "The critics are right. I think Troy is one of the *pretty people*. The kids love him. They think he's beautiful. They don't love him because he's a good actor."

"They think *I'm* a great actor," Troy said. "But the highbrows, the New York people, the *New Yorker*, the *Saturday Review* group – they joke about the fact that we're physically attractive. They joke about our being 'America's darlings.' They don't try to understand us. I *despise* the intellectuals. I'd rather be a bum on a beach than a highbrow intellectual all over Europe."

When his working partnership with Delmer Daves ended, Troy felt lost and vulnerable. The studio was displeased with Troy's seemingly unappreciative rant in the press about the state of his career. Perhaps as a punishment, he was cast along with many other Warner contract players in the lightweight, "beach party in the desert" movie, *Palm Springs Weekend* in 1963. Troy balked and refused to accept the role. "They wanted me to play a college basketball player," he said. "I was too old for that." The studio immediately suspended him. "I was living like a movie star," he recalled. "I lived way over my head and got into great trouble and lost everything." He had no choice but to accept the role in *Palm Springs Weekend*.

Troy couldn't connect with the director, and became convinced his career was careening off the track. Drugs and alcohol deadened his pain. Troy recalled, "I was loaded all the time. I'd wake up about 6:30 in the morning, take three aspirins mixed with codeine, slug down half a pint of vodka and then do four lines of cocaine. That was just so I could get the front door open to peek out and see if I could face the day."

To make matters worse for Troy, he was pushed into recording a couple of singles for Warner Bros. Records that year including "Somebody Loves Me," and "Live Young," which he sang in the film *Palm Springs Weekend*. His recordings never placed on the Billboard Chart. He considered singing a waste of time, and a drag on his acting career.

In June, 1963, Troy went to Flagstaff, Arizona to begin work on a western film, *A Distant Trumpet*. He was reunited with fellow actors Diane McBain and Suzanne Pleshette, who co-starred in the film. Troy's on-again, off-again flirtation with Suzanne became a serious romance in the desert dust of Arizona. Hollywood journalists were hot on their trail.

Diane McBain recalled, "I liked Suzanne. I never met a girl like her. I'd never heard a woman use four-letter words before. And she managed to slip a few into almost every sentence she uttered. She was funny, and loved to laugh. Troy was so delicate. He was certainly fascinated by her. I was surprised by their romance, but I guess it proved that opposites attract. And I think Suzanne appreciated that she got so much publicity from dating a handsome, popular star."

If there is such a thing as a "good-time-boy," than Troy fit the bill. Suzanne said, "It takes more than love to make a good marriage. Fun and good times are fine, when you have nothing but fun on your mind. But you shouldn't think about marriage until you're ready for responsibility."

Troy and Suzanne married on January 4, 1964. A glamorous dinner and dance reception followed at the Beverly Hills Hotel on Sunset Boulevard. Hundreds of friends, family members, and co-workers, including numerous Warner Brothers contract players attended. Rock Hudson's "date," publicist Pat Fitzgerald, actually caught the bridal bouquet. Late that evening, the couple flew to Jamaica for their honeymoon.

When they returned to California, Suzanne moved into Troy's house in the Hollywood Hills. His grandmother moved out.

In April, Troy went to Japan for three weeks to promote his soon-to-be released films, *Palm Springs Weekend*, and *A Distant Trumpet*. When reporters asked him why he was traveling alone, he said, "Suzy can't go along. She has wardrobe tests and fittings for her next picture."

After a rocky few months, Troy and Suzanne announced their separation on June 3. Hedda Hopper's June 21 column in the *Los Angeles Times*, screamed, "Troy and Suzy – Who Said It Could Be Done?"

It may have taken Suzanne three years of on again-off again romance to decide to marry Troy, but it took her only two weeks after separating from him five months after the ceremony, to decide to file for divorce. She sued for divorce on June 29, charging him with the "infliction of grievous mental suffering."

Troy did not contest the action. Suzanne was granted a divorce in Los Angeles Superior Court on September 8 on a charge of mental cruelty. She told the court there was no community property, she waived alimony, and stated she wanted nothing more to do with him. Ever.

Troy's film, *A Distant Trumpet*, was released in May, 1964. The film bombed. He refused to do another TV series for the studio. "After two years of *Surfside 6*, and a stretch in *Hawaiian Eye*, I'd rather do pictures," he said. Later that year, he starred with Joey Heatherton in *My Blood Runs Cold*, a film about reincarnation that was filmed in Santa Cruz, and Monterey, California. He described it as "a piece of shit." The film was released in March, 1965, and was panned by critics and the public. Troy had fallen into a downward spiral. His increasing dependence on alcohol and drugs was destroying both his personal and professional lives.

In early 1965, he guest-starred in an episode of *The Patty Duke Show*, filmed in New York City. After the dismal reception of *My Blood Runs Cold*, Troy thought he would have better luck finding appropriate films if he was no longer under contract to Warner, and he asked to be released in January, 1966. "So I went to see Jack Warner and told him, 'I don't want to make any more dumb movies,' and he said, 'What'll you do?' and I said, 'What difference does that make to you, man?'

"So I walked out in 1966 and I had to sit out three years of my contract. I couldn't work anywhere."

He found the transition from a contract player to a free agent to be very difficult. "None of us knew what to do," Diane said. "After years of being told what to do every day, every minute of the week, it was like being cast overboard without a life jacket."

"Jack Warner called every studio and used his muscle to keep me busted," Troy said. "I was blackballed and everyone in the business knew it. By the time I could get work again, it was too late because my type was already out of fashion. Warner pumped me until the well ran dry.

"I was typecast from my first film at Warners," Troy explained. "I was usually cast with blondes. Since it worked for *A Summer Place*, they weren't going to break the mold. I guess because I was blond, blue-eyed and tanned, people associated me with all those beach movies that were around then, even though I never did one. I was always the goody-goody, the guy who did what he was supposed to."

In the spring of 1966, Troy flew to Jamaica to star in an independent film titled *Come Spy with Me*. He began a relationship with an actress, Valerie Allen, who had a small role in the film. In October, Troy flew to Ireland to begin work on another independent film, *Those Fantastic Flying Fools*, based on a story by Jules Verne. Valerie contacted Troy to tell him that she was pregnant.

"I was sure I loved her," Troy said. "I asked her to come over here to Ireland and marry me. She did. And we did."

The couple married on October 21, 1966. In December, Valerie suffered a miscarriage. The couple returned to Troy's home in Los Angeles in January, 1967. A few weeks later, Troy and Valerie flew to Mexico where Troy filmed *The Phantom Gunslinger* for director Albert Zugsmith – best remembered for

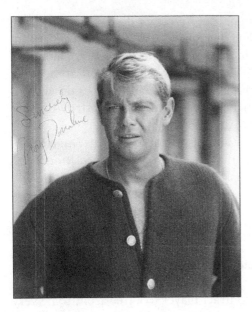

a string of "soft porn" films in the 1960s and 1970s. The miscarriage took an emotional toll on Valerie. Troy was drinking heavily. The low budget film, which provided him with his first starring role in a couple of years, was a disaster in the making. Troy suffered the effects of no direction on the set, and a serious language barrier. Valerie returned to Los Angeles before Troy's work was completed.

In April 1967, Valerie and Troy separated. They reconciled and separated several more times during the forthcoming months, but Troy wasted no time to be a celebrity bachelor contestant on the popular daytime show, *The Dating Game*, in May. With no work on the horizon, Troy accepted personal appearance jobs including that of a celebrity guest at the annual father-son banquet at St. Nicholas Cathedral in Los Angeles on June 10. And he and Diane McBain were reunited as celebrity judges for the annual West Coast rock music championship contest during the week of August 14 at the Hullabaloo Club in Hollywood.

Troy and Valerie reconciled one last time in October, 1967. They accepted a three-week Chicago theater engagement, starring together in the Jean Kerr comedy, *Poor Richard*. On November 7, Troy made the front page news when he walked out on his contract to perform at the Pheasant Run Playhouse. Carl Stohn, Jr., the theater producer, said Troy told him he decided to leave to prove to himself that he could run his own career. Troy told him, the producer explained, that he had been forced by managers and agents to do things in his career that he didn't want to do. The couple left, but went their separate ways. The Pheasant Run Playhouse sued Troy for more than $200,000 in damages. Eventually they won a judgment against him.

In February, 1968, Troy signed a one-year, exclusive contract with Universal covering feature films and television. Weeks later, on April 19, his estranged wife Valerie filed suit to end their marriage. She charged him with cruelty, sighting his alcoholism, and chronic infidelity. Troy did not contest the charges. Their divorce was finalized on November 16, 1968. They were married for eighteen months, but lived together for less than six months collectively.

Troy had filed for bankruptcy in September, to protect what few assets he had. Nevertheless, Valerie was awarded a substantial cash settlement, and Troy was ordered to give her his exclusive membership in The Factory, a West Hollywood disco.

Drug addiction was not conducive to a good marriage. "I would lie, steal and cheat, all those wonderful things that drunks do," Troy recalled. "I was crafty. Nobody knew how much I drank then. I filed bankruptcy, and lost my home. I went from a beautiful house, garden, swimming pool to living in shabby apartments," he said.

His contract with Universal provided him with a few first-class jobs. He guest-starred in a two-part episode of *Ironside*, broadcast on September 26, 1968. On October 18, he guest-starred on an episode of *The Name of the Game*. He played a bounty hunter on an episode of *The Virginian*, broadcast on April 2, 1969. He completed one made-for-television movie before Universal dropped him. *The Lonely Profession* aired on October 21, 1969, and drew positive reviews and a respectable audience.

In July 1969, Troy met a young Jamaican-born woman named Alma Sharpe who was on vacation in Los Angeles. The couple had a whirlwind romance, and married on November 15 in Roanoke, Virginia. Troy justified their union, "I couldn't take care of myself, and I knew this friend would take me under her wing."

Troy left Hollywood behind, and moved to New York City shortly after his wedding in late 1969. "The unknown scared me most when I started to fade in the late '60s," he said.

"It took guts to walk out of Hollywood," he told journalist Rex Reed, "but it would've been worse to stay. I had a house, seven black Cadillac convertibles and two wrecked marriages. I already had my head turned; turning my back was easy."

He recalled, "I let my hair grow and did quite a bit of dope. I was very, very gloomy." For six months in 1970, he played the role of R.B. Keefer, the drug-addicted scheming boyfriend of a hooker on the daytime soap opera, *The Secret Storm*. With his long, scruffy hair and droopy mustache, he was nearly unrecognizable.

Not surprisingly, Troy's addictions proved to be too

Jennifer Darling and Troy in *The Secret Storm.*

much for his new wife to bear. The couple separated several months after their marriage. They finalized their divorce in 1972.

Troy found himself homeless in Manhattan. But there *was* some little value to being "Troy Donahue." He was in his early thirties, and still looked reasonably well. For a while, he depended on strangers to feed him and give him a place to sleep. "There was always somebody who could be amused by Troy Donahue," he remembered. "I'd meet them anywhere, in a park, on the street, at a party, in bed. I lived in a bush in Central Park for one summer. I kept everything I had in a backpack."

In early 1971, Troy was cast as the lead in a low budget, independent film inspired by the 1969 Manson murders in Hollywood. He played the hippie leader of a sex cult who orders murders. The part was a true departure from his blonde, surfer-boy image. *Sweet Savior*, originally rated X, and edited to qualify for an R rating, was a bomb. Roger Greenspun reviewed the film for the *New York Times*. "Making fun of the screen career of Troy Donahue may now have become a reputable cottage industry among cultural commentators, and in recent months, nobody has been better at it than Troy Donahue, who is currently establishing a new image. And though I haven't seen all his work, it seems to me just possible that Donahue's first absolutely awful movie is *Sweet Savior*. The film is quite without performances except for Troy Donahue, who is helplessly inauthentic."

With the little bit of money he was paid for the film, Troy was able to get himself off the street, and move into a Holiday Inn motel. Rex Reed interviewed Troy at the bar there at the time.

"Everybody changes, man. Even the kids change. I had long hair a long time ago, but Warner Brothers threw a net over my head in *A Summer Place*, and never let me out. I was never the boy in the red windbreaker. I wanted them to burn the damn thing. They had to lock it up.

"That image of the All-American boy on the screen had nothing to do with me as a person. In the same day, they had me going from *Surfside 6* on one stage to playing a beach boy in some dumb Connie Stevens movie or another. They set a pattern to make money and wouldn't let me play anything else.

"But it doesn't matter if I have a beard or crew cut. People respond to me because I have a human quality. I know I'll be put down by Hollywood, but I don't speak to anybody out there anyway."

During the next couple of years, Troy accepted roles in embarrassingly bad low budget movies. "Lot's of location stuff," he explained. "It gave me a place to be." He played a sheriff in *The Last Stop*, and had a supporting role in *Cockfighter*. Both films were shot in Georgia. He traveled to the Philippines to film *South Seas*, which was released in 1974.

Troy played a supporting role in Oliver Stone's directorial feature film debut, a horror movie titled *Seizure*. The film was shot in Quebec on a shoe-string budget in early 1974. All the cast and crew stayed in the same house.

In 1974, he appeared in his first big budget film in ten years when he played the role of Talia Shire's boyfriend in *The Godfather, Part II*. His character's name was "Merle Johnson." "I went to summer camp with Coppola," Troy said. With the $10,000 he was paid, Troy moved back to Los Angeles.

"After years at Warners," he said, "I did a few independent films that never went any place. I travelled, played stickball, had a few marriages and many affairs. I just totally enjoyed myself and did the things I didn't get to do when I was a kid. Now I've decided I wanna go back to work again and I've been encouraged by a lot of people who feel that I have the talent and everything that goes with it."

Troy appeared in two films in 1977; *The Legend of Frank Woods*, and *Ultraje*. Both films were barely seen. But he had a successful run guest-starring in television programs including; *Ellery Queen* in 1976, and in 1978, *The Hardy Boys*, *CHiPs*, *Vega$*, *The Eddie Capra Mysteries*, and *Fantasy Island*.

Troy married for the fourth time on March 3, 1979. Vicki Taylor was a Los Angeles land-development manager. His highest profile job that year was a series of whiskey commercials for Japanese television. "But whatever money I made I put into cocaine," he said. His inability to support himself, and his drug abuse ended his marriage in 18 months. The couple divorced in 1981.

Work was difficult to come by. He was a guest-star on *The Love Boat* in 1980, and made his second, and last, appearance on *Fantasy Island* in 1981.

"I was whipped," he said. "Powerless. But the worst thing, I was in pain. Ironically that helped me. In May of 1982, I decided to get sober." He joined Alcoholics Anonymous, and achieved sobriety.

In 1983, a short time after he stopped drinking, Troy ran into a woman he had once dated. "She walked over and introduced herself," he recalled, "and I remembered that we had been together four or five times in Los Angeles in 1969. She said, 'I'm glad I saw you. I've always wanted to tell you about something. Look over there, Troy.' I looked across the room and I saw a 13-year old spitting image of what I looked like when I was young. 'This is your son, Sean,' she said. 'He's known all his life that you are his father.' Now he calls me 'Dad,'" Troy said. "The whole thing was so natural, the three of us accepted it so easily. I see him every couple of weeks now."

Between 1983 and 1999, Troy dabbled in screenwriting, and appeared in more than thirty low budget horror and sexploitation films, many going directly to video distribution, but never enough work to make for a comfortable life. The only memorable films he completed during that time were *Grandview, U.S.A.* in 1984, and John Waters' *Cry Baby* in 1990.

"I spent a lot of time judging beauty contests and opening banks," Troy recalled.

In January, 1998, be began a five-month, national tour in Long Beach, California, in the musical *Bye, Bye, Birdie*. The production traveled from Washington to Florida to Illinois, and eventually Hawaii. "I've had many opportunities to do theater in the past, both at resident companies and on tour, but the time wasn't right," he explained, "*Birdie* will give me an opportunity to connect with my friends and fans across the country."

Troy also participated in "celebrity" cruises. Passengers booked a short cruise, usually in the Gulf of Mexico, that was attended by celebrities who introduced their films being shown in the ship theater, and conducted question and answer, and meet and greet sessions with the fans. "I write, I teach, I direct," he said. "I sail around the world for Holland America two months out of every year doing a seminar where we discuss film or theater and do improvisations."

It was on one of those cruises in October, 1995, where Troy met Chinese-born, American operatic mezzo-soprano, Zheng Cao. "I was doing my seminar," Troy recalled. "She was going to the Curtis Institute of Music in Philadelphia. She read a thing in the paper that said, 'Sail the South Seas and sing on a ship.' So she signed on and sang on the ship, and that's where we met." In spite of their thirty-year age difference, they began a relationship. When Cao graduated from the Curtis Institute, the couple moved to Santa Monica, California, where they rented a small, one-bedroom apartment. They divided their time between Santa Monica and San Francisco. Cao was an Adler Fellow with the San Francisco Opera.

Cao was best known for playing the role of Suzuki in *Madame Butterfly*, and her role of Cherubino in *The Marriage of Figaro*. When Troy was not working on an occasional film, he spent all his time with her. "We travel a lot because her singing career takes her all over the world. We're very serious, very committed to each other. It's the greatest relationship I've ever had in my life." The couple became engaged in 1999.

Troy and his former film leading lady Sandra Dee reunited in 1997, when they hosted a special screening of their 1959 hit film, *A Summer Place*, in New York City. The program drew a sold-out crowd. "It was like going to the *Rocky Horror Picture Show*," Troy recalled. "They had about two thousand people in there of all ages, and everybody knew all the lines! I was amazed! I didn't even know all the lines." After so many years, *A Summer Place* was considered a cult classic by many fans.

"I hadn't seen it on the big screen in more than twenty-five years," Troy said. "I was mesmerized by my own image up there. I thought, 'Man, that's what they were talking about.' Because you forget. It was so beautifully photographed. And seeing your face along with Sandra's up there in this huge, huge close-up. And being that young and beautiful, both of us – that's pretty heady stuff."

Troy played his final role in 2000 in the independent film, *The Boys Behind the Desk*. Directed by Sally Kirkland, the film was never released.

On August 30, 2001, Troy suffered a heart attack and was taken to Saint John's Health Center in Santa Monica. Upon his arrival, he required immediate angioplasty surgery. The procedure seemed to be a success, but the next day he suffered a second heart attack. He underwent a heart bypass operation. He did not regain consciousness, and died on September 2. He was 65 years old.

"We spoke on the phone now and then until shortly before he died," Diane McBain recalled. "The last time I saw him we were at the same audition. I asked him for a ride home. He had a jeep. He looked awful, so washed out. Just a shadow of himself. But he was sober. He told me he'd slept on the beach the night before. In a way, he always seemed a little lost to me. We talked about what we'd been up to, and he said he had struggled for a long time, but was feeling good. He told me he was finally happy with a young Asian opera singer. He lived with her in Santa Monica. He was a sweet man. It was awful to see him that way, and I was heartbroken when he died. I delivered the eulogy at his service."

A couple of years before his death, a journalist asked Troy his opinion of himself as an actor. Troy laughed, "I've always thought I was as good as my material. And that was pretty funny stuff."

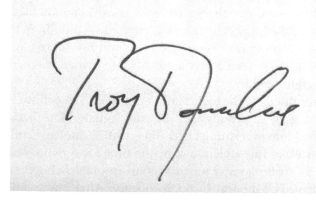

Van Williams

Van Williams played the role of Ken Madison, the second of the three private detectives. He was born Van Zandt Jarvis Williams on February 27, 1934. "I was born in a little train stop of a place called Avondale, Texas, about twelve miles outside of Ft. Worth," Van recalled. "Nobody's ever heard of it, so I just say I'm from Ft. Worth. There's nothing much to the town except a general store and some cattle pens for the railroad.

Van Williams.

"We had to travel to Ft. Worth to go to school and for almost everything else, too. I guess I had a boy's ideal of a real nice place to grow up in. Our ranch was great. I suppose living in such a real big stretch of country gave us that much more room for making mischief in! My older brother, Bernie, and I really had fun growing up." Bernard "Bernie" Williams Jr. later became a Trappist monk.

"The Van Zandts and the Jarvises were there when Ft. Worth was really just a fort," Van explained. His great-grandfather was a Major in the Confederate Army, and a pioneer of Texas. His grandfather was mayor of Fort Worth, and president of the board of trustees at Texas Christian University. He inaugurated the Southwest Exposition and Stock Show, and was a director of the biggest bank in the city. His father, Bernard Cardwell Williams, was a leading rancher in the area, and owned one of the largest ranches in Texas. Van lived a privileged life. He owned his own jeep when he was in the eighth grade.

He later admitted that he took a lot for granted. "I'm definitely not one to follow rules set up by somebody else," he said, "but, as I look back at things, I see I was pushed into everything I ever did – until I came to California.

"My father was a fine athlete, and by the time I was two years old, he was sure I'd be a football player. I was. I was on my high school All-American team, and I played all the way through college." After high school, he was a pre-med student at the University of Texas. A football scholarship landed him at Texas Christian University where he studied business administration.

"My mother, Priscilla Jarvis, was active socially, and she guided my social life. She was very strictly reared in the South's tradition of being a lady, and she has rigid ideas about right and wrong. Nevertheless, I was pretty wild."

Van had a good relationship with his father, although they often butted heads. He planned to follow his father's footsteps and become a rancher. "We never thought he'd do anything but ranch," his father recalled. "He's about as good a cattleman as I know." Van's dad, "Blackie" Williams, cast a long and imposing shadow. He was a strong-willed man who expected his son to obey him. But Van was independent minded. "Nobody ever knew me as Van Williams," he said. "I was always Blackie Williams' son, and I was sick of it."

When he was a freshman at Texas Christian University he met a co-ed named Drucilla Greenhaw. They eloped in 1953 when she became pregnant. The couple had twin daughters, Lisa and Lynne. They divorced less than two years later. Bored with school, he dropped out in 1956. His father wanted him to assume more responsibilities on the ranch, but feeling frustrated and rebellious, Van surprised his family when he decided to move to Hawaii.

"In 1957, just before my senior year at TCU," Van said, "I got the travel bug. I'd been asked to come over to Hawaii to play football for the University there. I went. But the islands proved too much of a diversion for me to spend my days in a classroom, so I quit. My favorite sports are water skiing, swimming, skin-diving and surfing. In fact, I'd been content to spend the rest of my days on a beach if I could. But I was lucky enough to get hired at the Hawaiian Village Hotel as a skin-diving instructor. Imagine getting paid for that!"

While working at the hotel, Van met a man who would change his life. "That's when I met Mike Todd," he recalled. "He and Elizabeth Taylor were there on a combination business-pleasure trip. Mr. Todd took a liking to me. I was to be the assistant manager of a new theater chain he was setting up. The deal never came off. But Mike would talk for hours and hours with such enthusiasm about show business, I'd just sit there spellbound, listening. One day, out of the clear blue, he looked at me and said, 'Kid, you should be in the movies.'

"It came as quite a surprise. I'd never thought about it before. Then he asked me about myself, my background, and when he found out I had a year to go to graduate from college, he said, 'Kid, go back to school and get that degree. After you get your degree, come to Hollywood and look me up. I'll help open as many doors as I can for you.'

"I took Mike's advice and went back to TCU. It was while I was still in school that Mike was killed in a plane crash in March, 1958. I graduated that June, and decided to give Hollywood a try anyway. I set myself a time limit – three years – then if nothing happened I'd go back home and into ranching, or oil, or something.

"When I got to Hollywood, even though Mike wasn't there anymore, he was with me in spirit. He'd already told some of his friends about me and they were very helpful and encouraging. I was told to get myself a good drama coach to help me lose my Texas drawl, so I studied for six months until I got to talking like a regular Yankee!"

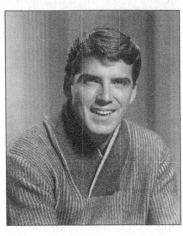

Van took odd jobs to survive, and took some acting lessons. He managed to get a small role on an episode of the CBS series, *General Electric Theater*, titled "The Castaway," which aired on October 12, 1958. A few months later, on January 25, 1959, he appeared again in another episode of *General Electric Theater*, titled "Bill Bailey Won't You Please Come Home?" The episode was actually an unsold pilot.

"Then, Revue Television Studios optioned me," Van recalled, "but they let me go after six months."

In the meantime, William T. Orr, the chief of television production at Warner Brothers., saw the pilot, and optioned Van. "Instead of a screen test," Van recalled, "they gave me a few small parts." His first work at the studio included the *Lawman* episode, "The Young Toughs," broadcast in April, 1959, and a *Colt .45* episode, "The Sanctuary," broadcast in May 1959. Orr was impressed enough to offer Van a contract with the studio.

He was immediately cast in a new private detective series titled *Bourbon Street Beat*. The ABC-TV presentation concerned a detective agency based in the Absinthe House on Bourbon Street in the French Quarter of New Orleans. The cast included Richard Long, Andrew Duggan, and Arlene Howell. Van

played the role of investigator Kenny Madison.

"I got lucky with *Bourbon Street Beat*," he said at the time. "And the funniest thing is that now I have to talk with a sort of drawl, so here I am learning to talk Southern again – and after all those drama lessons! But I'm not complaining – this movie making is sure as exciting as roping steers any day!"

Despite his background as a Texas rancher, Van was never professionally identified with Westerns. "I guess Warner Brothers pictured me as a guy in a suit and tie."

Before his career began to blossom, he was side-lined for a short time when a malfunctioning kidney required surgical removal in the summer of 1959. "I had a little kidney problem," he told a reporter at the time. "I'd lived with it my whole life and it never really interfered with my being just as active as possible. When I started out at Warner, it began acting up. I had some pain but I was just about to start work on *Bourbon Street Beat*, and didn't want to go to the hospital until I'd at least done a few shows first. But between the doctors and Vicki being so persuasive, I found myself at UCLA Medical Center. So I just let them operate. They removed one kidney. I'm fine now. Feel wonderful."

In March 1959, Van had met a young woman named Vicki Flaxman at the beach. She was an accomplished and well-known "Malibu girl surfer." He said she was "about the best woman surfer there is." They had been introduced by mutual friends. Vicki was finalizing her divorce from actor Jeff Richards, with whom she had a daughter named Nina. Van and Vicki began dating in April, and quickly fell in love. But Van had a difficult time convincing Vicki to marry him.

Van recalls that she told him, "This may sound crazy, but I don't want a life of nothing but fun. I don't want everything to go right all the time. In life, it almost never does, anyway, and you've never been up against big trouble. I don't know how it would affect you. If I marry again, I want a few problems, because good marriages grow and strengthen through problems. A couple with nothing to work toward and nothing to surmount soon has nothing."

"I had a hard time convincing Vicki that we should marry," Van said. "She had just ended an unhappy marriage, and she didn't want to risk another one. She had to be convinced that I was serious about wanting a home and a family more than a constant good time."

The wedding was called off three times because the bride and groom got cold feet. Finally, the couple came to terms with their doubts, and planned to marry in March, 1960, in San Francisco. The Christmas holiday break in the production schedule for *Bourbon Street Beat* gave them time to drive to Texas to visit Van's family.

"On the way back from Texas," Van recalled, "we decided that we had waited long enough." Vicki's mother flew to Los Angeles from San Francisco, and the couple married at the Wayfarer's Chapel in Palos Verdes, California, on December 31, 1959.

The first of thirty-nine episodes of *Bourbon Street Beat* was broadcast on October 5, 1959. Van was assured that his role on the program would develop and evolve into a solid lead, but that didn't happen. The series never caught on with the television audience, and was cancelled after one season. The final episode was broadcast on July 4, 1960.

While most Warner contract players were busy making feature films for the studio, Van was kept busy with television assignments. Without missing a beat, his *Bourbon Street Beat* character, Ken Madison, was written into a new series titled, *Surfside 6*, which premiered on October 3, 1960.

Van was grateful for the chance to improve his acting skills on the new show. "And I finally got a chance to prove myself through an accident," he recalled. "Lee Patterson fell ill one night out of town just before he was to play the leading part in a *Surfside* episode. He sent a telegram saying he wouldn't be at work the next day, and then went to bed.

"The telegram didn't arrive. Nobody knew where Lee was. In desperation, the director called me and asked whether I thought I could play the role which had been tailored to fit Lee. I said sure, and it worked out to my advantage."

"I first met Van when I did an episode of *Bourbon Street Beat*," Diane McBain recalled. "I guest-starred in a few episodes of that show in early 1960. I loved Van. He was a terrific guy. He was a very secure fellow, and he seemed well-off financially. He wasn't the 'show-biz' type at all. He didn't have a lot of range as an actor, but that wasn't required for our show. He was handsome and clean-cut, and very relaxed and easy to work with. It was all a lot of fun for him, and that played well on camera. He was recently married when we started the show, and his wife was lovely. For some reason, the studio paired us in many magazine photo shoots frolicking on the beach or playing volley ball in our bathing suits. It was ridiculous. We were more like brother and sister. We remained friends for the rest of his life."

Van, Diane and Cocquette.

Van's first national magazine interview was uninhibited, and frank. He said he was strict with his young stepdaughter. "I wouldn't want Nina to go out with boys as wild as I was when I was growing up. Child-rearing theories alternate with each generation. My mother was very strictly brought up, but I did as I wanted. I hope I won't be too strict with Nina, but a girl who is allowed too much freedom is a lousy wife."

He said he believed a woman's place was in the home. "I don't want my wife to have a career, other than being my wife. Vicki agrees with me. If Nina wants to be an actress someday, that's her business, but I certainly wouldn't want her to be a child actress."

The studio publicity department expressed their dismay with their star. "I remember after that first interview," he said, "I was warned to think before I spoke. But I still say what I believe."

Later in 1960, Vicki miscarried the couple's first child – a boy. They were heartbroken, and Van rarely mentioned it except to say, "Of course, we were sorry. But the baby might not have been normal if it had lived, the doctor told me, so I guess, in a way, we were lucky." In 1961, Vicki gave birth to a daughter they named, Tia.

Before *Surfside 6* was cancelled, Van and Troy – playing their characters Ken Madison and Sandy Winfield – made a cameo appearance in an episode of the popular Warner series, *77 Sunset Strip*, titled "Hot Tamale Caper: Part I." It was a failed attempt to bolster audience interest in *Surfside.*

With the exception of one feature film, *The Caretakers*, released in 1963, the studio did not give any movie roles to Van. He had played the small role of an air force sergeant in a U.S. government sponsored short film about communist aggression, titled *Red Nightmare*, in 1962. In 1963, Van guest-starred in several Warner television productions including, *Cheyenne, 77 Sunset Strip, The Gallant Men*, and *Hawaiian Eye*. On January 30, 1964, he guest-starred in *Temple Houston* in an episode titled, "Ten Rounds for Baby." The one-hour Western-themed series starred Jeffrey Hunter. Warner Bros. Studios dropped Van's contract, but he remained good friends with Hunter until Hunter's untimely death in 1969.

Van's first acting job, post Warner Brothers, found him co-starring with Walter Brennan in a series produced by Danny Thomas Productions. *The Tycoon* concerned an eccentric business tycoon who helps young people in need. Van played the role of the tycoon's personal pilot. Brennan, a three-time Oscar winner, was professional and easy to work with, but he owned a piece of the show, and he wasn't about to let anyone overshadow him. "I was just an errand boy for Brennan," Van said. The first of thirty-two episodes was broadcast on September 15, 1964. The half-hour program never caught on with the audience and was cancelled after the final episode aired on April 27, 1965. Later that year, he guest-starred in an episode of *The Dick Van Dyke Show*, and *The Beverly Hillbillies*. He lent his vocal talents – with a thick, Texas drawl – to provide the voice of President Lyndon Johnson in *Batman, the Movie*, released in the summer of 1966.

Van's business training enabled him to manage and leverage his money to his advantage. "I've still got the first dollar I ever earned. I'm a tightwad," he joked. In 1965, he incorporated a bank with his business manager, and actor James Garner. He maintained an interest in the family ranch in Texas, and, with his parents, he owned a shopping center and a downtown office building in Ft. Worth. "But I don't have to do anything with any of them," he said. Producer Richard Bluel, who had known Van since *Bourbon Street Beat*, said, "Van is secure, personally and financially. He does this [acting] because he really enjoys it."

Even when he was busy with work, Van maintained a private, and very ordinary life in Southern California. He lived in a comfortable but modest home at the foot of a canyon in Pacific Palisades. "It's like living out in the country," he said. "I never have been able to get used to city life. We spend ninety percent of the time outdoors surfing, swimming, playing tennis, and skiing. We're day people."

Van with his family.

Each summer, his parents came for an extended visit. They brought his twin daughters, who they helped raise. "They're growing up – blossoming out, getting all their femininities," he told the *TV Guide* in 1966.

In early 1966, Van filmed a TV pilot, *Pursue and Destroy*. The pilot went unsold, but he soon landed the role that would bring him more fame than he ever counted on. William Dozier, who produced the camp hit TV series, *Batman*, presold a proposed series titled *The Green Hornet* without making a pilot episode. *The Green Hornet* was an adaptation of the radio serial that debuted in the 1930s. The story concerned Britt Reid, a playboy editor/publisher who inherited *The Daily Sentinel* newspaper from his father who was framed for a crime, and died in jail. Reid "disguised" himself with a green mask, a fedora and a long overcoat, and chased bad guys as the Hornet. His manservant, Kato, drove him around the city in a gadget-packed car they called Black Beauty.

Many actors tested for the role of Britt Reid. But George Trendle who created *The Green Hornet* as a radio show said, "All of a sudden you see someone who fills the bill perfectly, and Van Williams was it."

"When I was a kid," Van recalled, "I had actually been a fan of *The Green Hornet* when it was on the radio, and in those serials at the theater, but I didn't know if I wanted to star in a TV series like that. It was very similar to Adam West's *Batman*, with the same producer Bill Dozier, and seemed like something that would probably be the kiss of death to my career. You do that type of show and become so identified with it, like *Superman*'s George Reeves was, and you can never get away from it. But my agency, William Morris, really wanted me to do *The Green Hornet*, so that is what I did."

In April, Adam West introduced Bruce Lee and Van as the newly cast Green Hornet and Kato at a press luncheon complete with green corsages, and green-tinted water. Dozier assured reporters that the Hornet was nothing like Batman. "Not in any sense," he said. "This will not be a camp show – whatever that is. But, there will be a very heavy overlay of gimmicks, gadgets, flair, pace and excitement. When the Green Hornet was on radio, you could only hear the Black Beauty. Now, you'll be able to see it, and it will make the James Bond car look like a baby buggy."

While the Hornet drove around in his Black Beauty, in real life Van drove a 1959 Pontiac station wagon. When he was offered the role, he needed the work. He was working outside of show business, and doing volunteer work for the Sheriff's Department. "When I signed on for the series," he recalled, "I bought a brand new Chevrolet. Vicki got the new Chevy, but I was still driving the station wagon!"

Production of *The Green Hornet* began at 20th Century-Fox Studios on June 6, 1966. Unlike the television hit, *Batman*, *The Green Hornet* was played "straight." Van recalled, "I told Bill Dozier that I didn't want to go running around in tights like Batman. The Hornet is a pretty dead-pan guy." And that was how Van played the role. "And lots of action – that's what makes a show," he added. In fact, Van nixed several Hornet scripts because there was too much dialog. "Let's face it," he told *TV Guide* in September, 1966, "you just can't tell stories any more about normal people and real-life situations to the TV viewer or the movie-goer. You know, there are a lot of fine Shakespearean actors who are starving."

On September 9, the *Los Angeles Times* printed an interview with Van conducted by Vernon Scott. "Thank God for television," Van said, "you have room for mistakes. Very few actors come out here with enough training, and TV gives you the opportunity to learn while you earn. When I first came out here the method was very large. Now they're not hiring those types anymore. Then it was the freak phase for foreign guys with long hair. Now the all-American look is back again. And that's where I come in.

"Acting is here today and gone tomorrow. I've been in the business eight years now and the bubble hasn't burst yet. Every series, every change in my career has been a step upward. I fought the teenage image, the fan magazine stories and the gimmicks. I just wanted to learn my trade."

About his latest assignment as the Hornet, Van said, "Our budget is double *Surfside 6*. And that was an hour show. So you can see the difference. I'd like to do movies someday, but meanwhile I don't have to go off on location, and the money is very nice indeed."

In the months leading up to the premiere, Van promoted the show on *The Mike Douglas Show*, and Van and Bruce Lee appeared on an episode of the daytime, teen program *Where the Action Is*, filmed at Malibu beach. On September 7, Van and Bruce in their Green Hornet costumes made an appearance at Dodger Stadium in a pre-game activities program for the fans, benefitting the YMCA.

The first episode of *The Green Hornet* was broadcast on ABC-TV on September 9, 1966. To further promote the new show, Van – as Green Hornet, and Adam West – as Batman, made a cameo appearance on *The Milton Berle Show* on September 16.

Dozier felt it was essential to present the show in a one-hour format to give time to develop more intricate plots. He also wanted to be able to present the Hornet in international story lines. "I think the major mistake was the network not giving the show an hour to begin with," Van recalled, "because they could have done so much more with it. There were problems in time in setting up the image of an international situation. James Bond never got involved in anything minor. It was either internationally on the edge of disaster, or Britain on the edge of disaster, but it was never just petty crooks stealing a few pennies, or small crimes. So they set up a very simple plot, a very simple introduction of the Green Hornet to the plot, and the rest of the show was figuring out how to solve the crime using all the gimmicks, basically because they wanted to sell the merchandising. I think they were too wrapped up in that. The problem, in my estimation, was that they set up these minor crooks and we went through all of this fancy stuff to solve the problems when it didn't take all of that. Even in *Batman*, even though it was a joke, they set up these people and elaborate schemes because they wanted to control the world and Gotham City, and it wasn't just a petty criminal. The network also treated it as a kiddie show, putting it on Friday night at 7:30, and that's not what it was. We had more college students and older students interested in it because of Bruce Lee."

Dozier tried to tie-in *The Green Hornet* with the huge success of *Batman*. Van and Bruce Lee made three guest appearances in character on *Batman*. They first made a "bat-climb" cameo in the episode, "The Spell of Tut," on September 28, 1966. They later guest-starred in a two-part episode, "A Piece of the Action," broadcast on March 1, 1967, and "Batman's Satisfaction" on March 2nd.

"I played Pinky Pinkston on the two-part cross-over episode on *Batman* with Van," Diane McBain recalled. "We had always stayed in touch, but that was the first time working together again since *Surfside 6*. We had a great time. It was lots of fun."

In a last ditch effort to promote the show that was failing in the ratings, Van was booked as a celebrity guest on *The Hollywood Squares Daytime* game show in February, 1967.

The Green Hornet did not endure, but Bruce Lee did. "Bruce was a very nice boy. His wife Linda was nice and his son was about two when we started the show. Bruce was very content. I can't say that he really wanted to be an actor necessarily. He wanted to show off his "jeet-kun-do" as he called it, and he did a pretty good job. He died very young, but he went on to have a big international career. I liked him very much and we became good friends. We spoke often afterwards, and got together for lunch whenever we could."

The final episode of the series was broadcast on March 24, 1967. *The Green Hornet* was cancelled after only twenty-six episodes.

Van and Bruce Lee in *The Green Hornet*.

After *The Green Hornet* ended, Van worked infrequently on television. He guest-starred in *The Big Valley* in 1968. In 1970, he appeared on *Mannix, Love,*

American Style, and *Nanny and the Professor*. He guest-starred in an episode of *Ironside* in 1971, and an episode of *Mission: Impossible* in 1972. *Apple's Way* and *Gunsmoke* provided him guest-star roles in 1974. Van appeared on *The Manhunter* in 1975, and shared top-billing with Dorothy McGuire in the made-for-television film, *The Runaways*, which was broadcast on April 1, 1975. The film which concerned a teenage boy and an escaped leopard was the most viewed primetime program in the U.S. for the week when it debuted.

In the early summer of 1975, Van and his family relocated to Hawaii to begin production of an NBC-TV Saturday morning program titled, *Westwind*. The story concerned an underwater photographer, played by Van, his marine biologist wife and two children who sail around remote islands in the Pacific, encountering exotic dangers and adventures on their twin-mast yacht called "Westwind." John Carradine played the villainous Captain Hooks.

The show premiered on September 6, 1975 and was a hit with a young audience. However, after thirteen episodes, the series was cancelled because of the excessive production costs involved with location shooting, and the elaborate underwater photography. The final episode was broadcast on November 29, 1975. Van enjoyed the assignment ("One of my favorite acting jobs"), and loved Hawaii even more. He bought a home there during the production of the series.

During the next four years, Van starred in the made-for-television movies *You Gotta Start Somewhere*, in 1977, *Colorado C.I.*, in 1978, and *The Night Rider*, in 1979, and guest-starred in numerous TV series including *The Streets of San Francisco*, *Tales of the Unexpected*, *Barnaby Jones*, *The Red Hand Gang*, *How the West Was Won*, *Centennial*, and *Mrs. Columbo*. He retired from acting after his final television appearance on *The Rockford Files* in 1979.

Van was never interested in celebrity or being in the limelight. He approached acting as a business, strictly as a means of earning a living. "I'd like to be a success," he said, "but I never counted on it. It's too harum-scarum. By the time *The Green Hornet* came along, I had pretty well decided to get out of the television business. About the only thing I enjoyed about those years was the location work. Basically, I'm a shy person. I knew that public appearances and autographs and all that are a necessary part of the business, but it wasn't for me."

In the later 1970s, Van became a volunteer with the Malibu station of the Los Angeles County Sheriff's Department, and worked for its search and rescue team. He was not afraid of challenges, and jumped in whenever called upon. On one dangerous assignment, his lungs were singed while working as a volunteer firefighter, and he suffered permanent bronchial problems. He even suffered back injuries on the job. "I did some of my own stunts on film," he said, "but it was nothing compared to real physical challenges law enforcement officers face every day."

In 1982 he opened a communications company in Santa Monica that leased time on six two-way radio repeater stations. "I got involved with a governmental agency that was not really law enforcement," he explained in a 1988 interview. "And in working with them, I worked with law enforcement agencies. I did a lot of work with the Los Angeles Police Department, and the Los Angeles County Sheriff's Department. After *Hornet* was cancelled, I decided I didn't want to depend upon that business fully, as a livelihood, for the rest of my life. So I really started looking around for other things to do. That's why I got involved with the government. I didn't like what I was doing there, and I actually thought at one point of becoming a reserve deputy, not a regular deputy. At that particular point I was thirty-five years old, which was too old for that then. They would take you up to thirty-five and that was the cutoff, and they wouldn't waive it. But I don't think I would have enjoyed being a full-time law enforcement officer, especially starting at thirty-five years old. Being on *The Green Hornet* didn't help me because all of that stuff they film about police and all that has nothing to do with what goes on out there in the real world. You see these shows where there's pursuits and things going on in every show, but you could probably take one cop's career of twenty-five years and expand it into all the action that happens, and have one two-hour movie. There are some real anxious moments out there, but I've worked in law enforcement now for twenty years and I probably haven't had more than ten real anxious moments. The rest of the time is regular boring police work. Asking a lot of dumb questions. Writing reports. Being sure everything is exactly right because if it's not you know that it's going to get thrown out of court. There is a great burden on police officers not to get everything right, because if you don't, that's as far as it gets with the crime because it gets thrown out."

Van retired from acting in 1979, but returned in 1993 to play the cameo role of *The Green Hornet* director in the feature film, *Dragon: The Bruce Lee Story*. He told a reporter, "I didn't really care that much for the acting business. I didn't like the people in it, the way they operated and all the phoniness and back-stabbing. It was not a very pleasant education for a guy from Texas whose handshake was his word. Plus, I'd gone into acting looking at it as a business, not wanting necessarily to be a celebrity."

In the early 1990s, Van again surrendered to his love of "wide-open spaces" and moved to Hailey, Idaho, a town near Sun Valley. At last, Van was living in peaceful retirement. He and his wife traveled to Africa every year, and hosted their kids and grandchildren for holidays and during summer vacations. He also enjoyed mountain biking, and spent many hours fishing with actor Adam West, who was a neighbor.

In 2011, Van found himself again the subject of tabloids and entertainment publications. On October 3rd of that year, he suffered a serious heart attack at his home. "It happened around 9:30 in the morning," he told a reporter. "What I was doing at the time was that I was on my back, in my garage, trying to fix a dead battery in my motorcycle. Had the battery not been dead – I likely would have been out dirt-bike riding – and in these parts, you go a few miles from our house and it's completely wilderness – there's bears, elks, moose, deer, you name it wildlife. I don't want to think what would have happened if I had been out riding when I was stricken. I likely would have been a goner. It's so rural out there to get reception I sometimes have to use a satellite phone. And I don't often pack it on my cycle because I keep the bike stripped down.

"I knew instantly it was a heart attack. I've never felt pain like that in my life. It was excruciating. I've been in rodeo accidents, stunts gone wrong, but nothing ever like that."

He was airlifted to a nearby hospital. "The chopper rescued me and got me to the hospital. They were able to put a stent in. I had one hundred percent blockage, but they were able to remove the blockage. Then they discovered I had pancreatitis. I had to stay in the hospital for a week."

After his heart attack, Van and his wife decided to leave the wilderness of Idaho, and move to a warmer, drier climate. They bought a home in Scottsdale, Arizona. Van lived a quiet life with his family, and occasionally ventured out to attend autograph conventions and fan meet-and-greet events. In the fall of 2016, his deteriorating health necessitated moving him to an assisted care facility near his home. He died there of kidney failure on November 28, 2016. He was 82 years old. He was survived by his wife of fifty-five years, his twin daughters Lisa and Lynne, his two children with Vicki, Tia and Britt, his step-daughter Nina, and nine grandchildren.

"He had a wonderful, caring, and kind heart, "Vicki said. "He was a wonderful husband; he was a fabulous father, and a devoted grandfather."

Lee Patterson

Lee Patterson played the role of Dave Thorne, the third of the three private detectives. Born Beverley Frank Atherly Patterson on March 31, 1929 in Vancouver, British Columbia, he was the second-eldest of four sons, and considered the most rebellious. Lee's father, a former London stage and screen actor, was a bank teller, and his mother a housewife. The family struggled financially, and his parents had a rocky marriage.

Lee Patterson.

When he was a young boy, Lee contracted Polio. He was confined to his home, and his slow recovery included learning to walk again. He wasn't able to attend school until after his sixth birthday, and was bullied for his slow-to-heal awkward gait, and the ill-fitting hand-me-down clothes he wore. His high school years were challenging. If he wasn't getting into fights at school, he was stepping between his battling parents at home, often trading shoves and punches with his father. His mother tried to intercede and defend him, but over time, he came to resent her for staying in an abusive marriage.

To control his frustrations, he played hockey in high school, and was a champion middleweight and light heavyweight boxer. To please his mother, he learned to play the trombone. His skills as a hockey player earned him several offers from professional hockey teams.

Lee ran errands and made deliveries for the local pharmacy and grocery store to earn pocket money. When he was fifteen, life at home became unbearable. His parents' fights and arguments became more frequent and more violent. His battles with his father worsened. He ran away from home after a fistfight that bloodied father and son.

"I had a dollar eight or two thirty or some ridiculous sum in my pocket when I ran away from home," he recalled, "and it lasted two days." When he was sixteen years old, he left home for good with one of his buddies. "I had only the clothes on my back – a sports jacket, a pair of flannel pants, a shirt. My family didn't know I was leaving – I just disappeared," he said. "I traveled around, worked at many jobs, and hitched thousands of miles. I could just about eat and try to stay alive."

For the next three years, he worked as a jack of all trades. He worked in restaurants as a waiter, busboy, bartender, and dish washer. He worked as a car-washer, a golf caddy at Banff (he caddied for Jack Benny who holidayed at the resort), and conducted surveys. He worked on barges on the Great Lakes, mined in Northern Quebec, and worked in a lumber mill in British Columbia.

"A friend and I were working our way through Canada," he recalled. "We were sixteen and trying to make enough money to get down to the southern part of the country when we got mining jobs. It was wild country. Nobody seemed to think it strange for a sixteen-year-old boy to be in a mine. If there were child labor laws against it, nobody up there had heard about them."

They had to purchase work equipment at the company store on credit. The cost would be deducted from their pay. The arrangement put the boys in debt, so there was no turning back.

"The shaft was about 3,000 feet deep, and the miners were let down in a skip that was run by a fellow who seemed more interested in a card game than in the passengers' safety. A skip is a little cage on a cable, with a dial at the top of the shaft to show how far the cage has dropped. Force of gravity pulls it down, and an operator at the mouth of the entrance is supposed to stop it at various levels by pulling a lever. The madman who operated this skip never looked at the dial! He played cards while the cable reeled out and the cage plunged toward destruction. Then, just before the cage crashed, some instinct would alert the operator, and he would jerk the lever, still studying his card hand.

"I asked him once, 'Don't you ever look at that dial?' 'Nah,' he said."

One day, Lee found himself in a dark, narrow tunnel with one other fellow, an older man who spoke only French. Lee did not speak French. The fellow handed him a bucket, and motioned for the young man to follow him.

"I don't know when I realized that I was carrying dangerous explosives, but it came to me. I didn't know where I was going or what was going to happen, so, with the blind confidence of youth, I followed the Frenchman. At the end of the tunnel, he began boring holes in the rock, and planting explosive charges. I was working with a blaster. He knew what he was doing, I think, but I didn't, and he didn't bother to tell me. Of course, if he had tried, I wouldn't have known what he was talking about anyway."

When the charges were planted, the older man started to walk back towards the skip. Then, he suddenly began to run. Lee didn't know what to do, so he ran after him. He wondered what was going on, and then realized, "That old fool had set off a fuse or something, and the tunnel was going to collapse. He didn't even warn me!"

Lee heard the explosion behind him. The ground shook and the tunnel walls began to fold. The shoring was snapping around them, and dirt and dust was pelting from every direction. Lee began to gasp for breath.

"I thought I'm going to die. How many more minutes do I have to live?! Did that Frenchman make a mistake, or doesn't he give a damn that I'm going to get trapped?! He's getting away!"

As they approached the skip, the man tossed Lee a face mask. They reached the surface without barely acknowledging each other, the dust cloud rising in the shaft below them. Lee and his buddy quit their mining job that day. They left, not even earning enough to pay back the cost of their equipment.

The two boys traveled to the north woods in search of work. They were hired as day laborers at a lumber company, clear-cutting trees. Again, Lee found himself working at an unsafe job site where blasting was taking place.

"Nobody told me anything about where or when the next blast was set. I don't know what warned me, but suddenly some instinct told me that I better clear out. I jumped over a knoll, and as I did, the place I'd been standing at blew sky high!"

Lee and his buddy continued to work their way through the north country of Canada. "I was working as a bushwhacker clearing brush with an axe. The axe slipped and went through my boot and right into my foot. The foreman sent me back to camp. I had to walk about a mile. The blood was spilling out of the sliced leather. The pain was sickening. I had to do something to stop the bleeding, and luckily I found some spruce gum. That's an Indian remedy. I packed the wound with spruce gum and managed to get to camp. When I got there, the supervisor told me that I didn't have to cut any more brush that day, but that I could carry some cord wood instead. An hour and a half after the bushwhacking crew had come back in, I was still carrying wood."

Despite the dangers, Lee never regretted his youthful adventures. "A boy has to have his freedom to learn how to take care of himself. I took my younger brother out of college in Canada and sent him to Paris for a year to the Sorbonne where he was on his own and had to learn French. When he went back to school, he finished in half the time."

Lee joked, "I don't think I take more chances than other people. The Hollywood Freeway is as dangerous – more dangerous – than most of the other places I have been."

Lee discovered an inborn artistic talent and began painting and sculpting when he finally settled in Toronto. He enrolled in the Ontario College of Art and Design. He created decorative papier-mâché floats for the city's annual Christmas Parade. His skills earned him commissions to design floats for Montreal's legendary Santa Claus Parade.

When he was twenty-one years old, he moved to Paris to study art. After a very short time, he became disenchanted with the Paris "art scene." He thought the profession was "overrun with dilettantes and sub-masculine types." He left France, and crossed the channel to London. "I told my mother I'd look up some relatives in Ireland, and she said, 'Son, it's never a good idea to look up relatives!'

"In England," he explained, "I worked at many different jobs again – as an usher, a trucker, and as boss of a roofing gang made up of Polish immigrants who were tearing down old Army camps outside London. There were some rough times – fights, knifings."

He finally abandoned "hard-knock" jobs, and landed a job at the British Broadcasting Company in London as a stage manager and set designer. One day, he was asked to pick up an actor's check at the agent's office and bring it back to the BBC office. "I had to walk all the way. I had no money even for bus fare." When the agent saw the tall, handsome, curly-haired brunette, he asked him if he was an actor. Lee lied. "I said I was. I don't know what made me decide to go into acting – it was a fluke, really. Originally, I liked my design job at the BBC. I just fell into the whole thing,"

A short time later, he snuck onto a train without paying the fare to get to a part of London where he auditioned for the role of Happy in a production of *Death of a Salesman*. He nailed the audition, and landed the part, and began his acting career at the Theatre Royal in Windsor, England. He then appeared in a theatrical production of *Johnny Belinda*, for which he also designed the sets.

Lee made his London West End debut playing the son of Mary Martin in the musical, *South Pacific*. He then appeared in other London productions including, *Stalag 17*, *The Troublemakers*, and *The Man*.

Lee first appeared on the British screen in an uncredited role in the 1953 feature film, *Malta Story*. His first credited screen role was in the 1954 film noir, *The Good Die Young*, starring Laurence Harvey, Gloria Grahame, Richard Basehart, and Joan Collins.

During the next seven years, he acted in radio plays, appeared in numerous television dramas and twenty-eight feature films including *The Passing Stranger* (1954), *The Story of Esther Costello* (1957), *Jack the Ripper* (1959), and *The 3 Worlds of Gulliver* (1960). He worked in Spain, Italy, France, Switzerland, Germany, Denmark, and England. With a few exceptions, most of his motion pictures were "B" films, but he achieved a certain stardom. "My name was above the film title on the marquee," he said. "I did stuff like *Timelock*, which was Arthur Hailey's first film, and *Gulliver's Travels* – you can call that my smallest part. I really loved it. I was head of the little people.

"Another one of my favorites was *Spin in the Dark* in 1956." Lee played the role of a Canadian in London try- ing to succeed as a prizefighter. In the process, he gets mixed up with the local mob boss's sister, played by Faith Domergue. "Talk about life imitating art," he joked.

In spite of working virtually non- stop in European films and televi- sion, he was not satisfied. In addition, homesickness set in, and he decided to leave England.

He returned to Canada and guest-starred in the television series, *Encounter*, for the CBC. The episode, "You Win, You Lose," aired on January 24. 1960. Lee moved to Hollywood at William Orr's invitation. He had plenty of acting experience, so he wasn't asked to screen test for Warner Brothers, instead he guest-starred in two epi- sodes of *The Alaskans*. He also had a guest-starring role on Henry Fonda's TV series, *The Deputy*, filmed at Universal Studios.

"I was always a free soul," Lee explained. "Originally, a lot of the studios were offering me contracts, but I didn't want them. I wanted freedom. I'd do a movie and take three weeks off to go sailing. Do another movie and take three months off for skiing, another movie and take six months off for both sailing and skiing."

He entered into a difficult, six-week negotiation with William Orr and Warner Brothers to co-star in their new detective series, *Surfside 6*. Although he had heard of Lee's reputation as a "hard-head," Orr wondered why a vir- tual unknown actor in Hollywood would not jump at the chance for a seven- year contract with one of the biggest movie studios in America.

"Because," Lee recalled, "when I put my signature on a contract, I'm going to honor it."

Ultimately, Lee refused to be tied down to a long-term contract with Warner Brothers, but in early 1960 he did agree to co-star in the studio's new primetime series titled, *Surfside 6*. "There was a whole slew of those detective- type shows then. Our show was based in Miami. I played the older detective and Troy Donahue played the younger one. The show lasted two years, and was syndicated into reruns for another two, and I loved the whole thing. It was the slick professionalism of an American crew I admired, as opposed to the other crews I worked with around the world."

Van Williams, Lee, Diane McBain.

In the spring of 1960, production on *Surfside 6* began with a couple of weeks' location shooting in Miami Beach, before moving to the studio back-lot. He hoped the series would give him the Hollywood stardom he desired. He was happy living in America, as well, and applied for citizenship soon after arriving in California.

"I couldn't be more American than I am," he said at the time. "I'm so pro-American that I'll attack my American friends if they criticize the country. I've built a home here. This is the hand that feeds me. And once I'm a citizen I'll have the right to comment. I don't feel that I have, now."

He told a reporter, "Do you know how wonderful it is to live here? To be able to go twenty-four hours a day and get cigarettes because everybody has that kind of money in his pocket! You get the slightest feeling you're thirsty, and you can turn on the tap and get a glass of water! There are countries in Europe where you have to buy the water! I've seen people go thirsty all day because they're allowed only one glass of water. They can't afford any more. When you see this kind of stuff, boy, you gotta know you're lucky."

He said that he's often known "the wrong end of the stick." Nevertheless, he said, he felt that he had matured, and had shaken the chip on his shoulder. His up and down life experiences "had enriched rather than enraged him."

Lee and Diane.

He added, "I could have gone two ways. Sure, I could have been bitter, but that would have meant shutting my eyes to everything good that's happened to me."

Diane McBain recalls, "I liked Lee. He was reliable and professional. He was very independent, and didn't reveal much about himself. He never spoke about his childhood. We dated for a short time during the filming of the first season. And we went on a few publicity junkets together to promote the show. I was trying to get over my affair with Richard Burton while we filmed *Ice Palace*. I was lonely. Lee hadn't been in Hollywood very long. He didn't know a lot of people. He asked me out, and we spent some time together. He was not the sort of guy who would commit to anyone. When he got what he wanted, the thrill was gone for both of us. But I liked him, and felt like I never really got to know him very well."

Lee was a self-proclaimed bachelor. He dated numerous women, but was never interested in matrimony. "I've been accused of not having a sense of responsibility, but actually, it's to the contrary," he said. "There would be nothing I would like better at six in the morning when I'm getting ready to go to the studio than to have a woman there to fix my coffee, but I can't use women like that. Marriage is for some people and not for others, and it is not for me. I know myself too well. If I have a few days off, I like to take off for

Lee, Margarita, and Diane.

Bermuda, go to London, go sailing, go sport fishing – and I'd be very unhappy if I couldn't live that way. I have found that a woman finds that exciting for a while, but sooner or later, she wants a more settled way of life. When that happens, it's time for me to say adios. I try not to hurt anyone, and don't think that I have, but I do believe in doing my own thing.

"My goal is living. The idea is not to make things happen but to allow things to happen. This can be very pleasant, and it's the opposite of planning in great detail for the future. The people who plan and plan are likely to be disappointed. So many are so busy planning tomorrow that they don't enjoy today! I believe in today. I like the unexpected, the sudden surprises.'

His role as Dave Thorne on *Surfside 6* did not give him the "movie leading-man" status he had hoped for. When the series was cancelled, his contract obligations to Warner Brothers ended. His refusal to sign a seven-year contract with the studio backfired professionally, since he was never offered any film roles there during the two years he filmed *Surfside 6*. His refusal to commit to the studio discouraged the production chief from investing in Lee's career.

He returned to the stage for his first acting assignment in the summer of 1962, starring with Arlene Dahl in *Roman Candle* for the Kenley Players in Ohio. Later that year, he made a controversial, adult-themed feature film in Spain titled *The Ceremony*, starring Laurence Harvey. He then went to London to film guest-starring roles in the TV series *The Avengers* and *ITV Play of the Week*.

Lee filmed a guest-starring role on the series *Arrest and Trial*, at Universal Studios, which was broadcast on March 29, 1964. In October, he traveled to New York City to begin rehearsals for his Broadway debut. *P.S. I Love You*, starring Geraldine Page opened on November 19, 1964. The comedy concerned the infidelity of two married couples – an American couple stationed in Paris for business and a French couple they befriend. Lee played the role of Page's American husband. Howard Taubman, reviewing the play for *The New York Times*, was not impressed. He wrote, "You could die of boredom waiting for something titillating to happen. You could also perish waiting for someone to say something bright or comic." The only thing about the play that earned a positive mention was Geraldine Page's couture gowns and diamond jewelry. *P.S. I Love You* closed after only twelve performances on November 28. It was a disappointing experience for Lee.

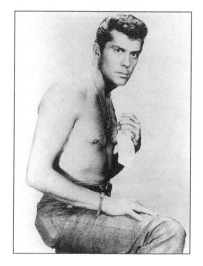

In June, 1965, Lee guest-starred in an episode of *Kraft Suspense Theater*. He was then offered a role that would forever change the trajectory of his career. He was cast in a daytime drama produced by Doris Quinlan titled *The Nurses*.

He played the role of Brad Kiernan for two years (making him one of the first film and primetime television stars to appear on daytime TV), and he continued to accept guest-starring roles on several television series including *Combat*, *The Virginian*, *Perry Mason*, *12 O'Clock High*, and *Bonanza*. In 1967, he joined an all-star cast in an unsold television pilot for NBC called *Stranded*. The story concerned a jetliner from Miami to Caracas that crashes in the Venezuelan jungle, stranding the surviving passengers and crew in exotic and dangerous surroundings. Filmed on the Universal Studios' backlot, the title was changed to *Valley of Mystery*, and broadcast as a television film. The following year he starred in a made-for-TV film titled *Power Trip*, for the CBC, and starred in *The Search for the Evil One*, a feature film about a Nazi hunter who investigates a report that a group of Nazis rescued Hitler and have hidden him in a castle in Argentina where they plan a Fourth Reich. "*Evil One* is a very good film," Lee recalled. "It was a low budget, actually *no* budget, independent movie. If it was made or distributed by a major film company, it would have done really well. But it wasn't. And it didn't."

Lee's father died in 1967. His mother then moved to Toronto to be near his brothers Jack and Paul who had relocated there to pursue their business interests. His brother Neil lived in San Francisco and worked in the publishing business.

In 1968, Quinlan called Lee again and offered him a plum role on another daytime drama she produced titled *One Life to Live*. The program was taped in New York City. He was living in California at the time, but immediately moved to New York. "When Doris told me the part was that of an Irish newspaper man, Joe Riley, I groaned, 'I did that for you on *The Nurses*!' And she said, 'You'll do it till you get it right!'"

Lee played the role of Joe Riley on *One Life to Live* from 1968 until (in soap opera fashion) his character's presumed death in 1970. "I thought that was it," he recalled. "I decided to move back to California." He gave up his New York apartment, and shipped his furniture, antiques and art to a newly rented Hollywood house. One of his hobbies was collecting antiques. "I have an old spinning wheel, and an 1827 sextant I'll use some day in navigating a ship I plan to buy," he said. "And I collect military silks, all made in China, of British battalions. They're like flags, and hard to get."

Once back in Hollywood, he filmed a guest role in 1970 on the television series *The Immortal* at Paramount. And then the travel bug called his name. He moved to London, where he rented a flat. He filmed a role in the Charles Bronson film *Chato's Land*. Although the story was set in New Mexico, the film was shot in Spain. Lee also played the role of an international art thief in a two-part, 1971 episode of the British series *Jason King*.

After two years in Britain, he returned to New York to reprise his role of Joe Riley on *One Life to Live* in 1972, and remained a romantic lead on the show until 1979. "Doing a serial is a tough business and requires high competence. It's not for inexperienced actors. You've got little time for preparation and you've got to get it right the first time!"

He gave up his rented Hollywood home, and moved his things to a condo in Palm Desert, California. "I bought it because I like to play golf now and then," he said. But Lee made New York City his home base for the next eight years. He lived in a residential hotel on the Upper West Side, overlooking Central Park. "The exciting thing about New York is that no three people think or act the same. There are rednecks everywhere – even in New York! Some bars in the lower East Side are doing a number on every ethnic group. But they wouldn't do that Uptown; they know they'd get punched out up here! We'll always have those types of 'frontier' problems, because we have frontiers."

In 1973, he built a Newporter ketch for $60,000, which he moored in Milford, Connecticut. "It's my real home," he said. "The apartment hotel is only where I sleep. I'm out on my ship all the time when I'm not working. Summers. Weekends. Days off. Even in the winter. And the sea follows me into my apartment which I decorated with nautical curios that I collected for years.

"I started sailing as a child. My father was a sailor, too. He had a boat and I stole a bed sheet and made a sail for it. This is typically Irish. I got the hell beaten out of me for stealing the sheet, and a pat on the back for having the ingenuity to do it.

"I can't ever remember not loving the sea. When I travel, the first thing I do is head for the coastline. I was born by the Pacific Ocean, but I don't know if that's the reason I love the sea so much. After all, there are people from landlocked Iowa who love the sea. It goes deeper than remembering the sea as a child."

After years of working, Lee enjoyed a good life. "I have my yacht, my two Lincoln cars, my comforts, a nice apartment…but it's the sea and sailing that mean the most. My ship is a floating city with all the comforts. I love it, even though it has a narrow bed for me, whereas in my apartment I have a king-sized bed." Lee admitted to being a very happy man. "Just think! I live two lives…acting and sailing…and they're both great! And to think some people can't make it with one life…and I have two! I move a lot. I travel. I have a profound interest in the whole world. I'm interested in everything."

He described himself as a realist. "I try to remember that what seems a disaster today usually turns out not to be so bad after all. We survive! I try not to be crushed by trouble or sadness. I take the bull by the horn and say, 'I'll make it!' And I do!" Lee remembered a comment his mother made one day at the dinner table. "A pessimist says, 'Pass the milk.' An optimist says, 'Pass the cream,' and the realist says, 'Pass the jug.' Well, I think I'm the realist who isn't sure whether there's milk or cream in the jug, and just wants the jug and will accept whatever is in it."

Lee joked that he had one foot on a soundstage and the other on his boat. When he was working on *One Life to Live*, he said he concentrated totally on his role. "I'm a pro," he said. "I'm disciplined. I take my work seriously even though I seem casual about it. But when I'm at sea, I think only of sailing. I have my charts; I know what I'm doing: I'm ready for any emergency. I know the dangers as well as the thrills of handling a big sailboat."

Although his boat was equipped so that one person could sail it alone, he often invited his co-stars and friends on board. "They're not special, though," he said. "No visiting royalty, they're a member of the crew. I want them totally involved. I want them to participate. I give a guided tour and explain all the equipment and what it does, and then teach them how to work some part of the boat. They have a better experience that way."

When the last day of shooting is over, Lee hit the road. He might go to Los Angeles for work, or to Boston to check on a plastics business he owns. But it's more likely he headed to where his boat was docked. "While driving up to the boat," he said, "I listen to tapes of scenes I've done the previous week, listen to see if they make sense. But once I'm on board, that's it. The minute my feet hit the plank, everything is shut out. I can put up with all the irritating things that go on in show business, in any business, because of sailing. It's all trivia. Looking back at the land helps you see how small it is and you can sort through all the garbage.

"I can stand anything but stupidity. I'm quiet for the longest time, but a small thing can send me flying, because it's usually unnecessary. If a camera breaks down, I'll sit around all day and wait for it to be fixed. But if some jerk is too selfish or too crazy to do something about it because he's involved in some kind of power play, I'll go off the wall! I'll go for the throat!"

Acting provided Lee a steady source of income since he was a young man, but he was also involved in different side businesses. "Money is the key to freedom," he said. "It allows you objectivity and honesty. I'm not money-mad, but I saw to it many years ago that I would be secure. If I was offered a part, I could say no if it was wrong, and afford not to do it. I take my work seriously, but I don't take my life seriously. People will forgive you anything but success. I worked at NBC for so long because I'm good. I was with Doris Quinlan because I was good. Bull to luck. I believe people make their own opportunities.

"Look at women. I always worked in show business with successful, strong women. One of the toughest women I ever knew was also the most gracious – my mother. Yet, when a woman is successful, there are always questions – who did she sleep with? That sort of thing. But, that's their problem."

After months of backstage turmoil, NBC fired Doris Quinlan from her producer position on *One Life to Live* in 1977. "I had a gut feeling that when Doris left, I should have left," Lee recalled. But he stayed on for nearly two more years. "But the quality of the show fizzled out." He left *One Life to Live* in 1979 to play the role of Dr. Kevin Cook on a few episodes of *Another World*, and then played the same character on a new daytime soap opera titled *Texas*, from 1980 until 1981. He returned to play the role of Tom Dennison, Joe Riley's twin brother, on *One Life to Live* from 1986 until 1988.

Lee told a reporter in 1981 that he dreamt of sailing away into the sunset one day, but his longest solo sailing trip was from Annapolis, Maryland to Newport, Rhode Island. "Someday I'll sail it alone across the Atlantic. Ten years from this very moment I will be drinking a glass of very fine wine and say, 'Well, Fiji is quite pretty.'"

In 1982, with his soap opera work behind him, he moved back to Los Angeles. That year he had a small role in the feature film *Airplane II: The Sequel*, and appeared on *The Fall Guy* and *Magnum, P.I.* "I did *Magnum* so I could go sailing in Hawaii where it was shot," he said.

He played the role of the President in "All the Money in the World," an episode of *ABC Weekend Specials*, and guest-starred in an episode of the series *Matt Houston*, in 1983. The next year he guest-starred on *Riptide*, *The A-Team*, *Hunter*, and *Scarecrow and Mrs. King*. He played the small role of a newscaster in the feature film *Death Wish 3*, released in 1985.

Lee returned to his London flat in 1984 to begin rehearsals for a stage production of *The Caine Mutiny Court Martial* starring Ben Cross and Charlton Heston. The drama previewed on February 4, 1985 at the Theatre Royal in Brighton, and showcased at the Palace Theatre in Manchester from February 18 until February 23. *The Caine Mutiny Court Martial* opened at Queens Theatre in London on February 26, and played through June 29 earning respectable reviews and large audiences. Before returning to America, Lee guest-starred in an episode of *Lytton's Diary*, and filmed a supporting role in the television movie *The Last Days of Patton*, starring George C. Scott.

In May, 1986, Lee reprised his role in *The Caine Mutiny Court Martial* at the Henry Fonda Theater in Hollywood. Lee did not appear in the Washington D.C. engagement of the play in June. He butted heads with Heston, who also directed, one too many times. "I don't get along with actors who think they're artists," he said. "The writer is the artist. I can say that because I am an artist. I sculpt and paint – that's artistic."

Lee played a role in the ambitious TV mini-series *War and Remembrance*, broadcast on November 15, 1988. A few months later, he guest-starred on an episode of the series *MacGyver*. He returned to his London flat for the last time in 1991. He filmed a supporting role in the feature film *Bullseye!*, starring Michael Caine and Roger Moore, and played a guest-starring role in the TV series *Zorro*, which was filmed in Spain. Lee didn't appear on screen again for nearly three years. He played a supporting role in the 1994 feature film *Healer*, memorable for starring Turhan Bey in his first film in forty-one years. Lee's final acting role was a guest-star appearance in an episode of the Fox-TV series *Shadow*, which was broadcast in 1996.

Lee retired from acting in 1995, and lived a private life on a boat on Lake Travis in the small town of Lago Vista, Texas. He suffered ill health for a couple of years, and was hospitalized on several occasions. He died in a Galveston Island hospital of congestive heart failure complicated by lung cancer and emphysema on February 14, 2007. He was 77 years old. His death was not reported for nearly a year. Lee Patterson never married. He left the bulk of his estate to St. Jude Children's Hospital in honor of his friend, Danny Thomas.

Diane McBain

Diane McBain.

Diane McBain played the role of socialite Daphne Dutton who berths her yacht, Daffy II, next to the Surfside houseboat. Daphne was a good friend of the Surfside "boys," and was often involved in their cases, misadventures and investigations.

Diane was born on May 18, 1941 in Cleveland, Ohio. Her mother, Cleo Ferguson, was a housewife. Her father, Walter McBain, was a bus driver who loved to play the horses. In 1944, when her father was drafted to serve in the Navy during the waning years of WWII, Diane's mother, her aunt, and both of her grandmothers packed up and moved by train to Glendale, California. Word was left for her father to join them when he returned from the Navy. "I was raised by strong, independent women," she said.

Growing up, Diane was a bit of a tomboy, and loved playing ball games with her male friends. When she was a young teenager, she worked several menial jobs for pocket money. "When I was fifteen years old," she recalled, "I was still a tomboy at heart. To *feminize* me, my mother and grandmother pooled their resources and enrolled me in the John Robert Powers Modeling School. I could earn money modeling and pay for my eventual college tuition."

Diane's first modeling job introduced her to Hollywood. She was asked to pose in the background with actress Jayne Mansfield and her infamous pink Cadillac. Diane won a few minor beauty contest titles, and was named "Miss Days of the Verdugos" in May, 1957. A photograph of her riding atop a float in the annual Days of the Verdugos parade appeared in the *Los Angeles Times*.

"A family friend suggested I audition for the role of the ingénue lead at the tiny Glendale Centre Theater. I was accepted, and cast in my first play, *Love Comes in Many Colors*, in March, 1958."

Diane's smiling face began to appear on numerous magazine covers. She signed an early contract with Revlon to model and promote the company's cosmetics. "The television commercials I landed and my work at the Glendale Centre Theater proved much more interesting than modeling, though."

In the fall of 1958, an agent expressed an interest in representing her. "He assured my mother and me that television acting was easy. I read for and won a small role on Robert Young's hit TV series, *Father Knows Best*, playing his daughter's high school friend. I loved the experience, and all the activity on the sound stage at Columbia Studios in Hollywood. I loved the $200 pay-check, too."

Following her appearance on the show, she was invited to take acting, diction, and poise classes at Universal-International Studios. Solly Biano, a leading talent scout for Warner Brothers, saw Diane in a play in Glendale. Biano was always on the lookout for new talent for the studio. He invited her to Warner Brothers to read for the casting department. "After a few audi-

tions, I was cast in an episode of the hit television show *Maverick* that was filmed at Warner. I was intrigued by the enormous studio, and the sprawling backlot with a realistic Western set. James Garner was terrific, and Jack Kelly, who played Maverick's brother, gave me my first screen kiss!

"It was a heady time. I continued my final year of high school in Glendale, my lessons at Universal, more frequent print model jobs, and television auditions at Warner. I liked the frantic pace."

Diane next guest-starred in an episode of the popular program *77 Sunset Strip.* "I was still a minor and my mother had to accompany me on the sets. I know she enjoyed herself. To find ourselves in such a situation was surreal. This was a profession people dream about and tirelessly seek. I never did. In a peculiar way, it almost threw itself at me. I felt more like a witness than a participant!"

Shortly after her eighteenth birthday in 1959, Diane signed a seven-year contract with Warner Brothers Studios. "I talked it over with my parents, who were enthusiastic, and we decided to accept the generous offer that provided me with a beginning salary of $250 per week. Although the men were paid more, young contract players were paid a similar amount at signing with escalating salary clauses kicking in each successive year. The contract provided for forty weeks of work with a twelve-week paid hiatus. There were no bonuses promised, and no bonuses were paid to me during my years at the studio. Every contract actor's status was reviewed each six months. If the actor wasn't producing, or had become a troublemaker, the studio could terminate the contract at the end of each six-month period."

Gossip queen Louella Parsons reported that Jack Warner was sitting in a projection room at his studio and saw the episode of *77 Sunset Strip* featuring Diane, and signed her to a contract immediately.

"I have no idea how it came to be that I was offered a long-term contract, but I met Jack Warner only once in passing at a studio function. I don't think he knew who I was."

By the end of the 1950s, television was charging ahead and devouring the feature film market. Like most of the movie studios, Warner Brothers was struggling to keep afloat. "Instead of capitulating to television," Diane recalled, "the studio created a television department that would rival all other contenders for several years to come. Executive Bill Orr was the head of television production on the lot. He was very creative, and powerful, he was married to Jack Warner's stepdaughter. Most television production had been based in New York. Orr moved all studio television production to Los Angeles, which saved money, created more jobs, and tapped into the movie star talent under contract to the studio. He negotiated an exclusive deal with ABC-TV to broadcast new series produced at Warner. Bill Orr personally supervised the ten leading TV series then produced by Warner for ABC. Bill, and his assistant Hugh Benson, were great guys."

In July, 1959, Diane began work on her first feature film, *Ice Palace.* The epic was filmed at the studio, and on location in Alaska. The cast included Robert Ryan, Shirley Knight, George Takei, Jim Backus, Martha Hyer, Carolyn Jones, and Richard Burton. "Richard played the role of my grandfather," Diane recalled, "although he was only thirty-two years old to my eighteen. I was served a large portion of Burton charm. I fell in love with him." Their affair continued during the making of the film, and for some time afterwards.

"Richard encouraged me to read," Diane said. "He advised me to find novels and stories that might be suitable for future roles, and to present them to my agent. He said I needed a better agent, and should never have signed a studio contract. He told me to stay away from television work. That it would destroy my movie career. But I had no choice."

When *Ice Palace* was finished, Diane guest-starred in another episode of *Maverick* and *77 Sunset Strip*. She also appeared on a Bob Hope TV special. "*Ice Palace* was a commercial and critical failure. The studio lost millions of dollars, and I lost my heart to Richard Burton."

In early 1960, Diane moved out from her parent's home on Verdugo Road in Glendale, and into a two-bedroom apartment on Scenic Drive in the Hollywood Hills that she shared with actress Sherry Jackson. "I had no idea how profoundly my life would change. I was assigned a studio publicist and instructed never to engage in a conversation with a critic or gossip columnist. I was told to be seen with certain actors who were also under contract to Warner. I posed for countless publicity photographs and pictorials for magazines. Don Ryber was the publicist who handled me. He was good at spinning stories, or keeping a secret. He was gay, and lived with his boyfriend, Ray. I liked Don and Ray very much, and spent a lot of time with them.

"Don was a great friend and a clever publicist. Through the years, I gave the poor guy plenty of gossip to handle. My family was conservative, and even though one of my best high school friends was gay, I was surprised to meet and work with so many homosexual men at the studio. They were involved in

every creative aspect of movie making, including hair, make-up, costuming, music, art and set design, lighting, and writing. Or course, many actors were gay, but they lived in the closet for fear of sabotaging their career goals. Making movies was deeply infused with homosexual aestheticism. I think their cultural influence was so powerful, it's mystifying to me that so many people – people who loved the movies – harbored homophobic prejudices. I never understood it."

Diane guest-starred in an episode of *The Alaskans* starring Roger Moore. "Roger was thirty-two years old. I didn't pay attention to him, and he didn't pay attention to me. He was too busy having an affair with his leading lady, Dorothy Provine.

"I then filmed three episodes of *Bourbon Street Beat*. This was another detective series using Warner's formula of a requisite team of detectives, an aspiring third detective, and an attractive female character. Sound familiar? Contract players Andrew Duggan, Richard Long, and Van Williams starred in this program set in New Orleans. It was actually shot on Stages 17 and 18 where *A Streetcar Named Desire* was filmed. What was most memorable about that assignment was the beginning of a life-long friendship with Van Williams. Little did we know that he and I would soon be starring in our own detective series at the studio."

Diane was kept busy with TV assignments. She guest-starred in *Sugarfoot*, *The Lawman*, and again on *77 Sunset Strip*. "In the midst of working twelve-hour days in sound stages and on the backlot, I was expected to be available for interviews, photo shoots, and personal appearances. Talented photographers took head and glamour shots of the studios' stars.

"One of the first things a person notices when they become a celebrity is that the people around them suddenly treat them differently. I enjoyed the special treatment. I loved being driven around in limousines and delighted to be adorned in fabulous clothing. The studio's chief costume designer, Howard Shoup, created spectacular outfits for me. Howard was a delightful gay man, and one of the dearest men I ever met in Hollywood, which says a lot. Another very talented gay man named John Brandt became my personal clothing designer."

In the spring of 1960, production began at the studio on a new feature film, *Parrish*, based on the novel by Mildred Savage. The film version was written and directed by Delmar Daves. The story concerned rival tobacco farmers in Connecticut. Dean Jagger, Karl Malden, and Claudette Colbert headlined the cast. Troy Donahue was cast as the title character, Parrish. Connie Stevens and Sharon Hugueny played two young woman chasing after Parrish's affections. Diane was cast in the role of Allison Post, Dean Jagger's manipulative and truculent daughter. "It was a choice role, and I was thrilled to be a part of it," Diane recalled.

In April, production moved to Windsor, Connecticut. "I had known Connie since our time at the Glendale Theater," Diane said. "And I began life-long friendships with Troy and Sharon during that film."

The film was released in early 1961 to mixed reviews, but drew large audiences.

"In 1960, I was on my contractual hiatus for most of the summer. I wasn't required to appear in front of the cameras, but I was still expected to grant interviews and pose for publicity pictures. Columnists speculated about my dating life, but there was nothing at all to report. In August, I was told that I

would be starring as a regular in a new, one-hour detective series set in Miami Beach called *Surfside 6*. I wanted to object, but legally I was required to comply with the studio's demands or face suspension. Burton had warned me that if the studio over-exposed me by too many television appearances, it would destroy my chances for a real career as a motion picture star. And he was right. In a way, I felt as though the studio put me out to pasture."

Diane recalled the genesis of *Surfside 6* in her book, *Famous Enough, A Hollywood Memoir*. "*Surfside 6* was created by studio chief William T. Orr and writer Hugh Benson. The storylines centered around a Miami Beach detective agency that used a sixty-foot, two-story houseboat as a home and office. "Surfside 6" was the telephone exchange that also included the marina slip number where the boat was docked. The detective team featured Troy Donahue as Sandy Winfield II, Van Williams as Ken Madison, and Lee Patterson as Dave Thorne. I was cast as Daphne 'Daffy' Dutton, a 'kooky socialite,' whose yacht was parked next to the boys' houseboat. Margarita Sierra played Cha Cha O'Brien, a singer who worked the Boom Boom Room at the majestic Fontainebleau Hotel across the street. The series also gave the studio another opportunity to use their contract players on a weekly basis. Perhaps the most memorable thing about the show was the popular theme song written by Jerry Livingston and David Mack.

"Though I was billed as a 'regular,' I did not appear in all seventy-four episodes broadcast over the next two years, but I did appear in most. The

Troy, Lee,
Diane, and Van.

show gave the three handsome leading men plenty of opportunity to take their shirts off, Margarita to shimmy and shake, and me to prance around like a zany debutant in outlandishly stylish clothing.

"The show was filmed on Stages 20 and 24 at Warners, as well as on the backlot. There were only two permanent sets specific to *Surfside 6* – the boys' houseboat and the hotel lobby and adjoining nightclub. In the summer, we traveled to Miami Beach and filmed 'B-roll' for a couple of weeks. 'B-roll' was additional footage that could easily be cut into the primary film. In our case, it was little more than 'stock footage' for the producers and directors to use and re-use. For the most part, our Miami location scenes consisted of the boys and me driving up to or away from the houseboat, or dashing back and forth across the busy boulevard that separated the boat from the hotel. Costuming had to be simplified since those shots were later edited into whatever was filmed at the studio to give the viewers the mistaken idea that the entire program was filmed on location in Florida. I usually wore a tennis outfit, and the boys wore shorts or simple t-shirts and jerseys to make it easier for the sake of continuity to match the costumes in the edited shots. This is why the boys were bare-chested in so many scenes. No costumes were required to match one bare-chested shot to another.

"The work environment on the set was jovial; we all got along very well. There was a lot of teasing and laughter. Our natural chemistry and playfulness made the show easy to watch. The boys had a great time together, and their camaraderie was apparent on the screen. I loved them all for different reasons. Troy was billed as the star of the show. He was a good-natured, gentle soul. He didn't take himself or his blonde, Ivy-League good looks seriously. Van was a gentleman and a cool cat. He was happily married with kids, and always in a good mood. Lee was very independent. He was from Canada, and possessed no 'movie-star' attitude at all. He was a different kind of actor for me. Margarita Sierra was adorable. She was sweet and very funny, and we all loved her. I never experienced or witnessed any ego issues with the cast members.

"The order in which our scenes were filmed usually caused us to be on the set at different times. I might have

Van, Diane, and Troy.

had only a few scenes in an entire episode, so they tried to film all of them on the same day. Sometimes it took a couple of days. Of course, with me being a contract actor, they could have called me at midnight to come in and work, and they sometimes did.

"Since there were four of us credited as 'stars' of the show, each one of us was featured in individual episodes on a rotating basis. Each of those storylines was centered on a particular lead character. These shows were often filmed simultaneously at the studio. The producers realized that by doing so they could crank out more episodes without incurring a marked increase in production costs. Sometimes we actually shot two or three shows at the same time. There were days when I had no idea what the story concerned that I was working on. And I still don't know, because I rarely watched the finished product.

"I actually saw more of my co-stars at lunchtime in the studio commissary. Besides providing us all with a break from work, it was a great time to socialize and catch up with our co-workers and friends.

"The storylines of *Surfside 6* were less than lightweight. Some of the highlights of the first season included stories about a hated dictator living in exile in Miami Beach who was murdered at a birthday party by a performing clown named Pepe; a mind-reader in a trance who was instructed to commit a heinous murder; a diver who turned up dead after he claimed a portion of the gold coins he discovered in a shipwreck; a voodoo-practicing poisonous snake importer who killed someone at a carnival in Jamaica; a performer in a water-ski show who blackmailed her ex-boyfriend into forfeiting his multi-million dollar inheritance, and a Treasury Department money

engraver who was kidnapped on his honeymoon and forced to work for a counterfeiter. Very heady stuff. You get the picture.

"Ray Danton, playing an ex-con, guest-starred in our premiere episode titled 'Country Gentlemen,' which aired on October 3, 1960. My friend, Sherry Jackson, appeared in our second episode titled 'High Tide,' which was written and directed by her stepfather, Montgomery Pittman. Sherry played a 'bored stenographer on vacation,' who enlisted the boys' help after she discovered she was being followed by a couple of thugs played by Max Baer, Jr. and Chad Everett.

"Monty Pittman was not just a talented writer with infallible directing instincts. He looked like a character out of central casting. He was frumpy, and he could easily have played the role of a vagabond. What he lacked in formal education he made up for with his wit, his gregarious nature, and down-to-earth sensibility. The stinky odor of his cigar always heralded his entrance. He adored Sherry and doted on her.

"We had been on the air for just a few months, when the *Pittsburgh Press* put our show into perspective on January 1, 1961. They wrote, 'One of the few bright spots of *Surfside 6* is the good looks of Diane McBain. *Surfside 6* is a detective series with a Miami Beach locale. It has the quality of a game being played by a group of attractive youngsters, with luxurious cars, boats, and clothes as toys. As with many games of childhood, the players' reasons for doing whatever they do are vague, sort of made up as they go along, to create action and excitement. Diane appears every week, and approximately each fifth week has a major part. The rest of the time she is largely decorative.' I couldn't have said it better myself. We didn't showcase serious material like that featured on *Studio One* or *Omnibus*. *Surfside 6* was created for the youth market. We presented good old 'T&A,' and for a time, the audience hungrily tuned in.

"*Surfside 6* was successful, and like the stars of most successful television shows, we all quickly became household names. In a short time, we were deluged with fan mail, and movie magazine polls named me a fan favorite. The studio was thrilled with the advertising dollars and the marketing revenue from books, posters, photographs, board games, and other merchandise tie-ins. A firm in Miami built and sold replicas of the *Surfside 6* houseboat. The actors, though, were paid no more as a result of this windfall. We had no share of advertising or merchandizing revenue. For the first time, I realized the downside of fame. All of us did. I couldn't walk down the street without someone calling out to me, 'Hey, Daffy!'

Diane with Lee, and with Margarita, on publicity tours.

Van and Diane at the beach for publicity shots.

Van and Diane at the beach for publicity shots.

"I sensed a change in the way the studio intended to market me before we shot our first episode. Studio photographers were summoned, and the boys and I were readied for a new round of glamour shots. Only this time, we were required to wear bathing suits. Warner decided to market us as sex symbols."

To promote the show, Warner sent the cast members on press junkets around the country. They visited radio and local television stations, and were fair game for hundreds of interviews. Diane was a celebrity presenter at the 1961 Golden Globe Awards, and again in 1963. "I attended movie openings," Diane said, "county fairs, sporting events, golf and tennis tournaments, and other innocuous happenings, such as ribbon cuttings for store openings. We never got paid for these countless appearances. Warner Brothers charged from $5,000 to $10,000 for my personal appearance at an event, but I never got a dime of those fees. None of us did."

In 1960, Jack Warner optioned Erksine Caldwell's 1958 potboiler, *Claudelle Inglish*. Production of the film began in mid-December 1960 with Diane playing the enviable title role of Claudelle Inglish. After the Christmas holiday, filming moved from the studio to location work in Stockton, California. "While I was making the film," Diane said, "*Surfside 6* went on without me for several weeks."

The production of *Claudelle Inglish* dragged on for a couple of months. Diane worked nearly every day on the sets. "I was the star of the film," she recalled, "and I felt a very heavy burden to deliver." When there was a spare moment, she was sent out to publicize the upcoming second season of *Surfside 6*.

"In August 1961, production resumed on the second – and thankfully last – season of *Surfside 6*," Diane said. "We again filmed a couple of weeks on location in Miami, and then we were sentenced to the cavernous Warner Brothers sound stages. Our second season provided more ridiculous storylines concerning marital triangles, mobsters, mistaken identities, and murderous high school reunions. Some of the more absurd plots included a ventriloquist whose dummy is kidnapped for a ransom, the mentally unstable head of a flourishing swimsuit company who vanished when her husband turned up dead, and the director of a lingerie show who became the main suspect in the murder of one of his models. Some of our new interesting guest stars included Dennis Hopper, Lon Chaney, Jr., Bruce Dern, Mary Tyler Moore, Sally Kellerman, Ellen Burstyn, Jack Cassidy, Harvey Korman, George Kennedy, John Marley, and Chad Everett.

"About midway through our second season, we filmed a 'cross-over' episode that featured two main characters from the hit series, *77 Sunset Strip*. This was a common tactic by the television production department at the studio to bolster interest in a show that was failing in the ratings. Our ratings had begun to sag after riding a wave of popularity that had lasted for a little more than a year. The idea was that viewers would tune in to see their favorite characters from *77 Sunset Strip* appear in an episode of *Surfside 6*. Dean Riesner wrote the clever episode titled 'Love Song for a Deadly Redhead.' The producers thought the show would be the ratings boon that we needed. They were wrong.

"As our ratings declined, so did our production budget. The editors began to use 'stock footage' of our reaction shots from previous episodes. Several times, Margarita's musical production numbers were reused in the second season. If viewers were paying attention, they would have seen the same singing interludes previously broadcast. Continuity was nonexistent. Production values were abandoned. The sets were so poorly constructed that the walls wobbled!

"My character, Daffy, was featured in several episodes during our second season; Daffy befriended five retired, elderly crooks who shared a house and were victimized by a young hoodlum they had taken in, Daffy was kidnapped on the way to attend her friends' wedding in Nassau, Daffy fell in love with a mysterious young nomad, and Daffy took detective measures into her own hands when one of her party guests was murdered."

Claudelle Inglish was released in October, 1961. The film drew large audiences, and Diane earned her best reviews. In December, while still working on *Surfside 6*, Diane began work on her fourth studio film, *Black Gold*. "My father visited the set," she recalled. "He had a great time. He was very proud of me."

Diane broke the news that *Surfside 6* was cancelled after two seasons when she wrote a note dated April 21, 1962 for the spring issue of her fan club newsletter, *Diane's Doings*.

"Dear friends," she wrote. "Spring is here, and as usual, the air is light and breezy, the birds are full of song, and the flowers are blooming all around us. But, somehow, spring is always different for me. Winter, summer, and fall, always seem very much the same – but, spring always manages to change from year to year. Last year, spring was rather hectic, and this year is just plain lazy. Of course, it is just me!

"As I am sitting her now, and looking out my window, I can see pretty flowers blooming, the trees swaying in the soft breeze, and there is a blue jay perched on the window sill. It all sounds very romantic and beautiful, and it is, but I just feel tired and kind of empty. Love is all around me. Everywhere I look, I see lovers walking hand in hand, or sitting in deep conversation, or dancing along without a care in the world.

"That's the way spring should be. Full of love and happiness – and here I sit, all alone. I'm not feeling sorry for myself, mind you. This emptiness is very restful – and believe me, I need the rest. I don't want it, but I need it. So, I'm getting it all in one big lump.

"You see, the studio put me on lay-off. This is a period of one to twelve weeks during which the studio has the right to cease payment of my salary. So, quite frankly, I'm broke! I have to laugh right now as I sit here thinking about it. This whole situation strikes me funny.

"As you have probably heard, the series has been cancelled. It's official. No more *Surfside 6*. You will be seeing it until the end of summer, but we have finished it. I am not unhappy about it, because for me, it is a good break. Now, I'll be able to do some outside films – if Warner lets me. My hopes are that I will be doing pictures only from now on. Of course, I'll be guesting on TV shows at Warner. So, you will be seeing me on that old TV screen from time to time.

"That's all the news I can think of right now, so I shall sign off until next time."

In May, 1962, Warner lent Diane to Paramount to appear in the film *The Caretakers*. The story was set in a mental hospital, and starred Robert Stack and Joan Crawford. "Between running from the *Surfside* set to a movie set, the studio kept me very busy," Diane recalled. "And of course, I had to deal with Crawford the iron maiden."

"Midnight for Prince Charming," was the last episode of *Surfside 6*. It aired on June 25, 1962. "I hoped the studio would think I had paid my dues and would concentrate on feature film assignments for me. I had gained some excellent experience in the pressure-cooker atmosphere of episodic television production. We had worked with some wonderful directors, including Monty Pittman, Irving Moore, Charles Rondeau, Sidney Salkow, Richard Benedict, Jeffrey Hayden, and Robert Altman. Dean Reisner, a terrific writer who went on to write several hit feature films for Clint Eastwood, had given us several funny scripts. Still, I was happy and relieved to move on to more satisfying projects.

"But," Diane explained, "my next assignment at the studio was not a film at all, but a guest-shot on *77 Sunset Strip*."

Troy and Diane in *A Distant Trumpet*.

Dozens of television guest-starring roles followed. Diane made two more feature films for Warner Brothers – *Mary, Mary* with Debbie Reynolds and Barry Nelson released in 1963, and *A Distant Trumpet*, which reunited Diane with Troy Donahue, released in 1964.

After she finished *A Distant Trumpet*, the studio informed her she would next play a minor role in their upcoming production of *Sex and the Single Girl*. "It was an insult," she said. "In the script, the character didn't even have a name!"

With a studio contract, she had little choice. If she refused the job, the studio could terminate her services. "I passed on *Sex and the Single Girl*," Diane said. "I just couldn't bring myself to accept such a throw-away minor role because the studio couldn't see me in anything else. I told them I wouldn't take the part. I was politely shown the door. They told me I was relieved from my contractual obligations to them. In October, 1963, I gathered my few belongings and left Warner Brothers Studio as a contract player for the last time. I was twenty-two years old."

During the following thirty-plus years, Diane worked steadily in films, television, summer stock, and regional theater. She guest-starred in four episodes of *Burke's Law*, and two episodes of *The Wild, Wild West*, and *The Man from U.N.C.L.E.*. In 1966, she was Elvis Presley's leading lady in the film, *Spinout*. "Fans ask me about Elvis all the time," she said. "There was no flirting or romance at all. He was very sweet and respectful. We talked about religion a lot, and he gave me a few books about his spiritual beliefs. Yes, he was terribly handsome, and everyone asks me if he was a good kisser. What do you think!?"

Diane with Elvis Presley in *Spinout*.

In December 1966, she was asked by Johnny Grant to join him and Tippi Hedren on a two-week holiday tour entertaining American troops in Vietnam. She returned again in December 1967. "Spending time with our troops, most of them no older than teenagers, in the jungles and the mud was the greatest and hardest thing I ever did," she recalled.

Television fans fondly remember her for playing the role of Pinky Pinkston in a two-part episode of *Batman* in 1967. "The episode was a crossover with *The Green Hornet*. I was so happy to work with Van Williams again. We had a great time. And Adam was great. I was fascinated to see that he used a teleprompter on the set. I'd never seen an actor do that before. Adam was at Warner Brothers in the early 1960s, so it was pleasantly nostalgic for the three of us to be together again. That was the last time I'd work with Van, and I am so happy, it was so much fun."

Beginning in 1967, she starred in a series of low budget films including *Thunder Alley* (1967) and *Maryjane* (1968) with Fabian, *The Mini-Skirt*

Adam West with Diane in *Batman*.

Mob (1968), and *I Sailed to Tahiti with an All-Girl Crew* (1968) with Gardner McKay.

Diane made her summer stock debut in June, 1968 in Denver, Colorado. She starred in the Neil Simon comedy *The Star-Spangled Girl*, with Edd Byrnes and Carleton Carpenter. The tour took them up the Eastern Seaboard from New York to Maine. "Working for a live audience was such a departure for me. No audiences on a television or movie set. And the audiences – which were always different – affected the actors on stage. But it was exciting, and I enjoyed the time on the road. I liked doing comedy, which rarely came my way."

In 1969, she co-starred in *Five the Hard Way*. Her later films include *The Delta Factor, The Wild Season, Wicked, Wicked, The Deathhead Virgin, The Christmas Path, Donner Pass: The Road to Survival, Once Upon a Starry Night, The Red Fury, Puppet Master 5*, and *The Broken Hearts Club*. Her many television appearances include *Mannix, Land of the Giants, Mod Squad, Police Story, Marcus Welby, M.D., Hawaii Five-O, Charlie's Angels, Eight is Enough, Dallas, Airwolf, Knight Rider, Sabrina the Teenage Witch*, and *Dr. Quinn, Medicine Woman*, among others. "I appeared in the requisite television game shows, made an unsold pilot in 1992 called *The Streets of Beverly Hills*, and managed a funny episode titled "Love and the Roommate" on *Love, American Style* in 1969. I loved doing comedy, and I so rarely had the chance."

Diane also played the roles of Foxy Humdinger on the daytime soap opera *Days of Our Lives* (1982-84), and Claire Howard on *General Hospital* (1988).

"In the midst of it all," she recalled, "I got married, had a son,

and got divorced. And then I played the real life role of a single mother trying to support her child."

Diane garnered unfortunate news headlines in December, 1982. She arrived home after attending a holiday party in the early morning hours of Christmas Day when she was ambushed in her garage by two men who brutally beat and raped her. "It was unimaginable," she said. "Terrifying. They left me tied to my car bumper with my nylons. It was a deeply life-changing experience. And the police never found the rapists."

For five years, Diane worked as a counselor for rape victims and battered women. She also delivered meals for Project Angel Food during the early years of the AIDS epidemic, and worked with homeless organizations and animal rights charities.

In 2001, Diane retired from acting and reclaimed a private life. She moved to a small mountain village in California, and worked with me on her autobiography, *Famous Enough, A Hollywood Memoir*. In 2020, she published her first novel, *The Laughing Bear*, and her second novel, *The Color of Hope*, was published in 2021.

Margarita Sierra

Margarita Sierra played the role of Cha Cha O'Brien, the feisty headliner in the Boom Boom Room of the Fontainebleau Hotel in Miami Beach. Sierra was a ball of fire in real life, and fit the role of the nightclub singer/dancer perfectly. In real life, she was as exotic as the character she played.

Maria Margarita Suarez Sierra, professionally known as Margarita Sierra, was born on January 5, 1936 in Madrid, Spain. Her father, Jose Sierra, an artist and theatrical designer, was Spanish. Her mother, Maria Virginia, was American born.

By the age of four, Margarita was an accomplished tap dancer, and performed in local productions. She stud-

Margarita Sierra.

ied flamenco dancing and singing, and at age eight, she starred in a Spanish all-kiddie movie titled *Little Heroes of the Neighborhood*. Her performance earned her the nickname of the "crazy cute Shirley Temple of Spain." When she was ten, she replaced a twelve-year old girl in a musical comedy extravaganza that toured Barcelona, Valencia, and Seville. Her father designed the scenery for the show. At the tender age of seventeen, she was featured in a nightclub act at Madrid's famous Club Pasapoga.

Accompanied by her mother, she left Spain in 1954 and toured the nightclub circuits in Mexico City, Venezuela, and Chile. In 1956, she was spotted by an American producer when she was appearing at the Nacional Hotel in Havana. He brought her to the United States where she made her American debut at the Nautilus Hotel in Miami Beach.

After taking in her show in Miami Beach, producer Angel Lopez hired her to star in his new Latin-American revue "Tropical Holiday," at the Chateau Madrid on West 58th Street, the largest Latin-American cabaret in the East. She followed up with successful supper club engagements at Max Lowe's Viennese Lantern on 79th Street, where she turned in three grueling shows nightly, and at the fabled Maisonette Room of the St. Regis Hotel.

After a successful Chicago engagement, she was booked in early 1957 at the prestigious Persian Room in the Plaza Hotel in Manhattan. Columnist Walter Winchell often mentioned her in his column, "Broadway at Night." Following one of her late night performances, Winchell interviewed her at

Lindy's Deli. He reported that she had eaten her weight in dinner – steak, potatoes, and strawberry shortcake. She told him, "Helps me overcome my insomnia."

She rented an apartment in Manhattan with her mother, and made New York her new home and professional base.

On September 10, 1957, she made her national television debut on the popular *The Tonight Show* hosted by Jack Paar to promote her new Latin Pop LP, *Margarita Sierra: The Sparkling Senorita from Spain*. The audience and the host were enchanted. On October 15, and October 17, she returned to sing on the program. For months, she performed nightly at the Persian Room, and appeared again on *The Tonight Show* on March 5, and October 14, 1958.

Sierra made her West Coast debut in 1958 at the Hollywood Bowl. On August 23, she appeared as a soloist at the Bowl's annual Fiesta program in a salute to Latin America and Mexico. She sang "Malaguena," and several other popular songs.

In January 1959, she played a return engagement at the St. Regis Hotel, and in February, she stepped in for an ailing Edith Piaf at the Waldorf.

In the spring of 1960, Sierra was playing to sold out crowds at the Persian Room. One evening, William T. Orr, executive producer of Warner Brothers Television, and his assistant, Hugh Benson, caught her act at the Plaza. "I was working in Persian Room at Plaza Hotel in March," she recalled, "and two men send cards with notes to dressing room. They offer me movie job at Warner Brothers in Hollywood. I think they nobody and throw cards in drawer." She had never heard of

Warner Brothers Studios, and thought Orr and his assistant "were just blah blah people from Hollywood."

"They must find MCA my agent," she explained. "MCA call and say, 'you talk to Warner men?' They order me to be polite and see them. Mr. Orr and Mr. Benson fly from Florida, I think, to keep appointment. I like very much. But I never in life interested in movies. Like be with audience. Maybe I strange woman. I am un-believable."

Orr offered her a recurring, featured role in the upcoming Warner Brothers' television series *Surfside 6*, that was in pre-production. The primary cast members were in Miami Beach, filming location footage. But acting on screen was a goal that never interested the singer. "If I no be myself," she said, "I no happy. I had lots of 'fraid. I no speak English! What I going do!?"

A television contract would limit her nightclub engagements and challenge her limited skills speaking English. She told her agent she would consider the offer, and promptly left New York for a previously scheduled cross-country nightclub tour, ending with an extended appearance in Puerto Rico.

"I gone five months," she said. "All time, much telephone calls every place. Then I go back to New York for four days and MCA tells me I crazy. Then I get convinced when Mr. Orr send plane tickets to visit Hollywood to look and talk.

"Right away, he show me the Boom Boom Room, my set, and it is so beautiful. He say, 'This where you sing and dance.' That is thing I like very best."

"I wonder how I going to learn anything when I can't read English. How I study the script? How I know what's going on when I speak only few words of English? I thought perhaps I miss the audience too much, but they tell me at Warner Brothers that I still have an audience. And the extras they use for the audience don't applaud by the director. The applaud for the song I sing. That make me feel good."

By the time she decided to accept the offer, filming was underway in Hollywood. She purchased a rambling nine-room house at 16201 Meadow Ridge Way in Encino, and moved to California with her mother and five dogs. She quickly fell into the life of a twenty-two-year-old Hollywood star, and bought herself a new red Thunderbird to drive to and from the studio.

The sleek car, and perhaps her pretty and quickly recognizable good looks, often drew the attention of police officers. It may have been her tendency to drive too fast, as well. She began to collect speeding tickets, and told a *TV Guide* reporter that she thought her language, and not her driving, prompted her latest traffic ticket. "When I am estop by the policemen," she laughed, "the only English I can think to say is 'I hate you!'"

The character of Cha Cha O'Brien – a spirited girl singer and dancer – seemed written just to suit Sierra. Her appearances on screen exploded with energy and humor. When they weren't chasing suspects, contemplating clues, planning strategies, or engaged in fisticuffs, the three young detectives often dropped into the jumping Boom Boom Room for a rendezvous, to grab a drink at the bar, or to just enjoy the lively gyrations of Cha Cha on stage. Over time, as the television audiences embraced Sierra's character, Cha Cha got mixed up in their cases, and even had to be rescued now and then.

Months after settling into the role, and adjusting to a busy TV shooting schedule, Sierra told a reporter, "I love the work now. They like me to talk like myself and always audience on set, when I sing. And so interesting. Every week, different story. It is much fun to not know never what's going on."

Diane McBain, who played the role of Daphne Dutton, recalled, "Margarita fit right in with the gang. Right away. She was lovely, very funny, and so talented. We loved working with her."

Sierra picked her own songs for the show, using some from her nightclub act, and introduced a few traditional Spanish songs, too. She usually steered away from the better known American ballads, though. "I still do not understand English enough to always know what I am singing. Those make it hard to the feeling of a ballad. When I do a happy song, a fiery one where I can move my eyes, then I feel good."

Despite studying English on her own, when asked by a reporter if she was learning proper English, she said, "No. I never do classes and the studio won't coach me!" The reporter, sharing breakfast with the actress at the famed Hollywood Brown Derby on Vine Street, asked if perhaps the studio

Margarita in *Surfside 6*.

didn't want her to lose her accent. "I theenk," Sierra laughed, "you are pooling my feet!"

In the first few months, *Surfside 6* became a popular show. Sierra was a fan favorite, and the studio busied her with numerous interviews to promote the series. In February, 1961, she spoke with columnist Lydia Cane over lunch in the Polo Lounge of the Beverly Hills Hotel. She said she had gotten into the habit of "counting calories" to maintain her figure. "Cottage cheese and fruit three times a day," she explained. When asked about her beautiful skin and beauty tips for young women,

Sierra explained, "I never use soap. I clean my face with cream and never rub it hard enough to stretch the skin.

"My grandmother had the most exquisite complexion, and I follow the advice that she gave me. I follow it religiously. She told me to use apples. When I come home at night, I prepare them for the next day. I take two fresh apples, slice and cover them with water. Then I cook them, how you say, simmer them for forty-five minutes. I let them stay overnight covered in the

pan. The next morning, I drain off the juice and drink it. Then I put the apples in a dish and with my fingers I pat them all over my clean face. I keep pressing the apples right on my skin and I lie down with the soft apples like a mask on my face. In ten minutes, I take it off and I find color in my skin and my complexion is like a baby's. You know, they say that an apple a day keeps the doctor away – well, you try my apple a day on your face and you'll keep the lines away."

In March 1961, AP reporter Bob Thomas wrote, "Close your eyes and you think you're hearing Carmen Miranda. Open them, and

you see an entirely different doll. Margarita Sierra is tiny and vivacious like the great Miranda. She has the same bright, chirping voice. But Margarita is more of a sexpot, any red-blooded American male can tell." He asked her why there were no romantic story lines with her costars Troy Donahue, Van Williams and Lee Patterson. She answered, "I don't know. There doesn't seem to be any time for romance on the show!"

She continued, "That's the trouble with American men. They don't take time for romance. They make wonderful husbands, but poor lovers. They are so considerate of their wives; they do the dishes and mind the baby, something European men never do. But as lovers, they are too fast. They want to do everything in a hurry. In Spain, the boy takes his time. Perhaps you will exchange glances with him for weeks before he will speak to you. Then he will send you notes and flowers until you finally agree to go out with him. If an American asks you for a date and you say no, he gives up!"

During the course of *Surfside 6*, Sierra actually appeared on fifty-eight episodes, and sang on thirty-eight shows. In 1962, Warner Brothers Records released her only single, "Cha Cha Twist." When the series ended, Sierra discovered that her characterization of the fiery, flirtatious singer had typecast her. There were few acting opportunities, and her single never placed on the charts. Warner Brothers studio did not offer to extend her contract. She returned to nightclub performing, and did not appear on screen again.

While working in New York City in early 1963, she expressed her impatience with constantly being compared to Carmen Miranda and Lupe Velez. She told a UPI reporter," Carman Miranda wore all sorts of funny hair-

dresses, some made of bananas, and I have never done that. Miss Velez, on the screen, was a spitfire type while I prefer happy-go-lucky parts."

Sierra returned to her home in Encino in May, 1963. She complained of fatigue, and during the course of a check-up, it was discovered that her heart had damaged valves. Doctors told her that she would require surgery, and she was ordered to rest at home for several months before undertaking serious open-heart surgery.

On Thursday, September 5, a team of specialists performed the serious heart operation at

St. Vincent's Hospital in Los Angeles. Before undergoing the procedure, it was clearly understood that her case was complicated by a congenital weakness in the wall of her aorta. Her condition was listed as serious following the nine-hour operation, but she did not recover, and died on Friday, September 6. She was twenty-five years old.

"I was stunned," Diane McBain recalls. "We all were. She was so young, and was so lively. No one knew she had any potential heart problems. I don't think she knew, either. It was just terrible."

A devout Catholic, a rosary was recited for her at the Cunningham & O'Connor Mortuary in Hollywood on Monday evening, September 9. Sunday and Monday a visitation was hosted by the mortuary. Her funeral mass was held on Tuesday, September 10, at St. Cyril's Church in Encino. Her mother was her only family member at the service. Her father remained in Spain. There were only sixty invited mourners to the private mass. Among her show business friends were Connie Stevens and Diane McBain. Serving as pallbearers were her *Surfside* 6 costars Troy Donahue and Van Williams, actor Chad Everett, music arranger Earl Brent, Mort Lichter of Warner Brothers publicity department, and Phil Paladino, who handled the actress' public relations.

At the request of her mother, there was no eulogy. Following the service, she was buried at Holy Cross Catholic Cemetery in Culver City, California.

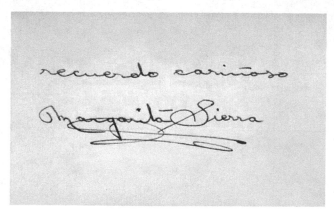

We Built this Original SURFSIDE 6 FLOATING HOME as shown on television.

Surfside (6) *Floating Homes, inc.,* 2000 S. W. 20th Street, Ft. Lauderdale, Florida

[Write for information concerning other models]

TERMS ARRANGED

Country Gentleman

Season 1, Episode 1

Broadcast on ABC TV on October 3, 1960
Directed by Irving J. Moore
Teleplay by Anne Howard Bailey and M.L. Schumann from a story by M.L. Schumann
Producer: Jerry Davis
Executive Producer: William T. Orr

Cast:

Lee Patterson	Dave Thorne
Troy Donahue	Sandy Winfield II
Van Williams	Ken Madison
Diane McBain	Daphne Dutton
Margarita Sierra	Cha Cha O'Brien
Paul "Mousie" Garner	Mousie
Don "Red" Barry	Lt. Snedigar
Ray Danton	Marty Hartman
Janet Lake	Paula Gladstone
Frank DeKova	Stinger
Fredd Wayne	Allan Abbott
John Hubbard	Roger Fielding
Robert Burton	Commodore Gladstone
Gary Conway	Ted Watson

Credits:

Cinematography by Harold E. Stine
Film Editing by David Wages
Art Direction by Howard Campbell
Set Decoration by William L. Kuehl

Makeup Supervisor: Gordon Bau
Hair Stylist: Jean Burt Reilly
Assistant Director: Gene Anderson Jr.
Props: Roy Moore
Sound: Samuel F. Goode
Supervising Editor: James Moore
Theme Music Composers: Mack David and Jerry Livingston
Music Editor: Charles Paley
Music Supervisors: Paul Sawtell and Bert Shefter
60 minutes/Black and White
Production Company: Warner Bros. Television
Filmed at Warner Bros. Studios on Stages 20 and 24
Margarita Sierra sang "Cielito Lindo" in this premiere episode.

Notes on the case:

Sandy drops in on Dave, Ken, and Daphne on the houseboat. He informs them that an ex-con by the name of Marty Hartman – a gangster Dave helped put in prison – is free and just bought the Gladstone mansion. Marty is attempting to buy respectability in the community, but when a meddlesome reporter named Fielding writes a revealing and damaging column about him, Miami high-society shuts Hartman out. A real estate deal Hartman had with Commodore Gladstone is ditched, causing him to lose a fortune. When Gladstone turns up dead, the Surfside detectives must determine who drowned him. There are many suspects including Hartman, his right-hand-man Stinger, a man named Abbott who is deeply in debt to Gladstone, the Commodore's daughter Paula who is romantically entangled with Hartman, and Ted Watson, Paula's boatman who is secretly in love with her.

Don "Red" Barry played the role of Lt. Snedigar in 28 episodes on the first season of *Surfside 6*. He was born on January 11, 1912 in Houston, Texas. After schooling in Texas, he moved to Los Angeles to work in advertising. He first appeared on screen in 1933, and played bit roles for the next six years. In 1935, he toured the country in the play *Tobacco Road*. Standing at only 5' 4" allowed him to often play juveniles in film. His career trajectory changed for the better when he played the title role in the 1940 film *Adventures of Red Ryder*. The film was so memorable, he adopted the nickname of "Red" for the rest of his life. He was a reliable character actor, and specialized in "tough guy" roles, and B-Westerns. He worked under contract to Warner Brothers beginning in the late 1950s and appeared in *Sugarfoot, Colt .45, Bourbon Street Beat, Maverick, Lawman, 77 Sunset Strip*, and *Bronco*. Barry played recurring characters on the series *Little House on the Prairie* and *Police Woman*, and is remembered for appearances on *Ironside* and *Batman*. His final acting role was in the feature film *Back Roads*, which was released after his death. Despite playing well over 300 roles in films and television shows, Barry never achieved stardom. He was a heavy drinker, and he earned the reputation of being difficult on the set early in his career. His personal life earned more attention than his work in Hollywood. In November 1955, Jil Jarmyn, an actress he dated after his second divorce, walked in unexpectedly on Barry and actress Susan Hayward in his bedroom. The two women got into a physical fight, and the reluctant threesome made newspaper headlines. On July 17,

Don Barry.

1980, Barry shot himself to death in his North Hollywood home after being questioned by police about a complaint of domestic abuse filed by Barbara Patin, his estranged third wife, and mother of his two children. Don "Red" Barry was 68 years old.

Paul "Mousie" Garner played the role of Mousie in 18 episodes on the first season of *Surfside 6*. Garner was born in Washington, D.C. on July 31, 1909. He made his stage debut in 1913, and worked in vaudeville for many years. Between 1922 and 1937, Garner worked in a musical comedy trio called the The Gentlemaniacs on stage and in several feature films. He served in the U.S. Army during World War II, and was injured twice. After he recovered, he joined the U.S.O. and toured throughout Europe starring in the Olsen and Johnson show *Sons O' Fun*. He continued to perform for troops during the Korean and Vietnam wars. Until retiring in 1994, he played dozens of comedic roles in films and television programs. He was a regular cast member of the 1957 series *The Spike Jones Show*. In the early 1960s, he worked under contract to Warner Brothers and appeared in most of the studio's television productions. Paul Garner died of kidney failure in Glendale, California on August 8, 2004. He was 95 years old.

Ray Danton played the role of Marty Hartman. Danton was born in New York City on September 19, 1931. He began his show business career as a child radio actor in 1943. He appeared on stage with Tyrone Power in *Mister Roberts* in London. When he returned to New York, he began working in television in 1951, but his career was put on hold while he served in the United States Army infantry during the Korean War from 1951 until 1953. He returned to television work, then signed a contract with Universal. His early films there include *The Looters, I'll Cry Tomorrow,* and *The Spoilers.* In 1958, he moved to Warner Brothers and appeared in *Too Much Too Soon, The Beat Generation, Ice Palace,* and *The Rise and Fall of Legs Diamond.* He appeared in most of the studio's television productions, and starred as Nifty Cronin in the Warner series *The Alaskans* (1959-60). When his contract expired, he moved to Europe for several years, and starred in half a dozen films. He formed a production company in Europe and produced and directed several films in the early 1970s. When he returned to the United States, he resumed acting but more frequently worked as a stage and television director. Ray Danton died in Los Angeles of kidney failure on February 11, 1992. He was 60 years old. He was married to actress Julie Adams from 1954 until 1981.

Fredd Wayne played the role of Allan Abbott. Wayne was born on October 17, 1924 in Akron, Ohio. After graduating high school, he traveled to Hollywood and got a job in the mail room at Warner Brothers Studio. He was drafted into the U.S. Army during World War II, and served in the 63rd Infantry Division as an "Entertainment Specialist." He fought in the Battle of the Bulge in 1944. After VE-Day, he was directed to put together a show for service members. He created *G.I. Carmen* and performed in drag in what would become one of the most successful G.I. touring shows. When he returned to New York, he studied at the American Theater Wing. Wayne appeared on Broadway, and first appeared on screen in 1949. During the following 50 years, he played more than 150 roles in television dramas and comedies. In 1964, he created a one-man show based on the papers of Benjamin Franklin. For more than a decade, he starred in *Benjamin Franklin, Citizen,* touring the United States. Fredd Wayne retired in 1999. He died in Santa Monica, California on August 17, 2018 at the age of 93.

Frank DeKova played the role of Stinger. DeKova was born in New York City on March 17, 1910. He was a school teacher in New York before beginning his acting career in 1947 on Broadway in *Heads or Tales.* In 1949 he starred in the hit Broadway show *Detective Story.* Hollywood type-cast him as a tough guy, a Mafia gangster, a Mexican, or more commonly as an American Indian in dozens of films, and hundreds of television roles. His films include *Viva Zapata!, The Big Sky, The Ten Commandments, Cowboy,* and *The Mechanic.* He played the recurring role of Tobeel, a Kiowa Indian friend to Marshal Matt Dillon on *Gunsmoke,* but is best remembered for playing the role of Wild Eagle, chief of the Hekawi tribe on the western-themed situation comedy *F-Troop,* from 1965 until 1967. Frank DeKova died of heart failure at his home in North Hills, California on October 15, 1981. He was 71 years old.

Janet Lake played the role of Paula Gladstone. Lake was born in Norristown, Pennsylvania on March 11, 1936. She was a professional model and cover girl before beginning her acting career in 1956. She had small roles in several films, and guest-starred in many Warner Brothers television shows including *Colt .45*, *Sugarfoot*, *77 Sunset Strip*, *Maverick*, and *Hawaiian Eye*. She was married to actor Robert Dix from 1956 until 1959. She remarried, and retired from acting in 1965 to raise two children. Her daughter, Paige Livingston, is a film and television producer.

John Hubbard played the role of Roger Fielding. Hubbard was born on November 6, 1914 in East Chicago, Indiana. He studied at the Goodman Theatre in Chicago, and made his film debut in 1937. His feature films include *The Housekeeper's Daughter*, *Turnabout*, *Maisie*, *Mexican Hayride*, *You'll Never Get Rich*, and *Out West with the Hardies*. He served in the U.S. military from 1944 until 1947. He resumed his acting career with independent films, but found sustained success as a television actor. He played Mr. Brown on *The Mickey Rooney Show* (1954-55), and had recurring roles in several series including *My Little Margie*, *Don't Call Me Charlie!*, and *Family Affair*. He frequently guest-starred in Warner Brothers television programs, and worked on stage and on radio. He retired in 1974, and died in Camarillo, California on November 6, 1988. John Hubbard was 74 years old, and survived by his wife of 50 years, and three children.

Robert Burton played the role of Commodore Gladstone. Burton was born in Eastman, Georgia, on August 13, 1895. He worked in theater and summer stock before making his film debut in 1952. During the following ten years he played more than 200 supporting roles in film and television productions. His feature films include *Above and Beyond*, *Fearless Fagan*, *My Man and I*, and *The Slime People*, which was released posthumously. He worked until this death at the Motion Picture Country Home in Woodland Hills on September 29, 1962. Robert Burton was 67 years old.

Gary Conway played the role of Ted Watson. Conway was born on February 4, 1936 in Boston. He studied art at UCLA, and supplemented his income as a nude model for art classes and physique magazines in the early 1950s. He made his acting debut playing the title character in the 1957 cult-classic film *I Was a Teenage Frankenstein*. In 1958, Conway married Marian McKnight, Miss America, 1957. In 1960, he began working for Warner Brothers, and appeared in most of the studio's television productions including *Colt .45*, *Bourbon Street Beat*, *Lawman*, *Maverick*, *77 Sunset Strip*, and *Hawaiian Eye*. He starred as Det. Tim Tilson in the series *Burke's Law* (1963-1965), and played the role of Capt. Steve Roberts in the series *Land of the Giants* (1968-70). Conway worked steadily in film and television until retiring in 2000. He is an accomplished painter. Since his retirement, he is the proprietor of Carmody McKnight Estate Winery in Paso Robles, California.

Diane McBain recalled, "I was little more than a decoration on this first show. I only worked with the boys on a couple of short bits. I didn't have high hopes for the series. And I was right. After working on some good films, I really thought I was being thrown out to dry with television work. Maybe if the writing and production values had been better, or if I had been given a real supporting role to play, it might have been better. We did have many wonderful guest stars and supporting players, many were under contract to the studio. But the show was really about the boys. And they were great, and had great chemistry. And they usually had the best lines."

Sandy: I spoke to my father this morning.

Dave: He wants you back on Wall Street in a gray flannel suit?

Sandy: Yeah, but I told him I was working for you guys.

Dave: Yeah? Then what did he say?

Sandy: He wants me to go back to New York.

Ken: And what are you gonna do?

Sandy: Stop answering the phone.

"I know Red Barry was in a number of episodes," Diane recalled, "but what I remember most about him was his short height. In heels, I towered over him. He was a little like the cliché of the short guy who overcompensates by trying to be a tough guy. And for some reason, he was quite a ladies' man. To me, he was always very polite and good natured.

High Tide

Season 1, Episode 2

Broadcast on ABC TV on October 10, 1960
Directed by Montgomery Pittman
Teleplay by Montgomery Pittman and Robert J. Shaw from a story by Robert J. Shaw
Producer: Jerry Davis
Executive Producer: William T. Orr

Cast:

Lee Patterson	Dave Thorne
Troy Donahue	Sandy Winfield II
Van Williams	Ken Madison
Diane McBain	Daphne Dutton
Margarita Sierra	Cha Cha O'Brien
Paul "Mousie" Garner	Mousie
Don "Red" Barry	Lt. Snedigar
Sherry Jackson	Jill Murray
Chad Everett	Don Whitman
Gregg Palmer	Lou Montell
Howard McLeod	Miller
Dicky Haynes	Drunk
Max Baer Jr.	Party Guest
Jeff Daley	Denver
Carolyn Komant	Girl
Alfred Shelly	Ted
Voorheis J. Ardoin	Bartender
Jerry Eagle	Joe
Jack Bordeaux	Fight Spectator

Credits:

Cinematography by Harold E. Stine
Film Editing by Leo H. Shreve
Art Direction by Howard Campbell
Makeup Supervisor: Gordon Blau
Hair Stylist: Jean Burt Reilly
Supervising Editor: James Moore
Theme Music Composers: Mack David and Jerry Livingston
Music Editor: Ted Sebern
Music Supervisors: Paul Sawtell and Bert Shefter
60 minutes/Black and White
Production Company: Warner Bros. Television
Filmed at Warner Bros. Studios on Stages 20 and 24.
Margarita Sierra sang "Rainy Night in Rio," and "I Do Do Do Like You" in this episode.

Notes on the case:

A beautiful young woman named Jill Murray ducks into the houseboat to avoid someone following her. Sandy is inside, and is instantly impressed with her good looks, and the two begin to chat. There is a knock at the door. Sandy opens the door and is met by a thug who says he wants the girl. Sandy refuses to let him in and pushes him outside. Two other thugs run up and the three get into a fight with Sandy. Ken is sunbathing on the roof of the boat. He hears the commotion and jumps down to join the fight. When the thugs dash off, Ken and Sandy go into the houseboat, and they ask Jill what's going on. She plays dumb and tells them that she is just a stenographer on vacation, but they soon discover that she is actually a dancer in low-class clubs. Her real name is McCreary, and she's the ex-girlfriend of crime boss, Lou Montell. When Jill disappears, the detectives must find out what happened to her, and what the real truth will reveal. The detectives telephone number was revealed in this episode – SurfSide 6-2345.

Sherry Jackson played the role of Jill Murray. Jackson was born in Wendell, Idaho on February 15, 1942. When her father died in 1948, her mother moved the family to Los Angeles. In 1952, her mother married writer Montgomery Pittman. Jackson first appeared on screen in the 1949 musical *You're My Everything*. Her other films include *The Lion and the Horse*, *Come Next Spring*, *The Breaking Point*, *The Miracle of Our Lady of Fatima*, and *Trouble Along the Way*. Many fans remember her for playing the role of Susie Kettle in *Ma and Pa Kettle Go to Town*, *Ma and Pa Kettle Back on the Farm*, *Ma and Pa Kettle at the Fair*, and *Ma and Pa Kettle on Vacation*. From 1953 until 1958, she played the role of Terry Williams on

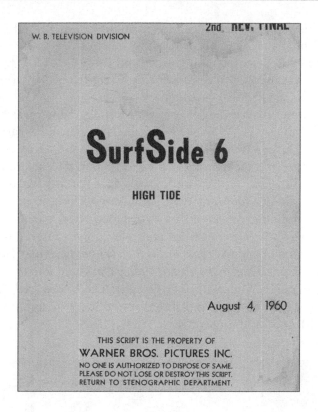

W. B. TELEVISION DIVISION

2nd REV, FINAL

SurfSide 6

HIGH TIDE

August 4, 1960

THIS SCRIPT IS THE PROPERTY OF
WARNER BROS. PICTURES INC.
NO ONE IS AUTHORIZED TO DISPOSE OF SAME.
PLEASE DO NOT LOSE OR DESTROY THIS SCRIPT.
RETURN TO STENOGRAPHIC DEPARTMENT.

The Danny Thomas Show. She made nearly 100 guest appearances on television programs during the 1960s and 1970s, including *Batman*, *Star Trek*, *Lost in Space*, and *The Wild, Wild West*, and many at Warner Brothers. Her later film work consisted mostly of B-exploitation movies including the 1968 drive-in flop, *The Mini-Skirt Mob*, which co-starred her friend, Diane McBain. Sherry Jackson retired from acting in 1982. She teaches acting, and is an animal rights activist.

Chad Everett played the role of Don Whitman. Everett (agent Henry Willson gave him his show business name) was born on June 11, 1937 in South Bend, Indiana. He graduated Wayne State University in Detroit with a degree in drama. In 1960, he became a contract player at Warner Brothers Studio. His first film there was *Claudelle Inglish*, with Diane McBain. Everett made his television debut in this episode of *Surfside 6*. He guest-starred in most of the Warner television productions including *Maverick*, *Lawman*, *Bronco*, *Cheyenne*, *77 Sunset Strip*, and *Hawaiian Eye*. He starred in the role of Dep. Del Stark in the series *The Dakotas* (1962-63). His numerous films include *The Singing Nun*, *Johnny Tiger*, *Return of the Gunfighter*, and *The Impossible Years*, among others. He is best known for playing the role of Doctor Joe Gannon on the long-running medical series *Medical Center*

(1969-76). His career stalled after *Medical Center*, and Everett fought alcoholism until finally tackling his drinking problem in 1986. He worked until his death in Los Angeles from lung cancer on July 24, 2012, at the age of 75. Chad Everett was married to actress Shelby Grant from 1966 until her death in 2011. The couple had two daughters.

Gregg Palmer played the role of Lou Montell. Palmer was born in San Francisco on January 25, 1927. He began his show business career in radio broadcasting. During World War II, he served in the Army Air Corps as a cryptographer. In the early 1950s, he was a contract player at Universal. His films there include *To Hell and Back, The Creature Walks Among Us, The Rebel Set, Zombies of Mora Tau, Taza, Son of Cochise*, and *Magnificent Obsession*. He found great success as a freelance actor, establishing himself as a reliable player in Western films and television dramas. His more than 150 acting credits include *Wagon Train, Cheyenne, Laramie, Tales of Wells Fargo, Daniel Boone, Gunsmoke, Death Valley Days*, and *Bonanza*. Beginning in 1969, he made five films with John Wayne: *The Undefeated, Chisum, Rio Lobo, Big Jake*, and *The Shootist*. Palmer retired in 1982, and died in Encino on October 31, 2015 at the age of 88.

Van, Diane, and Lee.

Diane recalled, "Sherry was my roommate. We were really great friends. Her father, Monty Pittman, wrote and directed this episode. She had terrible laryngitis when we filmed, and she wasn't able to come back and redub her dialogue. June Foray, a great voice-over artist who was the voice of Rocky the Squirrel on the *Bullwinkle* cartoon series dubbed Sherry's lines. I was working with Chad Everett on the film *Claudelle Inglish* on the lot at the same time we shot this episode. He was under contract to Warner. He was such a handsome guy, and a nice guy. He was always very gentlemanly with me. At the time, the studio arranged for publicity magazine shoots with us suggesting a romance. Nothing to it. But he was a great guy and I always enjoyed working with him, although our time together on this episode is very short."

The Clown

Season 1, Episode 3

Broadcast on ABC TV on October 17, 1960
Directed by Leslie H. Martinson
Teleplay by Lee Loeb from a story by Lee Loeb and Richard Lederer
Producer: Jerry Davis
Executive Producer: William T. Orr

Cast:

Lee Patterson	Dave Thorne
Troy Donahue	Sandy Winfield II
Van Williams	Ken Madison
Diane McBain	Daphne Dutton
Margarita Sierra	Cha Cha O'Brien
Paul "Mousie" Garner	Mousie
Don "Red" Barry	Lt. Snedigar
Vito Scotti	Pepe Alvarez
Joe De Santis	Silva
Ted De Corsia	Correro
Tina Carver	Elaine Alvarez
Joel Grey	Willy
Pepe Hern	Carlos
Jacqueline deWit	Manager
Del Moore	Airline Clerk
Burt Mustin	Student
Charles Alvin Bell	Dickinson
Charles Wagenheim	Little Man
Pedro Gonzalez-Gonzalez Jr.	Ricardo
Joe Garcio	Correro Butler
Sol Gorss	Thug
Sailor Vincent	Captain

Credits:

Cinematography by Harold E. Stein
Film Editing by Robert Watts
Art Direction by Howard Campbell and Perry Ferguson
Set Decoration by Ralph S. Hurst
Makeup Supervisor: Gordon Bau
Hair Stylist: Jean Burt Reilly
Assistant Director: Victor Vallejo
Sound: M.A. Merrick
Supervising Editor: James Moore
Theme Music Composers: Mack David and Jerry Livingston
Music Editor: Erma E. Levin
Music Supervisors: Paul Sawtell and Bert Shefter
60 minutes/Black and White
Production Company: Warner Bros. Television
Filmed at Warner Bros. Studios on Stages 20 and 24, July 14-20, 1960
Margarita Sierra sang "Dancing in the Dark" in this episode.

"The Clown" is perhaps the best remembered single episode of *Surfside 6*. The teleplay was well written with numerous twists and turns. An early draft of the script is included at the end of this book. Many talented character actors appeared in this episode.

Joe De Santis played the role of Silva. De Santis was born to Italian immigrants in New York City on June 15, 1909. He began his prolific career on radio in 1931. He appeared on Broadway a dozen times, and first appeared on screen in 1949. He moved to Los Angeles in 1956, and worked steadily in film and television, earning himself a reputation as one of Hollywood's most reliable character actors. Until his retirement from acting in 1978, he played more than 200 roles on screen. He moved to

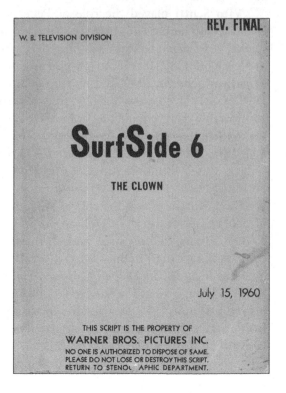

W. B. TELEVISION DIVISION

REV. FINAL

SurfSide 6

THE CLOWN

July 15, 1960

THIS SCRIPT IS THE PROPERTY OF
WARNER BROS. PICTURES INC.
NO ONE IS AUTHORIZED TO DISPOSE OF SAME.
PLEASE DO NOT LOSE OR DESTROY THIS SCRIPT.
RETURN TO STENOGRAPHIC DEPARTMENT.

Provo, Utah to be near his family, and created a second life for himself as a respected sculptor. Joe De Santis died in Provo on August 30, 1989 of chronic pulmonary disease. He was 80 years old.

Ted De Corsia played the role of Correro. De Corsia was born on September 29, 1903 in Brooklyn. He began his acting career in radio. De Corsia made his Broadway debut in 1929. He first appeared on film in the 1947 motion picture *The Lady from Shanghai*. His many films include *A Place in the Sun*, *Neptune's Daughter*, *The Life of Riley*, *Naked City*, *The Enforcer*, and *The Killing*, among others. He transitioned to television work in the late 1950s, and played more than 200 roles until this death from a heart attack on April 11, 1973 in Encino, California. Ted De Corsia was 69 years old.

Pepe Hern played the role of Carlos. Hern was born to Spanish immigrants in New Jersey on June 6, 1927. He made his film debut in the 1948 film *Bodyguard*. Until his retirement in 1985, he appeared in dozens of films, and many television dramas usually playing a Spanish or Latino character. His better known films include *Borderline*, *Make Haste to Live*, *Madigan*, *The Magnificent Seven*, and *Joe Kidd*. Between acting jobs in the 1960s, Hern worked as a substitute teacher for the Los Angeles School District. His brother was actor Tom Hernandez. Pepe Hern died in Los Angeles on February 28, 2009. He was 81 years old.

Vito Scotti played the role of Pepe Alvarez. Scotti was born in San Francisco on January 26, 1918. His family moved to Italy, and lived there for several years when he was a youngster. When they returned, the family lived in New York City, and Scotti worked as a magician and mime. He made his Broadway debut in 1939, and his film debut in 1949. Until his retirement in 1995, Scotti played more than 250 roles in films and television shows, moving comfortably from comedy to drama. He co-starred in numerous television series including *Life with Luigi* (1953), *The Flying Nun* (1967-69), *To Rome with Love* (1969-71), and *Barefoot in the Park* (1970). Vito Scotti died of lung cancer at the Motion Picture Country Home in Woodland Hills, California on June 5, 1996. He was 78 years old.

Burt Mustin played the role of Student. Mustin, one of the most recognizable character actors in Hollywood, was born in Pittsburgh on February 8, 1884. He worked on stage and on the radio until making his big screen debut at the age of 67 in the 1951 William Wyler film *Detective Story*. A few of his films include *The Desperate Hours*, *The Adventures of Huckleberry Finn*, *What a Way to Go!*, *The Adventures of Bullwhip Griffin*, and *Mame*. Until his retirement in 1976, he acted in more than 300 films and television shows. Comfortable with comedy or drama, his television appearances include *Leave It to Beaver*, *The Twilight Zone*, *The Abbott and Costello Show*, *The Lucy Show*, *Petticoat Junction*, *All in the Family*, *Gunsmoke*, and *The Outer*

Limits. Burt Mustin died in Glendale, California on January 28, 1977, at the age of 92. He was predeceased by his wife of 54 years, Frances Woods.

Joel Grey played the role of Willy. Grey was born in Cleveland, Ohio on April 11, 1932. He began his acting career on stage and in nightclubs, and made his Broadway debut in 1951. He appeared on television, and made several films, but is best remembered for his Oscar-winning performance as the master of ceremonies in the 1972 film *Cabaret*. In 1967, he won a Tony Award for playing the same role in the Broadway musical. During his long career, Grey has won a BAFTA, two Drama Desk Awards, one Golden Globe, and two Grammy Awards. He was nominated for an Emmy Award in 1993 for his guest-starring role in *Brooklyn Bridge*. He is the father of actress Jennifer Grey. In 2015, Joel Grey came out publicly as gay.

Pedro Gonzalez-Gonzalez, Jr. played the role of Ricardo. Gonzalez was born on May 24, 1925 in Aguilares, Texas. He made his acting debut in the 1953 film *Wings of the Hawk*. His memorable appearance with Groucho Marx on the television quiz show *You Bet Your Life* in 1953 was seen by John Wayne, who then cast Gonzalez in several of his films including *The High and the Mighty*, *Rio Bravo*, and *Hellfighters*. His comedic abilities secured for him consistent work on screen, but he was later accused of portraying Hispanic male characters in negative stereotypical ways. After more than 100 appearances on screen, he retired in 1998. Pedro Gonzalez-Gonzalez Jr. died at his home in Culver City on February 6, 2006 at the age of 80. He was survived by his wife of 64 years, and three children. His grandson is actor Clifton Collins, Jr.

Season 1, Episode 4

Broadcast on ABC TV on October 24, 1960
Directed by George Waggner
Teleplay by Philip Saltzman and Richard De Roy from a story by Hugh Benson
Producer: Jerry Davis
Executive Producer: William T. Orr

Cast:

Troy Donahue	Sandy Winfield II
Van Williams	Ken Madison
Lee Patterson	Dave Thorne
Diane McBain	Daphne Dutton
Margarita Sierra	Cha Cha O'Brien
Paul "Mousie" Garner	Mousie
Don "Red" Barry	Lt. Snedigar
Alvy Moore	Herbert Colter
Mike Road	Kip Daly
Joan Marshall	Vera Burnet
Anita Sands	Jenny Jo
Jane Betts	Woman on Ship
William Yip	Cook

Credits:

Cinematography by Harold E. Stine
Film Editing by Byron Chudnow
Art Direction by Howard Campbell
Set Direction by Ralph S. Hurst

Makeup Supervisor: Gordon Bau
Hairstylist: Jean Burt Reilly
Assistant Director: Richard Maybery
Sound: Samuel F. Goode
Supervising Editor: James Moore
Theme Music Composers: Mack David and Jerry Livingston
Music Editor: Joe Inge
Music Supervisors: Paul Sawtell and Bert Shefter
60 minutes/Black and White
Production Company: Warner Bros. Television
Filmed at Warner Bros. Studios on Stages 20 and 24
Margarita Sierra sang "You and the Night and the Music" and "The Gaucho Serenade" in this episode.

Notes on the case:

Insurance investigator Herbert Cotler hires Sandy to help him find $90,000 in bonds that were stolen seven years earlier, and never found. The man accused of the crime is about to be released, and Cotler claims that the insurance company now owns the missing bonds. They need to find the bonds before the newly released thief can retrieve them. When the thief turns up dead, the investigation takes many twists and turns that involve the criminal's former girlfriend, Vera, and Kip Daly, the young messenger who was originally robbed of the bonds.

Alvy Moore played the role of Herbert Colter. Moore was born in Vincennes, Indiana on December 5, 1921. He served in the U.S. Marine Corps during World War II, and fought in the Battle of Iwo Jima. After the war, he moved to Los Angeles, and studied acting at the Pasadena Playhouse. In 1950, he made his Broadway debut in *Mister Roberts*, and toured with the play for 14 months. Moore made his screen debut in the 1952 film *Okinawa*. His films include *The Wild One*, *The War of the Worlds*, *Susan Slept Here*, and *5 Against the House*, among many others. He worked successfully in film and television and played more than 100 roles. He is perhaps best known for playing the role of Hank Gimball in the situation comedy *Green Acres* from 1965 until 1971. He retired in 1995, and died of heart failure on May 4, 1997 at his Palm Desert, California home.

Mike Road played the role of Kip Daly. Road was born on March 18, 1918 in Malden, Massachusetts. He appeared on Broadway in *The Moon Vine* in 1943 and *Dear Ruth* in 1946. He first appeared on screen in 1943, and continued to work in the theater as an actor and director. Road became a Warner Brothers contract player in the late 1950s. He guest-starred in numerous series at the studio including *Colt .45*, *The Alaskans*, *Lawman*, *Bronco*, *77 Sunset*

Strip, Hawaiian Eye, and *Cheyenne.* He starred in the series, *The Roaring 20's* (1960-62). As a voice actor, Road performed in dozens of cartoon series in his later career, most notably as Race Bannon on *Johnny Quest.* Mike Road retired in 1981, and died in Los Angeles on April 14, 2013 at the age of 95.

Joan Marshall played the role of Vera Burnet. Marshall was born in Chicago, Illinois on June 6, 1931. She began her career as a showgirl in Chicago nightclubs. She made her film debut as a dancer in the 1945 movie *The Chicago Kid.* Marshall was a frequent guest star in episodic television throughout the 1950s and 1960s. She is best remembered for her appearances in the episodes "Dead Man's Shoes" on *The Twilight Zone,* and in "Court Martial" on *Star Trek.* Her final acting role was in the 1975 film *Shampoo,* directed by her ex-husband, Hal Ashby. Joan Marshall died at the age of 61 in Montego Bay, Jamaica.

Local Girl

Season 1, Episode 5

Broadcast on ABC TV on October 31, 1960
Directed by Charles R. Rondeau
Written by Richard De Roy
Producer: Jerry Davis
Executive Producer: William T. Orr

Cast:

Van Williams	Ken Madison
Lee Patterson	Dave Thorne
Troy Donahue	Sandy Winfield II
Diane McBain	Daphne Dutton
Margarita Sierra	Cha Cha O'Brien
Sue Ann Langdon	Darcy Peyton
Frank Ferguson	Earl Purdy
Tom Gilson	Billy Paris
Ric Roman	Ralph Shreiner
Jimmy Ames	Angel
Jeno Mate	Abe Shreiner
Edward Colmans	Minister
Mike Lally	Taxi Driver
Philo McCullough	Wedding Guest
Charles Morton	Bartender
Barbara Pepper	Waitress
Almira Sessions	Opal

Credits:

Cinematography by Roger Shearman
Film Editing by Holbrook N. Todd

Art Direction by Howard Campbell
Set Decoration by George James Hopkins
Makeup Supervisor: Gordon Bau
Hairstylist: Jean Burt Reilly
Assistant Director: Samuel Schneider
Sound: Francis E. Stahl
Supervising Editor: James Moore
Theme Music Composers: Mack David and Jerry Livingston
Music Editor: George Marsh
Music Supervisors: Paul Sawtell and Bert Shefter
60 minutes/Black and White
Production Company: Warner Bros. Television
Filmed at Warner Bros. Studios on Stages 20 and 24.
Margarita Sierra sang "Oh, Promise Me" in this episode.

Notes from the case:

Showgirl Darcy Peyton has stolen an envelope filled with $20,000 from her gangster boyfriend. She intends to return to her small hometown to flaunt her wealth in the faces of all the locals – especially her abusive father. She hires Ken as her bodyguard, knowing that her ex-boyfriend will send some of his men after her to get the money back. But the trip to her small town of Two Rivers takes many twists and turns, with gangsters in hot pursuit.

Sue Ann Langdon played the role of Darcy Peyton. Langdon was born in Paterson, New Jersey on March 8, 1936. She began her career as a singer at Radio City Music Hall. She made her television debut in 1959, and worked frequently, guest-starring in many series. She starred in several television series including *Bachelor Father* (1959-61), *Arnie* (1970-72), *Grandpa Goes to Washington* (1978-79), and *When the Whistle Blows* (1980). Langdon won a Golden Globe Award in 1971. Her films include *The Great Imposter*, *A Guide for the Married Man*, and *The Cheyenne Social Club*. In 1966, Langdon posed nude for *Playboy* magazine. She retired in 1990.

Frank Ferguson played the role of Earl Purdy. Ferguson was born in Ferndale, California on December 25, 1906. He studied speech and drama at the University of California, and earned a master's degree from Cornell University, where he later taught. He directed plays at the Pasadena Playhouse, and made his film debut in 1939 in *Gambling on the High Seas*. Until his retirement in 1977, Ferguson played more than 400 roles in feature films and episodic television. He was one of Hollywood's most reliable and recognizable character actors. Frank Ferguson died in Santa Monica of cancer on September 12, 1978 at the age of 71.

Barbara Pepper played the role of Waitress. Pepper was born in New York City on May 31, 1915. At the age of 16, she became a performing "Goldwyn Girl." She made her screen debut in the 1933 film *Roman Scandals*. Until her death in 1969, she played more than 200 roles in films and television, and is best known for playing the recurring character of Doris Ziffel on *Green Acres* (1965-68). Barbara Pepper died in Panorama City, California on July 18, 1969. She was 54 years old, and was survived by two sons.

Tom Gilson played the role of Billy Paris. Gilson was born in New York City on January 6, 1934. He began his film career in 1954. He was under contract to Warner Brothers, and played more than 50 roles until his death in 1962. Gilson married actress/March 1957 Playmate of the Month, Saundra Edwards in 1961. Edwards was under contract to Warner Bros. and first appeared on screen in 1958. The couple had a son, but Gilson's alcoholism and physical abuse caused Edwards to flee with their child to her sister's home in August, 1962. On October 6, Gilson broke into her house and threatened to kill her and their baby. She shot him to death with a shotgun. The shooting was later ruled a justifiable homicide. Gilson was good friends with Steve McQueen, who served as a pallbearer. Saundra Edwards' final role was in the Warner film *Parrish*, starring Diane McBain and Troy Donahue.

Almira Sessions played the role of Opal. Sessions was born in Washington D.C. on September 16, 1988. She began her show business career performing on stage, and in cabarets. In the 1930s, she performed with Bob Hope on the radio. She appeared in six Broadway productions including *Ethan Frome* (1936), *White Horse Inn* (1936-37), *Shadow and Substance* (1938), and *Yokel Boy* (1939-40). Her first credited screen role was in the 1940 motion picture, *Little Nellie Kelly*. Sessions more than 100 film appearances include *Sun Valley Serenade*, *Sullivan's Travels*, *My Sister Eileen*, *The Heat's On*, *Madame Curie*, *Henry Aldrich's Little Secret*, *The Miracle of Morgan's Creek*, *State Fair*, *It's a Wonderful Life*, *Monsieur Verdoux*, *The Bishop's Wife*, *The Bride Goes Wild*, *Fancy Pants*, *Summer Stock*, *Loving You*, *Harvey*, *The Lemon Drop Kid*, *Summer and Smoke*, *The Boston Strangler*, *Rosemary's Baby*, and *Willard*, among others. Her dozens of television appearances include *Adventures of Superman*, *Lassie*, *Cheyenne*, *The Donna Reed Show*, *The Munsters*, *F Troop*, *The Andy Griffith Show*, *Marcus Welby, M.D.*, *The Wild, Wild West*, *Night Gallery*, and *Love, American Style*. She retired in 1971. Almira Sessions died in Los Angeles on August 3, 1974 at the age of 85.

Par-a-Kee

Season 1, Episode 6

Broadcast on ABC TV on November 7, 1960
Directed by William J. Hole Jr.
Teleplay by William L. Stuart from a story by Mack David
Producer: Mack David
Executive Producer: William T. Orr

Cast:

Lee Patterson	Dave Thorne
Van Williams	Ken Madison
Troy Donahue	Sandy Winfield II
Diane McBain	Daphne Dutton
Margarita Sierra	Cha Cha O'Brien
Paul "Mousie" Garner	Mousie
Don "Red" Barry	Lt. Snedigar
Grant Williams	Keith Minter
Raymond Bailey	Reginald Dutton
Lyle Talbot	Alan Crandell
Michael Harris	Eddie Geer
J. Edward McKinley	Manders
Ben Welden	Joe Bundy
Mike Ragan	Monk
Roscoe Ates	Clem
Lewis Charles	Hood
Karl Lukas	Hood

Credits:

Cinematography by Ray Fernstrom
Film Editing by Robert Watts

Art Direction by Howard Campbell
Set Decoration by William L. Kuehl
Makeup Supervisor: Gordon Bau
Hairstylist: Jean Burt Reilly
Assistant Director: Claude Binyon Jr.
Sound: Samuel F. Goode
Theme Music Composers: Mack David and Jerry Livingston
Music Editor: Sam E. Levin
Music Supervisors: Paul Sawtell and Bert Shefter
60 minutes/Black and White
Production Company: Warner Bros. Television
Filmed at Warner Bros. Studios on Stages 20 and 24
Margarita Sierra sang "Par-a-kee" in this episode. The song was written by the show's theme song composers, Mack David and Jerry Livingston.

Notes from the case:

Someone tries to kill Daphne's prized race horse, Par-a-kee, before a big race. She arrives at the stables in time to foil the killer's murderous mission. Daphne's father hires Dave to investigate the disturbing incident. At the same time, a bookie begins spreading scandalous rumors about the Dutton family stable in an attempt to have Par-a-kee disqualified. Dave learns that the bookie who is spreading false rumors will lose a fortune if the Dutton horse wins the race. In desperation, before the race can take place, the bookie kidnaps Daphne to insure the horse will not run.

Grant Williams played the role of Keith Minter. Williams was born in New York City on August 18, 1931. He served in the U.S. Air Force from 1948 until 1952, and he was discharged as an Air Force staff sergeant. He studied at the Actors Studio under Lee Strasberg, and began his acting career on the New York stage. In 1955, Williams signed a contract with Universal-International, and starred in numerous B-films and horror movies including *The Monolith Monsters, The Leech Women*, and the 1957 classic *The Incredible Shrinking Man*. Universal dropped his contract in 1959, and he was signed by Warner Brothers in 1960. He appeared in films and television productions for the studio, and played the recurring role of detective Greg McKenzie on *Hawaiian Eye*. When his acting career declined, Williams operated an acting school in West Hollywood, California. His final television appearance was on the primetime game show *Family Feud* with his *Hawaiian Eye* cast mates in 1983. Grant Williams died on July 25, 1985 in Los Angeles at the age of 53. Williams was gay.

Raymond Bailey played the role of Reginald Dutton. Bailey was born in San Francisco on May 6, 1904. He began his acting career on Broadway, but left to travel around the world as a merchant seaman. In 1938, he began working in Hollywood films. He took time away from acting to serve in the U. S. Merchant Marine during WWII. After the war, he established himself on television, film, and on stage. Some of his better known films include *Sabrina, Picnic, Vertigo, No Time for Sergeants, I Want to Live!,* and *Band of Angels,* among others. Fans know Bailey best for playing the role of banker Milburn Drysdale on the long-running hit series *The Beverly Hillbillies.* In his later years, he suffered from Alzheimer's disease which forced him to retire in 1975. Raymond Bailey died in Irvine, California on April 15, 1980 at the age of 75.

Lyle Talbot was born in Pittsburgh on February 8, 1902. Talbot moved to Hollywood in 1931. His screen test at Warner Brothers earned him a contract along with Bette Davis and Humphrey Bogart. He first appeared on screen that same year. His better known film appearances include *The Life of Jimmy Dolan, Return of the Terror, The Dragon Murder Case, Our Little Girl, Go West Young Man,* and *Miracle on Main Street,* among others. Talbot worked steadily in film, and became a co-founder of the Screen Actors Guild. His activism in the union derailed his career opportunities as a leading man. Talbot began his stage career in 1940 in the Broadway drama *Separate Rooms.* He performed in summer stock and regional theater productions. By the time he retired from acting in 1987, he had played more than 400 supporting roles in feature films and on television. His final film role was in the 1987 cult film *Amazon Women on the Moon.* Lyle Talbot died at his San Francisco home on March 2, 1996. He was 94 years old.

Deadly Male

Season 1, Episode 7

Broadcast on ABC TV on November 14, 1960
Directed by Charles R. Rondeau
Written by Lee Loeb
Producer: Jerry Davis
Executive Producer: William T. Orr

Cast:

Lee Patterson	Dave Thorne
Troy Donahue	Sandy Winfield II
Van Williams	Ken Madison
Diane McBain	Daphne Dutton
Margarita Sierra	Cha Cha O'Brien
Don "Red" Barry	Lt. Snedigar
Robert Colbert	Gary Dawson
George Wallace	Jim Elliot
Victor Buono	Mr. Beamish
Laurie Mitchell	Gloria Elliot
Roger Til	Jacque Andre
Jered Barclay	Charlie
Frances Osborne	Mrs. Digby
Charles Alvin Bell	Bill McGraw
Barbara Wooddell	Mrs. Gilbert
Darlene Fields	Mrs. Haney
Carol Forman	Mrs. Jordan
Mike Lally	Bartender

Credits:

Cinematography by Edwin B. DuPar
Film Editing by Harvey Manger

Art Direction by Howard Campbell
Set Decoration by William L. Kuehl
Makeup Supervisor: Gordon Bau
Hairstylist: Jean Burt Reilly
Assistant Director: Gene Anderson
Sound: Samuel F. Goode
Theme Music Composers: Mack David and Jerry Livingston
Music Editor: John Allyn Jr.
Music Supervisors: Paul Sawtell and Bert Shefter
60 minutes/Black and White
Production Company: Warner Bros. Television
Filmed at Warner Bros. Studios on Stages 20 and 24
Margarita Sierra sang "Valencia" in this episode.

Notes from the case:

Gloria Elliot is two-timing her wealthy husband. She juggles her affection between a charming Frenchman, Jacques Andre, and an appealing beach boy, Gary Dawson. Her indiscretions lead her into a trap perpetrated by handsome young men who seduce married women, and then blackmail them. When Gloria refuses to pay, she is murdered. Her husband, fearing he will be blamed for her death, hires Dave and Ken to investigate the crime and track down the real killer. What the boys discover is a case of blackmail and a lucrative illegal jewel insurance racket. Events take a dangerous turn for Dave.

Laurie Mitchell played the role of Gloria Elliot. Mitchell was born on July 14, 1928 in Manhattan. She began work as a child model, and won several titles including "Miss Body Beautiful" and "Miss Bronx." Her family moved to Los Angeles when she was in her teens. She made her movie debut in the 1954 Kirk Douglas film *20,000 Leagues Under the Sea*. Her numerous films include *Calypso Joe* and *That Touch of Mink*. She may be best remembered for starring opposite Zsa Zsa Gabor in the camp-classic 1958 science-fiction film *Queen of Outer Space*. Mitchell guest-starred in dozens of television dramas and comedies before retiring in 1971. She died in Perris, California on September 20, 2018. Laurie Mitchell was 90 years old.

George Wallace played the role of Jim Elliot. Wallace was born in New York City on June 8, 1917. He joined the U.S. Navy in 1936 and served eight years through World War II. After the war, he worked as a singing bartender in Hollywood. Columnist Jimmie Fidler heard him sing and introduced him to his movie business friends. In 1952, Wallace played the starring role of Commando Cody in the film *Radar Men from the Moon*. Until his death, Wallace appeared in more than 250 films and television programs. He made his Broadway debut in the Rodgers and Hammerstein musical, *Pipe Dream*.

He also appeared with Mary Martin in the 1963 musical *Jennie*, and he appeared in the musical *Company* in 1971. While he was vacationing in Pisa, Italy, he was injured in a fall, and returned to Los Angeles. George Wallace died in Los Angeles on July 22, 2005. He was 88 years old, and survived by his wife of 40 years.

Victor Buono played the role of Mr. Beamish. Buono was born in San Diego on February 3, 1938. In 1956, he joined the Globe Theater Players in San Diego and acted in Shakespearean classics and modern plays. In the summer of 1959, a Hollywood scout found him, and he signed a contract with Warner Brothers. Buono appeared in many Warner television productions, and numerous films including *Hush, Hush Sweet Charlotte* and *Robin and the 7 Hoods*. He is best known for playing the role of Edwin Flagg in the classic 1962 film *Whatever Happened to Baby Jane?* Buono was nominated for an Academy Award and a Golden Globe Award for his performance in the film. His more than 150 appearances in film and television include his recurring role of the comically villainous King Tut on *Batman*. Buono performed on stage, and made his Broadway debut in *Camino Real* in 1970. He was a spoken word recording artist, and author. Victor Buono was gay. He died at his Apple Valley, California home on January 1, 1982. He was 43 years old.

Roger Til played the role of Jacques Andre. Til was born on January 5, 1909 in Paris, France. He made his acting debut in 1947 in French films. After moving to Hollywood, he appeared in more than 100 films and television shows, often playing the cliché role of a prickly maitre d'. Roger Til died in Los Angeles on June 28, 2002 at the age of 93.

Robert Colbert played the role of Gary Dawson. Colbert was born in Long Beach, California on July 26, 1931. He was serving in Japan with an American Military Police unit, and working as an evening disc jockey, when he was recruited to perform in a radio production of *The Caine Mutiny Court-Martial*. Colbert moved to Hollywood and worked in a few minor films before signing a contract in 1958 with Warner Brothers. He worked in a few films there, including *Claudelle Inglish*, but concentrated on television work. He guest-starred in most of the Warner television productions including *Maverick, Bourbon Street Beat, Colt .45, The Alaskans, Sugarfoot, Cheyenne, Hawaiian Eye, Bronco, The Roaring 20's*, and *77 Sunset Strip*. He is perhaps best known for playing the role of Doug Phillips in the science-fiction series, *The Time Tunnel* (1966-67). Robert Colbert retired in 1995.

"I loved Victor [Buono]," Diane recalled. "We made a terrible movie together in Mexico in 1970. It was not a great experience, but I was so thankful Victor was there. We had a wonderful time together in spite of it all. He found the most wonderful restaurants and antique shops and beautiful sites to see. He made it fun. He was funny, charming, and so erudite. He was a true delight."

Power of Suggestion

Season 1, Episode 8

Broadcast on ABC TV on November 21, 1960
Directed by Irving J. Moore
Written by Laszlo Gorog
Producer: Jerry Davis
Executive Producer: William T. Orr

Cast:

Lee Patterson	Dave Thorne
Troy Donahue	Sandy Winfield II
Van Williams	Ken Madison
Margarita Sierra	Cha Cha O'Brien
Don "Red" Barry	Lt. Snedigar
Shirley Knight	Miriam
Jody Baker	Bernie Bergen
Stephen Bekassy	Prof. Daniell
Oliver McGowan	Dr. Rose
Frank Leo	Clerk
Robert Millar	Medic
Dolores Erickson	Girl

Credits:

Cinematography by Edwin B. DuPar
Film Editing by Robert Watts
Art Direction by Howard Campbell
Set Decoration by Hoyle Barrett
Makeup Supervisor: Gordon Bau
Hairstylist: Jean Burt Reilly
Assistant Director: Rex Bailey

Sound: Ross Owen
Theme Music Composers: Mack David and Jerry Livingston
Music Editor: Lou Gordon
Music Supervisors: Paul Sawtell and Bert Shefter
60 minutes/Black and White
Production Company: Warner Bros. Television
Filmed at Warner Bros. Studios on Stages 20 and 24
Margarita Sierra sang "Portuguese Washerwoman" in this episode.

Notes from the case:

While watching a nightclub performance, Dave notices that Miriam, the beautiful assistant to a mentalist, looks frightened. After the show, Miriam approaches Dave and tells him that Prof. Paul Daniel, an evil-intentioned hypnotist, has given her a post-hypnotic suggestion to commit a murder after a failed stage performance. She asks Dave and Cha Cha to protect her, but shortly afterwards, the magician in the show is murdered.

Shirley Knight played the role of Miriam. Knight was born in Goessel, Kansas on July 5, 1936. After studying at the Pasadena Playhouse, she began her screen career in 1955. Throughout her long career, she appeared in more than 200 film and television productions. Her feature films include *Sweet Bird of Youth, The Dark at the Top of the Stairs, Ice Palace, The Group,* and *The Couch.*

Shirley Knight as Miriam.

She won a Golden Globe Award and three Emmy Awards for her acting, and was nominated for two Academy Awards. She won a Tony Award for the 1976 play *Kennedy's Children.* Shirley Knight died at her daughter's home in San Marcos, Texas on April 22, 2020 at the age of 83. She was survived by her two daughters.

Stephen Bekassy played the role of Prof. Paul Daniel. Bekassy was born in Nyiregyhaza, Hungary on February 10, 1907. He first appeared on screen in Hungary in 1930. He immigrated to the United States in 1944. His first American film was *A Song to Remember,* in 1945. His many films include

One Step Beyond, Beyond the Time Barrier, The Purple Mask, Hell and High Water, and *Prisoner of War.* In 1947, he starred in *The Whole World Over* on Broadway. His movie career was damaged during the "Red Scare" in the mid-1950s when Ronald Reagan accused him of being a Communist because he was Hungarian, despite the fact that he worked with Radio Free Europe, and rescued Jewish escapees. Because of his accent, he usually played a "menacing exotic." Bekassy guest-starred in dozens of television productions until his retirement in 1964, when he returned to Hungary. He died in Budapest, Hungary on October 30, 1995 at the age of 88.

Joby Baker played the role of Bernie Bergen. Baker was born in Montreal, Canada on March 26, 1934. He began his acting career in 1952. His films include *Gidget, Gidget Goes Hawaiian, Gidget Goes to Rome, Girl Happy,* and *The Wackiest Ship in the Army.* He appeared in the Disney Studios films *Superdad, Blackbeard's Ghost,* and *The Adventures of Bullwhip Griffin.* Baker guest-starred in dozens of television dramas and comedies, and may be remembered for playing the role of David Lewis in the 1967-68 series *Good Morning World.* He was married to actress Joan Blackman from 1959 until 1961, and married to songwriter Dory Previn from 1984 until her death in 2012. Joby Baker retired from acting in 1984, and has pursued a career as an abstract painter.

Odd Job

Season 1, Episode 9

Broadcast on ABC-TV on November 28, 1960
Directed by Robert Douglas
Written by William L. Stuart
Producer: Charles Hoffman
Executive Producer: William T. Orr

Cast:

Van Williams	Ken Madison
Troy Donahue	Sandy Winfield II
Paul "Mousie" Garner	Mousie
Robert Rockwell	Phillip Johns
Patricia Michon	Nan Dale
Wilton Graff	Stanley Williams
Regina Gleason	Zelda Arms
Clarke Gordon	Rodney Arms
Molly Magruder	Cupcake
Mack Williams	Carter Bell
Karl "Killer" Davis	Rudy Walper
Rusty Wescoatt	Pug Garnes
Claude Stroud	Maintenance Man
Dick Tulfeld	Announcer

Credits:

Cinematography by Harold E. Stine
Film Editing by David Wages
Art Direction by Howard Campbell
Set Decoration by William L. Kuehl
Makeup Supervisor: Gordon Bau

Hairstylist: Jean Burt Reilly
Assistant Director: Claude Binyon Jr.
Sound: B.F. Ryan
Theme Music Composers: Mack David and Jerry Livingston
Music Editor: Robert Phillips
Music Supervisors: Paul Sawtell and Bert Shefter.
60 minutes/Black and White
Production Company: Warner Bros. Television
Filmed at Warner Bros. Studios on Stages 20 and 24

Notes from the case:

Ken receives a telegram from a businessman in Fort Lauderdale offering him a job to provide security for a potentially contentious proxy business meeting. On his way to Fort Lauderdale, he is kidnapped by men posing as police officers. Ken escapes, and continues on to the meeting, but when he arrives he discovers that an imposter had arrived earlier and had contacted the businessman who hired him. Ken enlists Sandy's aid to play an imposter in a game of their own.

Robert Rockwell played the role of Phillip. Rockwell was born on October 15, 1920 in Lake Bluff, Illinois. He served in the U.S. Navy for four years during World War II. He studied at the Pasadena Playhouse, and first appeared on screen in 1948. He appeared in numerous films, and more than 300 television episodes. He had recurring roles in *Growing Pains, Days of Our Lives, Dallas, Different Strokes*, and *The Man from Blackhawk*. Rockwell is best remembered for playing the role of Philip Boynton in *Our Miss Brooks* on radio, and then from 1952 until 1956 in the television series. He retired in 1995. Robert Rockwell died of cancer at his Malibu home on January 25, 2003 at the age of 82. He was survived by his wife of 61 years and five children.

The International Net

Season 1, Episode 10

Broadcast on ABC-TV on December 5, 1960
Directed by William J. Hole, Jr.
Teleplay by Dean Riesner from a story by William Koenig
Producer: Mack David
Executive Producer: William T. Orr

Cast:

Van Williams	Ken Madison
Troy Donahue	Sandy Winfield II
Diane McBain	Daphne Dutton
Margarita Sierra	Cha Cha O'Brien
Paul "Mousie" Garner	Mousie
Don "Red" Barry	Lt. Snedigar
Myrna Fahey	Ann Trevor
Gladys Hurlbut	La Contessa
John Van Dreelen	Frederick Lundstrom
Albert Carrier	Andre Martine
George Latchford	Lanny Hogan
Claude Akins	Mike Hogan
Anna-Lisa	Alixe Hogan

Credits:

Cinematography by Harold E. Stine
Film Editing by Leo H. Shreve
Art Direction by Howard Campbell
Set Decoration by Georg James Hopkins
Makeup Supervisor: Gordon Bau
Hairstylist: Jean Burt Reilly

Assistant Director: C. Carter Gibson
Sound: M.A. Merrick
Theme Music Composers: Mack David and Jerry Livingston
Music Editor: Donald Harris
Music Supervisors: Paul Sawtell and Bert Shefter
60 minutes/Black and White
Production Company: Warner Bros. Television
Filmed at Warner Bros. Studios on Stages 20 and 24
Margarita Sierra sang "Boom Boom" in this episode. The song was written by
the theme song's composers Mack David and Jerry Livingston.

Notes from the case:

Producer Mike Hogan and his wife are visiting Miami. Hogan is seeking an
investor for a new show. His wife receives a mysterious note accusing her
husband of murder, and warning her that she will be his next victim. When
two people are murdered, including a man the producer hated and who was
a former rival for his wife's affections, Hogan is arrested. Ken and Sandy are
hired to find out who sent the note, and who committed the murders.

Claude Akins played the role of Mike Hogan. Akins was born on May
25, 1926 in Nelson, Georgia. He served in the U.S. Army during World War
II, and graduated from Northwestern University with a theater degree in
1949. He first appeared on screen in the 1953 film *From Here to Eternity*.
His other films include *Rio Bravo, Inherit the Wind, The Killers, Battle for the
Planet of the Apes, Witness to Murder, The Caine Mutiny,* and *The Human
Jungle*. Akins appeared in 100 films, and played more than 180 roles on television, making him one of Hollywood's most recognizable character actors.
Television audiences may remember him for playing the role of Sheriff Lobo
in the series, *B.J. and the Bear* (1978-79), and in *The Misadventures of Sheriff
Lobo* (1979-81). He appeared in dozens of television commercials in the
1970s. Claude Akins died of cancer on January 27, 1994 in Pasadena. He was
survived by his wife of 42 years and three children.

Anna-Lisa played the role of Alixe Hogan. Anna-Lisa was born in Oslo,
Norway on March 30, 1933. She worked there in the theater, and in 1954 she
travelled to Hollywood to visit her brother – and decided to stay. She made
her acting debut in 1958, and appeared in several Warner Brothers series.
She starred as Nora Travers in the series *Black Saddle* (1959-60). She guest-
starred on numerous television dramas and comedies until she returned to
Norway in the 1970s to work on stage. From 1976 until 1995, she was a puppeteer at the Oslo Nye Theatre. Anna-Lisa died in Oslo, Norway on March
21, 2018 at the age of 84.

John Van Dreelen played the role of Frederick Lundstrom. Van Dreelan was born on May 5, 1922 in Amsterdam, Netherlands. His father was a Dutch actor and his mother was the Countess de Labouchere of Paris. He studied at the Sorbonne. During the World War II German invasion of the Netherlands, he escaped capture and incarceration by disguising himself as a German officer. He made some European films, and came to New York from London in 1950 to recreate his role in the play *Daphne Laureola*. Van Dreelen played dozens of roles on television, and made several memorable films including *Madame X*, *Von Ryan's Express*, *Topaz*, *Lost Horizon*, *The Formula*, and *The Money Pit*. He maintained a successful, international stage career. He played the role of Professor Higgins in a memorable Dutch production of *My Fair Lady*, and toured America for nearly a year in the role of Baron von Trapp in *The Sound of Music*. John Van Dreelen was starring in the German television series, *Unsere Hagenbecks*, when he died on September 4, 1992 in Cap d'Agde, Herault, France at the age of 70.

Myrna Fahey played the role of Ann Trevor. Fahey was born on March 12, 1933 in Carmel, Maine. She entered and won several local beauty contests, which eventually led her to work as a fashion model on Los Angeles local television. She made her acting debut in 1954, and had small roles in several films and television shows. Fahey starred as Kay Banks in the series *Father of the Bride* (1961-62), and is best remembered for playing the role of Madeline Usher opposite Vincent Price in the 1960 film *House of Usher*. During the 1960s, she guest-starred in many television productions including *Perry Mason*, *Wagon Train*, *Gunsmoke*, *Batman*, *Thriller*, *Peyton Place*, and *The Time Tunnel*. She also appeared in many Warner Brothers series. Myrna Fahey died of cancer on May 6, 1973 in Santa Monica, California. She was 40 years old.

"Claude Atkins was a great guy," Diane McBain recalled. "I worked with him in *Claudelle Inglish* and *Black Gold*. He was a gentleman, a wonderful storyteller, and had a great sense of humor. I was good friends with Myrna. We met up on holiday in Hawaii once. And she bought my house in Beverly Hills. I liked her very much. It was horrible that she suffered with cancer for so long. She was lovely."

The Frightened Canary

Season 1, Episode 11

Broadcast on ABC-TV on December 12, 1960
Directed by Charles R. Rondeau
Written by Sonya Roberts
Producer: Jerry Davis
Executive Producer: William T. Orr

Cast:

Troy Donahue	Sandy Winfield II
Van Williams	Ken Madison
Lee Patterson	Dave Thorne
Diane McBain	Daphne Dutton
Paul "Mousie" Garner	Mousie
Don "Red" Barry	Lt. Snedigar
Nina Shipman	Nina Landis
Robert Ridgely	Eddy Harker
Hal Baylor	Marty Moran
Art Lewis	Luke Miles
Sam Gilman	Will Whitman
Paul Bryar	Denitch
Kathy Marlowe	Joy
Ray Danton	Danny Rome

Credits:

Cinematography by Edwin B. DuPar
Film Editing by Leo H. Shreve
Art Decoration by Howard Campbell
Set Decoration by Hoyle Barrett
Makeup Supervisor: Gordon Bau

Hairstylist: Jean Burt Reilly
Assistant Director: Gene Anderson Jr.
Sound: Francis E. Stahl
Theme Music Composers: Mack David and Jerry Livingston
Music Editor: Jack Wadsworth
Music Supervisors: Paul Sawtell and Bert Shefter
60 minutes/Black and White
Production Company: Warner Bros. Television
Filmed at Warner Bros. Studios on Stages 20 and 24
Nina Shipman sang "It Can't Be Wrong" and "You and the Night and Music" in this episode.

Notes from the case:

An obnoxious stand-up comedian becomes threatening and vindictive when a pretty nightclub singer – a friend of Sandy - rejects his advances. When she publicly embarrasses him, he vows revenge and frames her for a murder. Sandy works to expose his scheme.

Nina Shipman played the role of Nina Landis. Shipman was born into a show business family on August 15, 1938 in Los Angeles. She earned a degree in music at California State University, and studied acting with Sanford Meisner. She first appeared on screen in 1957. She was a starlet at 20th Century-Fox in the 1950s, and appeared in numerous films including *Blue Denim*, *High Time*, and *The Oregon Trail*. She worked at Warner Brothers in the early 1960s, and guest-starred on many of the studio-produced television shows including *Sugarfoot*, *Lawman*, *Hawaiian Eye*, *Maverick*, and *Bronco*. Shipman retired in 1987, and moved to Hawaii.

Girl in the Galleon

Season 1, Episode 12

Broadcast on ABC-TV on December 19, 1960
Directed by Frank Baur
Teleplay by Charles Hoffman and Oliver Gard from a story by Oliver Gard
Producer: Charles Hoffman
Executive Producer: William T. Orr

Cast:

Troy Donahue	Sandy Winfield II
Van Williams	Ken Madison
Lee Patterson	Dave Thorne
Diane McBain	Daphne Dutton
Don "Red" Barry	Lt. Snedigar
Andra Martin	Connie Taylor
Jackie Loughery	Hazel Haynes
Jean Willes	Eve Tibbles
Rhodes Reason	Martin Haynes
Dean Fredericks	Danny "Deep" Waters
Whit Bissell	Quincey Tibbles
Michael Garrett	Jason Westover

Credits:

Cinematography by Edwin B. DuPar
Editing by David Wages
Art Direction by Howard Campbell
Set Decoration by William L. Kuehl
Makeup Supervisor: Gordon Bau
Hairstylist: Jean Burt Reilly
Assistant Director: Claude Binyon Jr.

Sound: John K. Kean
Theme Music Composers: Mack David and Jerry Livingston
Music Editor: Erma E. Levin
Music Supervisor: Paul Sawtell and Bert Shefter
60 Minutes/Black and White
Production Company: Warner Bros. Television
Filmed at Warner Bros. Studios on Stages 20 and 24

Notes on the case:

The Maritime Museum hires a local salvage diver to explore an old sunken Spanish galleon. He discovers five boxes of gold doubloons – and a girl's body floating near the shipwreck. Later, the body of the girl disappears. Unbeknownst to the diver and authorities, criminals who stole a fortune in gold are making Spanish coins from the stolen gold and planting them in the shipwreck. The next day, the diver asks for his share of his find, but he soon turns up dead. Sandy and Ken investigate the mysteries, and capture the crooks in an undersea fight.

    Dean Fredericks played the role of Danny "Deep" Waters. Fredericks was born in Los Angeles on January 21, 1924. He served in the U.S. Army

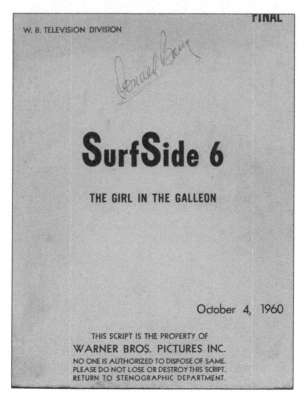

Calvary during WWII, and earned a Purple Heart. He made his acting debut in 1952, and appeared in numerous films and television shows. He was a recurring cast member on *Jungle Jim* (1955-56) and *Rin Tin Tin* (1954-57), and played the title role in the series, *Steven Canyon* (1958-59). Among his film appearances is the 1954 sci-fi cult-classic *Them!* Fredericks retired from acting in 1965. He died in Los Angeles on June 30, 1999 at the age of 75.

Andra Martin played the role of Connie Waters. Martin was born in Rockford, Illinois on July 15, 1935. She first appeared on screen in 1957. Her better known films include *Up Periscope* and the 1958 cult-classic *The Thing That Couldn't Die*. She was a contract player at Warner Brothers and appeared in most of their television productions including *Bronco*, *Lawman*, *77 Sunset Strip*, *The Alaskans*, *Hawaiian Eye*, *Bourbon Street Beat*, and *Maverick*. From 1958 until 1960, she was married to her fellow Warner contract player, Ty Hardin. The couple had twin boys. Martin's acting career ended when Warners terminated her contract in 1961. She married David May II, heir to the May Company department store chain, in 1962. In 1968, she was awarded a substantial monetary judgement when she divorced May, who was 23 years her senior.

Bride and Seek

Season 1, Episode 13

Broadcast on ABC-TV on December 26, 1960
Directed by Charles F. Haas
Teleplay by Anne Howard Bailey from a story by Steve Goodman
Producer: Jerry Davis
Executive Producer: William T. Orr

Cast:

Lee Patterson	Dave Thorne
Troy Donahue	Sandy Winfield II
Van Williams	Ken Madison
Diane McBain	Daphne Dutton
Margarita Sierra	Cha Cha O'Brien
Don "Red" Barry	Lt. Snedigar
Grant Williams	Frank Anders
Warren Stevens	Arnie Helmen
Kaye Elhardt	Lois Culver
Linda Bennett	Nancy Clayborne
Louise Lorimer	Mrs. Clayborne III
Paul Carr	Stan Ritchie
Charles Seel	Hotel Clerk
Mary Treen	Hotel Plaza Desk Clerk

Credits:

Cinematography by Robert Hoffman
Film Editing by Victor Lewis
Art Direction by Howard Campbell
Set Decoration by Hoyle Barrett
Makeup Supervisor: Gordon Bau

Hairstylist: Jean Burr Reilly
Assistant Director: James T. Vaughn
Sound: M.A. Merrick
Theme Music Composers: Mack David and Jerry Livingston
Music Editor: Erma E. Levin
Music Supervisors: Paul Sawtell and Bert Shefter
60 minutes/Black and White
Production Company: Warner Bros. Television
Filmed at Warner Bros. Studios on Stages 20 and 24
Margarita Sierra sang "New Moon" and "Softly as in a Morning Sunrise" in this episode.

Notes on the case:

Frank Anders is part of an extortion ring that preys on single women from wealthy families. His criminal intent was to romance and elope with a young woman from a very rich New York family. He would then go about getting money from her wealthy grandmother. But before his planned elopement, he goes missing, and one of his ex-girlfriends hires Dave to find him. Two other racketeers are looking for Anders, too, so Dave has to determine who everybody really is and what they all really want.

Warren Stevens played the role of Arnie Helman. Stevens was born on November 2, 1919 in Clarks Summit, Pennsylvania. He served in the U.S. Army Air Forces during World War II. Stevens was a founding member of The Actor's Studio in New York, and made his Broadway debut in *The Life of Galileo* in 1947. He also starred in the Broadway hit, *Detective Story* (1949-50). He first appeared on television in 1948. Stevens' feature films include *The Frogmen, Phone Call from a Stranger, Wait Till the Sun Shines Nellie, The Barefoot Contessa*, and *Intent to Kill*. He is best remembered for playing the role of Doc Ostrow in the 1956 science-fiction classic, *Forbidden Planet*. He guest-starred in more than 150 television programs until his retirement in 2007. Warren Stevens died at his Sherman Oaks, California home on March 27, 2012 at the age of 92. He was survived by his wife, actress Barbara French, and three children.

Paul Carr played the role of Stan Ritchie. Carr was born on January 31, 1934 in Marrero, Louisiana. As a teenager, he moved to New York and studied acting at the American Theatre Wing. He served two years in the U.S. Marine Corps, and began working on stage in New Orleans. He made his television debut in 1955, and first appeared on screen in the 1956 Hitchcock thriller *The Wrong Man*. Carr performed on Broadway, off-Broadway, and in summer stock and regional theater. He also was a successful and award-winning stage director, writer, and producer. His film appearances include

Jamboree, and *The Young Don't Cry*. He guest-starred in more than 150 television episodes before his retirement in 2002. Paul Carr died in Los Angeles of lung cancer on February 17, 2006 at the age of 72. He was survived by his wife and three kids.

Kaye Elhardt played the role of Lois Culver. Elhardt was born in Los Angeles on August 28, 1935. She made her screen debut in 1956. Her films include *The Crimson Kimono, Violent Midnight, Dr. Goldfoot and the Bikini Machine*, and *The Navy vs. the Night Monsters*. She guest-starred frequently on episodic television programs including *Highway Patrol, Sea Hunt, Wagon Train, Perry Mason, My Three Sons, Family Affair, Maverick, Colt .45, Bourbon Street Beat, Bronco, 77 Sunset Strip*, and *Hawaiian Eye*. She worked in regional theater before retiring in 1977. Kaye Elhardt died on September 1, 2004 at the Motion Picture Country Home in Woodland Hills, California at the age of 69. She was survived by her son.

Louise Lorimer played the role of Mrs. Clayborne III. Lorimer was born in Newton, Massachusetts on July 14, 1898. She began her acting career on Broadway in 1925, and appeared in five productions during the following three years. Lorimer returned to Broadway in 1944 to appear in the hit *I Remember Mama*. She first appeared on screen in 1934. Lorimer's films include *Gentleman's Agreement, The Glass Menagerie, The Sun Sets at Dawn, Marnie*, and *Compulsion*, among others. She earned more than 125 acting credits in film and on television until her retirement in 1982. She appeared numerous times on *Hopalong Cassidy, Dragnet, Dennis the Menace, Window on Main Street, Alfred Hitchcock Presents, Hazel*, and *Perry Mason*. Louise Lorimer died at her home in Newton, Massachusetts on August 11, 1995 at the age of 97.

Little Star Lost

Season 1, Episode 14

Broadcast on ABC-TV on January 2, 1961
Directed by Charles R. Rondeau
Written by Richard De Roy
Producer: Jerry Davis
Executive Producer: William T. Orr

Cast:

Troy Donahue	Sandy Winfield II
Van Williams	Ken Madison
Lee Patterson	Dave Thorne
Diane McBain	Daphne Dutton
Margarita Sierra	Cha Cha O'Brien
Don "Red" Barry	Lt. Snedigar
Shirley Knight	Linda Lord
Constance Ford	Sybil Lord
David White	Arnold Plagermann
Marjorie Reynolds	Mrs. Phelps
Gayla Graves	Myra Kane
Don Ross	Eddie Stark
Dick Tufeld	Announcer

Credits:

Cinematography by Roger Shearman
Film Editing by Noel L. Scott
Art Direction by Howard Campbell
Set Decoration by George James Hopkins
Makeup Supervisor: Gordon Bau
Hairstylist: Jean Burt Reilly

Assistant Director: Bernard McEveety
Sound: Francis E. Stahl
Theme Music Composers: Mack David and Jerry Livingston
Music Editor: Joe Inge
Music Supervisors: Paul Sawtell and Bert Shefter
60 minutes/Black and White
Production Company: Warner Bros. Television
Filmed at Warner Bros. Studios on Stages20 and 24
Margarita Sierra sang "It's Magic" in this episode.

Notes on the case:

Starlet Linda Lord returns to her home town of Miami to work on a film. She discovers that the woman traveling with her, whom she believed to be her mother, is actually her adoptive mother. A crooked lawyer has hatched a scheme to use her real mother to cash in on Linda's fortune. Faked documents, deception, and murder soon follow. Linda hires her old friend Sandy to find her birth mother, and to protect her from the shady lawyer's extortion attempt.

Constance Ford played the role of Sybil Lord. Ford was born in the Bronx, New York, on July 1, 1923. She worked as a print and catalog model until making her Broadway debut playing the role of Miss Forsythe in *Death of a Salesman* (1949-50). Her other Broadway appearances include *See the Jaguar, Say Darling, Golden Fleecing, Nobody Loves an Albatross,* and *UTBU.* She first appeared on television in 1950, and became a Warner Brothers con-

tract player in the late 1950s. Her feature films include *A Summer Place, Claudelle Inglish, Rome Adventure, House of Women, The Caretakers,* and *All Fall Down.* Ford guest-starred in many dramatic television productions, but found her greatest television success in soap operas. She is best remembered for playing the role of Ada Hobson on *Another World* from 1967 until her retirement in 1992. Constance Ford died of cancer on February 26, 1993 in Manhattan. She was 69 years old, and had no survivors.

Troy and Constance Ford.

David White played the role of Arnold Plagermann. White was born in Denver, Colorado on April

4, 1916. He moved to Los Angeles and began acting at the Pasadena Playhouse. White served in the U.S. Marine Corps during World War II. After his discharge, he made his Broadway debut in *Leaf and Bough* in 1949. In the 1950s and 1960s, White, equally adept at drama and comedy, played more than 125 roles in films and television shows. His films include *Sweet Smell of Success, The Apartment, Sunrise at Campobello, The Great Imposter,* and *Brewster's Millions.* His several engagements on Broadway include the 1957-58 hit play *Romanoff and Juliet.* Fans remember White from his memorable supporting role of Darrin Steven's boss, Larry Tate, on the long-running hit situation comedy *Bewitched* (1964-1972). His first wife, actress Mary Welch, died suddenly after her second pregnancy. Their son, Jonathan White, died in the downing of Pan Am Flight 103 over Lockerbie, Scotland, on December 21, 1988. He was 33 years old. David White died of a heart attack on November 27, 1990 in North Hollywood, California. He was 74 years old, and survived by his wife of 31 years, Lisa Figus, and two children.

Marjorie Reynolds played the role of Mrs. Phelps. Reynolds was born on August 12, 1917 in Buhl, Idaho. Her family moved to Los Angeles when she was three years old, and she began dancing lessons. She first appeared on screen in the 1923 silent film *Scaramouche.* Over the next 30 years, she appeared in more than 50 films including *Dixie, Star Spangled Rhythm, Duffy's Tavern, The Fatal Hour, Ministry of Fear, The Time of Their Lives, Monsieur Beaucaire,* and the 1942 classic musical/comedy *Holiday Inn,* among others. She began working in television in 1951. She guest-starred in many television shows, and is perhaps best remembered for playing the role of Peg Riley in the 1953-58 series *The Life of Riley.* Marjorie Reynolds suffered a heart attack and died while walking her dog in Manhattan Beach, California on February 1, 1997 at the age of 79. She was survived by her daughter.

Diane McBain recalled, "I worked with Constance a few times. She played my mother in *Claudelle Inglish.* I played the title character, and felt the weight of that picture on my shoulders. It was daunting. Constance was a terrific actress, always playing strong female types. We argued so much of the time on screen in that movie, but there was one scene where I make a confession to her, and I'm very distraught. I was supposed to cry, and I had a hard time crying on cue. She was very helpful, and grabbed me in her arms, to comfort me, which surprised me a little, but she did help me get through the scene. She was very generous, and supportive. She was a lesbian, which never bothered me at all. There were so many actors who were gay and living under the radar then. She was a wonderful actress. It was always great to work with a pro."

Heels Over Head

Season 1, Episode 15

Broadcast on ABC-TV on January 9, 1961
Directed by John Ainsworth
Written by Michael Cramoy
Producer: Jerry Davis
Executive Producer: William T. Orr

Cast:

Lee Patterson	Dave Thorn
Van Williams	Ken Madison
Diane McBain	Daphne Dutton
Margarita Sierra	Cha Cha O'Brien
Paul "Mousie" Garner	Mousie
Don "Red" Barry	Lt. Snedigar
Carlos Romero	Juan Escudero
Berry Kroeger	Homer Garson
George Kennedy	Gabe Buchanan
William Phipps	Al Owens
Paul Collins	Bertie Simms
Tim Rooney	Jimmy Degan

Credits:

Makeup Supervisor: Gordon Bau
Hairstylist: Jean Burt Reilly
Theme Music Composers: Mack David and Jerry Livingston
60 minutes/Black and White
Production Company: Warner Bros. Television
Filmed at Warner Bros. Studios on Stages 20 and 24.

Notes on the case:

Although Dave and Ken refuse to be hired by a man named Juan Escudero because he's too closed-mouth about the details, they agree to hold an envelope on his behalf, but Escudero soon disappears. The envelope has a fake address, but is filled with $70,000 in illicit cash that Escudero stole from gangster Homer Garson. Dave and Ken find themselves intermediaries between dangerous factions vying for the money. Garson kidnaps Dave and Cha Cha in order to get back his money.

Berry Kroeger played the role of Homer Garson. Kroeger was born on October 16, 1912 in San Antonio, Texas. He began his show business career as a radio announcer, and acted on the radio in *The Falcon*, *Big Sister*, and *Young Doctor Malone*. Kroeger made his Broadway debut in 1943 in *The World's Full of Girls*. His other Broadway credits include *Reclining Figure*, *Julius Cesar*, *The Tempest*, and *Shangri-La*. He began his film career in 1948 in the film *The Iron Curtain*. Often playing a villain, his films include *Act of Violence*, *Cry of the City*, *Gun Crazy*, and the camp classics *Chamber of Horrors* (1966) and *The Incredible 2-Headed Transplant* (1971). Before his retirement in 1977, he guest-starred in dozens of television comedies and dramas. Berry Kroeger died of kidney failure on January 4, 1991 in Los Angeles at the age of 78. He was survived by his wife of 20 years.

Carlos Romero played the role of Juan Escudero. Romero was born on February 15, 1927 in Hollywood. His father was a choreographer and director of ice shows including the *Polarink Follies*, and the more well-known *Ice Follies*. Romero, billed as Carlos Romero Jr., began performing as a skater in the *Ice Follies of 1944*. He toured with the *Ice Follies of 1945*, as well, before taking leave to serve in the U.S. Army from 1945 until 1947. After his military service, he returned to professional skating and toured with the *Ice Follies of 1948*. He worked with the *Ice Follies* for the next two years, and made his stage acting debut in 1951 in a Los Angeles production of *Light Up the Sky*. He starred again in 1953 in a stage production of *The Two Mrs. Carrolls*. He made his acting debut on television in 1957. His dozens of television appearances include *Bronco*, *Cheyenne*, *Bourbon Street Beat*, *Zorro*, *Maverick*, *77 Sunset Strip*, *Wagon Train*, *Rawhide*, *I Spy*, *Perry Mason*, *Death Valley Days*, *Mod Squad*, *The Virginian*, *Family Affair*, *Falcon Crest*, and *L.A. Law*, among many others. His feature films include *They Came to Cordura*, *The Young Land*, *Island of Blue Dolphins*, *The Professionals*, and *Soylent Green*. Romero retired in 1989. He was married and divorced twice. Carlos Romero died on June 21, 2007 in Ferndale, California. He was 80 years old, and survived by one child.

George Kennedy played the role of Gabe Buchanan. Kennedy was born on February 18, 1925 in New York City. He made his stage debut at age two in a touring production of *Bringing Up Father*. He enlisted in the U.S. Army during World War II, and served for 16 years, retiring as a Captain. He made his television debut in 1956 playing the role of M.P. Sgt. Kennedy in *The Phil Silvers Show* (1956-1959). Until his retirement in 2014, he appeared in more than 100 films and television productions. His feature films include *Lonely are the Brave, Strait-Jacket, McHale's Navy, Hush Hush Sweet Charlotte, In Harm's Way, The Sons of Katie Elder, The Boston Strangler*, and *The Dirty Dozen*. In 1967, Kennedy won an Academy Award for Best Supporting Actor for playing Dragline in *Cool Hand Luke*. Younger audiences may know him for his appearances in all four *Airport* films, and playing Captain Ed Hocken in the *Naked Gun* film series. He wrote two novels, and his autobiography, *Trust Me*. George Kennedy died of heart failure on February 28, 2016 in Middleton, Idaho, at the age of 91. He was survived by his six children.

Tim Rooney played the role of Jimmy Degan. Rooney was the son of Mickey Rooney. He was born in Birmingham, Alabama on January 4, 1947. Warner Brothers offered him a contract in 1960, and he made his television debut in this episode of *Surfside 6*. He guest-starred in the Warner programs *Maverick*, and *77 Sunset Strip*, and co-starred in the 1962 series *Room for One More*. He acted in several movies including the 1965 cult-classic *Village of the Giants*. Rooney also co-starred with his father in the 1964-65 series, *Mickey*. His final film was the 1975 made-for-television movie *Motor Scouts*. He was a cartoon voice-over artist in his later years. Tim Rooney contracted and recovered from polio when he was a little boy. He died at his Hemet ranch on September 23, 2006 from pneumonia, complicated by a muscle disease known as dermatomyositis. He was 59 years old.

Facts on the Fire

Season 1, Episode 16

Broadcast on ABC-TV on January 16, 1961
Directed by Charles R. Rondeau
Teleplay by Al C. Ward from a story by William Koenig
Producer: Jerry Davis
Executive Producer: William T. Orr

Cast:

Van Williams	Ken Madison
Lee Patterson	Dave Thorne
Diane McBain	Daphne Dutton
Margarita Sierra	Cha Cha O'Brien
Paul "Mousie" Garner	Mousie
Don "Red" Barry	Lt. Snedigar
Julie Adams	Merilee Williams
Dorothy Green	Crystal Martel
Robert Knapp	Philip Baine
Richard Webb	Jock Lansford
Max Baer Jr.	Joe Wilk
Thomas Browne Henry	Larry

Credits:

Cinematography by Edwin B. DuPar
Film Editing by Fred Bohanan
Art Direction by Howard Campbell
Set Decoration by Hoyle Barrett
Makeup Supervisor: Gordon Bau
Hairstylist: Jean Burt Reilly
Assistant Director: C. Carter Gibson

Sound: M.A. Merrick
Theme Music Composers: Mack David and Jerry Livingston
Music Editor: Charles Paley
Music Supervisors: Paul Sawtell and Bert Shefter
60 minutes/Black and White
Production Company: Warner Bros. Television
Filmed at Warner Bros. Studios on Stages 20 and 24
Margarita Sierra sang "Begin the Beguine" in this episode.

Notes on the case:

Ken is hired by a woman who wants him to prove that she's guilty of murdering her millionaire husband – even though she was cleared of the crime in an inquest, and never charged with murder. She told police that she thought he was a prowler, and shot him – killing him. Before he begins his investigation, Ken is beaten up by self-described "admirers" of the dead man. They advise him to make certain he proves that she was guilty, but the more he digs, the more complicated the case becomes and he wonders if she wasn't the intended victim.

Julie Adams played the role of Merilee Williams. Adams was born on October 17, 1926 in Waterloo, Iowa. She began her acting career at Universal-International in 1949. Her many films include *Red Hot and Blue*, *The Dalton Gang*, *Bend of the River*, *The Lawless Breed*, *The Mississippi Gambler*, *The Man from the Alamo*, *The Looters*, *How to Marry a Millionaire*, *Four Girls in Town*, and *Tickle Me*. She is best remembered for playing the role of Kay Lawrence in the 1954 science-fiction classic *Creature from the Black Lagoon*. Throughout the 1960s, until her last credited role in 2007, Adams guest-starred in more than 100 television episodes. She had recurring roles in *The Jimmy Stewart Show* (1971-72), *Code Red* (1981-82), and *Murder She Wrote* (1987-93). In 1984, she played the role of Paula Denning on the soap opera *Capitol*. Adams was married to actor Ray Danton from 1954 until they divorced in 1981. Her autobiography, *The Lucky Southern Star: Reflections from the Black Lagoon*, was co-written by her son Mitchell Danton, and published in 2011. Julie Adams died on February 3, 2019 in Los Angeles at the age of 93. She is survived by her sons, Emmy Award winning television editor Mitchell, and actor/director Steve Danton.

Dorothy Green played the role of Crystal Martel. Green was born in Los Angeles on January 12, 1920. She was an occasional model, and was discovered when she was appearing with a theater group in Manhattan Beach, California. She first appeared on television playing a small role on *The Jack Benny Show* in 1953. Until her retirement in 1997, she played supporting roles in more than 125 films and television shows. Her films include *The Big*

Heat, Bad for Each Other, The Helen Morgan Story, Man-Trap, It Happened at the World's Fair, Critic's Choice, Palm Springs Weekend, Zebra in the Kitchen, and *Tammy and the Millionaire.* Dorothy Green died at her Los Angeles home after suffering a heart attack on May 8, 2008. She was 88 years old, and survived by her three children.

Max Baer, Jr. played the role of Joe Wilk. Baer was born on December 4, 1937 in Oakland, California. He is the son of boxing champion Max Baer. He graduated from Santa Clara University with a Bachelor's Degree in Business Administration. In 1960, he signed a contract with Warner Brothers, and became a frequent guest star in the studio's television productions including *Maverick, Cheyenne, Hawaiian Eye, 77 Sunset Strip, Bronco, The Roaring 20's,* and *Sugarfoot.* In 1962, he was cast in the role of Jethro Bodine in *The Beverly Hillbillies.* The role changed his life and his career. He starred in the hit situation comedy from 1962 until 1971. He acted infrequently after the series ended, but became a successful film producer and director. His producer credits include *Two for the Money, Macon County Line, The Wild McCullochs, Ode to Billy Joe,* and *Hometown U.S.A.* Max Baer Jr. retired from acting in 1991. In his later years, he invested in the gambling industry.

Richard Webb played the role of Jock Lansford. Webb was born in Bloomington, Illinois on September 9, 1915. He began his film career at Paramount in 1940. His films there include *I Wanted Wings, Sullivan's Travels,* and *This Gun for Hire.* He served in the U.S. Army during WWII. He returned to Hollywood after the war ended, and signed a contract with Warner Brothers in 1951. He appeared in dozens of films and television shows, and played the title role in the 1954-55 series *Captain Midnight.* He worked steadily until his retirement in 1978. In his later life he authored several books about psychic phenomena. After suffering a debilitating long-term respiratory illness, he died of a self-inflicted gunshot wound at his Van Nuys home on June 10, 1993. Webb was 77 years old.

Yesterday's Hero

Season 1, Episode 17

Broadcast on ABC-TV on January 23, 1961
Directed by Charles R. Rondeau
Written by Richard De Roy
Producer: Jerry Davis
Executive Producer: William T. Orr

Cast:

Lee Patterson	Dave Thorne
Van Williams	Ken Madison
Margarita Sierra	Cha Cha O'Brien
Paul "Mousie" Garner	Mousie
Don "Red" Barry	Lt. Snedigar
Merry Anders	Chris Karns
Joe De Santis	Emilio Mendez
Ernest Sarracino	Silva
Craig Hill	Robbie Karns
Miguel Angel Landa	Captain Rivas
Viviane Cervanese	Carmen Mendez
Dick Tufeld	Announcer

Credits:

Cinematography by Ralph Woolsey
Film Editing by David Wages
Art Direction by Howard Campbell
Set Decoration by Hoyle Barrett
Makeup Supervisor: Gordon Bau
Hairstylist: Jean Burt Reilly
Assistant Director: Claude Binyon Jr.

Sound: M.A. Merrick
Theme Music Composers: Mack David and Jerry Livingston
Music Editor: Donald Harris
Music Supervisors: Paul Sawtell and Bert Shefter
60 minutes/Black and White
Production Company: Warner Bros. Television
Filmed at Warner Bros. Studios on Stages 20 and 24
Previous footage of Margarita Sierra singing "Dancing in the Dark" (first seen in Episode 3 "The Clown") and "You and the Night and the Music" (first seen in Episode 4 "According to Our Files") was used in this episode.

Notes on the case:

Dave's best combat buddy from the Korean War was reported executed by the dictator of the Caribbean island nation of San Doro. His widow shows up in Miami Beach and seeks Dave's assistance. She says that she recently wired her husband money long after his alleged execution. Dave struggles with his feelings because he blames her desire for money for driving his buddy to drink, and his ultimate death in the Caribbean. But she insists her husband is alive, and she needs Dave to find him. His investigation reveals that his execution was faked to cover up his betrayal of the rebels he had been working with as a mercenary.

Merry Anders played the role of Chris Karns. Anders was born on May 22, 1934 in Chicago. She and her mother moved to Los Angeles in 1949. She began working as a "junior" model, and was signed to a film contract with 20th Century-Fox in 1951. She made her film debut that same year. Her numerous films include *The Farmer Takes a Wife*, *All That Heaven Allows*, and *Desk Set*. In 1954, Fox dropped her contract. She worked on stage, and continued to work in film and television, and played the role of Mike McCall in the 1957-59 television series, *How to Marry a Millionaire*. In the early 1960s, Anders guest-starred in several Warner Brothers television productions including *Bronco*, *Maverick*, and *Hawaiian Eye*. In 1965, she costarred with Elvis Presley in *Tickle Me*. While her career waned, and fewer jobs came her way, she worked as a receptionist at Litton Industries in Beverly Hills. She eventually became a customer relations coordinator for the company. She retired from acting in 1971, and retired from Litton in 1994. She was married and divorced once, and married and widowed once. Merry Anders died in Encino, California on October 28, 2012 at the age of 78.

Craig Hill played the role of Robbie Karns. Hill was born in Los Angeles on March 5, 1926. He began his acting career as a contract player for 20th Century-Fox in 1950. His early films include *Cheaper by the Dozen*, *Fixed Bayonets*, *What Price Glory*, *Detective Story*, *A Christmas Carol*, and *Tammy* *and the Bachelor.* He costarred in the series *Whirlybirds* (1957-60). In 1960, he moved to Warners for one year and appeared in several television programs there including *Bourbon Street Beat, Sugarfoot,* and *Hawaiian Eye.* Hill appeared in numerous films and television dramas. In the mid-1960s, he moved to Spain and starred in several "Spaghetti Westerns." In 1990, he married Teresa Gimpera, a Catalan fashion model and actress. Craig Hill died in Barcelona, Spain of natural causes on April 21, 2014. He was 88 years old.

Ernest Sarracino played the role of Silva. Sarracino was born in Valdez, Colorado on February 12, 1915. His six-decade career as a character actor began in 1939 with several film serials for Republic Pictures including *Zorro's Fighting Legion, Drums of Fu Manchu, Adventures of Red Ryder, Mysterious Doctor Satan,* and *Adventures of Captain Marvel.* His other films include *Santiago, Castle of Evil, Chubasco, A Dream of Kings,* and *The Hudsucker Proxy,* which provided him with his final acting role. Sarracino's numerous television appearances include *Private Secretary, You Are There, The Adventures of Rin Tin Tin, Father Knows Best, Peter Gunn, Perry Mason, Thriller, Rawhide, The Flying Nun, Here's Lucy, Eight is Enough,* and *Charlie's Angels.* He retired in 1994. Ernest Sarracino died in Los Angeles on May 20, 1998 at the age of 83.

Thieves Among Honor

Season 1, Episode 18

Broadcast on ABC-TV on January 30, 1961
Directed by Robert Altman
Teleplay by Anne Howard Bailey and Leo Solomon from a story by Leo
  Solomon
Producer: Jerry Davis
Executive Producer: William T. Orr

Cast:

Troy Donahue	Sandy Winfield II
Van Williams	Ken Madison
Diane McBain	Daphne Dutton
Margarita Sierra	Cha Cha O'Brien
Paul "Mousie" Garner	Mousie
Don "Red" Barry	Lt. Snedigar
Alex Gerry	Dr. Bernard Ostrow
Myron Healey	Dan Zeeman
Harry Holcombe	Mayor White
Ellen Corby	Addie Horton
Jane Wald	Joanne White
Peter Breck	Mark Goodwin
Lee Patterson	Dave Thorne
Dick Tufeld	Announcer

Credits:

Cinematography by J. Peverell Marley
Film Editing by William W. Moore
Art Direction by Howard Campbell

Set Decoration by Mowbray Berkeley
Makeup Supervisor: Gordon Bau
Hairstylist: Jean Burt Reilly
Assistant Director: Richard L'Estrange
Sound: B.F. Ryan
Theme Music Composers: Mack David and Jerry Livingston
Music Editor: Ted Sebern
Music Supervisors: Paul Sawtell and Bert Shefter
60 Minutes/Black and White
Production Company: Warner Bros. Television
Filmed at Warner Bros. Studios on Stages 20 and 24

Notes on the case:

Ken and Sandy take Dave to the airport where he catches a plane to Baltimore for a job. They literally bump into a man who later becomes an integral character in their newest case. Daphne has undertaken a project to help her friend, Dr. Ostrow, raise money for a hospital he proposes to build. She meets two men who offer to help her fundraising efforts. The two men are swindlers who intend to abscond with the donations. Sandy becomes suspicious, but only alienates Daphne when he tries to intervene. The more that Sandy investigates, the more suspicious he becomes of Dr. Ostrow, himself.

Alex Gerry played the role of Dr. Bernard Ostrow. Gerry was born in Manhattan on October 6, 1904. He began his film career in 1948. Gerry was a reliable character actor in dramas and comedies, and played more than 125 roles in films and television productions until his retirement in 1977. His films include *Funny Face*, *The Bellboy*, *Back Street*, and *Love is Better than Ever*, among many others. And his numerous television appearances include *Mannix*, *The F.B.I.*, *Bewitched*, and *The Wild, Wild West*. He was married to actress Toni Gerry from 1948 until 1959. Alex Gerry died in Ventura County, California on May 18, 1993 at the age of 89.

Myron Healey played the role of Dan Zeeman. Healey was born on June 8, 1923 in Petaluma, California. He served in the U.S. Air Force during World War II, and continued in the Air Force Reserve before retiring in the early 1960s. He made his film debut in the 1943 movie *Young Ideas*. Until his retirement from acting in 1994, Healey appeared in more than 350 films and television productions. He was usually cast in Westerns, and his television credits include *The Adventures of Kit Carson*, *Colt. 45*, *The Lone Ranger*, *The Roy Rogers Show*, *The Life and Legend of Wyatt Earp*, *The Virginian*, *Death Valley Days*, *Laramie*, and *The Gene Autry Show*. His feature film work includes more than 80 Westerns, three serials including *Bomba*, *Jungle Jim*, and *Panther Girl of the Kongo*, and two classic science-fiction films, *Varan the Unbelievable*, and *The Incredible Melting Man*. Myron Healey died in Simi Valley, California on December 21, 2005 after sustaining a broken hip in a fall at his home. He was 82 years old.

Peter Breck played the role of Mark Goodwin. Breck was born in Rochester, New York on March 13, 1929. He served in the U.S. Navy post-World War II, and played professional basketball during the 1948-49 season for *The Rochester Royals*. He made his television debut in 1956, and his first film, *The Beatniks*, in 1958. His numerous films include *Thunder Road, Lad: A Dog, Shock Corridor*, and *The Crawling Hand*. Breck found his true success in television. From 1959 until 1960, he starred in the Western series, *Black Saddle*. He guest-starred on many shows including *Sea Hunt, Wagon Train, Tombstone Territory, The Outer Limits, Bonanza*, and *The Virginian*. He was a contract player with Warner Television, and appeared on many of the studio's productions including *Maverick, Lawman, Cheyenne, 77 Sunset Strip, Hawaiian Eye, Bronco, Sugarfoot*, and *The Roaring 20's*. Breck is best remembered for playing the role of Nick Barkley in the long-running series *The Big Valley* (1965-69). In the 1970s, he continued to work in television, appearing on *Alias Smith and Jones, Mission: Impossible, Fantasy Island*, and *The Fall Guy*, among others. In the 1980s, he and his wife and son moved to Vancouver, British Columbia, where he opened an acting school called "The Breck Academy." He retired from acting in 2004. He suffered from dementia in his later years, and died in Vancouver on February 6, 2012 at the age of 82. He was survived by his wife of 62 years. Their son died of leukemia shortly after moving to Canada.

Ellen Corby played the role of Addie Horton. Corby was born on June 3, 1911 in Racine, Wisconsin. She moved to Hollywood in 1932 and worked as a script girl at RKO Studios and Hal Roach Studios. During the 1930s and 1940s, she played bit roles in dozens of films including *Babes in Toyland* (1934), and *It's a Wonderful Life* (1946). Her first major role was in the 1945 RKO film *Cornered*. Corby was nominated for an Academy Award for her performance in the 1948 film classic *I Remember Mama*. Her numerous films include *The Glass Bottom Boat, The Ghost and Mr. Chicken, The Caretakers*, and *Pocketful of Miracles*. She guest-starred in nearly 100 television series including *Trackdown, The Andy Griffith Show, Wagon Train, Cheyenne, The Rifleman, Hazel, I Love Lucy, Batman, The Lucy Show, Get Smart, The Addams Family, Lassie*, and *Night Gallery* among many others. In 1971, she played the role of Grandma Walton in the TV-movie *The Homecoming: A Christmas Story*. The film served as the pilot for the series *The Waltons*, which premiered in 1972. Corby played the role of Grandma Walton on the series until she suffered a stroke in 1976. She returned to the series in 1977, and appeared on the show until 1979. She returned in the role in five *Waltons* reunion films. Grandma Walton was the final role she played in her six-decades-long career in the 1997 TV-film, *A Walton Easter*. Corby earned three Emmy Awards for her work on *The Waltons*. She was also a screenwriter. Ellen Corby died on April 14, 1999 at the Motion Picture Country Home in Woodland Hills, California at the age of 87. Corby was gay. She was survived by her partner of more than 40 years, Stella Luchetta.

License to Steal

Season 1, Episode 19

Broadcast on ABC-TV on February 6, 1961
Directed by Charles R. Rondeau
Teleplay by Paul Savage and John D.F. Black from a story by John D.F. Black
Producer: Jerry Davis
Executive Producer: William T. Orr

Cast:

Lee Patterson	Dave Thorne
Van Williams	Ken Madison
Margarita Sierra	Cha Cha O'Brien
Paul "Mousie" Garner	Mousie
Don "Red" Barry	Lt. Snedigar
Jil Jarmyn	Sue Morrison
Hardie Albright	Mr. Adam
Vito Scotti	Marcus
Sam Gilman	Dan Norwin
Joseph Ruskin	Christy
Jason Wingreen	Simm
Leonard Stone	Konie
Jim Goodwin	Frankie
Les Hellman	George
Ralph Manza	Delcastro
Dick Tufeld	Announcer

Credits:

Cinematography by Glen MacWilliams
Film Editing by Byron Chudnow
Art Direction by Howard Campbell

Set Decoration by Hoyle Barrett
Makeup Supervisor: Gordon Bau
Hairstylist: Jean Burt Reilly
Assistant Director: John Francis Murphy
Sound: John K. Kern
Theme Music Composers: Mack David and Jerry Livingston
Music Editor: Lou Gordon
Music Supervisors: Paul Sawtell and Bert Shefter
60 minutes/Black and White
Production Company: Warner Bros. Television
Filmed at Warner Bros. Studios on Stages 20 and 24
Jil Jarmyn sang "You Go to My Head" and "Who Cares" in this episode.

Notes on the case:

Sue Morrison, a former USO singer who Dave knew in Korea, has booked herself in a Miami nightclub. To attract more attention, she wears $130,000 worth of diamonds on stage. In the middle of her show, thieves raid the club and make off with her glittering jewels. Dave investigates the crime and discovers evidence that points to the insurer of the jewelry being behind the theft.

Jil Jarmyn played the role of Sue Morrison. Jarmyn was born in Batavia, Illinois on October 8, 1926. She worked as a model, and made her film debut in 1952. For the next 12 years, she guest-starred in numerous television shows including *My Little Margie, The Millionaire, Dragnet, I Love Lucy, Cheyenne, Dr. Kildare, Death Valley Days,* and *The Beverly Hillbillies.* Her several films include *Swamp Women,* and *Tarzan's Fight for Life.* She was married to actor James Craig from 1959 until 1962.

Hardie Albright played the role of Weldon J. Adam. Albright was born in Charleroi, Pennsylvania on December 16, 1903. He made his stage debut at the age of seven in his parents' vaudeville act. He graduated from Carnegie Tech in 1926 with a degree in drama. He first appeared on Broadway in the 1926 play *Saturday Night.* During the next 12 years, he appeared in 11 other Broadway shows including *Twelfth Night* (1926-27) and *The Merchant of Venice* (1928). Albright made his film debut in the 1931 movie *Young Sinners.* Until his retirement in 1946, he starred in many films including *The Song of Songs, The Ninth Guest, White Heat, The Scarlet Letter, Carolina Moon, Saboteur, The Loves of Edgar Allan Poe, Sunset at El Dorado, The Jade Mask, The Mad Doctor of Market Street,* and *Angel on My Shoulder.* Albright became a drama teacher at UCLA, and wrote several books about film acting and directing. In the 1960s, he returned to acting and guest-starred on numerous television shows including *Hazel, Leave It to Beaver, Bewitched,*

Perry Mason, Rawhide, Laramie, The Twilight Zone, and *Gunsmoke.* Hardie Albright suffered congestive heart failure, and died on December 7, 1975 in Mission Viejo, California at the age of 71. He was survived by his wife of 30 years, actress Arnita Wallace.

Dick Tufeld was the narrator. Tufeld was born in Los Angeles on December 11, 1926. He earned a Bachelor's Degree in Speech from Northwestern University, and began his career as a voice actor/narrator/announcer on radio in the early 1950s. His first announcing job on television was for the show, *Space Patrol,* in 1953. His hundreds of assignments include *Annie Oakley, The Magical World of Disney, The Roaring 20's, The Gallant Men, The Judy Garland Show, Voyage to the Bottom of the Sea, The Time Tunnel, Peyton Place, The Julie Andrews Hour, The Fantastic Four, Spider Woman, Spider Man and His Amazing Friends, Super Friends: The Legendary Super Powers Show, Histeria, The Simpsons,* and 11 episodes of *Surfside 6.* Audiences best remember him for providing the voice of the Robot on the television series *Lost in Space* (1965-1968), and in the 1998 feature film, *Lost in Space.* Dick Tufeld was widowed in 2004, and died of congestive heart failure on January 22, 2012 at the age of 85. He was survived by his four children, and numerous grandchildren.

Race Against Time

Season 1, Episode 20

Broadcast on ABC-TV on February 13, 1961
Directed by Charles R. Rondeau
Written by Joan Scott
Producer: Jerry Davis
Executive Producer: William T. Orr

Cast:

Troy Donahue	Sandy Winfield II
Van Williams	Ken Madison
Lee Patterson	Dave Thorne
Margarita Sierra	Cha Cha O'Brien
Don "Red" Barry	Lt. Snedigar
Angela Greene	Barbara Manning
Nancy McCarthy	Pamela Wiley
John Archer	Arnold Henderson
William Lanteau	Steve Crest
Brad Johnson	Mr. Maxwell
Darlene Fields	Mrs. Carpenter
H.E. West	Mr. Carpenter
Pat McCaffie	First Detective
Lionel Ames	Dr. Michaels
Fred Crane	Policeman
Robert Shield	Announcer
Dick Tufeld	Announcer

Credits:

Cinematography by Edwin B. Dupar
Film Editing by William W. Moore

Art Direction by Howard Campbell
Set Decoration by William L. Kuehl
Makeup Supervisor: Gordon Bau
Hairstylist: Jean Burt Reilly
Assistant Director: C. Carter Gibson
Sound: B.F. Ryan
Theme Music Composers: Mack David and Jerry Livingston
Music Editor: Erma E. Levin
Music Supervisors: Paul Sawtell and Bert Shefter
60 minutes/Black and White
Production Company: Warner Bros. Television
Filmed at Warner Bros. Studios on Stages 20 and 24

Notes on the case:

Dave is poisoned on a flight from New York to Miami. Since doctors cannot identify the toxin, they are unable to prescribe an antidote. Ken and Sandy try to outrun the clock and find out who committed the crime. The passengers on the flight are not forthcoming, and the investigation is threatened by the murder of the prime suspect, a man Dave once prosecuted.

Angela Greene played the role of Barbara Manning. Greene was born in Dublin, Ireland on February 24, 1921. She was adopted by her uncle when she was six, and moved to Flushing, New York. She was a model for the John Robert Powers Agency, and made her acting debut in the 1944 film *Mr. Skeffington*. Her 100 acting credits include numerous films including *Jungle Jim in the Forbidden Land*, *A Perilous Journey*, and *Night of the Blood Beast*, and dozens of television programs including *Thriller*, *Cheyenne*, *Bachelor Father*, *Lawman*, *77 Sunset Strip*, *Batman*, *Ben Casey*, and *Mod Squad*, among many others. She played the role of Tess Trueheart in the 1950 television series *Dick Tracy*. History buffs remember Greene for dating Navy Lieutenant John F. Kennedy in 1945. Angela Greene suffered a stroke, and died in Los Angeles on February 9, 1978. She was 56 years old.

John Archer played the role of Arnold Henderson. Archer was born on May 8, 1915 in Osceola, Nebraska. His family moved to California in 1920. He studied cinematography at the University of Southern California in Los Angeles. Archer worked as a radio announcer, and played the role of Lamont Cranston in the radio show *The Shadow* in 1944. He made his Broadway debut in 1944, and appeared in seven productions including *The Day Before Spring*, *Strange Bedfellows*, and *Captain Brassbound's Conversion*. Archer first appeared on film in 1938. Some of his films include *Hello Frisco Hello*, *Guadalcanal Diary*, *White Heat*, *Destination Moon*, *Rock Around the Clock*, *She Devil*, *Blue Hawaii*, and *How to Frame a Figg*. He guest-starred in dozens of television comedies and dramas until his retirement in 1996, including *Perry Mason*, *Bonanza*, *The Twilight Zone*, and *The Name of the Game*. From 1941 until 1953, he was married to actress Marjorie Lord. The couple had a son, and a daughter, actress Anne Archer. John Archer died of lung cancer in Redmond, Washington on December 3, 1999 at the age of 84.

Troy, Lee, and Van.

Black Orange Blossoms

Season 1, Episode 21

Broadcast on ABC-TV on February 20, 1961
Directed by Robert B. Sinclair
Written by Von Stuart
Producer: Jerry Davis
Executive Producer: William T. Orr

Cast:

Troy Donahue	Sandy Winfield II
Van Williams	Ken Madison
Margarita Sierra	Cha Cha O'Brien
Paul "Mousie" Garner	Mousie
Kathleen Crowley	Lady Kay Smallens
David Frankham	Ian Smallens
Errol John	Young Charlie
Karen Parker	Barbara Page
Howard Wendell	Mr. Page
Doris Packer	Mrs. Page
Lester Matthews	Inspector Campbell
Jack Livesey	Dr. McLeod
Alan Caillou	Sir Niles Smallens
Mittie Lawrence	Cogee
Charles Lampkin	Monsieur Servat
Dick Tufeld	Announcer

Credits:

Cinematography by J. Peverall Marley
Film Editing by Victor Lewis
Art Direction by Howard Campbell

Set Decoration by Hoyle Barrett
Makeup Supervisor: Gordon Bau
Hairstylist: Jean Burt Reilly
Assistant Director: Jack Stubbs
Sound: John K. Kean
Theme Music Composers: Mack David and Jerry Livingston
Music Editor: John Allyn Jr.
Music Supervisors: Paul Sawtell and Bert Shefter
60 minutes/Black and White
Production Company: Warner Bros. Television
Filmed at Warner Bros. Studios on Stages 20 and 24

Notes on the case:

Sandy vacations in Jamaica to celebrate a local festival at the invitation of his friend, Barbara. But a friend of her father, plantation boss Sir Niles Smallens, dies suddenly from a poisonous snake bite. The mystery deepens when Sandy learns there are no poisonous snakes native to Jamaica. One of the plantation workers who has been accused of importing poisonous snakes for his voodoo rituals in the past becomes the prime suspect. Barbara and Sir Smallens' plantation workers ask Sandy to investigate the suspicious death.

Alan Caillou played the role of Sir Smallens. Caillou was born on November 9, 1914 in Surrey, England. He served with the Palestine Police from 1936 until 1939. He married Aliza Sverdova in 1939, and studied acting until 1941. In 1940, he joined the Royal Army Service Corps, and was captured and imprisoned in North Africa. He escaped, joined the British forces in Solerno, and then served in Yugoslavia. He wrote about his experiences in *The World is Six Feet Square*, published in 1954. He returned to work with the Palestine Police in 1946, and served as a Police Commissioner in Somaliland from 1947 until 1952. He wrote about those experiences in his book, *Sheba Slept Here*. He then worked as a professional hunter in Canada, and began acting on Canadian television. He wrote dozens of novels, and numerous television episodes and feature films in Hollywood. He made his acting debut in Hollywood in 1959 on the series *Have Gun – Will Travel*. His films include *Five Weeks in a Balloon*, *Clarence the Cross-Eyed Lion*, *The Rare Breed*, *The Devil's Brigade*, *Herbie Goes to Monte Carlo*, and *The Sword and the Sorcerer*. He acted in many television shows including *Maverick*, *Sugarfoot*, *Cheyenne*, *Bronco*, *Thriller*, *Adventures in Paradise*, *77 Sunset Strip*, *The Rogues*, *Daktari*, and *Daniel Boone*. He played the role of Jason Floor in the 1966 series *Tarzan*, and played the role of "The Head" in the 1977-78 series *Quark*. He retired in 1984. Alan Caillou died in Sedona, Arizona on October 1, 2006. He was 91 years old, and survived by his wife of 67 years.

Kathleen Crowley played the role of Lady Kay Smallens. Crowley was born in Washington Township, New Jersey on December 26, 1929. She won the title of Miss New Jersey in 1949. She studied at New York's American Academy of Dramatic Arts, and began working on live television. Crowley first appeared on screen in 1951. Until her retirement in 1970, she appeared in dozens of television shows including *Climax, Cheyenne, Wagon Train, Rawhide, Laramie, Maverick, 77 Sunset Strip, Route 66, My Three Sons, Perry Mason, Bonanza*, and *Batman*. Her feature films include *The Silver Whip, The Farmer Takes a Wife, Target Earth, Female Jungle, City of Shadows, The Rebel Set, Downhill Racer*, and *The Lawyer*. Kathleen Crowley died at her home in Green Bank, New Jersey on April 23, 2017. She was 87 years old, and survived by her son, and husband of 48 years.

The Chase

Season 1, Episode 22

Broadcast on ABC-TV on February 27, 1961
Directed by Allen Baron
Written by Roger Smith and Montgomery Pittman
Producer: Jerry Davis
Executive Producer: William T. Orr

Cast:

Lee Patterson	Dave Thorne
Troy Donahue	Sandy Winfield II
Van Williams	Ken Madison
Margarita Sierra	Cha Cha O'Brien
Reggie Nalder	The Hunter (Dmitri Grajian)
Tim Graham	Old Man
Jerry O'Sullivan	Officer
George Werier	Hotel Manager

Credits:

Cinematography by Robert Tobey
Film Editing by Elbert K. Hollingsworth
Art Direction by Howard Campbell
Set Decoration by William L. Kuehl
Makeup Supervisor: Gordon Bau
Hairstylist: Jean Burt Reilly
Assistant Director: Victor Vallejo
Sound: Ross Owen
Theme Music Composers: Mack David and Jerry Livingston
Music Editor: Joe Inge
Music Supervisors: Paul Sawtell and Bert Shefter

60 minutes/Black and White
Production Company: Warner Bros. Television
Filmed at Warner Bros. Studios on Stages 20 and 24

Notes on the case:

As a favor to Dave, Cha Cha drives through the Everglades to deliver some important papers to him. On a small back road, she witnesses a man dumping a woman's body into a swamp. The killer spots her, and chases her into a ghost town. Dave tracks them down, and becomes a target of the murderer, as a mystery man talks Dave and Cha Cha through the abandoned town.

Margarita.

Reggie Nalder played the role of Oren Jackson. Nalder was born on September 4, 1907 in Vienna, Austria. He performed as an Apache dancer in Vienna theaters and Paris cabarets in the 1930s. After World War II ended, he worked for the German language service of the BBC. He suffered burns on his face and neck in an accident during his youth. The severe scars contributed to him being cast in villainous roles. He first appeared on screen in 1938. His films include *Jericho*, *The Man Who Knew Too Much*, *The Manchurian Candidate*, *Mark of the Devil*, *Fellini's Casanova*, and *The Devil and Max Devlin*, among many others. His television guest-starring appearances include *77 Sunset Strip*, *It Takes a Thief*, *Thriller*, *McCloud*, *I Spy*, *Adventures in Paradise*, *Combat*, *Star Trek*, *The Man from U.N.C.L.E.*, and *The Wild, Wild West*. Fans remember him for playing the role of vampire Kurt Barlow in the television adaptation of *Salem's Lot* in 1979. Reggie Nalder was gay. He died of bone cancer in Santa Monica, California on November 19, 1991 at the age of 84.

Ghost of a Chance

Season 1, Episode 23

Broadcast on ABC-TV on March 6, 1961
Directed by Frank Baur
Written by Gerald Drayson Adams
Producer: Charles Hoffman
Executive Producer: William T. Orr

Cast:

Van Williams	Ken Madison
Margarita Sierra	Cha Cha O'Brien
Paul "Mousie" Garner	Mousie
Claire Kelly	Pat Wheeler
John Gabriel	Johan Starr
Russ Conway	Brockton Starr
Danielle De Metz	Naomi
Slim Pickens	Muskrat George
Billy M. Greene	Lige
Johnny Seven	Deke
Theodore Newton	John Norton
Stella Garcia	Nina
Nicky Blair	Waiter
Dick Tufeld	Announcer

Credits:

Cinematography by Robert Hoffman
Film Editing by Milt Kleinberg
Art Direction by Howard Campbell
Set Decoration by Hal Overell
Makeup Supervisor: Gordon Bau

Hairstylist: Jean Burt Reilly
Assistant Director: Bernard McEveety
Sound: John K. Kean
Theme Music Composers: Mack David and Jerry Livingston
Music Editor: Robert Phillips
Music Supervisor: Paul Sawtell and Bert Shefter
60 minutes/Black and White
Production Company: Warner Bros. Television
Filmed at Warner Bros. Studios on Stages 20 and 24
Johnny Seven sang "I Only Have Eyes for You" in this episode.

Notes on the case:

A retired engraver for the Federal Mint disappears while on his honeymoon
vacation in Catfish Bayou. Pat Wheeler, a Federal agent with the Treasury
Department, is assigned to find the missing man. The government fears the
engraver has been kidnapped by counterfeiters who want to use his expertise.
Since Catfish Bayou and nearby Bass Creek are favorite vacation spots for
Ken, the Federal agent engages his services to help in the search. They pose as
a married couple, but when they arrive, Ken is surprised that his old friends
have all been replaced by unfriendly business owners.

    Claire Kelly played the role of Pat Wheeler. Kelly was born in San
Francisco on March 15, 1934. She worked as a model and cover girl, and
studied at the Neighborhood Playhouse in New York. She first appeared on
screen in the 1955 film *Son of Sinbad*. Her films include *The Badlanders,
Party Girl, Ask Any Girl, The Loved One, A Guide for the Married Man,* and
What Ever Happened to Aunt Alice? She guest-starred in numerous television dramas and comedies including *The Bob Cummings Show, Tightrope,
The Adventures of Rin Tin Tin, Bachelor Father, Burke's Law, The Monkees,*
and *The F.B.I.* She retired in 1972. Her first three marriages ended in divorce.
Claire Kelly died in Palm Springs on July 1, 1998 at the age of 64. She was
survived by her fourth husband, and one son.

    John Gabriel played the role of Jonah Starr. Gabriel was born on May 25,
1931 in Niagara Falls, New York. He first appeared on television in 1953. He
guest-starred in dozens of programs including *Hawaiian Eye, The Lawless
Years, Bachelor Father, 77 Sunset Strip, The Flying Nun, The Big Valley,* and
The Love Boat. He played the role of Andy Rivers on *The Mary Tyler Moore
Show* from 1973 until 1975. Gabriel made his film debut in the 1958 musical
South Pacific. His other films include *The Young Lions, The Story of Ruth,
Sex and the College Girl,* and *El Dorado.* He starred in numerous daytime
dramas including *General Hospital, Loving, Ryan's Hope, Generations,* and
Days of Our Lives. Gabriel was an accomplished singer, and recording artist.

He appeared on Broadway in *The Happy Time*, and *Applause*. He performed as a singer on many variety programs, memorably *The Ed Sullivan Show*, *The Merv Griffin Show*, and *The Mike Douglas Show*. John Gabriel died at his New York home on June 11, 2021 of complications from Alzheimer's disease. He was survived by his wife of 53 years, and their two daughters, actresses Andrea and Melissa Gabriel. John Gabriel was 90 years old.

Slim Pickens played the role of Muskrat George. Pickens was born in Kingsburg, California on June 29, 1919. He began performing in the rodeo, and served in the U.S. Army during World War II. He made his acting debut in 1946. Until his death in 1983, he appeared in dozens of films and television shows, often playing cowboy roles. His films include *Blazing Saddles*, *1941*, *One-Eyed Jacks*, *An Eye for an Eye*, *The Cowboys*, *Tom Horn*, *The Getaway*, *Rancho Deluxe*, *Pat Garrett and Billy the Kidd*, and *Dr. Strangelove*. He worked on radio, and guest-starred in many television dramas including *Mannix*, *Cheyenne*, *The Lone Ranger*, *Frontier Doctor*, *Gunsmoke*, *Maverick*, *Hawaii Five-O*, and *The Legend of Jesse James*. He suffered a brain tumor and died on December 8, 1983 in Modesto, California at the age of 64. He was survived by his wife of 33 years, and their three children.

Johnny Seven played the role of Deke. Seven was born in Brooklyn on February 23, 1926. He served in U.S. Army during World War II, and performed with the U.S.O. He began working on stage in New York. He first appeared on screen in a bit role in the 1954 film *On the Waterfront*. His other films include *Johnny Gunman*, *Cop Hater*, *The Last Mile*, *The Apartment*, *What Did You Do in the War Daddy*, and *The Destructors*. His many television credits include *Bonanza*, *Gunsmoke*, *Naked City*, *Batman*, *Death Valley Days*, *The Rockford Files*, and *Charlie's Angels*. Seven played the recurring role of Lt. Carl Reese on the 1968-1975 series *Ironside*. He retired in 1995. For many years he owned a real estate development business in the San Fernando Valley. Johnny Seven died of lung cancer on January 22, 2010 in Mission Hills, California at the age of 84. He was survived by his wife of 61 years and a son.

Nicky Blair played the role of the waiter. Blair was born in Brooklyn on July 26, 1926. Beginning in 1949, Blair played bit roles in dozens of films and television shows. His films include *Viva Las Vegas*, *Ocean's Eleven*, *Hell to Eternity*, *Operation Petticoat*, *Rocky V*, *True Crime*, and *The Godfather Part III*. Blair is best known for owning Nicky Blair's Italian restaurant on Sunset Strip in Hollywood which opened in 1986. Blair was the perfect host for some of Hollywood's most famous stars, and often cooked in his restaurant's kitchen for his celebrity friends. Nicky Blair suffered ill health for several years, and died of liver cancer on November 22, 1998 in Los Angeles. He was 72 years old.

The Impractical Joker

Season 1, Episode 24

Broadcast on ABC-TV on March 13, 1961
Directed by Charles R. Rondeau
Written by Lee Loeb
Producer: Jerry Davis
Executive Producer: William T. Orr

Cast:

Van Williams	Ken Madison
Troy Donahue	Sandy Winfield II
Lee Patterson	Dave Thorne
Margarita Sierra	Cha Cha O'Brien
Paul "Mousie" Garner	Mousie
Don "Red" Barry	Lt. Snedigar
Karen Steele	Jean Pappas
Mala Powers	Millie Pierce
Peter Mamakos	George Pappas
Robert Colbert	Stephen Wade
John Compton	Jack Larson
Ted Knight	Tod Edwards
Judith Rawlins	Actress
Joseph Forte	Maitre d'
Harold J. Stone	Harry Wilde
Dick Tufeld	Announcer

Credits:

Cinematography by Louis Jennings
Film Editing by William W. Moore
Art Direction by Howard Campbell

Set Decoration by Hoyle Barrett
Makeup Supervisor: Gordon Bau
Hairstylist: Jean Burt Reilly
Assistant Director: Russell Llewellyn
Sound: Samuel F. Goode
Theme Music Composers: Mack David and Jerry Livingston
Music Editor: Ted Sebern
Music Supervisors: Paul Sawtell and Bert Shefter
60 minutes/Black and White
Production Company: Warner Bros. Television
Filmed at Warner Bros. Studios on Stages 20 and 24
Previous footage of Margarita Sierra singing "You and the Night and the Music" (first seen in Episode 4 "According to Our Files") was used in this episode.

Notes on the case:

Businessman Harry Wilde planned to threaten his partner's life as a practical joke. But the joke backfires when he kills his partner with a gun that was supposed to be loaded only with blanks. Was it really an accident? Harry is charged with murder. Ken and Dave are hired to find the real murderer.

Harold J. Stone played the role of Harry Wilde. Stone was born on March 3, 1913 in New York City. He began his acting career on the New York stage, and made his Broadway debut in 1933 in *Honeymoon*. Stone starred in numerous Broadway shows including *Stalag 17*, *A Bell for Adano*, *Morning Star*, *Irma la Douce*, and *One Touch of Venus*. He returned to the New York theater later in his career to direct off-Broadway and Broadway productions. Stone made his screen debut in the 1946 classic *The Blue Dahlia*. His dozens of films include *The Harder They Fall*, *The Wrong Man*, *Spartacus*, *The Chapman Report*, *The Man with the X-Ray Eyes*, *Girl Happy*, and *The Greatest Story Ever Told*. Often playing a tough guy, his many television appearances include *Bonanza*, *Daniel Boone*, *The Rifleman*, *The Untouchables*, *The Twilight Zone*, *Route 66*, *Gilligan's Island*, *Hogan's Heroes*, *Hawaii Five-O*, *Welcome Back Kotter*, and *Charlie's Angels*. He was nominated for an Emmy Award for his performance in *The Nurses* in 1964. He had recurring roles in the series *My World and Welcome to It* and *Bridget Loves Bernie*. He retired in 1986. Harold J. Stone died at the age of 92 at the Motion Picture Country Home in Woodland Hills, California on November 18, 2005.

Karen Steele played the role of Jean Pappas. Steele was born in Honolulu, Hawaii on March 20, 1931. She nearly lost her leg in a surfing accident when she was 13 years old. It took twenty-two operations and months of rehabilitation to get her back on her feet. She studied acting at Rollins College in Florida, and worked as a model and cover girl when she was young. Her first acting job was on the radio, and she made her film debut in 1953 in *The Clown*. Her other films include *Man Crazy, Marty, Toward the Unknown, The Rise and Fall of Legs Diamond, 40 Pounds of Trouble, A Boy...A Girl*, and *The Happy Ending*. Her many television appearances include *Climax, The Millionaire, Bat Masterson, Mannix, Hogan's Heroes, Star Trek, Get Smart, Voyage to the Bottom of the Sea, Perry Mason*, and *Naked City*. She retired in 1972. She married Dr. Maurice Boyd Ruland, a psychiatrist, in 1973. The couple settled in Arizona, where she died from cancer on March 12, 1988 in Kingman, Arizona. Karen Steele was 56 years old, and survived by her husband.

Mala Powers played the role of Millie Pierce. Powers was born on December 20, 1931 in San Francisco. She attended the Max Reinhardt Junior Workshop in Los Angeles, and made her film debut in 1942 in *Tough as They Come*. She performed in radio dramas, and began working steadily as a film actress in 1950. Her feature films include *Edge of Doom, Cyrano de Bergerac, City Beneath the Sea, City That Never Sleeps, Bengazi, Rage at Dawn, The Unknown Terror, The Colossus of New York, Tammy and the Bachelor*, and *Daddy's Gone A-Hunting*. She guest-starred in more than 100 television episodes including *Wagon Train, Maverick, Bonanza, The Man from U.N.C.L.E., Mission: Impossible, Rawhide, Perry Mason, The Wild, Wild West, Wanted: Dead or Alive*, and *The Man and the City*. She played the recurring role of Mona in the final season of *Hazel*. Powers also wrote several children's books. She trained with Michael Chekhov for many years in Hollywood. From 1993 until 2006, she taught the Chekhov Technique at the University of Southern Maine during summer acting sessions. She retired from acting in 2005. Mala Powers died from leukemia on June 11, 2007 in Burbank, California. She was 75 years old, and survived by her only son.

Peter Mamakos played the role of George Pappas. Mamakos was born on December 14, 1918 in Somerville, Massachusetts. His family was Greek and owned the Pilgrim restaurant chain in New England. He went to California to scout locations for more restaurants, but abandoned the restaurant business and pursued acting roles in Hollywood. He made his film debut in the 1949 movie *Trail of the Yukon*. Typecast in ethnic roles, he appeared in dozens of films including *For Pete's Sake, Ship of Fools, Island of Love, City Beneath the Sea, Bandits of Corsica, Forbidden, Ain't Misbehavin', Desert Sands, The Searchers, Tarzan and the Slave Girl*, and *The Ten Commandments*. His more than 100 television appearances include *The Adventures of Jim Bowie, Perry Mason, Batman, The Lone Ranger, The Adventures of Superman, Daniel Boone, Zorro, Cisco Kid, Night Gallery, Kojak*, and *Fantasy Island*. He retired in 1990. Peter Mamakos died on April 27, 2008 at the age of 89 in Paso Robles, California. He was survived by his daughter.

Ted Knight played the role of Tod Edwards. Knight was born in Terryville, Connecticut on December 7, 1923. He dropped out of high school to enlist in the U.S. Army during World War II. After the war, he became a puppeteer and ventriloquist, and hosted his own kiddies show in Rhode Island from 1950 until 1955. He made his national television debut in 1958. His proficient voice-over skills provided him steady work for the next three decades. His feature films include *Cold Turkey, Cry for Happy, Hitler, Countdown, The Candidate,* and the memorable comedy *Caddyshack.* Knight's greatest successes were on television. He guest-starred in dozens of comedies and dramas, and starred in his first series, *The Young Marrieds,* in 1964. Fans remember him for playing the role of stuffy newscaster Ted Baxter on *The Mary Tyler Moore Show* from 1970 until 1977. The role earned him six Emmy Award nominations, with two wins. From 1980 until 1987, he starred in the situation comedy *Too Close for Comfort.* A recurrence of cancer forced him to stop working in 1986. Ted Knight died of cancer on August 26, 1986 at the age of 62. He was survived by his wife of 38 years, and their three children.

Judith Rawlins played the role of "actress". Rawlins was born in Milwaukee, Wisconsin on June 24, 1936. Her family moved to Sherman Oaks, California when she was young. She studied at the Valley Community Players and The Walt Disney Players Group. She married film editor David Rawlins in 1954. The marriage was short-lived. Rawlins dated Errol Flynn's son Sean, Elvis Presley, and Bobby Rydell, before marrying Vic Damone in 1963. She made her screen debut in a small role in the Elvis Presley film *G.I. Blues* in 1960. She guest-starred in several television shows including *The Rebel, Bat Masterson, Wanted: Dead or Alive, The Real McCoys,* and *77 Sunset Strip,* and had a small role in the 1961 film, *20,000 Eyes.* Rawlins retired from acting when she married Damone, and worked as his secretary. In March, 1964, she and Damone were seriously injured in a single car accident in Italy. She suffered a critical back injury that became a chronic problem for her until her death. The couple had three children before divorcing in 1971. On March 28, 1974, Rawlins' five-year-old daughter found her dead in their Mandeville Canyon home. She died from a prescription drug overdose of the pain-killer Darvon. Judith Rawlins was 36 years old.

Judith Rawlins.

Inside Job

Season 1, Episode 25

Broadcast on ABC-TV on March 30, 1961
Directed by Charles R. Rondeau
Written by Philip Saltzman
Producer: Charles Hoffman
Executive Producer: William T. Orr

Cast:

Lee Patterson	Dave Thorne
Van Williams	Ken Madison
Diane McBain	Daphne Dutton
Margarita Sierra	Cha Cha O'Brien
Paul "Mousie" Garner	Mousie
Don "Red" Barry	Lt. Snedigar
Dolores Donlon	Laurie Ames
Mary Tyler Moore	Kathy Murlow
Don Burnett	Hal Murlow
Jeffrey Stone	Barney Michaels
Joe Sawyer	Leon Huff
Tol Avery	Mr. Wylie
Robert Burton	Arthur Camden
Michael Harris	Ted Briller

Credits:

Cinematography by Ray Fernstrom
Film Editing by Robert L. Wolfe
Art Direction by Howard Campbell
Set Direction by Hoyle Barrett
Makeup Supervisor: Gordon Bau

Hairstylist: Jean Burt Reilly
Assistant Director: Fred Scheld
Sound: Ross Owen
Theme Music Composers: Mack David and Jerry Livingston
Music Editor: Sam E. Levin
Music Supervisors: Paul Sawtell and Bert Shefter
60 minutes/Black and White
Production Company: Warner Bros. Television
Filmed at Warner Bros. Studios on Stages 20 and 24
Margarita Sierra sang "Por tu Amor" in this episode.

Notes on the case:

A man believes his bank is going to be robbed because he has discovered some suspicious activity among his employees. However, the police won't act simply on someone's hunch, so the banker hires Dave to work undercover as a teller. He learns one of the other tellers has a unsavory friend, Barney Michaels, who is a notorious bank robber. When the banker is murdered, Dave must infiltrate the gang he now suspects is planning a heist.

Mary Tyler Moore played the role of Kathy Murlow. Moore was born in New York City on December 29, 1936. She began her acting career in 1952. Her early television appearances include *The Adventures of Ozzie and Harriet, Steve Canyon, The George Burns Show, Richard Diamond, Private Detective, Bronco, Bourbon Street Beat, 77 Sunset Strip, The Millionaire, The Tab Hunter Show, Riverboat, Bachelor Father, Hawaiian Eye,* and *Thriller.* From 1961 until 1966 she starred as Laura Petrie in *The Dick Van Dyke Show.* From 1970 until 1977 she starred as Mary Richards in the *The Mary Tyler Moore Show.* She was nominated for 14 Emmy Awards, with seven wins. Her early feature films include *Operation Mad Ball, Change of Habit,* and *Thoroughly Modern Millie.* Moore was nominated for an Academy Award for her performance in the 1980 film *Ordinary People,* and won a Tony Award for her performance in the 1980 Broadway drama *Whose Life Is It Anyway?* On October 14, 1980, her only son, Richard, died of an accidental gunshot wound to his head when he was handling a shotgun. He was 24 years old. Moore continued to work until shortly before her death at the age of 80 in Greenwich, Connecticut on January 25, 2017. She was survived by her husband of 34 years, Dr. Robert Levine.

Jeffrey Stone played the role of Barney Michaels. Stone was born in Detroit, Michigan on December 16, 1926. He was raised in an orphanage after the death of his father. He served in the U.S. Navy during World War II. Stone first appeared on screen in 1948. His early films include *Army Bound, Fighter Attack, Bad for Each Other, Wonder Valley, Drive a Crooked Road,*

Edge of Hell, The Girl in the Kremlin, The Big Beat, Damn Citizen, When the Girls Take Over, and *The Thing That Couldn't Die.* He was the model for Prince Charming in the Disney animated classic *Cinderella,* in 1950. Stone began his voice-over career providing voices for other characters in the film. In 1954, he starred in the Italian television series *The Three Musketeers.* He made other films in Spain and Mexico. His guest-starring roles on American television include *The Californians, The Millionaire, Death Valley Days, The Outer Limits,* and *Adventures in Paradise.* Stone was married three times. His first wife was actress Barbara Lawrence, and his second wife was French actress Corinne Calvet, with whom he had one child. Stone retired in 1964, and moved to Penang, Malaysia. He traveled through Southeast Asia, wrote several novels, and his autobiography was published in 2010. Jeffrey Stone died at his home in Penang on August 22, 2012 at the age of 85.

Donald Burnett played the role of Hal Murlow. Burnett was born in Los Angeles on November 3, 1930. He attended officer's school and served in the U.S. Army in the early 1950s. He made his film debut in 1955. His films include *Hell's Horizon, Tea and Sympathy, Untamed Youth, Raintree County, Jailhouse Rock, Damon and Pythias,* and *Don't Go Near the Water.* He starred as Ensign Langdon Towne in the 1958-59 television series *Northwest Passage,* and guest-starred in a few television dramas including *Bonanza, Hawaiian Eye,* and *Stagecoach West.* In 1962, Burnett retired from acting after starring in his final film, *The Triumph of Robin Hood.* In 1959, he married actress Gia Scala. She suffered clinical depression, and the couple divorced in 1970. Burnett married actress Barbara Anderson in 1971. He had to obtain a restraining order against Scala in 1971 to stop her harassment and threats toward him and Anderson. Scala committed suicide by a drug and alcohol overdose in 1972. After his retirement from acting, Donald Burnett worked as a successful stockbroker. He met Rock Hudson at a Malibu house party, the two became good friends, remaining so until Hudson's death, and often sailed and fished together off the Southern California coast.

Invitation to a Party

Season 1, Episode 26

Broadcast on ABC-TV on March 27, 1961
Directed by Paton Price
Written by Erna Lazarus
Producer: Jerry Davis
Executive Producer: William T. Orr

Cast:

Troy Donahue	Sandy Winfield II
Van Williams	Ken Madison
Margarita Sierra	Cha Cha O'Brien
Paul "Mousie" Garner	Mousie
Don "Red" Barry	Lt. Snedigar
Elizabeth MacRae	Carla Wilson
Kaye Elhardt	Virginia Barker
Ed Nelson	Eddie Grant
George Margo	Bunny Lewis
Tony Travis	Billy Lee
Alan Dexter	Morrie Herbert
Sally Kellerman	Roxy

Credits:

Cinematography by Jacques R. Marquette
Film Editing by George R. Rohrs
Art Direction by Howard Campbell
Set Decoration by Jack H. Allen
Makeup Supervisor: Gordon Bau
Hairstylist: Jean Burt Reilly
Assistant Director: Chuck Hansen

Sound: Thomas Ashton
Theme Music Composers: Mack David and Jerry Livingston
Music Editor: Charles Paley
Music Supervisors: Paul Sawtell and Bert Shefter
60 minutes/Black and White
Production Company: Warner Bros. Television
Filmed at Warner Bros. Studios on Stages 20 and 24
Tony Travis sang "Oh, Lady Be Good," "April in Paris," "Tea for Two," and "What's New?" in this episode.

Notes on the case:

A wealthy young woman named Virginia Barker believes she is the victim of blackmail after she injured a woman named Carla Wilson in an auto accident in the parking lot of the Club Imperio. She hires Sandy to investigate the incident. She feels she is being blackmailed to keep the accident out of the news which would ruin her father's chances at a run for political office. Sandy goes to the scene of the accident just in time to see Carla get killed in

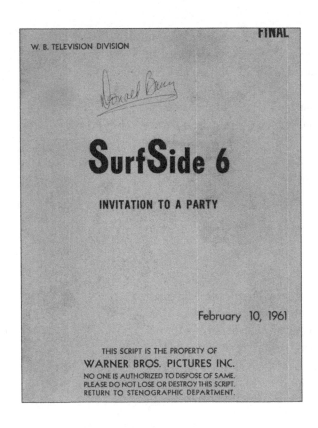

another accident. He suspects that the owners of the club are staging phony accidents to blackmail wealthy customers. Sandy then poses as the wild son of a multi-millionaire who is in danger of having his inheritance cut off it he gets into trouble.

Elizabeth MacRae played the role of Carla Wilson. MacRae was born in Columbia, South Carolina on February 22, 1936. She first appeared on screen in 1959. Her films include *Love in a Goldfish Bowl, Everything's Ducky, Wild is My Love, For Love or Money,* and *The Conversation,* among others. She had recurring roles in the daytime dramas *Search for Tomorrow, Days of Our Lives, General Hospital, Another World,* and *Guiding Light.* Her many television guest-starring roles include *Naked City, Dr. Kildare, Rawhide, Burke's Law, Gunsmoke, Route 66, Rhoda, Mannix,* and *Petrocelli.* Fans remember her for playing the role of Lou Ann Poovie in the series, *Gomer Pyle: U.S.M.C.* (1966-69). Elizabeth MacRae retired in 1989.

Ed Nelson played the role of Eddie Grant. Nelson was born on December 21, 1928 in New Orleans. He left Tulane University in Louisiana to study at the New York School of Radio and Television Technique. He served as a radioman in the U.S. Navy, and later became a program director at a local television station in New Orleans. In 1956, he moved to Los Angeles and worked for B-movie producer Roger Corman. Nelson's early films include *Swamp Women, Attack of the Crab Monsters, Rock All Night, Carnival Rock, Night of the Blood Beast, The Cry Baby Killer, Teenage Cave Man, A Bucket of Blood, The Brain Eaters,* and *Devil's Partner.* Until his retirement in 2003, he guest-starred in more than 100 television shows including *Thriller, The Rifleman, Bonanza, Zane Grey Theatre, Perry Mason, The Rebel, Highway Patrol, Gunsmoke, Johnny Ringo,* and *Murder She Wrote.* He is best remembered for playing the role of Michael Rossi on the 1964-69 prime time soap opera *Peyton Place.* He worked steadily on television, and in feature films, and on stage. In his later years, he taught acting and screenwriting at two universities in New Orleans. Ed Nelson died in Greensboro, North Carolina of heart failure on August 9, 2014. He was 85 years old, and survived by his wife of 63 years, six children, and numerous grandchildren. One of his sons is actor Christopher S. Nelson.

Alan Dexter played the role of Morrie Herbert. Dexter was born on October 21, 1918 in Tulsa, Oklahoma. In 1939, he moved to New York to pursue acting. During World War II, Dexter served in the U.S. Army. He began his acting career in 1943. Until his retirement in 1978, he played more than 150 roles in films and television. His feature films include *Pushover, It Came from Outer Space, Operation Petticoat, Kiss Me Stupid, Paint Your Wagon, Step Down to Terror, I Married a Monster from Outer Space,* and *Gable and Lombard,* among others. Dexter's many television guest-starring appearances include *Whirly Birds, Hennesey, The Twilight Zone, Time Limit,*

Racquet Squad, Dragnet, Perry Mason, The Untouchables, The Virginian, Ironside, and *Marcus Welby, M.D.* He played a recurring role on the daytime drama *Days of Our Lives* (1965-66). Alan Dexter died from a heart attack in Oxnard, California on December 19, 1983 at the age of 65.

Sally Kellerman played the role of Roxie. Kellerman was born on June 2, 1937 in Long Beach, California. She attended Los Angeles City College, and studied acting with Jeff Corey. In the later 1950s, she joined Actors Studio West. She made her screen debut in the 1957 film *Reform School Girl*. She appeared on stage at the Pasadena Playhouse, and began to work in television. Her early television work includes *Bachelor Father, The Twilight Zone, My Three Sons, Star Trek, The Outer Limits,* and *Ben Casey.* She is a voice-over artist in advertising, and numerous animated series. Her many films include *Brewster McCloud, Welcome to L.A., The Player, Last of the Red Hot Lovers, The Boston Strangler, The April Fools, It's My Party,* and *Ready to Wear.* She is best known for playing the role of Hot Lips in the 1970 film *M*A*S*H,* which earned her an Academy Award nomination. Kellerman remains busy with television and movie roles, and has toured the country for years singing in night clubs.

Spring Training

Season 1, Episode 27

Broadcast on ABC-TV on April 3, 1961
Directed by Charles R. Rondeau
Teleplay by Ed Jurist and Leo Solomon from a story by Leo Solomon
Producer: Ed Jurist
Executive Producer: William T. Orr

Cast:

Van Williams	Ken Madison
Troy Donahue	Sandy Winfield II
Lee Patterson	Dave Thorne
Margarita Sierra	Cha Cha O'Brien
Don "Red" Barry	Lt. Snedigar
Gigi Perreau	Robin Phillips
Barry Kelley	Matty Phillips
Bing Russell	Ron Kaslow
George N. Neise	Mitch Mitchell
Pitt Herbert	Mr. Parsons
Gerald Milton	Delsey
Baynes Barron	Carter
Will Hutchins	Arky Cooper
Murray Alper	Mitchell's waiter

Credits:

Cinematography by Louis Jennings
Film Editing by William W. Moore
Art Direction by Howard Campbell
Set Decoration by Hoyle Barrett

Makeup Supervisor: Gordon Bau
Hairstylist: Jean Burt Reilly
Assistant Director: Richard L'Estrange
Sound: Ross Owen
Theme Music Composers: Mack David and Jerry Livingston
Music Editor: Donald Harris
Music Supervisors: Paul Sawtell and Bert Shefter
60 minutes/Black and White
Production Company: Warner Bros. Television
Filmed at Warner Bros. Studios on Stages 20 and 24.
Margarita Sierra sang "When Yuba Plays the Rumba on the Tuba Down in Cuba" in this episode.

Notes on the case:

Ken's aspirations to become a pitcher when he was young help him in his latest assignment. The Bears baseball team is in spring training in Florida. The club owner, Matty Phillips, learns that Arky Cooper, his star pitcher is keeping time with shifty Mitch Mitchell, a well-known sports bookie. Phillips hires Ken to pose as a rookie ball player to keep tabs on Cooper. The young pitcher discovers that his girlfriend was involved with the bookie. Cooper beats him up. Mitchell is bent on revenge, but he is murdered before he has a chance to get even with Cooper. Unfortunately, Cooper is the prime murder suspect. Ken has to find out who the real killer is.

Will Hutchins played the role of Arky Cooper. Hutchins was born on May 5, 1930 in Los Angeles. He majored in Greek drama at Pomona College, and studied cinema at U.C.L.A. before serving two years in the U.S. Army Signal Corps as a cryptographer in Paris during the Korean War. He returned to cinema studies at U.C.L.A. after the war, and was discovered by a talent scout for Warner Brothers. Hutchins signed a contract with Warners in 1956, and first appeared on television in the series *Conflict*. He appeared in most of the Warner Brothers television productions including *Maverick, Cheyenne, 77 Sunset Strip, Bronco*, and *The Roaring 20's*. He starred as Tom Brewster in *Sugarfoot* from 1957 until 1961. Hutchins' Warner films include *Bombers B-52, Lafayette Escadrille, No Time for Sergeants, Young and Eager, Claudelle Inglish*, and *Merrill's Marauders*. He left Warner Brothers in 1962. His later television appearances include *Gunsmoke, The Alfred Hitchcock Hour, Perry Mason, Love American Style, Emergency!, The Streets of San Francisco*, and *The Quest*. Hutchins played the role of Woody Banner in the 1966-67 series *Hey Landlord*, and played the role of Dagwood Bumstead in the 1968-69 series, *Blondie*. His later films include *Spinout* and *Clambake* with Elvis

Presley, *The Shooting, The Horror at 37,000 Feet, The Romantics, Gunfighter*, and *The Happy Hooker Goes to Washington*. He retired in 2010, but occasionally appears as "Patches the Clown" in traveling American circuses. He was married to Carol Burnett's sister, Chris Burnett, from 1965 until 1969. The couple had one daughter.

Gigi Perreau played the role of Robin Phillips. Perreau was born in Los Angeles on February 6, 1941. She made her screen debut in the 1943 film *Madame Currie*. For more than a decade, she was a very successful child actress in Hollywood. Her films include *Mr. Skeffington, Shadow on the Wall, Song of Love, Green Dolphin Street, Song of Surrender, Never a Dull Moment, Dance with Me, Henry, Has Anybody Seen My Girl, Tammy Tell Me True*, and *The Man in the Grey Flannel Suit*. Her numerous television credits include *The Donna Reed Show, The Betty Hutton Show, Stagecoach West, The Islanders, The Rebel, Follow the Sun, Perry Mason, The Rifleman, Gunsmoke, Hawaiian Eye, Tarzan*, and *The Brady Bunch*. In 1977, she retired from acting, and taught drama classes at Immaculate Heart High School in Los Angeles for nearly 20 years. Since 2007, she has provided voice-over work for animated films and television programs. Gigi Perreau was Meghan Markle's drama teacher, and attended her 2018 wedding to Prince Harry in London.

Barry Kelley played the role of Matty Phillips. Kelly was born in Chicago on August 19, 1908. He studied at the Goodman School of Drama at the Art Institute of Chicago. He began acting on stage and made his Broadway debut in 1934. He appeared in 12 Broadway productions including *Hamlet, The Wingless Victory*, and *Oklahoma*. He first appeared on screen in 1947. His many films include *Ma and Pa Kettle, Mr. Belvedere Goes to College, Too Late for Tears, The Asphalt Jungle, Francis Goes to the Races, Flying Leathernecks, Ice Palace, Elmer Gantry, The Manchurian Candidate, Robin and the 7 Hoods, Boy Did I Get a Wrong Number!*, and *The Love Bug*. Kelly appeared in dozens of television dramas and comedies including *Petticoat Junction, The Lucy Show, The Lone Ranger, Mr. Ed, Mr. Roberts, Death Valley Days, Lawman, Laramie, Maverick*, and *Pete and Gladys*. He retired in 1969. Barry Kelley died on June 5, 1991 at the Motion Picture Country Home in Woodland Hills, California at the age of 82.

George Neise played the role of Mitch Mitchell. Neise was born on February 16, 1917. Beginning in 1937, he acted in local radio plays in Chicago. He worked in summer stock theater in 1938 and 1939, before serving for four-and-a-half years in the U.S. Army Air Corps during World War II. In 1942, he began his decades-long career as a reliable character actor in more than 150 films and television programs. His numerous films include *The Three Stooges Meet Hercules, Rome Adventure, The Three Stooges in Orbit*,

Did You Hear the One About the Traveling Saleslady?, *The Girl Who Knew Too Much*, *The Computer Wore Tennis Shoes*, *On a Clear Day You Can See Forever*, and *The Barefoot Executive*. His dozens of television appearances include *The Lone Ranger*, *Death Valley Days*, *Cheyenne*, *Zorro*, *Perry Mason*, *Thriller*, *The Lucy Show*, *The Addams Family*, *Get Smart*, *Gilligan's Island*, *Here's Lucy*, *Room 222*, and *Hogan's Heroes*. He retired in 1978. George Neise died of cancer at his Hollywood home on April 14, 1996. He was 79, and survived by his five children.

Troy, Van, and Lee.

Troy, Lee, Van, and Diane.

Double Image

Season 1, Episode 28

Broadcast on ABC-TV on April 10, 1961
Directed by Irving J. Moore
Teleplay by Bob Stuart from a story by Leo Townsend
Producer: Jerry Davis
Executive Producer: William T. Orr

Cast:

Troy Donahue	Sandy Winfield II
Van Williams	Ken Madison
Lee Patterson	Dave Thorne
Diane McBain	Daphne Dutton
Margarita Sierra	Cha Cha O'Brien
Don "Red" Barry	Lt. Snedigar
Ellen McRae (Burstyn)	Wandra Drake
Brad Dexter	Albie Banion
Ann Robinson	Gloria Hale
Richard Benedict	Mingo
Ric Roman	Joey
Robert Shayne	Dowell
David Alpert	Junior Billforth
Charles Seel	Harry Honnegger
Nora Marlowe	Woman outside Lupo's Apts

Credits:

Cinematography by Jacques R. Marquette
Film Editing by Noel L. Scott
Art Direction by Howard Campbell
Set Decoration by Jack H. Ahern

Makeup Supervisor: Gordon Bau
Hairstylist: Jean Burt Reilly
Assistant Director: Bernard McEveety
Sound: M.A. Merrick
Theme Music Composers: Mack David and Jerry Livingston
Music Editor: John Allyn Jr.
Music Supervisors: Paul Sawtell and Bert Shefter
60 minutes/Black and White
Production Company: Warner Bros. Television
Filmed at Warner Bros. Studios on Stages 20 and 24
Previously aired footage of Margarita Sierra singing "Par-a-Kee" (from Episode 6, "Par-a-Kee") was used in this episode.

Notes on the case:

Sandy meets, and seems to hit it off with a beautiful tourist named Wanda Drake. He is disappointed to learn that she is flirting with Albie Banion, a known social-ladder-climbing hoodlum. Sandy also learns that Wanda's father is serving a life-sentence for a crime she believes Banion really committed. He must investigate her seeming obsession with Banion, and determine who is the real criminal.

Ellen McRae (Burstyn) played the role of Wanda Drake. Burstyn was born on December 7, 1932 in Detroit, Michigan. As a young woman, she worked as a model and a showgirl on *The Jackie Gleason Show* in 1952. She worked as a dancer in Montreal nightclubs before making her Broadway debut in *Fair Game* in 1957. She would appear on Broadway seven more times in productions including *84 Charing Cross Road, Shirley Valentine*, and *Same Time Next Year*, for which she won a Tony and a Drama Desk Award in 1975. She made her television debut on *The Kraft Theatre* in 1958. She guest-starred in several television dramas including *The Loretta Young Show, Cheyenne, Dr. Kildare, Perry Mason, 77 Sunset Strip, Ben Casey,* and *Wagon Train*. Her appearance on this episode of *Surfside 6* was only her sixth television role. She starred as Dr. Kate Bartok in the 1965 series *The Doctors*, but it was her work in the 1964 films *For Those Who Think Young* and *Goodbye Charlie* that put her acting career into high gear. She continued to work in episodic television for a couple of years, but motion pictures dominated her acting opportunities until today. She is remembered by many fans for her starring role in the 1973 horror classic *The Exorcist*. Burstyn has been nominated for six Academy Awards with one win, seven Golden Globe Awards with one win, and eight Emmy Awards with two wins.

Brad Dexter played the role of Albie Banion. Dexter was born in Goldfield, Nevada on April 9, 1917. He was an amateur boxer as a young man, and studied acting at the Pasadena Playhouse. During World War II he served in the U.S. Army Air Corps. He made his film debut in the 1940 movie *The Mortal Storm*. His many films include *Winged Victory, Heldorado, Sinbad the Sailor, The Asphalt Jungle, Fourteen Hours, The Las Vegas Story, Macao, Untamed, Between Heaven and Hell, The Oklahoman, Run Silent Run Deep, The George Raft Story, The Magnificent Seven, Johnny Cool, Taras Bulba, Von Ryan's Express*, and *Shampoo*. He worked frequently in television as well, and guest-starred in dozens of television dramas including *Climax, Wagon Train, Pursuit, Bronco, Mr. Lucky, Hawaiian Eye, Mission: Impossible, Kojak, McCloud*, and *Death Valley Days*. He retired from acting in 1988, and transitioned into film production. He produced the 1980 television series *Skag* and the feature films *The Naked Runner, The Lawyer, Lady Sings the Blues*, and *Little Fauss and Big Halsey*. He was married to singer Peggy Lee for eight months in 1953. His second wife, Mary Bogdanovich, was the Star-Kist tuna heiress. They were married from 1971 until her death in 1994. That same year he married his third wife who survived him when he died of emphysema on December 11, 2002 in Rancho Mirage, California. Brad Dexter was 85 years old.

Ann Robinson played the role of Gloria Hale. Robinson was born in Los Angeles on May 25, 1929. She made her film debut in the 1950 movie *The Damned Don't Cry*. Her other films include *Abbott and Costello in the Foreign Legion, The Glass Wall, Gun Duel in Durango*, and *Imitation of Life*. She is best known for playing the role of Sylvia Van Buren in the classic 1953 science-fiction film *War of the Worlds*. She played the same character in the films *Midnight Movie Massacre* (1988), and *The Naked Monster* (2005). She also reprised the role in three episodes of the 1988 television series *War of the Worlds*, and played a cameo role in the 2005 Steven Spielberg film remake, *War of the Worlds*. Robinson appeared frequently on television. Her television guest-starring appearances include *Fury, Rocky Jones Space Ranger, Cheyenne, Perry Mason, Rawhide, Peter Gunn, Ben Casey*, and *Gilligan's Island*. She continues to act, and has made television commercials, and performs as a voice-over artist. Ann Robinson was married to the world famous matador, Jaime Bravo. The couple had two sons before divorcing in 1967.

Richard Benedict played the role of Mingo. Benedict was born in Palermo, Italy on January 8, 1920. He first appeared on screen in 1944. During the next 40 years he appeared in numerous films including *Ace in the Hole, Ocean's 11*, and the 1958 sci-fi cult classic *It! The Terror from Beyond Space*. His nearly 100 guest-starring television appearances include *Adventures of Superman, The Lone Ranger, Perry Mason, Zorro, Dragnet, Peter Gunn, Hawaii Five-O, Sugarfoot, The Roaring 20's, Bronco*, and *Lawman*. Benedict was also an accomplished film and television director. He directed two episodes of *Surfside 6*. Richard Benedict died of a heart attack in Studio City, California on April 25, 1984, at the age of 64. He is the father of actor Nick Benedict.

Circumstantial Evidence

Season 1, Episode 29

Broadcast on ABC-TV on April 17, 1961
Directed by Allen Baron
Written by Anne Howard Bailey
Producer: Jerry Davis
Executive Producer: William T. Orr

Cast:

Lee Patterson	Dave Thorne
Van Williams	Ken Madison
Diane McBain	Daphne Dutton
Margarita Sierra	Cha Cha O'Brien
Don "Red" Barry	Lt. Snedigar
Leslie Parrish	Sunny Golden
Lisa Gaye	Liz
John Lupton	Curt
John Beradino	Granger
Mario Roccuzzo	Rafael
Carolyn Komant	Dana
Dawn Wells	June

Credits:

Cinematography by Glen MacWilliams
Film Editing by Fred Bohanan
Art Direction by Howard Campbell
Set Decoration by Robert C. Bradfield
Makeup Supervisor: Gordon Bau
Hairstylist: Jean Burt Reilly
Assistant Director: John Francis Murphy

Sound: Thomas Ashton
Theme Music Composers: Mack David and Jerry Livingston
Music Editor: Lou Gordon
Music Supervisors: Paul Sawtell and Bert Shefter
60 minutes/Black and White
Production Company: Warner Bros. Television
Filmed at Warner Bros. Studios on Stages 20 and 24

Notes on the case:

Sunny Golden, a beautiful performing water skier in a water ski show, is blackmailing her ex-boyfriend. She discovered that he secretly married one of her rivals in the show. She knows he will lose a promised million-dollar inheritance if he gets married before he turns 30 years old. When Sunny is found dead, Cha Cha's nephew, Raphael, who worked at the hotel she was staying in, and had an obsession with her, is suspected of the crime. Cha Cha and Ken investigate what really happened, and discover a complicated and deadly romantic quadrangle. The water ski show footage used in this episode was shot at Cypress Gardens in Florida.

Leslie Parrish played the role of Sunny Golden. Parrish was born in Melrose, Massachusetts on March 18, 1935. She originally pursued a career in music, but her modeling led her to acting roles which provided her a means of supporting her family. She made her screen debut in the 1955 film *The Virgin Queen*. Her many feature films include *Daddy Long Legs*, *How to Be Very Very Popular*, *The Girl in the Red Velvet Swing*, *Li'l Abner*, *Portrait of a Mobster*, *The Manchurian Candidate*, *Sex and the Single Girl*, and *Crash*. Her dozens of television appearances include *Steven Canyon*, *Perry Mason*, *Hawaiian Eye*, *Bachelor Father*, *The Wild, Wild West*, *Batman*, *My Three Sons*, *Tarzan*, *Star Trek*, *The Man From U.N.C.L.E.*, *To Rome with Love*, *Logan's Run*, and *Police Story*. Parrish retired in 1978. For decades, she was a nationally recognized political, environmental, and

Leslie Parrish and Lee.

wildlife activist. Her second husband was writer Richard Bach, the author of *Jonathan Livingston Seagull*, *The Bridge Across Forever*, and *One*. They were married from 1981 until 1999.

Lisa Gaye played the role of Liz Perry. Gaye was born in Denver, Colorado on March 6, 1935. Her family moved to Los Angeles in the early 1930s. Her mother wanted her children to have careers in show business. Gaye's sisters were actresses Debra Paget and Teala Loring, and her brother, known professionally as Frank Griffin, was an actor and movie make-up artist. Gaye attended Hollywood's Professional School, and signed a contract with Universal Studios when she was 17 years old. She made her screen debut in the 1954 film *The Glenn Miller Story*. Her other films include *Drums Across the River*, *Magnificent Obsession*, *Rock Around the Clock*, *Shake Rattle and Roll!*, *Ten Thousand Bedrooms*, *Night of Evil*, *Castle of Evil*, and *The Violent Ones*. Her numerous television credits include guest-starring roles in *Annie Oakley*, *The Adventures of Jim Bowie*, *Have Gun – Will Travel*, *Perry Mason*, *Sea Hunt*, *Wanted: Dead or Alive*, *Cheyenne*, *Rawhide*, *Death Valley Days*, *Wagon Train*, *The Wild, Wild West*, *The Time Tunnel*, *Get Smart*, *The Flying Nun*, and *The Mod Squad*. Gaye was married to Bently C. Ware from 1955 until his death in 1977. The couple had one daughter. Lisa Gaye died in Houston, Texas on July 14, 2016 at the age of 81. She was survived by her daughter, her sister, Debra Paget, and her brother, Frank Griffin.

John Lupton played the role of Curt Maxon. Lupton was born in Highland Park, Illinois on August 23, 1928. He attended New York's American Academy of Dramatic Arts, and worked in stock theater companies until signing a contract with MGM Studios. He first appeared on screen in the 1949 film *On the Town*. His many films include *The Great Locomotive*, *Shadow in the Sky*, *Julius Caesar*, *The Band Wagon*, *Battle Cry*, *The Clown and the Kid*, *Jesse James Meets Frankenstein's Daughter*, *Airport 1975*, *The Greatest Story Ever Told*, *The Day of the Wolves*, *Cool Breeze*, *Napoleon and Samantha*, *The Phantom of Hollywood*, *The World's Greatest Athlete*, and *The Secret of Lost Valley*. His dozens of television appearances include *Climax*, *Broken Arrow*, *The Millionaire*, *U.S. Marshall*, *Sea Hunt*, *Perry Mason*, *Alfred Hitchcock Presents*, *Rawhide*, *Flipper*, *The Time Tunnel*, *The F.B.I.*, *S.W.A.T.*, and *Who's the Boss?*. He played the role of Dr. Tom Horton Jr. on the daytime drama *Days of Our Lives*. John Lupton died in Los Angeles on November 3, 1993 at the age of 65. He was survived by his second wife of 31 years, Dian Friml, the granddaughter of music composer Rudolf Friml, and one daughter.

John Beradino played the role of Al Granger. Beradino was born on May 1, 1917 in Los Angeles. After attending U.S.C., Beradino was a major league baseball player from 1939 until 1952 – with time out for service in the U.S. Naval Reserve during World War II from 1942 until 1945. He first appeared on the screen in the 1948 film *The Winner's Circle*. His films include *The Kid from Cleveland, The Kid from Left Field, Them!, The Killer is Loose, Seven Men from Now, The Naked and the Dead, North by Northwest, Seven Thieves*, and *Young Doctors in Love*. He began his television career in 1954 and appeared in dozens of television episodes and made-for-television films including *Adventures of Superman, Sea Hunt, Lawman, Route 66, The New Breed, Bronco, Batman, The Love Boat*, and *The Fresh Prince of Bel Air*. He played the role of Sgt. Vince Cavelli on the 1961-62 series *The New Breed*. Beradino is best known for playing the role of Dr. Steve Hardy from 1963 until 1996 on the daytime drama, *General Hospital*. John Beradino died of pancreatic cancer at his Los Angeles home on May 19, 1996 at the age of 79. He was survived by his third wife of 25 years, and four children.

Dawn Wells played the role of June. Wells was born on October 18, 1938 in Reno, Nevada. In 1959, she was crowned Miss Nevada. She graduated from the University of Washington in 1960 with a degree in theater arts and design. In 1961, she signed a contract with Warner Brothers and began working frequently on the studio's television productions including *The Roaring 20's, Maverick, Cheyenne, 77 Sunset Strip, Lawman, Laramie*, and *Hawaiian Eye*. Her other television appearances include *Wagon Train, The Love Boat, Fantasy Island, The Wild, Wild West, Bonanza, Growing Pains*, and *Columbo*. Her feature films include *Palm Springs Weekend, The New Interns, The Town that Dreaded Sundown, Winterhawk, Lover's Knot, Forever for Now*, and *Return to Boggy Creek*. Fans remember her best for playing the role of lovable Mary Ann in the classic 1964-67 comedy series *Gilligan's Island*. She reprised the role for several made-for-television movies including *Rescue from Gilligan's Island* (1978), *The Castaways from Gilligan's Island* (1979), and *The Harlem Globetrotters on Gilligan's Island* (1981). In her later years, she enjoyed a successful theatre career in regional and summer stock productions, and national tours including *Chapter Two* and *They're Playing Our Song*. She was involved with many humanitarian organizations, and wrote *Mary Ann's Gilligan's Island Cookbook* (1993), and *What Would Mary Ann Do? A Guide to Life* (2014). Dawn Wells died of COVID-19 complications on December 30, 2020 in Los Angeles at the age 82.

Dawn Wells.

Vengeance Is Bitter

Season 1, Episode 30

Broadcast on ABC-TV on April 24, 1961
Directed by Frank Baur
Written by Lee Loeb
Producer: Charles Hoffman
Supervising Producer: Howie Horwitz
Executive Producer: William T. Orr

Cast:

Lee Patterson	Dave Thorne
Troy Donahue	Sandy Winfield II
Van Williams	Ken Madison
Margarita Sierra	Cha Cha O'Brien
Don "Red" Barry	Lt. Snedigar
Linda Watkins	Mrs. Denning
Claire Griswold	Patricia Carver
Neil Hamilton	Judge Denning
Guy Stockwell	Robert Carver
James Seay	Phillip Lordan
Lori Kaye	Gloria Randall
Lorrie Richards	Cleo
Jodi McDowell	Miss Ryan
Peggy McCay	Ann Wayne

Credits:

Cinematography by Robert Tobey
Film Editing by Noel L. Scott
Art Direction by Howard Campbell
Set Decoration by Hoyle Barrett

Makeup Supervisor: Gordon Bau
Hairstylist: Jean Burt Reilly
Assistant Director: Fred Scheld
Sound: Samuel F. Goode
Theme Music Composers: Mack David and Jerry Livingston
Music Editor: Erma E. Levin
Music Supervisors: Paul Sawtell and Bert Shefter
60 minutes/Black and White
Production Company: Warner Bros. Television
Filmed at Warner Bros. Studios on Stages 20 and 24
Margarita Sierra sang "Let's Put Out the Lights (and Go to Sleep)" in this
episode.

Notes on the case:

Bob Carver and his wife Patricia, prominent members of the community, are
informed that a new book scheduled for publication, slanders them, actually
alleging that one of them committed an unsolved murder. They hire Dave to
find a way to stop publication of the book. Before he can make any headway,
the publisher is murdered. And it looks like one of the Carvers committed
the crime.

Guy Stockwell played the role of Bob Carver. Stockwell was born on
November 16, 1933 in New York City. His father was actor/singer Harry
Stockwell, and his mother was singer/dancer Elizabeth Veronica. He began
his acting career on stage, appearing in the 1943 Broadway production of
The Innocent Voyage. He also starred in the Broadway hit *Chicken Every
Sunday* (1944-45). Stockwell made his screen debut in the 1946 film *The
Green Years*. His numerous films include *The Romance of Rosy Ridge,
The Beat Generation, Please Don't Eat the Daisies, Three Swords of Zorro, The
War Lord, The Plainsman, Beau Geste, Tobruk, The Monitors, It's Alive,* and
Airport 1975. Stockwell's many television appearances include *Adventures
in Paradise, The Roaring 20's, Perry Mason, Simon & Simon, Tales of the
Gold Monkey, The Eddie Capra Mysteries, Magnum, P.I., Murder She Wrote,
Land of the Giants, Gunsmoke, The Virginian,* and *Return to Peyton Place*. He
retired in 1990. Guy Stockwell died on February 6, 2002 in Prescott, Arizona
of complications from diabetes. He was 68 years old. He was married and
divorced three times, and survived by three children, and his brother, actor
Dean Stockwell.

Claire Griswold played the role of Patricia Carver. Griswold was born
in Honolulu, Hawaii on October 30, 1936. She worked as a model, and
made her acting debut on television in 1958. She guest-starred in numerous
shows including *Studio One in Hollywood, Wanted: Dead or Alive, Hawaiian*

Eye, Checkmate, Lawman, Perry Mason, 77 Sunset Strip, The Twilight Zone, Bonanza, and *The Alfred Hitchcock Hour.* In 1958, she married director Sydney Pollock and the couple had three children. She retired in 1967 to raise their children. Claire Griswold died of Parkinson's Disease in West Hollywood on March 28, 2011 at the age of 74. She was predeceased by her husband of 50 years in 2008. She was survived by two daughters.

Neil Hamilton played the role of Judge Denning. Hamilton was born on September 9, 1899 in Lynn, Massachusetts. He learned his acting trade in stock and professional stage productions. He made his screen debut in the 1918 silent film *The Beloved Imposter.* His film acting transitioned silent movies, and he eventually appeared in more than 250 feature films including *The White Rose, Isn't Life Wonderful?, Beau Geste, Mother Machree, The Dawn Patrol, Laughing Sinners, Tarzan the Ape Man, What Price Hollywood?, Tarzan and His Mate, Since You Went Away, When Strangers Marry, Brewster's Millions, The Patsy, The Family Jewels, Madame X, Strategy of Terror,* and *Which Way to the Front?* Hamilton's many television appearances include *Perry Mason, 77 Sunset Strip, Maverick, The Real McCoys, Mister Ed, Bachelor Father, The Outer Limits,* and *The Cara Williams Show.* He starred on Broadway in *Many Happy Returns* (1945), *The Men We Marry* (1948), *To Be Continued* (1952), and *Late Love* (1953-54). He is best remembered for playing the role of Police Commissioner Gordon in the classic series *Batman* (1966-68) and in the 1966 feature film *Batman, the Movie.* He retired in 1971. Neil Hamilton suffered an asthma attack and died in Escondido, California on September 24, 1984 at the age of 85. He was survived by his wife of 62 years, and one child.

Peggy McCay played the role of Ann Wayne. McCay was born in Manhattan on November 3, 1927. She performed in regional and repertory theater before studying with Lee Strasberg in New York. She later was instrumental in establishing his West Coast studio. She made her television debut in 1949. McCay's television guest-starring roles include *Perry Mason, Maverick, Gibbsville, Lou Grant, Appointment with Adventure, Room for One More, The Andy Griffith Show, The Virginian, Love of Life, The Roaring 20's, The Greatest Show on Earth,*

Troy and Peggy McCay.

Barnaby Jones, *The Fugitive*, and *Laramie*. In the 1970s, she played memorable roles in *Eleanor and Franklin: The White House Years*, *How the West Was Won*, *The Lazarus Syndrome*, and *John O'Hara's Gibbsville*. Her feature films include *Uncle Vanya*, *Lad: A Dog*, *Promises in the Dark*, *Bustin' Loose*, *Second Thoughts*, *Daddy's Girl*, and *James Dean*. She won an OBIE Award for her off-Broadway performance in *Uncle Vanya* in 1956. McCay is perhaps best remembered for playing the role of Caroline Brady on the daytime drama *Days of Our Lives* from 1983 until 2017. She was nominated for five Daytime Emmy Awards and two Prime Time Emmy Awards, with one win for Outstanding Supporting Actress in a Drama Series, *The Trials of Rosie O'Neill*, in 1991. She retired in 2017, and died at her Los Angeles home on October 7, 2018 at the age of 90. Peggy McCay never married or had children.

Little Mister Kelly

Season 1, Episode 31

Broadcast on ABC-TV on May 1, 1961
Directed by Charles R. Roneau
Written by Erna Lazarus
Producer: Jerry Davis
Supervising Producer: Howie Horwitz
Executive Producer: William T. Orr

Cast:

Van Williams	Ken Madison
Troy Donahue	Sandy Winfield II
Lee Patterson	Dave Thorne
Diane McBain	Daphne Dutton
Don "Red" Barry	Lt. Snedigar
Biff Elliot	Hank Kelly
Irene Hervey	Mrs. Gardiner
Eve McVeagh	Blossom McKenzie
Sam Gilman	Jack Miller
John Goddard	Smiley Jackson
Ed Peck	Mack Neilly
Eddie Quillan	Chuck
Jack Kosslyn	Alex Boles
Charles Horvath	Ralph Stringer
Richard Benedict	Sam Norton
Ronnie Dapo	Little Kelly
Billy Nelson	Al

Credits:

Cinematography by Ralph Woolsey
Film Editing by Stefan Arnsten
Art Direction by Howard Campbell
Set Decoration by Robert C. Bradfield
Makeup Supervisor: Gordon Bau
Hairstylist: Jean Burt Reilly
Assistant Director: Phil Rawlins
Sound: Samuel F. Goode
Theme Music Composers: Mack David and Jerry Livingston
Music Editor: Ted Sebern
60 minutes/Black and White
Production Company: Warner Bros. Television
Filmed at Warner Bros. Studios on Stages 20 and 24

Notes on the case:

Professional boxer Hank Kelley's sparring partner is found dead. The police dismiss the death as a suicide, but Hank suspects foul play. When he learns his young son is in danger, he hires Ken to explore his suspicions. Ken's investigation uncovers a dangerous fight-fixing ring.

Biff Elliott played the role Hank Kelly. Elliott was born in Lynn, Massachusetts on July 26, 1923. His family moved to Presque Isle, Maine when he was 16. He became interested in boxing and eventually became the Northern Maine champion. He boxed his way to the New England regional championship before his mother coaxed him to quit. His attendance at the University of Maine was interrupted when he joined the U.S. Army in 1943. He returned to college after the war, and moved to New York to pursue a writing career. While in New York City, he took acting lessons at the famed Actors Studio, and began working on television in 1950. He moved to Hollywood in 1953 to star as Mike Hammer in the first adaptation of Mickey Spillane's *I, the Jury*. During the 1950s, Elliott appeared in many films including *Good Morning Miss Dove*, *Between Heaven and Hell*, *The Enemy Below*, *Pork Chop Hill*, and *PT 109*. He transitioned into television work, and guest-starred in dozens of programs including *Alfred Hitchcock Presents*, *Star Trek*, *Mission: Impossible*, *Cannon*, and *Falcon Crest*, until his retirement in 1986. In his later years, he worked for CBS Radio Network covering Los Angeles Sports. He died at his Studio City, California home on August 15, 2012. Biff Elliott was 89 years old.

Ronnie Dapo played the role of Little Kelly. Dapo was born on May 8, 1952 in Plattsburgh, New York. His family moved to Los Angeles, and Dapo signed a five-year contract with Warner Brothers in 1959. He guest-starred on many Warner Brothers television shows including *Sugarfoot, Maverick, 77 Sunset Strip, The Roaring 20's,* and *Hawaiian Eye.* He played the role of Flip Rose on the 1962 series *Room for One More,* and the role of Andy in the 1964 series *The New Phil Silvers Show.* His several feature film appearances include *The Music Man* and *Kisses for My President.* Dapo retired from acting in 1966 at the age of 14. He spent many years as a touring musician.

Irene Hervey played the role of Mrs. Gardner. Hervey was born in Venice, California on July 11, 1909. She signed a contract with MGM in 1933, and first appeared on screen in *The Stranger's Return.* During her five-decade career, she starred in dozens of films including *The Count of Monte Cristo, With Words and Music, The League of Frightened Men, Destry Rides Again, The Girl Said No, The Boys from Syracuse,* and *Mr. Peabody and the Mermaid.* Hervey guest-starred in dozens of television shows, and earned an Emmy nomination for her guest-starring role in *My Three Sons* in 1969. She was married to actor Allan Jones from 1936 until 1957. The couple had one son, singer Jack Jones. After retiring from acting, Hervey worked at a travel agency in Los Angeles. Irene Hervey died at the Motion Picture Country Home in Woodland Hills on December 20, 1998. She was 89 years old, and survived by her son.

Eddie Quillan played the role of Chuck. Quillan was born into a family of vaudeville performers on March 31, 1907 in Philadelphia. As a child he toured with his family, and eventually came to California in the mid-1920s. He first appeared on screen in Mack Sennett silent film comedies. Quillan played the role of a vaudeville dancer in his first feature film, *Show Folks,* in 1928. The following year, he signed a contract with Cecil B. DeMille's Pathe Film Corporation, and starred in the feature film *The Godless Girl.* Throughout his sixty-year career he appeared in more than 150 films including *Mutiny on the Bounty, Young Mr. Lincoln, The Grapes of Wrath, Brigadoon, Alaska Highway,* and *It Ain't Hay,* among many others. Equally adept at drama or comedy, he transitioned to television work in the 1950s, and guest-starred in dozens of programs. Quillan was one of the busiest and more reliable character actors in Hollywood. He retired in 1987, and died of cancer on July 19, 1990 in North Hollywood. Eddie Quillan was gay.

Spinout at Sebring

Season 1, Episode 32

Broadcast on ABC-TV on May 8, 1961
Directed by Charles R. Rondeau
Teleplay by Whitman Chambers from a story by Whitman Chambers and
    Fred Schiller
Producer: Jerry Davis
Supervising Producer: Howie Horwitz
Executive Producer: William T. Orr

Cast:

Troy Donahue	Sandy Winfield II
Van Williams	Ken Madison
Lee Patterson	Davie Thorne
Margarita Sierra	Cha Cha O'Brien
Sue Randall	Maggie Littrell
Jorja Curtright	Lorraine Littrell
Alejandro Rey	Tony Ricardo
Alan Marshal	Larry Littrell
Andre Philippe	Jacques Monte
John Graham	Dr. Bertram
Elizabeth Harrower	Miss Thompson
Andrew Orapeza	Benito
John Van Dreelen	Martin Harriby

Credits:

Cinematography by Ralph Woolsey
Film Editing by Robert Crawford
Art Direction by Howard Campbell
Set Decoration by Hoyle Barrett

Makeup Supervisor: Gordon Bau
Hairstylist: Jean Burt Reilly
Assistant Director: Samuel Schneider
Sound: Everett A. Hughes
Theme Music Composers: Mack David and Jerry Livingston
Music Editor: Robert Phillips
Music Supervisors: Paul Sawtell and Bert Shefter
60 minutes/Black and White
Production Company: Warner Bros. Television
Filmed at Warner Bros. Studios on Stages 20 and 24
Previous footage of Margarita Sierra singing "Dancing in the Dark" (first seen in Episode 3 "The Clown") was used in this episode.

Notes on the case:

Sandy's favorite pastime is race car driving. A young woman, Maggie Littrell, approaches Sandy and expresses her concern that her mother is plotting with her attorney to murder her father, Martin Harriby. Maggie's boyfriend, a champion sports car racer named Tony Ricardo, and Sandy enter the Sebring Grand Prix twelve-hour endurance race in order to disrupt any murder plans. But Harriby is killed in an accident during the race, and Maggie's mother is struck and killed by a car. Sandy has his hands full with a complicated investigation.

Sue Randall played the role of Maggie Littrell. Randall was born in Philadelphia on October 8, 1935. In 1953, she moved to New York to attend the American Academy of Dramatic Arts. She moved to Hollywood in 1950, and appeared in the 1957 Tracy/Hepburn film *Desk Set*. Until her retirement from acting in 1967, she played supporting roles in more than 60 television dramas including *The Rifleman*, *The Real McCoys*, *77 Sunset Strip*, *Bronco*, *Thriller*, *Perry Mason*, and *Death Valley Days*. She is perhaps best known for playing the role of school

Sue Randall and Troy.

teacher Miss Landers on *Leave It to Beaver* (1958-1962). In 1969, she moved back to Philadelphia where she worked in the private sector and supported numerous charities. Sue Randall died of lung cancer on October 26, 1984 in Philadelphia. She was 49 years old.

Jorja Curtright played the role of Lorraine Littrell. Curtright was born in Amarillo, Texas on August 14, 1923. She began her acting career in 1943, and appeared in numerous films including *M*, *Whistle Stop*, *Love Is a Many Splendored Thing*, and *The Revolt of Mamie Stover*. Until her retirement from acting in 1967, she guest-starred in more than 30 television shows including *City Detective*, *Gunsmoke*, *Perry Mason*, *The Rogues*, and *Bonanza*. She married writer Sidney Sheldon in 1951. In her later life, she was a successful interior decorator. She suffered a heart attack and died in Los Angeles on May 11, 1985. Jorja Curtright was 61 years old.

Alejandro Rey played the role of Tony Ricardo. Rey was born on February 8, 1930 in Buenos Aires, Argentina. He began working in Argentinian films in 1953 and worked steadily until moving to the United States in 1960. This episode of *Surfside 6* was Rey's introduction to American television audiences. During the next 25 years, he played more than 100 roles in films and television, and directed for television. His American films include *Fun in Acapulco*, *Mr. Majestyk*, *The Swarm*, and *Moscow on the Hudson*. His many television credits include *Perry Mason*, *Thriller*, *Voyage to the Bottom of the Sea*, *Run for Your Life*, *Gunsmoke*, *Night Gallery*, *Fantasy Island*, and *Dallas*. He is best remembered for playing the role of casino owner and playboy Carlos Ramirez on the television series *The Flying Nun* (1965-69). He became a naturalized citizen of the United States in 1967. Rey died from lung cancer on May 21, 1987 in Los Angeles. Alejandro Rey was 57 years old. He is survived by his son, actor Brandon Rey.

Alan Marshal played the role of Larry Littrell. Marshal was born in Sidney, Australia on January 29, 1909. His parents were both successful stage and screen actors in Australia before moving to America in 1914. Marshal made his Broadway debut in the 1923 production of *The Swan*. Over the next 12 years he appeared in ten Broadway shows including *The Merchant of Venice*, *The Game of Love and Death*, *Death Takes a Holiday*, *Going Gay*, *While Parents Sleep*, and *The Bishop Misbehaves*. A talent scout for Selznick International Studios discovered Marshal on Broadway, and brought him to Hollywood. He made his screen debut in the 1936 film *The Garden of Allah*. His many films include *After the Thin Man*, *Night Must Fall*, *I Met My Love Again*, *Invisible Enemy*, *The Road to Reno*, *Dramatic School*, *Four Girls in White*, *Exile Express*, *The Adventures of Sherlock Holmes*, *The Hunchback of Notre Dame*, *Married and in Love*, *Irene*, *He Stayed for Breakfast*, *The Howards of Virginia*, *Tom Dick and Harry*, *Lydia*, *The While Cliffs of Dover*, and *Bride by Mistake*. In 1945, he suffered a nervous breakdown and was unable to work for several years. In the 1950s, he began to act on television. His appearances include *Climax!*, *The Clock*, *Perry Mason*, *Wagon Train*, *Rawhide*, *Alfred Hitchcock Presents*, *The Ann Sothern Show*, *Buckskin*, and several shows at Warner Brothers including *77 Sunset Strip*, *Sugarfoot*, and *Bourbon Street Beat*. Marshal returned to feature films briefly in the later 1950s, and played supporting roles in *The Opposite Sex*, *House on Haunted Hill*, and *Day of the Outlaw*. Alan Marshal suffered a heart attack and died on July 9, 1961, in his Chicago hotel room. At the time, he was co-starring with Mae West in her play *Sextette* at the Edgewater Beach Playhouse. His son, actor Kit Marshal, took over the role for his father for the duration of the engagement. Alan Marshal was 52 years old. This episode of *Surfside 6* was his final on screen appearance.

The Bhoyo and the Blonde

Season 1, Episode 33

Broadcast on ABC-TV on May 15, 1961
Directed by Michael O'Herlihy
Written by Sonya Roberts
Producer: Jerry Davis
Supervising Producer: Howie Horwitz
Executive Producer: William T. Orr

Cast:

Lee Patterson	Dave Thorne
Troy Donahue	Sandy Winfield II
Van Williams	Ken Madison
Diane McBain	Daphne Dutton
Margarita Sierra	Cha Cha O'Brien
Don "Red" Barry	Lt. Snedigar
Sean McClory	Kevin Flanagan
Sue Ann Langdon	Renee
Paula Raymond	Kathleen
Anthony Caruso	Hobey
Paul Debov	2nd Thief
John Craig	1st Craig
Marjorie Bennett	Mrs. Shaw
Robert Logan	Bellboy

Credits:

Cinematography by Louis Jennings
Film Editing by John Joyce
Art Direction by Howard Campbell
Set Decoration by Hoyle Barrett

Makeup Supervisor: Gordon Bau
Hairstylist: Jean Burt Reilly
Assistant Director: Bernard McEveety
Sound: Everett A. Hughes
Theme Music Composers: Mack David and Jerry Livingston
Music Editor: Sam E. Levin
60 minutes/Black and White
Production Company: Warner Bros. Television
Filmed at Warner Bros. Studios on Stages 20 and 24

Notes on the case:

Kevin Flanagan, an Irish novelist known for his womanizing and drinking skills as much as his writing, is on holiday in Miami Beach with his wife, Kathleen. While drunk one night, Flanagan attempts to pick up a beautiful blonde who is driving a criminal's getaway car. Unfortunately, he accidently witnesses a gangland killing. The murderer can't be sure if Flanagan will remember what he saw, so he is marked for murder, too. Kathleen knows the mob will soon find her husband, so she hires Dave to protect him. The mob sends a hit woman to shoot the author, but Ken and Sandy capture her in time.

Sean McClory played the role of Kevin Flanagan. McClory was born on March 8, 1924 in Dublin, Ireland. He attended the National University of Ireland Medical School, and served in the Irish Army Medical Corps during World War II. He began acting on stage in comedies at the Abbey Theater. He appeared on Broadway in 1951 in *The King of Friday's Men*, and later, in many regional theatre productions in America. A European scout for RKO Pictures discovered McClory acting at the Abbey Theatre, and brought him to Hollywood in 1947, where he made his screen debut in *Dick Tracy Meets Gruesome*. His many other films include *Dick Tracey's Dilemma*, *The Daughter of Rosie O'Grady*, *The Glass Menagerie*, *David and Bathsheba*, *What Price Glory*, *Them!*, *Ring of Fear*, *Charade*, *The Long Gray Line*, *The Quiet Man*, *Cheyenne Autumn*, *Mary Poppins*, *The Gnome-Mobile*, *The Happiest Millionaire*, *Roller Boogie*, and *My Chauffeur*. McClory guest-starred in dozens of television shows including *Bring 'Em Back Alive*, *The Californians*, *Overland Trail*, *Pony Express*, *The Man from Blackhawk*, *The Islanders*, *Adventures in Paradise*, *The Rifleman*, *Lost in Space*, *Perry Mason*, *Bonanza*, *Death Valley Days*, and *Mannix*. He retired in 1993. One of his favorite past times was gold mining on the California-Nevada border. Sean McClory died of heart failure at his Hollywood home on December 10, 2003 at the age of 79. He was survived by his fourth wife of 20 years, actress Peggy Webber.

Paula Raymond played the role of Kathleen Flanagan. Raymond was born in San Francisco, California on November 23, 1924. She studied ballet, piano, and singing, and was a member of the San Francisco Opera Company and the San Francisco Children's Opera Company. She worked as a print model and magazine cover girl, and made her screen debut in the 1938 film *Keep Smiling*. Her films include *Crisis, Devil's Doorway, Texas Carnival, The Bandits of Corsica, City That Never Sleeps, The Beast from 20,000 Fathoms, King Richard and the Crusaders, The Human Jungle, Hand of Death, Blood of Dracula's Castle, Five Bloody Graves*, and *Mind Twister*. Her numerous television appearances include *Perry Mason, Maverick, Hawaiian Eye, M Squad, 77 Sunset Strip, Peter Gunn, Gunsmoke, Rawhide, Death Valley Days, The Life and Legend of Wyatt Earp, Bat Masterson*, and *Have Gun – Will Travel*. In 1962, Raymond was involved in a car accident in Hollywood. Her nose, which was severed by the rear view mirror, required extensive and numerous plastic surgeries. It took a year to recover from her injuries. She suffered several accidents in her later life that left her with a broken ankle, a broken shoulder, and two broken hips. She retired from acting in 1993. Paula Raymond died of respiratory failure in West Hollywood on December 31, 2003 at the age of 79.

Anthony Caruso played the role of Hobey. Caruso was born in Frankfort, Indiana on April 7, 1916. His family moved to Long Beach in 1926. Caruso studied at the Pasadena Playhouse, and worked with The Hart Players, the Federal Theatre Project, and appeared in plays at the Hollywood Playhouse. He made his screen debut in the 1940 film *Johnny Apollo*. His film credits include *Tall Dark and Handsome, Always in My Heart, Lucky Jordan, Pride of the Marines, Tarzan and the Leopard Woman, The Blue Dahlia, Wild Harvest, Devil Ship, Anna Lucasta, The Asphalt Jungle, Walk the Proud Land, Tarzan and the Slave Girl, Phantom of the Rue Morgue, Cattle Queen of Montana, Escape from Zahrain, Young Dillinger*, and *Sylvia*, among many others. His television credits include *Gunsmoke, Crusader, Have Gun – Will Travel, The Restless Gun, Buckskin, Wanted: Dead or Alive, Sugarfoot, The Untouchables, Riverboat, Get Smart, Star Trek, The Time Tunnel, Zorro*, and *The Addams Family*. He retired in 1990, after playing his final role, that of Don Carlos in the film *The Legend of Grizzly Adams*. Anthony Caruso died at the age of 86 at his Brentwood, California home on April 3, 2003. He was survived by his wife of 63 years, and their son Tonio, who died a year later. Caruso was predeceased by his daughter, Valentina.

Robert Logan played the role of the Bellboy. Logan was born on May 29, 1941 in Brooklyn, New York. He was the eldest of seven children. He attended the University of Arizona at Tucson on a baseball scholarship where he was discovered by a Warner Brothers talent scout. He signed a contract with the studio and first appeared on screen in 1961 on *Maverick*. He played the role of J.R. Hale on *77 Sunset Strip* from 1961 until 1963, and appeared in the 1961 Warner film *Claudelle Inglish*. His other television credits include *Mr. Novak*, and a recurring role as Jericho Jones on *Daniel Boone* (1965-66). Logan's other films include *Beach Ball*, *The Bridge at Remagen*, *Catlow*, *Across the Great Divide*, *The Sea Gypsies*, *Snowbeast*, *A Night in Heaven*, *Scorpion*, *Man Outside*, *Born to Race*, and *Patriots*. He played the role of Skip Robinson in the family film series *The Adventures of the Wilderness Family*, *The Further Adventures of the Wilderness Family*, and *Mountain Family Robinson*. Robert Logan retired in 1997, and reclaimed a private life.

An Overdose of Justice

Season 1, Episode 34

Broadcast on ABC-TV on May 22, 1961
Directed by Michael O'Herlihy
Written by Richard De Roy
Producer: Jerry Davis
Supervising Producer: Howie Horwitz
Executive Producer: William T. Orr

Cast:

Lee Patterson	Dave Thorne
Van Williams	Ken Madison
Margarita Sierra	Cha Cha O'Brien
Mara Corday	Bonnie Scott
Edward Platt	Phil Molloy
Judy Lewis	Mary Regis
Richard Coogan	Eddie Regis
Donna Douglas	Paula Creston

Credits:

Cinematography by Harold E. Stine
Film Editing by Fred Bohanan
Art Direction by Howard Campbell
Set Decoration by Hoyle Barrett
Makeup Supervisor: Gordon Bau
Hairstylist: Jean Burt Reilly
Assistant Director: Chuck Hansen
Sound: Samuel F. Goode
Theme Music Composers: Mack David and Jerry Livingston
Music Editor: Joe Inge

60 minutes/Black and White
Production Company: Warner Bros. Television
Filmed at Warner Bros. Studios on Stages 20 and 24
Margarita Sierra sang "Little Romero with a Big Sombrero" in this episode.

Notes on the case:

Eddie Regis, a thief who successfully pulled off a major payroll robbery, flees to Miami with his girlfriend, Bonnie Scott. Insurance investigator Phil Molloy enlists Dave's help to track down the stolen $75,000. In a surprise twist, they both get assistance from the thief's larcenous girlfriend.

Richard Coogan played the role of Eddie Regis. Coogan was born on April 4, 1914 in Madison, New Jersey. He appeared on Broadway in several productions including *The Rainmaker* and *Diamond Lil*, starring Mae West. He worked in numerous films including *Three Hours to Kill, The Revolt of Mamie Stover*, and *Girl on the Run*. Coogan co-starred in the Western television series *The Californians* (1957-59), and guest-starred in many television dramas, but is perhaps best remembered for playing Captain Video in five episodes of *Captain Video and His Video Rangers*. He retired from acting in 1963. He became a professional golfer and golf instructor in his later life. Richard Coogan died in Los Angeles on March 12, 2014. He was 99 years old.

Mara Corday played the role of Bonnie Scott. Corday was born in Santa Monica on January 3, 1930. When she was a teenager, she worked as a showgirl at the Earl Carroll Theater in Hollywood. She worked there for nearly three years before being spotted by a casting agent. In 1951, she signed a contract with Universal-International Pictures. She appeared in small roles in numerous films until she was cast as the leading lady in the 1955 cult-classic film *Tarantula*. In 1957, she co-starred in two other sci-fi/horror films; *The Black Scorpion*, and *The Giant Claw*. During the 1950s, she was a pinup in many men's magazines, and she was the *Playboy* Playmate of the Month in October 1958. She married actor Richard Long in 1957. The couple had three children, and remained married until Long's death in 1974. Mara Corday retired from acting in 1990.

Edward Platt played the role of Phil Molloy. Platt was born in Staten Island, New York on March 19, 1916. He studied at the Juilliard School, and Princeton University. He served in the U.S. Army during WWII. Platt appeared on Broadway in the musical *Allegro*, and *The Shrike*. He made his film debut in 1955. His films include *Rebel Without a Cause, The Helen Morgan Story, The Lieutenant Wore Skirts, The Steel Jungle*, and *Serenade*. Platt guest-starred in dozens of television shows, but is best remembered for playing Chief in the long-running television comedy classic *Get Smart* (1965-70). For many years, he suffered from depression. He committed suicide in his Santa Monica apartment on March 19, 1974. Edward Platt was 58 years old. He was survived by his wife of 20 years, and four children.

Judy Lewis played the role of Mary Regis. Lewis was born in Venice, California on November 6, 1935. She was the "love child" of actors Loretta Young and Clark Gable. For most of her adult life, she believed she had been adopted by Young. She first appeared on screen in 1958, and played numerous roles in film, television shows, and soap operas including *The Doctors* and *Secret Storm*. Lewis played the recurring role of Connie Masters on the series *Outlaws* (1961-62). She retired from acting in 1977, but remained active in show business. From 1980 through 1982 she produced the soap opera *Texas*. In 1994, she published her autobiography, *Uncommon Knowledge*, in which she revealed her true parentage. Her mother, Loretta Young, barely spoke to her again for the rest of her life. Judy Lewis died on November 25, 2011 in Gladwyne, Pennsylvania. She was 76 years old.

Count Seven!

Season 2, Episode 1

Broadcast on ABC-TV on September 18, 1961
Directed by Richard C. Sarafian
Teleplay by William Bruckner from a story by Robert Martin
Producer: Joel Rogsin
Supervising Producer: Howie Horwitz
Executive Producer: William T. Orr

Cast:

Van Williams	Ken Madison
Lee Patterson	Dave Thorne
Margarita Sierra	Cha Cha O'Brien
Jason Evers	Don Canfield
Shirley Ballard	Kay Canfield
Richard Crane	Lt. Gene Plehn
Russell Arms	Ralph Truitt
Lisa Plowman	Annie Canfield
Max Slaten	Jackson
Owen Bush	Mitch
Grace Lee Whitney	Lorraine Eldridge
Benny Baker	Joe, the Waiter
Robert Glenn	Sgt. Woodley

Credits:

Cinematography by J. Peverell Marley
Film Editing by David Wages
Art Direction by Howard Campbell
Set Decoration by Hoyle Barrett
Makeup Supervisor: Gordon Bau

Hairstylist: Jean Burt Reilly
Assistant Director: Richard L'Estrange
Sound: Stanley Jones
Theme Music Composers: Mack David and Jerry Livingston
Music Editor: Erna E. Levin
60 minutes/Black and White
Production Company: Warner Bros. Television
Filmed at Warner Bros. Studios on Stages 20 and 24
Margarita Sierra sang "You Must Have Been a Beautiful Baby" in this episode.

Notes on the case:

A perplexing crime is committed when seven-year-old Annie Canfield's birthday present of a stuffed poodle is stolen at gunpoint. Her father, a pilot, and her mother have divorced recently, and to complicate matters, her father's new fiancée is found murdered in his apartment. Ken is hired to investigate the theft, but the investigation widens when others show an interest in the stolen stuffed toy. Annie helps Ken solve the case which involves a smuggling ring.

Jason Evers played the role of Don Canfield. Evers was born in New York City on January 2, 1922. After leaving high school, Evers enlisted in the U.S. Army. He made his acting debut on Broadway in the 1941 production *Popsy*. His Broadway appearances include *Pie in the Sky* (1941), *Janie* (1942-44), *Grandma's Diary* (1948), *Angel in the Pawnshop* (1951), *A Date with April* (1953), and *Fair Game* (1957-58). Evers made his screen debut in the 1943 film, *Guadalcanal Diary*. His other films include *Pretty Boy Floyd*, *The Brain That Wouldn't Die*, *House of Women*, *The Green Berets*, *The Illustrated Man*, *Escape from the Planet of the Apes*, *Claws*, and *Barracuda*. His more than 150 television appearances include *The Phil Silvers Show*, *Cheyenne*, *The Rebel*, *77 Sunset Strip*, *Perry Mason*, *Bonanza*, *Tarzan*, *Felony Squad*, *The Wild, Wild West*, *The Guns of Will Sonnett*, *Star Trek*, *Mission:Impossible*, *Cannon*, *Hawaii Five-O*, *The Streets of San Francisco*, *Barnaby Jones*, *The Rockford Files*, *The Fall Guy*, *The Dukes of Hazzard*, *Murder She Wrote*, and *Matlock*. Evers was married and divorced twice. His first wife (1953-1966) was actress Shirley Ballard. Jason Evers died in Los Angeles on March 13, 2005 of heart failure. He was 83 years old.

Shirley Ballard played the role of Kaye Canfield. Ballard was born in Los Angeles on September 21, 1925. She worked as a model, and was Miss California 1944. She made her screen debut in the 1946 movie *The Kid from Brooklyn*. She played small roles in numerous films including *Easter Parade*, *A Song Is Born*, *The Petty Girl*, *Frenchie*, *The Laughing Policeman*, and *The Second Woman*. She guest-starred in many television programs including *Sea*

Hunt, Shotgun Slade, Perry Mason, Cheyenne, Bonanza, The Rebel, Ben Casey, The Twilight Zone, Channing, and *Bronk.* She retired from acting in 1976, and worked as a script and continuity supervisor on several films including *Mad Max, The Still Point,* and *Best Enemies,* and the television series *Water Under the Bridge,* and *The Sullivans.* Ballard was married to actor Jason Evers from 1953 until their divorce in 1966. She retired from show business in 1993. Shirley Ballard died in New York on October 27, 2012. She was 87 years old.

Grace Lee Whitney and Van.

Grace Lee Whitney played the role of Lorraine Eldridge. Whitney was born in Ann Arbor, Michigan on April 1, 1930. She began her career as an entertainer singing on local radio, and later in Chicago nightclubs. She made her Broadway debut in the comedy *Top Banana,* and appeared in the 1954 film adaptation. She guest-starred in dozens of television shows including *Mike Hammer, Bat Masterson, The Real McCoys, Gunsmoke, The Rifleman, 77 Sunset Strip, The Untouchables, The Outer Limits, Run for Your Life, Batman, Death Valley Days, The Bold Ones, Cannon, Hart to Hart,* and *Bewitched.* Her several films include *Some Like It Hot, House of Wax, The Naked and the Dead, Pocketful of Miracles, A Public Affair, The Man from Galveston,* and *Irma la Douce.* Whitney is best remembered for playing the role of Janice Rand on the original *Star Trek* television series, and in four of the subsequent *Star Trek* films. In the 1960s and 1970s she resumed her music career, and sang with orchestras and big bands, and released two song collections. She retired from acting in 2007, and moved to the small town of Coarsegold, California, near Yosemite National Park, to be near one of her sons. Whitney was a recovering alcoholic, and worked to help others. Grace Lee Whitney died at her home in Coarsegold on May 1, 2015 at the age of 85. She was survived by her two sons.

Russell Arms played the role of Ralph Truitt. Arms was born in Berkeley, California on February 3, 1920. He studied at the Pasadena Playhouse, and performed on radio. In 1946, he graduated from the Signal Corps OCS program at Ft. Monmouth, New Jersey, and followed with further studies there from 1951 until 1953. He was a contract actor with Warner Brothers in the early 1940s. He made his screen debut in the 1942 film *The Man Who Came to Dinner*. His other films include *Captains of the Clouds, Always in My Heart, Wings for the Eagle, The Fighting Vigilantes, The Checkered Coat, Daredevils of the Clouds, Quick on the Trigger, Smokey Mountain Melody,* and *By the Light of the Silvery Moon*. His many television acting credits include *December Bride, Border Patrol, Gunsmoke, Lock Up, Rawhide, Gibbsville, Perry Mason, Marcus Welby M.D., Mod Squad, The Sixth Sense, Man from Atlantis,* and *Hardcastle and McCormick*. Fans may remember him best as a popular recording artist. From 1952 until 1957, he was a vocalist on the hit television series *Your Hit Parade*. In 1957, he was a singer on the syndicated quiz show *The Hidden Treasure*. He retired in 1985. Russell Arms died on February 13, 2012 in Hamilton, Illinois at the age of 92. He was survived by his wife of 37 years.

Richard Crane played the role of Lt. Gene Plehn. At the conclusion of Season One, Don Barry's character, Lt Snedigar, was written off the show. Veteran actor Richard Crane was cast to play the role of "official" police officer, Lt. Gene Plehn. He appeared in that role for the duration of Season Two. Crane was born on June 6, 1918 in New Castle, Indiana. He first appeared on screen in 1940. During his three-decade long career in film, television, and on stage, he played more than 150 roles. Fans remember him from the cult classic films *Mysterious Island* (1951), and *The Alligator People* (1959), and for his starring roles in the 1954 series *Rocky Jones, Space Ranger* and the 1955 series *Commando Cody: Sky Marshall of the Universe*. On March 9, 1969, he died of a heart attack in Hollywood. He was survived by his wife of 25 years, B-actress Kay Morley (1920-2020). Richard Crane was 50 years old.

The Wedding Guest

Season 2, Episode 2

Broadcast on ABC-TV on September 25, 1961
Directed by Irving J. Moore
Teleplay by Philip Saltzman from a story by Vicki Shill
Producer: Joel Rogosin
Supervising Producer: Howie Horwitz
Executive Producer: William T. Orr

Cast:

Troy Donahue	Sandy Winfield II
Van Williams	Ken Madison
Diane McBain	Daphne Dutton
Kaye Elhardt	Millie Owens
Joan Marshall	Delia Long
Ed Kemmer	Matt Kerwin
Tony Travis	Alec Hartley
Walter Woolf King	Ralph Owens
Meg Randall	Meg Leach
Brendan Dillon	Bertram Leach
Ronald Long	Captain Boothbay

Credits:

Cinematography by Robert Hoffman
Film Editing by David Wages
Art Direction by John Ewing
Set Decoration by Hoyle Barrett
Makeup Supervisor: Gordon Bau
Hairstylist: Jean Burt Reilly
Assistant Director: Sergei Petschnikoff

Sound: Samuel F. Goode
Theme Music Composers: Mack David and Jerry Livingston
Music Editor: Joe Inge
60 minutes/Black and White
Production Company: Warner Bros. Television
Filmed at Warner Bros. Studios on Stages 20 and 24

Notes on the case:

Daphne travels to Nassau to attend the wedding of her friend, Millie Owens. She arrives safely, but her plans for a happy time are dashed when she's kidnapped. Sandy arrives to track her down, and discovers that Millie's prospective groom is a gigolo con-artist who marries women and swindles them out of their money.

Edward Kemmer played the role of Matt Kerwin. Kemmer was born on October 29, 1921 in Reading, Pennsylvania. During World War II, he served as a fighter pilot. He was shot down over France and spent 11 months in a POW camp. He made his acting debut in 1950 playing the role of Cmdr. Buzz Corry in the live television science-fiction series *Space Patrol*, and played the part until 1956. His many other television credits include *Alfred Hitchcock Presents*, *Men of Annapolis*, *Target*, *Bronco*, *Trackdown*, *Richard Diamond*,

Private Detective, Hawaiian Eye, Maverick, Cheyenne, The Rebel, Perry Mason, The Twilight Zone, The Fugitive, 77 Sunset Strip, The New Breed, and the 1983 mini-series, *Kennedy*. He had recurring roles on several daytime dramas including *The Clear Horizon, The Edge of Night, Somerset*, and *As the World Turns*. Kemmer made his big screen debut in the 1956 film *Behind the High Wall*. His other films include *The Hot Angel, Giant from the Unknown, Too Much Too Soon, Earth vs. the Spider, Hong Kong Confidential*, and *The Crowded Sky*. He retired in 1983. He was married to actress Elaine Edwards from 1946 until their divorce in 1966. Edward Kemmer suffered a stroke and died in New York City on November 9, 2004 at the age of 83. He was survived by his second wife of 35 years, actress Fran Sharon, and their three children.

Tony Travis played the role of Alec Hartley. Travis was born in New York City on March 4, 1926. His family moved to Los Angeles in 1936. He attended Beverly Hills High School, and joined the school band. After high school, he studied acting at the Pasadena Playhouse. Travis served in the U.S. Navy for two and a half years, then pursued a career in music. He recorded several songs on small labels, and performed locally at music events. Eventually, he enjoyed some success as a recording artist on the RCA label. He had a brief acting career, beginning in 1956. Travis appeared in the 1957 film *Jamboree!* and starred as Eddy Crane in the 1960 film *The Beatniks*. His several television credits include *Playwrights '56, The Veil, M Squad, Steven Canyon, Goodyear Theatre, Perry Mason, 77 Sunset Strip*, and the 1959 made-for-television movie, *The Fat Man: The Thirty-Two Friends of Gina Lardelli*. Travis was married and divorced twice, and had three children. At one time, he was engaged to actress Jane Wyman. He retired from acting in 1961, after his guest-starring roles on two episodes of *Surfside 6*. Tony Travis died in Pasadena on May 24, 2018 at the age of 92.

One for the Road

Season 2, Episode 3

Broadcast on ABC-TV on October 2, 1961
Directed by Robert Douglas
Written by Richard H. Landau
Producer: Joel Rogosin
Supervising Producer: Howie Horwitz
Executive Producer: William T. Orr

Cast:

Troy Donahue	Sandy Winfield II
Lee Patterson	Dave Thorne
Van Williams	Ken Madison
Diane McBain	Daphne Dutton
Margarita Sierra	Cha Cha O'Brien
James Best	Ernie Jordan
Elizabeth MacRae	Margia Knight
Richard Crane	Lt. Gene Plehn
Larry J. Blake	Square Deal Brady
Don Ross	Mort Packard
Benny Baker	Joe
Louie Elias	Truck Drive
Robert Glenn	Sgt. Woodley

Credits:

Cinematography by Robert Hoffman
Film Editing by Elbert K. Hollingsworth
Art Direction by Howard Campbell
Set Decoration by George James Hopkins
Makeup Supervisor: Gordon Bau

Hairstylist: Jean Burt Reilly
Assistant Director: Sergei Petschnikoff
Sound: Francis E. Stahl
Theme Music Composer: Mack David and Jerry Livingston
Music Editor: Norman Bennett
60 minutes/Black and White
Production Company: Warner Bros. Television
Filmed at Warner Bros. Studios on Stages 20 and 24

Notes from the case:

A mysterious drifter using the assumed name Ernie Jordan crosses paths with Daphne. She soon falls for the man. Sandy, Ken and Dave warn her to take her time because Jordan will not talk about his past, or his future plans. Their concerns fall on Daphne's deaf ears. But when they investigate the man, and his mysterious past, they discover he may be involved in a murder.

James Best played the role of Ernie Jordan. Best was born on July 26, 1926 in Powderly, Kentucky. His mother's brother, Ike Everly, was the father of the singing Everly Brothers. When his mother died, he was sent to an orphanage at three years old. He was later adopted by the Best family and moved with them to Corydon, Indiana. He served in the U.S. Army near the end of World War II, and was part of an army unit of performers that traveled through Europe entertaining Allied troops. Best made his screen debut as a contract player with Universal Studios in 1949. His many films include *Last of the Badmen, Cole Younger, Gunfighter, The Naked and the Dead, Ride Lonesome, The Killer Shrews, Black Gold, Shock Corridor, Three on a Couch, Firecreek, Sounder, Ode to Billy Joe, Nickelodeon,* and *Return of the Killer Shrews.* He guest-starred more than 250 times in many television series including *The Lone Ranger, Death Valley Days, The Andy Griffith Show, The Twilight Zone, Alfred Hitchcock Presents, Perry Mason, The Green Hornet, Mod Squad, The Dukes of Hazard,* and *In the Heat of the Night.* He retired from acting in 2013. In his later years, Best taught acting in Los Angeles, the University of Central Florida, and the University of Mississippi. He was a painter, and guitarist. Best was married and divorced twice. James Best died of pneumonia on April 6, 2015 in Hickory, North Carolina. He was 88 years old, and survived by his third wife of 29 years, actress Dorothy Collier, and three children.

Larry Blake played the role of Square-Deal Brady. Blake was born in Brooklyn on April 24, 1914. He began his performing career in vaudeville, and night clubs. He made his screen debut in the 1937 film *Secret Agent X-9.* During the next 40 years, he played small and supporting roles in more than 300 films and television shows. His early films include *The Road Back, Trouble at Midnight, The Jury's Secret, State Police, The Nurse from Brooklyn,*

Air Devils, Sinners in Paradise, and *The Boys from Syracuse.* Blake served in the U.S. Navy during World War II. During that time, he suffered severe alcoholism. When he was discharged, he was treated at a California military hospital. There he became involved with Alcoholics Anonymous. In 1947, he founded the first Motion Picture AA group, and worked as a counselor until his death. His post-war films include *Sunset Boulevard, High Noon, Seven Brides for Seven Brothers, The Werewolf, Earth vs. the Flying Saucers, Portrait of a Mobster, The Shaggy Dog, Herbie Rides Again,* and *Time After Time.* His many television credits include *The Pride of the Family, Topper, The Lone Ranger, Young Derringer, The Life and Legend of Wyatt Earp, The Twilight Zone, Lawman, Wagon Train, Gunsmoke, Perry Mason, The Beverly Hillbillies, Night Gallery, Here's Lucy,* and *Kung Fu.* Blake retired in 1979, and died of emphysema in Los Angeles on May 25, 1982. He was 68 years old, and survived by his wife of 46 years, actress Teresa Blake, and their son, actor/author/makeup artist Michael F. Blake.

Don Ross played the role of Mort Packard. Ross was born on April 4, 1920 in Missoula, Montana. He made his screen debut in 1949. His feature films include *Walk the Dark Street, Anatomy of a Murder, Psycho, The Absent-Minded Professor, What Ever Happened to Baby Jane?,* and *Airport.* Ross's many television credits include *Bat Masterson, Sea Hunt, Peter Gunn, Adventures in Paradise, The Outer Limits, I Spy, The Fugitive, Get Smart, Gunsmoke, The F.B.I., The Wild, Wild West, Dragnet, The Governor and J.J., Ironside, Adam 12, Cannon,* and the daytime drama *The Bold and the Beautiful.* Don Ross retired in 2002, and died in Los Angeles on January 15, 2011 at the age of 90.

Daphne, Girl Detective

Season 2, Episode 4

Broadcast on ABC-TV on October 9, 1961
Directed by Leslie Goodwins
Teleplay by Herman Groves from a story by J.P. Taylor
Producer: Jerry Davis
Supervising Producer: Howie Horwitz
Executive Producer: William T. Orr

Cast:

Van Williams	Ken Madison
Lee Patterson	Dave Thorne
Diane McBain	Daphne Dutton
Margarita Sierra	Cha Cha O'Brien
Bruce Dern	Johnny Page
Grace Raynor	Vanessa James
Lori Kaye	Sally Page
Richard Crane	Lt. Gene Plehn
John Considine	Director
Robert Glenn	Sgt. Woodley

Credits:

Cinematography by Louis Jennings
Film Editing by William W. Moore
Art Direction by Howard Campbell
Set Decoration by Hoyle Barrett
Makeup Supervisor: Gordon Bau
Hairstylist: Jean Burt Reilly
Assistant Director: John Francis Murphy
Sound: Everett A. Hughes

Theme Music Composer: Mack David and Jerry Livingston
Music Editor: Sam E. Levin
60 minutes/Black and White
Production Company: Warner Bros. Television
Filmed at Warner Bros. Studios on Stages 20 and 24
Previous footage of Margarita Sierra singing "Begin the Beguine" (first seen in Season 1, Episode 16 "Facts on Fire") was used in this episode.

Notes from the case:

Daphne invites her friend, Sally, and her actor husband, Johnny Page, to a party on the Surfside houseboat. The couple argue, and leave, going their separate ways. Then Sally disappears. Daphne's distrust of Johnny is reinforced when she sees him kissing another woman. When Sally is found dead, a suspected suicide, Daphne suspects Johnny had something to do with it. Lt. Plehn and the Surfside detectives seem to accept the explanation of Sally's death as a suicide, but Daphne refuses to accept that idea. She decides to take matters into her own hands, and begins an investigation of her own.

Bruce Dern played the role of Johnny Page. Dern was born in Chicago, Illinois on June 4, 1936. His paternal grandfather was a Governor of Utah and Secretary of War. His maternal grandfather was president of a chain of department stores. His granduncle was poet Archibald MacLeish. Dern was a track star in school, and attended the University of Pennsylvania. His first professional acting job was on stage in the Philadelphia premiere of *Waiting for Godot*. He appeared on Broadway in *The Shadow of a Gunman* (1958-59) and *Sweet Bird of Youth* (1959-60). Dern made his screen debut in the 1960 film *Wild River*. The better known of his more than 100 films include *Marnie, Hush...Hush Sweet Charlotte, Will Penny, Hang 'Em High, Support Your Local Sheriff, They Shoot Horses Don't They?, Drive, He Said, The*

Diane McBain

Cowboys, Silent Running, The King of Marvin Gardens, The Great Gatsby, Family Plot, Black Sunday, Tattoo, That Championship Season, Mulholland Falls, The Haunting, All the Pretty Horses, Django Unchained, Nebraska, Once Upon a Time in Hollywood, and *Death in Texas,* among others. His more memorable television appearances include *Naked City, Stoney Burke, The Outer Limits, The Fugitive, The Alfred Hitchcock Hour, The Big Valley, Space, Big Love, CSI: NY,* and *Mr. Mercedes.* Dern's many television films include *Uncle Tom's Cabin, The Court-Martial of Jackie Robinson, Mrs. Munck,* and *Pete's Christmas.* His acting has earned him two Academy Award nominations, three Golden Globe Award nominations, and one Emmy Award nomination. Dern has been married three times. His second wife was actress Diane Ladd. Oscar, Emmy, and five-time Golden Globe winning actress Laura Dern is their daughter.

John Considine played the role of Director. Considine was born on January 2, 1935 in Los Angeles. He is the son of producer John Considine Jr. His grandfathers were early theater and vaudeville impresarios, John Considine Sr. and Alexander Pantages. His younger brother is actor Tim Considine. He made his screen debut in the 1942 film *A Yank in Eton.* His other early films include *The Green Years* and *Reunion in France.* Considine's later films include *The Greatest Story Ever Told, Doctor Death: Seeker of Souls, Buffalo Bill and the Indians or Sitting Bull's History Lesson, Welcome to L.A., The Late Show, When Time Ran Out, Circle of Power, Endangered Species, Choose Me, Trouble in Mind, Fat Man and Little Boy, Coupe de Ville,* and *The Book of Stars.* He also appeared in the Robert Altman directed film *A Wedding,* which he wrote. Considine's other writing credits include episodes of *MacGyver, Legend, My Three Sons, Marcus Welby, M.D.,* and *Combat.* His many television appearances include *Adventures in Paradise, The Twilight Zone, The Outer Limits, Perry Mason, Marcus Welby, M.D., The Rockford Files, Mannix, Cannon, Taxi, Dynasty, Highway to Heaven, The Colbys, Murder She Wrote,* and *Boston Legal,* among others. He starred in the daytime dramas *Bright Promise* (1971-72), *The Young and the Restless* (1973-74), and *Another World* (1974-76) and (1986-88). John Considine retired in 2005.

The Empty House

Season 2, Episode 5

Broadcast on ABC-TV on October 16, 1961
Directed by Robert Douglas
Teleplay by Gloria Elmore and Herman Epstein from a story by Herman
  Epstein
Producer: Joel Rogosin
Supervising Producer: Howie Horwitz
Executive Producer: William T. Orr

Cast:

Van Williams	Ken Madison
Lee Patterson	Dave Thorne
Diane McBain	Daphne Dutton
Susan Seaforth (Hayes)	Shirley Battersea
Sherwood Price	Vince Lederer
Elaine Devry	Thelma Long
Richard Crane	Lt. Gene Plehn
Lauren Gilbert	Walter Battersea
Sheldon Allman	Les Cosgrove
Dan Stafford	Larry Baxter
Robert Glenn	Sgt. Woodley

Credits:

Cinematography by Ralph Woolsey
Film Editing by John Hall
Art Direction by Howard Campbell
Set Decoration by William L. Kuehl
Makeup Supervisor: Gordon Bau
Hairstylist: Jean Burt Reilly

Assistant Director: Richard L'Estrange
Sound: Samuel F. Goode
Theme Music Composers: Mack David and Jerry Livingston
Music Editor: John Allyn Jr.
60 minutes/Black and White
Production Company: Warner Bros. Television
Filmed at Warner Bros. Studios on Stages 20 and 24

Notes from the case:

Walter Battersea, a wealthy businessman, hires Ken to watch over his daughter, Shirley, who has fallen for a high society pretender named Vince. The man is an ex-con who owes a crime boss a large sum of money. Ken hits a proverbial brick wall, so he tries a different approach. He romances young Shirley Battersea. As they become involved, Vince is murdered. Shirley is accused of the murder, and Ken must find proof of her innocence.

Lauren Gilbert played the role of Walter Battersea. Gilbert was born in Kearney, Nebraska on April 8, 1911. He made his television debut in 1945. His many television appearances include *The Kate Smith Hour, Kraft Theater, Concerning Miss Marlowe, Thriller, Dennis the Menace, Dr. Kildare, Petticoat Junction, Hazel, Mr. Novak, Perry Mason, The Name of the Game, The F.B.I.,* and *Cannon.* He played a recurring role on the daytime drama *The Edge of Night* in 1956. Gilbert's films include *Girl of the Night, From the Terrace, The Unsinkable Molly Brown,* and *How to Murder Your Wife.* He retired in 1998. Lauren Gilbert died in Los Angeles on February 6, 1998 at the age of 86. He was survived by his wife of 58 years, actress Jackson Perkins, and their two children.

Susan Seaforth played the role of Shirley Battersea. Seaforth was born on July 11, 1943 in Oakland, California. She grew up in Hollywood. Her mother, actress Elizabeth Harrower (1918-2003), was also a screenwriter, and part of the writing teams for the daytime dramas *The Young and the Restless* and *Days of Our Lives.* Seaforth made her television debut in 1954. She has appeared in dozens of television programs including *Lassie, The Danny Thomas Show, The Life and Legend of Wyatt Earp, The Loretta Young Show, Bronco, Perry Mason, Cheyenne, Hawaiian Eye, Bonanza, Wagon Train, The Man from U.N.C.L.E., The Fugitive, My Three Sons, The Wild, Wild West, Matlock,* and *Sunset Beach.* She played the role of Carol West in *The Young Marrieds* (1964-66). Her feature films include *California, Dream Machine, Wrestling with God, Gunfight at Comanche Creek, Billie,* and *A Million Happy Nows.* She is best known for playing the roles of Joanna Manning on the daytime drama *The Young and the Restless* (1984-2010) and Julie Olson Williams on *Days of Our Lives* (1968-2021). She has been nominated for six Daytime

Emmy Awards, and won a Daytime Emmy Award for Lifetime Achievement in 2018. In 1974, Susan Seaforth married her co-star/leading man from *Days of Our Lives*, Bill Hayes.

Sherwood Price played the role of Vince Lederer. Price was born in Detroit, Michigan on April 4, 1928. He made his screen debut in the 1952 film *Scorching Fury*. His other films include *The Revolt of Mamie Stover, City of Fear, Blueprint for Robbery, The Man from Galveston*, and *Ice Station Zebra*. His many television appearances include *Highway Patrol, Perry Mason, Peter Gunn, Wagon Train, Cheyenne, Lawman, Hawaiian Eye, Rawhide, Bonanza, Ben Casey, Death Valley Days*, and *The Big Valley*. He was the production manager of the television series *The Protectors* (1972-74). Price was married to actress Kathie Browne from 1953 until their divorce in 1961. He was married to his second wife, actress Mary La Roche, from 1967 until her death in 1999. Sherwood Price died on January 13, 2020 at the age of 91.

Elaine Devry played the role of Thelma Lang. Devry was born on January 10, 1930 in Compton, California. She was a teenage model. In 1948, she married Dan Ducich, her high school sweetheart. The couple moved to Montana, but Ducich was convicted of felony robberies, and sentenced to probation. Devry divorced him in 1952, and moved back to Los Angeles. Ducich's gambling problems indebted him to organized crime. He was found dead in his Las Vegas Sahara Hotel room in June, 1954. Devry was discovered by a talent scout when she was working as a carhop at Dolores Drive-In on Wilshire Boulevard. She made her screen debut in 1953 in the film *A Slight Case of Larceny*. Her other films include *The Atomic Kid, China Doll, Man-Trap, The Last Time I Saw Archie, Diary of a Madman, A Guide to the Married Man, With Six You Get Eggroll, Once You Kiss a Stranger, The Cheyenne Social Club, Bless the Beasts and the Children, The Boy Who Cried Werewolf*, and *Herbie Rides Again*. Her many television appearances include *77 Sunset Strip, Hawaiian Eye, Ripcord, Burke's Law, Perry Mason, Family Affair, My Three Sons, Bourbon Street Beat, Laramie*, and *Marcus Welby, M.D.* Devry married actor Mickey Rooney in 1952. The couple had two children before divorcing in 1958. She married actor Will J. White in 1975. She was widowed in 1992. Devry retired in 1999.

Witness for the Defense

Season 2, Episode 6

Broadcast on ABC-TV on October 23, 1961
Directed by George Waggner
Written by Whitman Chambers
Producer: Joel Rogosin
Supervising Producer: Howie Horwitz
Executive Producer: William T. Orr

Cast:

Troy Donahue	Sandy Winfield II
Lee Patterson	Dave Thorne
Diane McBain	Daphne Dutton
Lon Chaney Jr.	Tank Grosch
Elisha Cook Jr.	Mike Pulaski
Kathleen Case	Betty Lawrence
Richard Crane	Lt. Glen Plehn
Bartlett Robinson	Sanford Winfield I
Marjorie Stapp	Goldie Locke
Charles Lane	Joseph Cooper
Phil Arthur	Phil Compton
Nelson Leigh	Judge

Credits:

Cinematography by Glen MacWilliams
Film Editing by Noel L. Scott
Art Direction by Howard Campbell
Set Decoration by William L. Kuehl
Makeup Supervisor: Gordon Bau
Hairstylist: Jean Burt Reilly

Assistant Director: Claude Binyon Jr.
Sound: Stanley Jones
Theme Music Composers: Mack David and Jerry Livingston
Music Editor: John Allyn Jr.
60 minutes/Black and White
Production Company: Warner Bros. Television
Filmed at Warner Bros. Studios on Stages 20 and 24

Notes on the case:

Sandy is attacked by a belligerent drunk. He slugs him away in self-defense, but a short time later, his attacker is found dead, and Sandy is the prime suspect. Dave investigates the crime, and to complicate matters, he discovers that the dead man is the ex-fiancé of the girl Sandy is dating.

Lon Chaney, Jr. played the role of Tanker Grosch. Chaney, the son of silent film icon Lon Chaney, was born in Oklahoma City, Oklahoma on February 10, 1906. His father discouraged him from show business, so he attended business school and worked in Los Angeles in the plumbing business. After Lon Chaney died of throat cancer on August 26, 1930, Chaney Jr. began to act in films. He made his screen debut in the 1931 film *The Galloping Ghost*. During his long career, Chaney appeared in more than 200 films and television shows. Some of his films include *The Three Musketeers, Ace Drummond, Charlie Chan on Broadway, Mr. Moto's Gamble*, and *Of Mice and Men*. He is best known for his portrayal of the Wolf Man, and for his many "horror" films including *Man-Made Monster, The Wolf Man, The Ghost of Frankenstein, The Mummy's Tomb, Frankenstein Meets the Wolf Man, Son of Dracula, Calling Dr. Death, Cobra Woman, The Mummy's Ghost, House of Frankenstein, The Mummy's Curse, House of Dracula*, and the classic comedy, *Abbott and Costello Meet Frankenstein*. His screen swan song was the 1971 film *Dracula vs. Frankenstein*. During the 1950s and 1960s, Chaney appeared in many television shows including *Have Gun – Will Travel, Wagon Train, The Red Skelton Show, Bat Masterson, Route 66, Lawman, The Rifleman, Pistols 'n' Petticoats*, and *The Monkees*. Lon Chaney Jr. died of heart failure at the age of 67 in San Clemente, California on July 12, 1973. He was survived by his wife of 36 years, and two sons.

Elisha Cook, Jr. played the role of Mike Pulaski. Cook was born on December 26, 1903 in San Francisco. He began his show business career in vaudeville and stock companies. He made his Broadway debut in 1926, and appeared in 15 Broadway productions through 1963, including *Ah, Wilderness!*, and *The Kingdom of God*. He first appeared on screen in the 1930 film *Her Unborn Child*. His more than 100 films include *Hellzapoppin', Phantom Lady, I the Jury, The Maltese Falcon, The Big Sleep, Born to Kill,*

Shane, The Killing, House on Haunted Hill, One-Eyed Jacks, Rosemary's Baby, Pat Garrett and Billy the Kid, and *Tom Horn.* He was a familiar face on television, and appeared in numerous shows including *Adventures of Superman, The Dennis Day Show, The Real McCoys, The Rebel, The Wild, Wild West, The Fugitive, Perry Mason, Star Trek, The A-Team, Alf, Batman,* and *The Bionic Woman.* Fans remember him for playing the role of "Ice Pick" Hofstetler on *Magnum P.I.* from 1981 until his retirement in 1988. Cook lived a solitary life, away from Hollywood. He maintained homes in Bishop, California, and nearby Lake Sabrina. Elisha Cook Jr. died of a stroke in Big Pine, California on May 18, 1995. He was 91 years old.

Cathy Case played the role of Betty Lawrence. Case was born in Pittsburgh on July 31, 1933. She made her television debut in 1951 as a guest-star in *The Adventures of Kit Carson.* She first appeared on screen in the 1952 movie *Junction City.* Her other films include *Human Desire, Running Wild,* and *The Second Greatest Sex.* Her numerous television appearances include *Father Knows Best, Sugarfoot, Bachelor Father, Death Valley Days, The Alaskans, Highway Patrol, Wagon Train,* and *The Deputy.* She retired from acting in 1961. Her final acting role was in this episode of *Surfside 6.* Case's personal life was more interesting than her professional life. She was engaged to marry singer Steve Rowland. The couple was friends with James Dean. Rowland was supposed to join Dean on his fateful last car trip in September, 1955. She was the on-again, off-again girlfriend of Elvis Presley. In May, 1959, she lost control of the speedboat she was piloting. Her injuries landed her in a Los Angeles hospital for two months. On February 5, 1967, the car she was driving collided head-on with the car of actor Dirk Rambo and his friend, Horace Hester. Rambo was killed in the resulting car fire. A Los Angeles judge dismissed felony drunk driving and manslaughter charges against her months later, ruling she was not responsible for the crash. Cathy Case died in North Hollywood on July 22, 1979 at the age of 45.

Laugh for the Lady

Season 2, Episode 7

Broadcast on ABC-TV on October 30, 1961
Directed by Leslie Goodwins
Written by Erna Lazarus
Producer: Jerry Davis
Producer: Howie Horwitz
Executive Producer: William T. Orr

Credits:

Lee Patterson	Dave Thorne
Van Williams	Ken Madison
Margarita Sierra	Cha Cha O'Brien
Barbara Stuart	Mitzi McCoy
Mark Roberts	Ted Walters
Julie Adams	Julie Owens
Claire Carleton	Katie Williams
Richard Crane	Lt. Gene Plehn
Benny Baker	Joe Gluck
Barry Russo	Vincent Barker
Art Lewis	Emery Lewis

Credits:

Cinematography by Louis Jennings
Film Editing by James W. Graham
Art Direction by Howard Campbell
Set Decoration by John P. Austin
Makeup Supervisor: Gordon Bau
Hairstylist: Jean Burt Reilly
Assistant Director: Fred Scheld

Sound: Stanley Jones
Theme Music Composer: Mack David and Jerry Livingston
Music Editor: Lou Gordon
60 minutes/Black and White
Production Company: Warner Bros. Television
Filmed at Warner Bros. Studios on Stages 20 and 24
Margarita Sierra sang "South American Way" in this episode.

Notes on the case:

Julie, Dave's old girlfriend, is brassy comic Mitzi McCoy's secretary. Mitzi
has come to Miami for nightclub work. Despite the tyrannical behavior of
the comic, Julie stays with her because she is having an affair with the comic's
husband, Ted. When Mitzi learns about the affair, Julie finds herself in danger. The revelation of the affair leads to a suicide attempt, and Dave has to
determine whether the failed suicide was actually an attempted murder.

Barbara Stuart played the role of Mitzi McCoy. Stuart was born on
January 3, 1930 in Paris, Illinois. She studied at the Schuster-Martin School
of Drama, and in New York with Uta Hagen and Stella Adler. She worked as
a model, and performed in the national tour of *Lunatics and Lovers*. She also
worked as a showgirl in Las Vegas. She made her television debut in 1954 and
guest-starred in dozens of television shows including *The George Burns Show*,
Perry Mason, *The Cara Williams Show*, *The Andy Griffith Show*, *The Twilight
Zone*, *Batman*, *Three's Company*, *The Untouchables*, and *Huff*. Fans remem-
ber her for playing the role of Bunny, Sgt. Carter's girlfriend on *Gomer Pyle,
U.S.M.C.* Her feature films include *One Step Beyond*, *Airplane!*, *Marines Let's
Go*, *Hellfighters*, *Bachelor Party*, and *Pterodactyl Woman from Beverly Hills*.
She often worked in summer stock and regional theater productions. Stuart
was married to actor Dick Gautier from 1967 until their divorce in 1979.
Barbara Stuart died of muscular disease at a nursing home in St. George,
Utah on May 15, 2011 at the age of 81.

Mark Roberts played the role of Ted Walters. Roberts was born in
Denver, Colorado on June 9, 1921. After college, Roberts screen-tested at
Columbia Pictures and won a long-term contract. He made his screen debut
in the 1938 film *Brother Rat*. He appeared in several films including *Those
Were the Days!* and *Remember Pearl Harbor*, and the Columbia serial *Black
Arrow*, before taking time to serve in the U.S. Army during World War II.
When he resumed his career, and until his retirement in 2002, he appeared
in more than 100 films including *Ten Cents a Dance*, *Life with Blondie*,
The Bandit of Sherwood Forest, *Gilda*, *It's a Wonderful Life*, *Exposed*, *The
Pride of St. Louis*, *Ma and Pa Kettle on Vacation*, *The Buster Keaton Story*,
Onionhead, *The Girl Who Knew Too Much*, and *Jacqueline Susann's Once Is*

Not Enough. Roberts' many television credits include *The Front Page, The Brothers Brannagan, Studio One, Cheyenne, Perry Mason, The Millionaire, Ironside, The Outer Limits, M Squad,* and *77 Sunset Strip*. He starred in the 1951 Broadway production of *Stalag 17*. Mark Roberts died on January 5, 2006 in Los Angeles at the age of 84. He was survived by his three children.

Claire Carleton played the role of Katie Williams. Carleton was born in New York City on September 28, 1913. She began her acting career on stage, and first appeared on Broadway in 1932 in *Blue Monday*. She starred in numerous Broadway shows through 1950 including *I Must Love Someone,* and *Clutterbuck*. Carleton made her screen debut in the 1933 short film *Seasoned Greetings*. She played minor roles in films until her first featured role in the 1940 movie *Millionaire Playboy*. Her many films include *On the Town, If You Knew Susie, Death of a Salesman, Girl from Havana, Gildersleeve on Broadway, The Great Train Robbery, A Night of Adventure, The Missing Lady, It's a Great Feeling, Poppa Knows Worst, Rookies in Burma, A Double Life, The Barkleys of Broadway, Born Yesterday,* and *Witness to Murder*. Carleton worked frequently in television, and appeared on numerous shows including *The Mickey Rooney Show, The Abbott and Costello Show, Hopalong Cassidy, Cimarron City, Perry Mason, Make Room for Daddy, Alfred Hitchcock Presents, Hazel, Wagon Train, The Munsters,* and *The Virginian*. She retired in 1969. Claire Carleton died from cancer on December 11, 1979 in Northridge, California at the age of 66.

The Affairs at Hotel Delight

Season 2, Episode 8

Broadcast on ABC-TV on November 6, 1961
Directed by Robert Douglas
Written by Montgomery Pittman
Producer: Joel Rogosin
Supervising Producer: Howie Horwitz
Executive Producer: William T. Orr

Cast:

Van Williams	Ken Madison
Leslie Parrish	Lavender Caviness
Jock Gaynor	Don Valentinas
Med Flory	Boffo
William Windom	Shrewdie
Dub Taylor	Tobin
Jack Mather	Sheriff Fitch
John Durren	Joel
Rush Williams	Undersheriff

Credits:

Cinematography by Robert Hoffman
Film Editing by David Wages
Art Direction by Howard Campbell
Set Decoration by William L. Kuehl
Makeup Supervisor: Gordon Bau
Hairstylist: Jean Burt Reilly
Assistant Director: John Francis Murphy
Sound: Ralph Butler
Theme Music Composer: Mack David and Jerry Livingston

Music Editor: Donald Harris
60 minutes/Black and White
Production Company: Warner Bros. Television
Filmed at Warner Bros. Studios on Stages 20 and 24

Notes on the case:

After a brief stay, Ken is about to check out of a tiny, rural hotel, when he stumbles on the body of Lavender Caviness, unconscious in the hotel hallway. When he revives her, she explains that she was on her way to pay a $50,000 ransom for her kidnapped boyfriend. Reluctantly, Ken stays in town and tries to help her, but his investigation reveals the missing boyfriend may be involved in a fake kidnapping in order to extort money from his girlfriend Lavender. To complicate matters, Ken has to deal with an uncooperative, grouchy hotel manager, a trio of bumbling kidnappers, and Lavender's uncontrollable fainting spells. In a rare turn, this episode was played for laughs.

Jock Gaynor played the role of Don Valentinas. Gaynor was born in New York City on September 14, 1929. He was a pitcher in a minor league baseball team, and began his show business career as a set designer and decorator. He made his television debut in 1960, and appeared on numerous television shows including *Bourbon Street Beat*, *Outlaws*, *Laramie*, *Hawaiian Eye*, *The Doctors*, *Batman*, *The F.B.I.*, *Voyage to the Bottom of the Sea*, *Cannon*, *Mannix*, and *Night Rider*. He produced the television series, *Buck Rogers in the 25ᵗʰ Century* (1979-80), and wrote and starred in the film, *The Deathhead Virgin*, in 1974. He retired in 1986. Jock Gaynor died in Los Angeles on April 2, 1998 at the age of 69. He was survived by his wife of 40 years, actress Grace Gaynor, and one child.

Med Flory played the role of Boffo. Flory was born in Logansport, Indiana on August 27, 1926. He served in the U.S. Army Air Force during World War II, and later earned a degree in philosophy from Indiana University. Flory was a jazz saxophonist, and played with Claude Thornhill, Woody Herman, Terry Gibbs, and Art Pepper. He made his television debut in 1956, playing with the Ray Anthony Orchestra on *The Ray Anthony Show* (1956-57). He acted in dozens of television shows including *Rifleman*, *Wagon Train*, *Perry Mason*, *Ripcord*, *Lawman*, *Route 66*, *F Troop*, *The Monroes*, *The Virginian*, *Daniel Boone*, *Lassie*, *Starsky and Hutch*, and *How the West Was Won*. His numerous films include *The Nutty Professor*, *Mike and the Mermaid*, *The Night of the Grizzly*, *The Trouble with Girls*, *Home for the Holidays*, *The Teacher*, *Let's Do It Again*, *Hustle*, and *The Gumball Rally*. In 1972, he cofounded the Grammy Award-winning jazz group, Supersax. Med Flory died in Hollywood of heart failure on March 12, 2014, at the age of 87. He was predeceased by his wife of 48 years in 2000. He was survived by the couple's two children.

William Windom played the role of Shrewdie. Windom was born in Manhattan on September 28, 1923. He attended Williams College before he enlisted in the U.S. Army during World War II. He made his Broadway debut in 1946 in *King Henry VIII*. During the following fourteen years, he starred in thirteen Broadway shows including *What Every Woman Knows* (1946-47), *Alice in Wonderland* (1947), and *Fallen Angels* (1956). He first appeared on television in 1949. Windom guest-starred in more than 100 television programs including *Star Trek, The Twilight Zone, Columbo, Gunsmoke, Mission: Impossible, Magnum, P.I., Newhart, L.A. Law, The Farmer's Daughter, The Donna Reed Show, Ally McBeal*, and *The District* among others. He earned an Emmy Award for playing the role of cartoonist John Monroe in the comedy *My World and Welcome to It* (1969-70). Fans remember him for his recurring role of Dr. Seth Hazlitt in *Murder She Wrote* (1984-96). Windom's feature films include *To Kill a Mockingbird, The Detective, Escape from the Planet of the Apes, Planes Trains and Automobiles, She's Having a Baby, Uncle Buck, True Crime*, and *Sommersby*. He worked frequently in regional theater, summer stock, dinner theater, and touring productions. He retired in 2006, after playing roles in more than 150 films. William Windom died at his home in Woodacre, California from congestive heart failure on August 16, 2012. He was 88 years old, and survived by his fifth wife of 36 years, and four children.

Dub Taylor played the role of Tobin. Taylor was born in Richmond, Virginia on February 26, 1907. He was a vaudeville performer, and made his screen debut in the 1938 film *You Can't Take It with You*. He had a small role in the 1939 classic *Mr. Smith Goes to Washington*. That same year, he created the character "Cannonball" in the film *The Taming of the West* and played that same role in dozens of films for the following ten years. His more than 100 film appearances include *A Star is Born, Them!, Tonka, No Time for Sergeants, Major Dundee, The Wild Bunch, The Cincinnati Kid, Sweet Bird of Youth, Parrish, Black Gold, Auntie Mame, Junior Bonner, The Getaway, Pat Garrett and Billy the Kid, Bonnie and Clyde, Thunderbolt and Lightfoot, The Undefeated, Support Your Local Gunfighter*, and *Back to the Future Part III*. Taylor was a recognizable presence in many television shows including *The Range Rider, Cheyenne, Death Valley Days, Perry Mason, The Lloyd Bridges Show, The Andy Griffith Show, Hazel, I Love Lucy, Laredo, The High Chaparral, The Cosby Show, Little House on the Prairie, Twilight Zone, The Wild, Wild West, Emergency!*, and *Designing Women*. In his later years, he was a television commercial actor and voice-over artist. Dub Taylor died after suffering a heart attack in Los Angeles on October 3, 1994 at the age of 87. He was predeceased by his wife of 57 years in 1987. He was survived by his daughter and his son, actor Buck Taylor.

Jonathan Wembley Is Missing

Season 2, Episode 9

Broadcast on ABC-TV on November 13, 1961
Directed by Irving J. Moore
Teleplay by William Bruckner from a story by William P. D'Angelo and Joel Rogosin
Producer: Jerry Davis
Supervising Producer: Howie Horwitz
Executive Producer: William T. Orr

Cast:

Troy Donahue	Sandy Winfield II
Van Williams	Ken Madison
Margarita Sierra	Cha Cha O'Brien
Elliot Reid	Rusty Bell
Joan O'Brien	Linda Farris
Donna Douglas	Amy Farris
Richard Crane	Lt. Gene Plehn
Benny Baker	Harry
Baynes Barron	Dick Hildebrand
Carole Kent	Martha McQuillian
Ray Montgomery	Sam Bennion
Paul Bryar	Chuck Landon

Credits:

Cinematography by Edwin B. DuPar
Film Editing by Robert L. Wolfe
Art Direction by Howard Campbell
Set Decoration by William L. Kuehl
Makeup Supervisor: Gordon Bau

Hairstylist: Jean Burt Reilly
Assistant Director: James T. Vaughn
Sound: Ross Owen
Theme Music Composer: Mack David and Jerry Livingston
Music Editor: Ted Sebern
60 minutes/Black and White
Production Company: Warner Bros. Television
Filmed at Warner Bros. Studios on Stages 20 and 24
Previous footage of Margarita Sierra singing "South American Way" (first seen in Season 2, Episode 7 "Laugh for the Lady") was used in this episode.

Notes on the case:

Amy Farris, a fetching young blonde, talks Sandy into helping ventriloquist Rusty Bell secure a booking at the Boom Boom Room at the Fontainebleau Hotel. When his dummy, Johnathan Wembley, disappears, thereby ending his act, Sandy is persuaded to find the missing dummy.

Donna Douglas.

Donna Douglas played the role of Amy Farris. Douglas was born on September 26, 1932 in Pride, Louisiana. Upon graduating high school, she was named Miss Baton Rouge, and Miss New Orleans in 1957. She moved to New York to pursue modeling. She made her television debut in 1951, and guest-starred on numerous shows including *Bachelor Father, The Detectives, Route 66, Thriller, Checkmate, Dr. Kildare, Mister Ed, The Twilight Zone, The Phil Silvers Show, The Adventures of Ozzie and Harriet, Night Gallery, McMillan and Wife, Love American Style,* and *The Steve Allen Show.* Her feature films include *Career, Li'l Abner, Bells are Ringing, Strangers When We Meet, Lover Come Back,* and *Frankie and Johnny* opposite Elvis Presley. Audiences remember her best for playing the role of Elly May Clampett on *The Beverly Hillbillies* (1962-71). She reprised the role for the 1981 television movie, *The Return of the Beverly Hillbillies.* When *The Beverly Hillbillies* finished production, Douglas performed as a gospel singer and recorded several albums, worked as a motivational speaker, wrote religious-themed children's books, and sold real estate. She was married and divorced twice. Her second husband, Robert M. Leeds, was the director of *The Beverly Hillbillies.* Donna Douglas died in Zachary, Louisiana of pancreatic cancer on January 1, 2015. She was 82 years old.

Elliott Reid played the role of Rusty Bell. Reid was born on January 16, 1920 in Manhattan. He attended the Professional Children's School, and made his acting debut in 1935 on the radio show *The March of Time.* He worked steadily on the radio in such programs as *Billy and Betty, Against the Storm, The United States Steel Hour, The Mercury Theatre on the Air, Theatre Guild on the Air, The Adventures of Philip Marlowe, Suspense,* and *CBS Radio Mystery Theater.* Reid's Broadway credits include *Julius Caesar* (1937-38), *The Shoemaker's Holiday* (1938), *Macbeth* (1948), *Two Blind Mice* (1949), *The Live Wire* (1950), *Two on the Aisle* (1951-52), and *From A to Z* (1960). He was an original member of The Actors Studio. He worked in regional theater and summer stock productions, and national tours. Reid made his screen debut in the 1940 movie *The Ramparts We Watch.* His other films include *The Story of Dr. Wassell, A Double Life, Gentlemen Prefer Blondes, Inherit the Wind, The Absent-Minded Professor, Son of Flubber, The Thrill of It All, It's a Mad, Mad, Mad, Mad World, The Wheeler Dealers, Move Over Darling, Follow Me Boys!, Blackbeard's Ghost,* and *Heaven Can Wait.* His many television appearances include *That Was the Week That Was, Miss Winslow and Son, Murder She Wrote, The Odd Couple, I Love Lucy, It's Always Jan, Barney Miller, Small Wonder, Perry Mason, The Munsters, Seinfeld,* and *Maybe This Time,* among others. He officially retired in 1995. Elliot Reid died on June 21, 2013 in Studio City, California of heart failure. He was 93 years old. Elliot Reid was gay.

Joan O'Brien played the role of Linda Farris. O'Brien was born in Cambridge, Massachusetts on February 14, 1936. Her family moved to California when she was a child and enrolled her in dance classes. Country music star Cliffie Stone hired her as a regular performer to sing and dance on his television variety show *Hometown Jamboree* in 1949. In 1954, she became a regular cast member on *The Bob Crosby Show* and stayed until 1958. She also sang on *The Liberace Show* and *Shower of Stars*. In the late 1950s, she turned to acting and guest-starred in dozens of television shows including *Riverboat, Bat Masterson, Wagon Train, Bronco, The Alaskans, Perry Mason, Bachelor Father, Adventures in Paradise, The Dick Van Dyke Show, The Man from U.N.C.L.E., The Virginian,* and *The Lieutenant.* Her feature films include *Handle with Care, Operation Petticoat, The Alamo, The Comancheros, We Joined the Navy, It Happened at the World's Fair,* and *Get Yourself* a *College Girl.* After only a decade, she retired from acting on screen to raise her two children. She later played the role of Ophelia in Robert Vaughn's production of *Hamlet* at the Pasadena Playhouse. In 1968, she sang with the Harry James band. Joan O'Brien has been married and divorced four times. She was widowed when her fifth husband of 25 years died in 2004.

The Old School Tie

Season 2, Episode 10

Broadcast on ABC-TV on November 20, 1961
Directed by Michael O'Herlihy
Written by Gloria Elmore
Producer: Joel Rogosin
Supervising Producer: Howie Horwitz
Executive Producer: William T. Orr

<u>Cast:</u>

Lee Patterson	Dave Thorne
Van Williams	Ken Madison
Diane McBain	Daphne Dutton
Gloria Talbott	Janice Walters
Margaret Lindsay	Millie Brenner
John Howard	Eric Brenner
Adam Williams	Mel Walters
Frances Helm	Helen Todd
Pamela Curran	Mari Winslow
Richard Crane	Lt. Gene Plehn
Benny Baker	Joe
Margarita Sierra	Cha Cha O'Brien

<u>Credits:</u>

Cinematography by Ralph Woolsey
Film Editing by John Joyce
Art Direction by Howard Campbell
Set Direction by Ralph S. Hurst
Makeup Supervisor: Gordon Bau
Hairstylist: Jean Burt Reilly

Assistant Director: Richard L'Estrange
Sound: Robert B. Lee
Theme Music Composers: Mack David and Jerry Livingston
Music Editor: Robert Phillips
60 minutes/Black and White
Production Company: Warner Bros. Television
Filmed at Warner Bros. Studios on Stages 20 and 24
Margarita Sierra sang "Baby Face" in this episode.

Notes on the case:

Dave's alma mater is holding its Class of 1951 reunion at the Fontainebleau Hotel. But, not unlike many class reunions, the event is fraught with more awkwardness and drama than fun, and opens up old resentments and wounds. When former classmate Mari Winslow is murdered, Mel Walters, a former college football star, becomes the prime suspect.

Pamela Curran played the role of Mari Winslow. Curran was born in New York City on February 6, 1930. She worked as a model until making her screen debut in 1957 in an uncredited role in *Desk Set*. Her other films include *The Blob*, *Who Was That Lady?*, *The Thrill of It All*, *Under the Yum Yum Tree*, *Girl Happy*, *Mutiny in Outer Space*, *The Loved One*, and *The Chase*. Her television credits include *Checkmate*, *The Detectives*, *Bachelor Father*, *Perry Mason*, *Thriller*, *Alfred Hitchcock Presents*, *Laramie*, *The Man from U.N.C.L.E.*, and *Love American Style*. Fans remember her for playing the role of Vanessa Vane on *The Green Hornet*. Curran has been married and divorced twice, and retired from acting in 1971. For many years she has been involved with rescue dogs.

Adam Williams played the role of Mel Walters. Williams was born on November 26, 1922 in New York City. He served in the U.S. Navy during World War II, and earned the coveted Navy Cross for his service. Williams made his screen debut in the 1951 movie *Flying Leathernecks*. His other films include *Without Warning!*, *Vice Squad*, *The Big Heat*, *The Proud and the Profane*, *The Garment Jungle*, *The Lonely Man*, *The Space Children*, *Darby's Rangers*, *North by Northwest*, *The New Interns*, *Helter Skelter*, and *This Is a Hijack*. Williams made a career of playing the "bad guy." His dozens of television credits include *Perry Mason*, *The Millionaire*, *Hawaiian Eye*, *Outlaws*, *The Roaring 20's*, *The Twilight Zone*, *The Detectives*, *Honey West*, *Cheyenne*, *The Rifleman*, *Rawhide*, *Voyage to the Bottom of the Sea*, and *Room 222*. Williams retired in 1978. He was an accomplished pilot and worked as an FAA examiner. He was married to actress Marilee Phelps from 1949 until 1971. The couple had three children. Adam Williams died of lymphoma in Los Angeles on December 4, 2006 at the age of 84. He was survived by his third wife, and six children.

Gloria Talbott played the role of Janice Walters. Talbott was born on February 7, 1931 in Glendale, California. She made her screen debut in the

1937 movie *Maytime*. Her films include *Sweet and Low-Down, We're No Angels, All That Heaven Allows, Lucy Gallant, A Tree Grows in Brooklyn, The Kettles on Old MacDonald's Farm, Crashout*, and *Strange Intruder*. She is perhaps best known for becoming a "scream queen" in films beginning in the 1950s, and starring in *The Cyclops, The Daughter of Dr. Jekyll, I Married a Monster from Outer Space*, and *The Leech Woman*. Talbott's numerous television credits include *Conflict, Sugarfoot, Adventures of Superman, The Cisco Kid, Sheriff of Chochise, Gunsmoke, Riverboat, The Roaring 20's, The Rebel, Bat Masterson, Rawhide, Perry Mason, Gunsmoke*, and *My Three Sons*. Talbott was married and divorced three times. She died on September 19, 2000 of kidney failure in Glendale, California. Gloria Talbott was 69 years old, and survived by her fourth husband of 30 years, and two children.

Margaret Lindsay played the role of Millie Brenner. Lindsay was born in Dubuque, Iowa on September 19, 1910. She studied at the American Academy of Dramatic Arts in New York, and made her stage debut in England. In London, she appeared in *Escape, Death Takes a Holiday*, and *The Romantic Age*. While living and working in England, she adopted a convincing British accent. She made her Hollywood screen debut in the 1932 film *Okay, America!* She appeared in a few films including *Once in a Lifetime*, and *Cavalcade*, before signing a contract with Warner Brothers. Lindsay's better known films include *Christopher Strong, Baby Face, Frisco Kid, Devil Dogs of the Air, "G" Men, Lady Killer, The Hard Boiled Canary, Fog Over Frisco, Dangerous, Bordertown, Jezebel, The Law in Her Hands, The House of Seven Gables, The Vigilantes Return, The Spoilers, Scarlet Street*, and *Tammy and the Doctor*. She played the role of Nikki Porter in *Ellery Queen, Master Detective* (1940), *Ellery Queen's Penthouse Mystery* (1941), *Ellery Queen and the Perfect Crime* (1941), *Ellery Queen and the Murder Ring* (1941), *A Close Call for Ellery Queen* (1942), *A Desperate Chance for Ellery Queen* (1942), and *Enemy Agents Meet Ellery Queen* (1942). Her television work included *The Ford Theatre Hour, Studio 57, Lux Video Theatre, Mike Hammer, Buckskin*, and *Pistol's 'n' Petticoats*. She retired in 1974. Lindsay was gay. Her life partner was actress Mary McCarty. McCarty died of an undetermined cause in the couple's West Los Angeles home on April 3, 1980. Margaret Lindsay died of emphysema on May 9, 1981 in Los Angeles. She was 70 years old.

John Howard played the role of Eric Brenner. Howard was born in Cleveland, Ohio on April 14, 1913. He became interested in performing while attending college, and took part in university productions. A talent scout spotted him in a production of *John Brown's Body*, and arranged for a screen test. Howard signed a contract with Paramount Pictures in 1934. His dozens of feature films include *Annapolis Farewell, Millions in the Air, Soak the Rich, Easy to Take, Let Them Live*, and *Mountain Music*. At Paramount, he starred as Captain Hugh C. "Bulldog" Drummond in *Bulldog Drummond Comes Back*

(1937), *Bulldog Drummond's Revenge* (1937), *Bulldog Drummond in Africa* (1938), *Arrest Bulldog Drummond* (1938), *Bulldog Drummond's Secret Police* (1939), and *Bulldog Drummond's Bride* (1939). For many fans, his most memorable films are *Lost Horizon, The Philadelphia Story,* and *Father Takes a Wife.* Howard interrupted his career to serve in the U.S. Navy as a lieutenant during World War II. He earned the Navy Cross, and the French Croix de Guerre. His film career never recovered from his years away from the screen. His later films include *Love from a Stranger, I, Jane Doe, The Fighting Kentuckian, The High and the Mighty,* and *Buck and the Preacher.* In 1953, he appeared in the Broadway production, *Hazel Flagg.* His numerous television credits include *Adventures of the Sea Hawk, Lawman, Wagon Train, Outlaws, 77 Sunset Strip, Hawaiian Eye, Perry Mason, Days of Our Lives, The Lucy Show, My Three Sons, Family Affair, To Rome with Love,* and *Little House on the Prairie.* He retired in 1979. In his later years, he taught English at Highland Hall Waldorf School. John Howard died of heart failure in Santa Rosa, California on February 19, 1995 at the age of 81. He was survived by his wife of 41 years, actress/dancer Eva Ralf, and their four children, including son actor/writer/director Dale Richard Howard. His grandson is actor Noel John Howard.

Frances Helm played the role of Helen Todd. Helm was born on October 14, 1923 in Panama City, Florida. She attended the College of William and Mary. Helm made her screen debut in the 1947 film *The Story of Mr. Hobbs.* Her other films include *Revolt at Fort Laramie, A Little Sex, Shakedown, Electric Moon, The Ugly American,* and *Love and Betrayal: The Mia Farrow Story.* Her numerous television appearances include *Kraft Theatre, Fireside Theatre, Mike Hammer, The Millionaire, Perry Mason, The Deputy, Gunsmoke, Hazel, Route 66, Kojak,* and the daytime dramas *The Edge of Night, The Secret Storm,* and *Dark Shadows.* She retired in 1995. Her first husband was actor Brian Keith. They married in 1948, and divorced in 1954. Frances Helm died on December 30, 2006 in Manhattan at the age of 83. She was survived by her second husband of 43 years, Walter Christopher Wallace, former Assistant Secretary of Labor during the Eisenhower administration, and their one child.

Diane and Van.

A Matter of Seconds

Season 2, Episode 11

Broadcast on ABC-TV on November 27, 1961
Directed by George Waggner
Teleplay by Stephen Lord from a story by Larry Cohen
Producer: Tom McKnight
Supervising Producer: Howie Horwitz
Executive Producer: William T. Orr

Cast:

Van Williams	Ken Madison
Troy Donahue	Sandy Winfield II
Lee Patterson	Dave Thorne
Diane McBain	Daphne Dutton
Margarita Sierra	Cha Cha O'Brien
Steve Brodie	Sergeant Carter
Ann McCrae	Maggie
Richard Crane	Lt. Gene Plehn
Alan Baxter	Swenson
William Schallert	Marty Kemp
Abigail Shelton	Gita
Jack Shea	Officer Toomey
Claude Akins	Harry Lodge
Murray Alper	1st Bartender at Terrace Club
Vincent Barbi	Hood
Sol Gorss	Hood

Credits:

Cinematography by Harold E. Stine
Film Editing by Milt Kleinberg

Art Direction by Howard Campbell
Set Decoration by William L. Kuehl
Makeup Supervisor: Gordon Bau
Hairstylist: Jean Burt Reilly
Assistant Director: Fred Scheld
Sound: Ross Owen
Stunts: Fred Carson
Theme Music Composers: Mack David and Jerry Livingston
Music Editor: Charles Paley
60 minutes/Black and White
Production Company: Warner Bros. Television
Filmed at Warner Bros. Studios on Stages 20 and 24
Previous footage of Margarita Sierra singing "You Must Have Been a Beautiful Baby" (first seen in Season 2, Episode 1 "Count Seven!") was used in this episode.

Notes on the case:

Professional boxer Harry Lodge, plagued with bad luck, is found at the scene of his girlfriend's murder by Sergeant Carter. In desperation, Lodge overpowers Carter and holds him hostage while he tries to engage the Surfside detectives to prove his innocence.

Steve Brodie played the role of Sgt. Carter. Brodie was born on November 21, 1919 in El Dorado, Kansas. After a series of odd jobs, Brodie became interested in acting and worked in summer stock before moving to Los Angeles in 1943. A talent scout discovered him while he was starring in the play *Money Girls* in Hollywood. He made his film debut in 1944. Not exactly the classic leading man type, Brodie became one of Hollywood's most reliable B-movie "heavies." His dozens of films include *A Walk in the Sun*, *The Falcon's Adventure*, *Desperate*, *Crossfire*, *Out of the Past*, *Armored Car Robbery*, *Kiss Tomorrow Goodbye*, *Joe Palooka in Triple Cross*, *The Story of Will Rogers*, *The Beast from 20,000 Fathoms*, *Donovan's Brain*, *The Caine Mutiny*, *Blue Hawaii*, *Roustabout*, *The Giant Spider Invasion*, and *Frankenstein Island*, among many others. From 1953 until 1957, he played the title role in the radio series, *Mike Malloy, Private Eye*. Brodie starred in the national touring company of *The Caine Mutiny Court Martial* in the 1950s. His decades-long career in television included appearances on *The Lone Ranger*, *Alfred Hitchcock Presents*, *Wanted: Dead or Alive*, *Thriller*, *Perry Mason*, *Daktari*, *Police Woman*, *Lassie*, *CHiPs*, *Sugarfoot*, and *The Alaskans*. He had recurring roles on *The Life and Legend of Wyatt Earp* (1960-61) and *Everglades* (1961-62). Steve Brodie died of cancer in West Hills, California on January 9, 1992 at the age of 72. He was survived by his third wife of 19 years, two children, including his son, actor Kevin Brodie, and his granddaughter, actress Farren Monet.

Ann McCrea played the role of Maggie. McCrae was born in Dubois, Pennsylvania on February 25, 1931. She made her film debut in 1952. She appeared as a chorus girl in her earliest films including *Singin' in the Rain*, *The Band Wagon*, and *Artists and Models*. She also appeared in *Will Success Spoil Rock Hunter?*, *Girls! Girls! Girls!*, *The War Wagon*, and *Welcome to Hard Times*. Her many television appearances include *Cheyenne*, *Perry Mason*, *Rescue 8*, *Rawhide*, *Death Valley Days*, *Wendy and Me*, *One Step Beyond*, and *My Three Sons*. She is perhaps best known for playing the role of Midge Kelsey on *The Donna Reed Show* (1963-66). Ann McCrea retired in 1971.

Alan Baxter played the role of Swenson. Baxter was born on November 19, 1908 in East Cleveland, Ohio. He was a classmate of Elia Kazan at Williams College, and studied in the 47 Drama Workshop at Yale University. He was later a member of the Group Theater in New York City, and began working on Broadway in 1932. He made his film debut in 1935, and his dozens of feature films include *Abe Lincoln in Illinois*, *Shadow of a Doubt*, *Saboteur*, *The Human Comedy*, *Judgment at Nuremberg*, and *This Property is Condemned*, among many others. Baxter served in the U. S. Army Air Corp during World War II. He was a familiar face on television as well, often playing the "bad guy," and guest-starred in more than 50 programs until his retirement in 1971. Alan Baxter died of cancer at the Motion Picture Country Home in Woodland Hills on May 7, 1976 at the age of 67. He was survived by his wife of 20 years, talent agent Christy Palmer.

William Schallert played the role of Marty Kemp. Schallert was born in Los Angeles on July 6, 1922. He is the son of *Los Angeles Times* drama critic Edwin Schallert, and movie magazine writer Elza Schallert. He studied acting at UCLA, and served in the Army Air Corps during World War II. In 1946, he founded the Circle Theater with Sydney Chaplin, and two years later was directed by Charlie Chaplin in the play *Rain*. He made his film debut in 1947, and until his retirement in 2014, he amassed more than 400 film and television credits. His films include *The High and the Mighty*, *Written on the Wind*, *The Incredible Shrinking Man*, *The Story of Mankind*, *Pillow Talk*, *Lonely Are the Brave*, *In the Heat of the Night*, *Will Penny*, *The Computer Wore Tennis Shoes*, *The Trial of the Catonsville Nine*, *Charley Varrick*, and *Twilight Zone: The Movie*. Schallert's television credits include *Leave It to Beaver*, *Father Knows Best*, *Peter Gunn*, *The Twilight Zone*, *Alfred Hitchcock Presents*, *The Many Loves of Dobie Gillis*, *The Hardy Boys/Nancy Drew Mysteries*, *Perry Mason*, *Star Trek*, *The Wild, Wild West*, *The Mod Squad*, *Lou Grant*, *In the Heat of the Night*, *The Partridge Family*, *My Name Is Earl*, *True Blood*, *How I Met Your Mother*, and *Desperate Housewives*, but fans know him best for playing the role of Patty Duke's father, Martin Lane, on *The Patty Duke Show*

(1963-66). Schallert was the president of the Screen Actors Guild from 1979 until 1981. During his term, he founded the Committee for Performers with Disabilities. Neuropathy forced him to use a wheelchair in later life. William Schallert died at his Pacific Palisades home on May 8, 2016, at the age of 93. He was predeceased by his wife of 56 years in 2015. He was survived by his four sons.

Troy and Lee.

Prescription for Panic

Season 2, Episode 12

Broadcast on ABC-TV on December 4, 1961
Directed by Sidney Salkow
Written by Douglas Morrow
Producer: Joel Rogosin
Supervising Producer: Howie Horwitz
Executive Producer: William T. Orr

Cast:

Troy Donahue	Sandy Winfield II
Lee Patterson	Dave Thorne
Margarita Sierra	Cha Cha O'Brien
Allison Hayes	Lotta
Richard Crane	Lt. Gene Plehn
Benny Baker	Waiter
Brad Weston	Chick
Phillip Angeloff	Sam
Douglas Henderson	Matt Spivic
Pamela Austin	Lucibelle
John Dennis	Frankie Merrill
Kathleen Crowley	Dr. Leslie Halliday

Credits:

Cinematography by Robert Tobey
Film Editing by James W. Graham
Art Direction by Howard Campbell
Set Decoration by William L. Kuehl
Makeup Supervisor: Gordon Bau
Hairstylist: Jean Burt Reilly

Assistant Director: Phil Rawlins
Sound: Ross Owen
Theme Music Composers: Mack David and Jerry Livingston
Music Editor: Joe Inge
60 minutes/Black and White
Production Company: Warner Bros. Television
Filmed at Warner Bros. Studios on Stages 20 and 24
Cha Cha sang "Bei Mir Bist Du Shon" in this episode.

Notes on the case:

As a favor for his friend, hotel waiter Joe, Sandy investigates the murder of the waiter's timid brother-in-law who was gunned down after visiting psychiatrist Leslie Halliday. At first, Halliday is reluctant to cooperate with any investigation. But Sandy's suspicion that she knows more than she's telling him is validated after someone tries to shoot them both.

Allison Hayes played the role of Lotta. Hayes was born in Charleston, West Virginia on March 6, 1930. She was a model, and won the title of Miss District of Columbia, and represented D.C. in the 1949 Miss America pageant. She made her screen debut in the 1954 film *Francis Joins the WACS*. Her numerous films include *Sign of the Pagan*, *The Prodigal*, *The Steel Jungle*, *Gunslinger*, *Zombies of Mora Tau*, *The Disembodied*, *Wolf Dog*, *A Lust to Kill*, *Hong Kong Confidential*, *The Hypnotic Eye*, *Who's Been Sleeping in My Bed?*, and *Tickle Me*. She is best remembered for playing the role of Nancy Fowler Archer in the 1958 cult classic *Attack of the 50 Foot Woman*. Her numerous television credits include *Death Valley Days*, *The Millionaire*, *Bat Masterson*, *Rawhide*, *The Alaskans*, *77 Sunset Strip*, *Perry Mason*, *Laramie*, *Ripcord*, *Bachelor Father*, *The F.B.I.*, *Gomer Pyle, U.S.M.C.*, and the daytime drama *General Hospital*. Hayes suffered injuries on two movie sets that eventually caused her to use a cane. She retired from acting in 1967. She experienced serious and mysterious health problems which she later discovered were the cause of prolonged acute lead poisoning from a calcium supplement a doctor had prescribed. She moved to an assisted care facility in San Clemente, California, and was diagnosed with leukemia in 1976. She died on February 26, 1977 at the University of California Medical Center in San Diego. Allison Hayes was 46 years old.

Benny Baker played the role of Joe. Baker was born on May 5, 1907 in St. Joseph, Missouri. He worked as a truck driver before finding his way into vaudeville and burlesque as a comic. He made his screen debut in the 1934 film *The Hell Cat*. His more than 50 film appearances include *Belle of the Nineties*, *The Big Broadcast of 1936*, *Murder with Pictures*, *Wild Money*, *Blonde Trouble*, *The Farmer's Daughter*, *Stage Door Canteen*, *Joe Palooka in* *the Knockout, Papa's Delicate Condition, Boy, Did I Get a Wrong Number!, Paint Your Wagon,* and *The Sting II.* His many television credits include *Maverick, The Thin Man, Leave It to Beaver, Alfred Hitchcock Presents, The Jack Benny Show, Cheyenne, 77 Sunset Street, Perry Mason, F Troop, Charlie's Angels,* and *The Love Boat.* He retired in 1991. Benny Baker died of heart disease on September 20, 1994 at the Motion Picture Country Home in Woodland Hills, California. He was 87 years old, and was survived by his second wife, and one child.

Troy and Margarita.

A Slight Case of Chivalry

Season 2, Episode 13

Broadcast on ABC-TV on December 18, 1961
Directed by Harold D. Schuster
Written by Michael Fessier
Producer: Joel Rogosin
Supervising Producer: Howie Horwitz
Executive Producer: William T. Orr

Cast:

Lee Patterson	Dave Thorne
Diane McBain	Daphne Dutton
Margarita Sierra	Cha Cha O'Brien
Roxanne Arlen	Chloe Childers
Ann Robinson	Penolope Carmody
George Petrie	Hubert Leebie
Richard Crane	Lt. Gene Plehn
John Dehner	Dan Castle

Credits:

Cinematography by Louis Jennings
Film Editing by Byron Chudnow
Art Direction by Howard Campbell
Set Decoration by Raphael Bretton
Makeup Supervisor: Gordon Bau
Hairstylist: Jean Burt Reilly
Assistant Director: Samuel Schneider
Sound: Samuel F. Goode
Theme Music Composers: Mack David and Jerry Livingston

Music Editor: Sam E. Levin
60 minutes/Black and White
Production Company: Warner Bros. Television
Filmed at Warner Bros. Studios on Stages 20 and 24
Margarita Sierra sang "Savage Serenade" in this episode.

Notes from the case:

Dave learns that his former New York business associate, Dan Castle, is hiding in Miami. They once worked together in a private investigation office in Manhattan. Castle has a $5,000 bounty on his head for committing a murder. A bounty hunter is on his trail, determined to bring him in dead or alive. And the wife of the man he is accused of killing is not far behind. Dave has to determine who is telling the truth about the murder, and find Castle before the bounty hunter does.

John Dehner played the role of Dan Castle. Dehner was born in Staten Island, New York on November 23, 1915. He studied art in New York, and worked as an animator at the Walt Disney Studios in Burbank. He worked on *Fantasia, The Reluctant Dragon,* and *Bambi.* He was a news editor and disc jockey at KFWB in Los Angeles, and had an impressive career in radio dramas including *The Whistler, Gunsmoke, Laramie, Philip Marlowe, The Trouble with the Truitts, The Judge, Family Skeleton, Escape, The Black Book,* and *Frontier Gentleman.* From 1941 until his retirement in 1986, he appeared in more than 125 feature films including *The Left Handed Gun, Scaramouche, Carousel, The Texas Rangers, The Man from Bitter Ridge, The Fastest Gun Alive, The Chapman Report, Critic's Choice, Youngblood Hawke,* and *The Boys from Brazil.* Dehner's dozens of guest-starring television appearances include *Wanted: Dead or Alive, Wagon Train, Maverick, The Rebel, The Doris Day Show, The Wild, Wild West, The Andy Griffith Show, Bonanza, The Twilight Zone,* and *The Virginian.* John Dehner died in Santa Barbara, California of emphysema and diabetes on February 4, 1992 at the age of 76. He was survived by his second wife of 19 years, and two children.

Roxanne Arlen played the role of Chloe Childers. Arlen was born in Detroit, Michigan on January 10, 1932. A former Miss Detroit, Arlen married actor Red Buttons in 1947, but the couple divorced two years later. She made her film debut in 1953, and played the role of the classic "dumb blonde" in numerous films including *Illegal, Hot Rod Girl, The Best Things in Life Are Free, Everything But the Truth, Bundle of Joy, The Young Stranger, The Big Caper, Bachelor Flat,* and *Gypsy.* In 1958, Arlen starred in the Broadway comedy *Who Was That Lady I Saw You With?* Her numerous television appearances include *77 Sunset Strip, Perry Mason, The Roaring 20's, Hawaiian*

Eye, Naked City, That Girl, and *Bewitched.* She retired in 1968, and moved to London with her fourth husband. Roxanne Arlen died in London on February 22, 1989 at the age of 57.

George Petrie played the role of Hubert Leebie. Petrie was born in New Haven, Connecticut on November 16, 1912. He had a successful acting career performing in radio dramas in the 1940s including *Charlie Wild, Private Detective, The Adventures of the Falcon, Call the Police,* and *Philo Vance.* He played a small role in the 1944 feature film *Winged Victory.* His later films include *Swiss Tour, At Sword's Point, Gypsy, Hud, Dead Ringer, Baby Boom,* and *Planes, Trains, and Automobiles,* among others. His more than 100 television appearances include *The Honeymooners, Leave It To Beaver, Alfred Hitchcock Presents, The Twilight Zone, The Addams Family, The Munsters, Cagney and Lacey, Wiseguy, Dallas, Herman's Head, Mad About You, St. Elsewhere, Night Court,* and the daytime drama *Search for Tomorrow.* He retired in 1996. George Petrie died of lymphoma on November 16, 1997 in Los Angeles at the age of 85. He was survived by his wife of many years, and their two children.

Pattern for a Frame

Season 2, Episode 14

Broadcast on ABC-TV on December 25, 1961
Directed by Irving J. Moore
Written by Herman Groves
Producer: Jerry Davis
Supervising Producer: Howie Horwitz
Executive Producer: William T. Orr

Cast:

Van Williams	Ken Madison
Troy Donahue	Sandy Winfield II
Lee Patterson	Dave Thorne
Margarita Sierra	Cha Cha O'Brien
Don "Red" Barry	Lt. Snedigar
Robert Cornthwaite	Jason Street
Kem Dibbs	Augie Dana
Myrna Fahey	Valerie Grant
Jack Mather	Jim Reagen
Adam Williams	Willie Cleveland

Credits:

Cinematography by Ralph Woolsey
Film Editing by Robert L. Wolfe
Art Direction by Howard Campbell
Set Decoration by Hoyle Barrett
Makeup Supervisor: Gordon Bau
Hairstylist: Jean Burt Reilly
Assistant Director: Fred Scheld
Sound: Ross Owen

Theme Music Composers: Mack David and Jerry Livingston
Music Editor: Erma E. Levin
60 minutes/Black and White
Production Company: Warner Bros. Television
Filmed at Warner Bros. Studios on Stages 20 and 24
Margarita Sierra sang "The Tourist Trade" in this episode.

Notes on the case:

Valerie Grant, the daughter of a judge, twists her ankle and falls on the beach near Ken. She flirts, and the two make a date to have dinner. When he goes to pick her up, he finds the body of mobster Augie Dana. Ken is accused of the murder and goes on the run to figure out what really happened. He learns that Grant is being blackmailed by a former bookie, Jason Street, whom Ken had sent to prison. Street, recently released from the pen, wants to regain control of his old rackets, and hatched the plan to lure Ken into a trap where he will be accused of killing one of his criminal rivals.

Robert Cornthwaite played the role of Jason Street. Cornthwaite was born on April 28, 1917 in Saint Helens, Oregon. He began acting in school productions at Reed College in Portland, Oregon. He later attended Long Beach City College and worked at local radio stations. He served in the U.S. Army Air Force during World War II as a radio-gunner, a radio operator, and an intelligence officer. After the war, he moved to Hollywood, and earned a degree from the University of Southern California. He made his screen debut in the 1950 film *Union Station*. During his career he appeared in more than 250 films and television shows. His better known films include *The Thing from Another World*, *Monkey Business*, *The War of the Worlds*, *Kiss Me Deadly*, *What Ever Happened to Baby Jane?*, *The Ghost and Mr. Chicken*, *Colossus: The Forbin Project*, *Futureworld*, and *The Naked Monster*. Cornthwaite's better known television credits include *Perry Mason*, *The Twilight Zone*, *Death Valley Days*, *Voyage to the Bottom of the Sea*, *Batman*, *The Monkees*, *Gidget*, *Laverne & Shirley*, *Dragnet*, *The Munsters*, and *Get Smart*. He played the role of Howard Buss from 1992 until 1994 on the acclaimed series *Picket Fences*. He retired in 2005. Robert Cornthwaite was a confirmed bachelor. He died at the Motion Picture Country Home in Woodland Hills, California on July 20, 2006 at the age of 89.

Kem Dibbs played the role of Augie Dana. Dibbs was born on August 12, 1917 in Zahle, Lebanon. He worked as a stock broker in New York before moving to California. Dibbs made his television debut in 1949. His ethnic looks typecast him in mostly villainous roles. Dibbs' many television credits include *Buck Rogers*, *Captain Video and his Video Rangers*, *Space Patrol*, *Captain Midnight*, *The Lone Ranger*, *The Adventures of Jim Bowie*, *The Life* *and Legend of Wyatt Earp, Maverick, Batman,* and *The Wild, Wild West.* His feature films include *Riders to the Stars, Suddenly, High Society, Abbott and Costello Meet the Mummy, Terror at Midnight, The Ten Commandments, Party Girl,* and *Paths of Glory.* Dibbs was a founder and former president of the show business charitable group called the Thalians. He helped raise more than $22 million for the Thalians Mental Health Clinic at Cedars-Sinai Medical Center in Los Angeles. Dibbs retired in 1970, and died at the age of 78 in Rancho Mirage, California on March 28, 1996.

The Roust

Season 2, Episode 15

Broadcast on ABC-TV on January 1, 1962
Directed by Robert Douglas
Written by John D.F. Black
Producer: Joel Rogosin
Supervising Producer: Howie Horwitz
Executive Producer: William T. Orr

Cast:

Lee Patterson	Dave Thorne
Van Williams	Ken Madison
Diane McBain	Daphne Dutton
Margarita Sierra	Cha Cha O'Brien
David White	Bernard "Chilly" Childress
Elizabeth MacRae	Marcy Johnson
Richard Crane	Lt. Gene Plehn
Vito Scotti	Marcus
Reedy Talton	Pete Minor

Credits:

Cinematography by Harold E. Stine
Film Editing by Robert B. Warwick Jr.
Art Direction by Howard Campbell
Set Decoration by William L. Kuehl
Makeup Supervisor: Gordon Bau
Hairstylist: Jean Burt Reilly
Assistant Director: Russell Saunders
Sound: Ross Owen
Theme Music Composers: Mack David and Jerry Livingston

Music Editor: Robert Phillips
60 minutes/ Black and White
Production Company: Warner Bros. Television
Filmed at Warner Bros. Studios on Stages 20 and 24

Notes on the case:

Dave runs into an old foe, "Chilly" Childress, in the Boom Boom Room. Childress is a dangerous criminal Dave unsuccessfully prosecuted in New York. The racketeer was responsible for Dave once being targeted for murder. Lt. Plehn informs Dave that he has information indicating that Childress is planning to move to Miami. Dave plans to do what he couldn't do in New York, send Childress to prison by goading him into making the same mistake he made in New York. Ken worries that Dave may put his ethics aside to carry out his vendetta.

Reedy Talton played the role of Pete Minor. Talton was born in Talladega, Alabama on December 11, 1921. He served in Company B of the U.S. Army during WWII. He made his television debut in 1951 on *Two Girls Named Smith*. His other television credits include *Man Against Crime, Studio One, The United States Steel Hour, The Jack Benny Show, The Deputy, 77 Sunset Strip, New York Confidential, Return to Peyton Place, Lock Up, Outlaws*, and *Suspense*. He may be best remembered for co-starring in the series, *Stanley* (1956-57). He starred in one motion picture, *Dead to the World*, in 1961. Talton retired from acting in 1964. He died in Los Angeles on May 8, 1987 at the age of 65.

The Quarterback

Season 2, Episode 16

Broadcast on ABC-TV on January 8, 1962
Directed by Paul Landres
Written by Herman Groves
Producer: Joel Rogosin
Supervising Producer: Howie Horwitz
Executive Producer: William T. Orr

Cast:

Troy Donahue	Sandy Winfield II
Van Williams	Ken Madison
Janet Lake	Myrna Weston
Richard Crane	Lt. Gene Plehn
Sandy McPeak	Tom Plehn
Bronwyn FitzSimons	Jenny
Al Avalon	Wally Barker
Tucker Smith	Turk Williams
Herman Rudin	Max Borden
Robert Shield	Harry Lyle
Lyle Latell	Coach Rice

Credits:

Cinematography by Robert Tobey
Art Direction by Howard Campbell
Set Decoration by William L. Kuehl
Makeup Supervisor: Gordon Bau
Hairstylist: Jean Burt Reilly
Assistant Director: Rex Bailey
Sound: Francis E. Stahl

Theme Music Composers: Mack David and Jerry Livingston
Music Editor: Erma E. Levin
60 minutes/ Black and White
Production Company: Warner Bros. Television
Filmed at Warner Bros. Studios on Stages 20 and 24

Notes on the case:

Lt. Plehn's younger brother Tom is a star quarterback set to play in the Orange
Bowl. Gambler Wally Barker concocts a plan to fix the upcoming game. He
sends his former girlfriend, Myrna Weston, to meet Tom. She claims to be
his brother's mistress, and says he has stolen evidence and is taking bribes.
She threatens to contact the District Attorney with this information and ruin
him if Tom doesn't throw the game. Tom falls for the story and refuses to
talk to his brother. Plehn asks the Surfside detectives to help him figure out
what's happened. Sandy becomes alarmed when he sees Tom talking with the
racketeer. With twenty-four hours until the game, they need to determine
what is going on.

Al Avalon played the role of Wally Barker. Avalon was born on August
10, 1932 in Boston. He directed the television series *Divorce Court* (1957-
58), and made his film debut providing the voice of a radio newscaster in
the 1957 film *The Astounding She-Monster*. He played small roles in several
films including *Breakfast at Tiffany's*, *Bushfire*, *Experiment in Terror*, and
Funny Girl. He played supporting roles in a few television programs including *Richard Diamond Private Detective*, *Bonanza*, *Barnaby Jones*, and *Hawaii
Five-O*. He was married and divorced from actress Marilyn Harvey. Al Avalon
retired from acting in 1978.

Sandy Kevin (McPeak) played the role of Tom Plehn. McPeak was born
on February 21, 1936 in Indiana, Pennsylvania. He began his acting career
as a contract player at Warner Brothers. He first appeared on screen in the
television show *Lawman* in 1961. His other Warner assignments were guest-
starring roles in *Hawaiian Eye*, and *77 Sunset Strip*. He played the role of
Pvt. Saunders in the series *The Gallant Men* (1962-63), and appeared in the
1963 film *Palm Springs Weekend*. The studio did not pick up his contract
option, so he worked as a free agent thereafter. His feature films include *The
Cincinnati Kid, Not With My Wife You Don't!, Patton, Kelly's Heroes, The
Man Who Loved Cat Dancing, Ode to Billy Joe, Walking Tall: Final Chapter,
Tarantulas: The Deadly Cargo, The Onion Field, The Osterman Weekend*, and
Born to Ride. His many television appearances include *Bonanza, Hank, The
Green Hornet, Lou Grant, Knight Rider, Hill Street Blues, Nasty Boys, L.A.
Law, The Felony Squad, Nanny and the Professor, Medical Center, Room 222,
Logan's Run, Baretta, Murder She Wrote, Charlie's Angels*, and *The Incredible*

Hulk. He played the role of Giggler on *Batman*, and played the role of Orion Hawk on the daytime drama *Days of Our Lives* from 1988 until 1989. He retired in 1994. Sandy Kevin (McPeak) died of a heart attack in Nevada City, Nevada on December 31, 1997. He was 61 years old.

Bronwyn FitzSimons played the role of Jenny. FitzSimons was the only child of actress Maureen O'Hara. She was born in Los Angeles on June 30, 1944. She entered show business with her mother's encouragement. She made her acting debut in this episode of *Surfside 6*. Before she quit acting in 1965 to be a mother to her son, she played guest roles on the television shows *Alcoa Premiere*, *The Virginian*, *McHale's Navy*, *The Alfred Hitchcock Hour*, and *The Ravagers*, and had a small role in the film *Spencer's Mountain*. In her later years, she lived with her mother in Glengarriff, Ireland. Maureen O'Hara died on October 24, 2015 in Boise, Idaho where she lived with her grandson. Bronwyn was found dead in the family's Glengarriff cottage on May 25, 2016. She died of natural causes. She was survived by her son, hairdresser/hair care products entrepreneur Conor Beau FitzSimons.

Bronwyn FitzSimons and Troy.

Separate Checks

Season 2, Episode 17

Broadcast on ABC-TV on January 15, 1962
Directed by Sidney Salkow
Written by Ed Waters
Producer: Joel Rogosin
Supervising Producer: Howie Horwitz
Executive Producer: William T. Orr

<u>Cast</u>:

Van Williams	Ken Madison
Lee Patterson	Dave Thorne
Margarita Sierra	Cha Cha O'Brien
Bruce Gordon	Joe Vodka
Roy Roberts	Cliff Thornton
Barbara Jo Allen	Elaine Bradford
Joseph Gallison	Joe-Too
Sandra Knight	Kathy
Richard Crane	Lt. Gene Plehn
Lewis Charles	Shoopy Jacobs
Gordon Jones	Garth
Jake Sheffield	Ralphie
Nora Hayden	Lynn

<u>Credits</u>:

Cinematography by Harold E. Stine
Film Editing by Robert L. Wolfe
Art Direction by Howard Campbell
Set Decoration by William L. Kuehl
Makeup Supervisor: Gordon Bau

Hairstylist: Jean Burt Reilly
Assistant Director: Gene Anderson Jr.
Sound: Robert B. Lee
Theme Music Composers: Mack David and Jerry Livingston
Music Editor: Lou Gordon
60 minutes/ Black and White
Production Company: Warner Bros. Television
Filmed at Warner Bros. Studios on Stages 20 and 24
Margarita Sierra sang "Lover Come Back to Me" in this episode.

Notes on the case:

Joe-Too, the son of gangster Joe Vodka, is suckered out of a large amount of money by a con-man named Cliff Thornton. The gangster is enraged that someone would bilk his son. He sets out to find, and kill, Thornton. For some reason, Joe-Too is more forgiving, and hires Ken to find the man before his father's hit-men do.

Bruce Gordon played the role of Joe Vodka. Gordon was born on February 1, 1916 in Fitchburg, Massachusetts. He began his impressive Broadway career in the 1937-38 play *The Fireman's Flame*. Gordon appeared in 11 more Broadway shows including *The Girl from Wyoming* (1938-39), *Arsenic and Old Lace* (1941-44), *Antony and Cleopatra* (1947-48), *Captain Brassbound's Conversion* (1950-51), *The Lark* (1955-56), and *Diamond Orchid* (1965). He made his screen debut in the 1948 film *The Naked City*. His numerous films include *The Street with No Name, Love Happy, The Buccaneer, Key Witness, Rider on a Dead Horse, Tower of London, Hello Down There, Piranha*, and *Timerider: The Adventure of Lyle Swann*. His dozens of television appearances include *Studio One, Whirlybirds, Tombstone Territory, Harbormaster, Perry Mason, Outlaws, The Lucy Show, It Takes a Thief*, and *Adventures in Paradise*. Gordon played the recurring role of Frank Nitti on *The Untouchables* (1959-63), and the role of Gus Chernak on *Peyton Place* (1965-68). He starred in the 1966 series, *Run, Buddy, Run*. He retired from acting in 1984. In his later years, he produced a couple of low-budget films, and became a restaurateur with eateries in Scottsdale, Arizona, and Kansas City, Missouri. After several years of failing health, Bruce Gordon died on January 20, 2011 in Santa Fe, New Mexico. He was 94 years old, and survived by his second wife.

Evan McCord played the role of Joe-Too. McCord was born in Boston on March 9, 1935. He first appeared on screen in 1960. He worked under contract to Warner Brothers for a couple of years and guest-starred in many of the studio's television productions including *Maverick, Bronco, The Roaring 20's, Lawman, Cheyenne, Hawaiian Eye*, and *77 Sunset Strip*. When he left

Warner Brothers, he reclaimed his birth name, Joseph Gallison, and continued to work in film and television. Gallison's television credits include *Arrest and Trial, Flipper, Quincy, M.E., Silk Stockings,* and *One Tree Hill.* He is best known for playing the role of Dr. Neil Curtis on the daytime soap opera *Days of Our Lives,* from 1974 until 1991. He was married to OBIE Award-winning playwright Maxine Klein from 1958 until 1959. His second wife (1967-1970) was actress Cornelia Sharpe. He married his third wife in 1980.

Roy Roberts played the role of Cliff Thornton. Roberts was born on March 19, 1906 in Dade City, Florida. He made his Broadway debut in 1931, and appeared in 14 Broadway productions including *Twentieth Century* (1932), *Pre-Honeymoon* (1936), and *My Sister Eileen* (1941-42). Roberts made his screen debut in the 1936 comedy short *Gold Bricks.* His dozens of films include *My Darling Clementine, The Shocking Miss Pilgrim, Force of Evil, He Walked by Night, Nightmare Alley, Borderline, The Enforcer, House of Wax, The Outfit,* and *Chinatown.* Roberts appeared in hundreds of television shows. He played the recurring characters of banker Mr. Cheever on *The Lucy Show,* bank president John Cushing on *The Beverly Hillbillies,* railroad president Norman Curtis on *Petticoat Junction,* and banker Harry Bodkin on *Gunsmoke.* He retired in 1975. Roy Roberts suffered a heart attack and died in Los Angeles on May 28, 1975. He was 69 years old, and was survived by his wife of 28 years.

Barbara Jo Allen played the role of Elaine Bradford. Allen was born in New York City on September 2, 1906. She lived with an aunt in Los Angeles after her mother died when she was a child. She studied at U.C.L.A. and Stanford University. She began performing on the radio in 1933, playing roles on *One Man's Family, Death Valley Days, I Love a Mystery, NBC Matinee,* and *Signal Carnival.* She created the character of "Vera Vague," and actually adopted that as her professional name in nearly 60 films made between 1938 and 1963. Her films include *Village Barn Dance, Broadway Melody of 1940, Melody Ranch, Kiss the Boys Goodbye, Ice Capades, Design for Scandal, Mrs. Wiggs of the Cabbage Patch, The Palm Beach Story, Henry Aldrich Plays Cupid, Rosie the Riveter, Earl Carroll Sketchbook,* and *Born to Be Loved.* She starred in dozens of comedy short films, and was a voice-over artist, providing the voice of Fauna, the green fairy, in *Sleeping Beauty* (1959), Goliath II's mother in *Goliath II* (1960), and the Scullery Maid in *The Sword in the Stone* (1963). Her television credits include *Hey Jeannie!, Maverick, General Electric Theatre,* and *The Greatest Man on Earth.* This episode of *Surfside 6* provided Allen with her final onscreen role. She was married and divorced twice. Her first husband was actor Barton Yarborough. The couple had a daughter. Barbara Jo Allen died on September 14, 1974 in Santa Barbara, California. She was 68 years old, and survived by her husband of 31 years, producer Norman Morrell, and two children.

The Artful Deceit

Season 2, Episode 18

Broadcast on ABC-TV on January 22, 1962
Directed by Charles R. Rondeau
Written by John O'Dea and Jack Jacobs
Producer: Joel Rogosin
Supervising Producer: Howie Horwitz
Executive Producer: William T. Orr

Cast:

Troy Donahue	Sandy Winfield II
Van Williams	Ken Madison
Margarita Sierra	Cha Cha O'Brien
Angela Greene	Marie Cameron
John Archer	Wilbur Law
Richard Crane	Lt. Gene Plehn
Danielle De Metz	Vicki Falvay
Christine Nelson	Peggy
Stephen Coit	Charles Bell
Marjorie Bennett	Abbie
Chad Everett	Roger Coleman

Credits:

Cinematography by Frank G. Carson
Film Editing by Lloyd Nosler
Art Direction by Howard Campbell
Set Decoration by Ralph S. Hurst
Makeup Supervisor: Gordon Bau
Hairstylist: Jean Burt Reilly
Assistant Director: Fred Scheld

Sound: Everett A. Hughes
Theme Music Composers: Mack David and Jerry Livingston
Music Editor: Donald Harris
60 minutes/ Black and White
Production Company: Warner Bros. Television
Filmed at Warner Bros. Studios on Stages 20 and 24
Cha Cha sang "She's a Latin from Manhattan" and – with Troy Donahue, "You're Getting to Be a Habit with Me" in this episode.

Notes on the case:

A prominent art dealer is mysteriously murdered. The prime suspect is Wilber Law, a local theatrical set painter. A police background investigation reveals that Law is the husband of a wealthy woman named Marie Cameron. They also learn that he supposedly committed suicide years before. Sandy and Cha Cha have been volunteering with the same theatrical group, and they decide to help with the investigation. They determine that a fellow acting student – a gifted mimic – could be involved with the perplexing crime.

    John Archer played the role of Wilbur Law. Archer was born in Osceola, Nebraska on May 8, 1915. His family moved to California when he was five years old. He attended Hollywood High School, and studied cinematography at the University of Southern California. He drifted into radio acting, and played the role of Lamont Cranston in *The Shadow* in 1944. He made his Broadway debut that same year. Archer starred in seven Broadway shows including *The Day Before Spring* (1945-46), *Strange Bedfellows* (1948), and *Captain Brassbound's Conversion* (1950-51). He made his film debut in the 1938 movie *Flaming Frontiers*. His better known films include *Cheers for Miss Bishop*, *King of the Zombies*, *Hello Frisco Hello*, *Sherlock Holmes in Washington*, *White Heat*, *Destination Moon*, *My Favorite Spy*, *Blue Hawaii*,

Margarita and Troy.

I Saw What You Did, and *How to Frame a Figg*. His many television credits include *Perry Mason*, *Bonanza*, *Lassie*, *McHale's Navy*, *Sea Hunt*, *Maverick*, *77 Sunset Strip*, *Wagon Train*, *Mannix*, *The Name of the Game*, and *Hazel*. Archer retired in 1996. He was married to actress Marjorie Lord from 1941 to 1953. The couple had two children including Oscar nominated and Golden Globe winning actress Anne Archer. John Archer died of lung cancer on December 3, 1999 in Redmond, Washington at the age of 84. He was survived by his second wife of 43 years, and four children.

Chad Everett.

Season 2, Episode 19

Broadcast on ABC-TV on January 29, 1962
Directed by Robert Douglas
Written by Sonya Roberts
Producer: Joel Rogosin
Supervising Producer: Howie Horwitz
Executive Producer: William T. Orr

Cast:

Lee Patterson	Dave Thorne
Van Williams	Ken Madison
Margarita Sierra	Cha Cha O'Brien
William Windom	Robby Brooks
Jeanne Cooper	Lois Brooks
Sallie Jones	Leda
John Hiestand	Henry Tewksbury
Max Showalter	Ned Martin
Richard Crane	Lt. Gene Plehn
Sid Kane	Elder
Glen Vernon	Trask

Credits:

Cinematography by Robert Hoffman
Film Editing by Clarence Kolster
Art Direction by Howard Campbell
Set Decoration by William L. Kuehl
Makeup Supervisor: Gordon Bau
Hairstylist: Jean Burt Reilly
Assistant Director: Phil Rawlins

Sound: B.F. Ryan
Theme Music Composers: Mack David and Jerry Livingston
Music Editor: Charles Paley
60 minutes/ Black and White
Production Company: Warner Bros. Television
Filmed at Warner Bros. Studios on Stages 20 and 24
Sallie Jones sang "Somebody Loves Me" in this episode.

Notes on the case:

Robby Brooks, a famous television star plans a gala TV special program to commemorate his wedding anniversary. But his wife, Lois, not only wants no part of it, she wants a divorce. Brooks hires Dave to look after her, explaining his fears that she is insane and might attempt suicide. The television star wants the special broadcast to begin his campaign for President. He also thinks that a murder (in the form of his wife's "suicide") would gain him sympathy votes. But Dave believes that Brooks' ego and abuse have driven his wife away.

Jeanne Cooper played the role of Lois Brooks. Cooper was born in Taft, California on October 25, 1928. She made her film debut in the 1953 movie *The Redhead from Wyoming*. Her numerous films include *The Man from the Alamo, The Naked Street, Over-Exposed, Rock All Night, Unwed Mother, Red Nightmare, The Glory Guys, Tony Rome, The Boston Strangler, There Was a Crooked Man, Kansas City Bomber*, and *Lethal Justice*. Her many television credits include *Cheyenne, Perry Mason, The Twilight Zone, Wanted: Dead or Alive, The Untouchables, Bonanza, The Big Valley, The Man from U.N.C.L.E.*, and *Daniel Boone*. She is perhaps best known for playing the role of Katherine Chancellor on the daytime drama *The Young and the Restless*, from 1973 until 2013. She was nominated for two Prime Time Emmy Awards, and ten Daytime Emmy Awards, with one win. Cooper was married to producer Harry Bernson from 1954 until their divorce in 1977. The couple had three children including Emmy and Golden Globe Award nominated actor Corbin Bernsen. Jeanne Cooper took ill while promoting the 40th anniversary of *The Young and the Restless*. She died in Los Angeles on May 8, 2013 at the age of 84. She was survived by her three children.

Sallie Jones played the role of Leda. Jones was born in Los Angeles on September 23, 1932. She attended Pasadena High School, and studied speech in Santa Cruz. In the 1950s, she sang in nightclubs where she was spotted by Vincente Minelli who gave her a small part in his 1960 film, *Bells Are Ringing*. She played a small role that same year in the film, *Please Don't Eat the Daisies*. She provided the voice of Honeydew Melon on the cartoon series, *Top Cat*, and guest-starred in a memorable episode of *The Dick Van Dyke Show*. She played the role of Miss Swenson in several episodes of *The Beverly Hillbillies* in 1964, and appeared on *The Joey Bishop Show*. Fans will remember her best for playing the role of Mona McKenzie in the 1976 series, *Mary Hartman, Mary Hartman*. In 1962, she married Perry Polski, a Culver City school teacher and educational activist. He was a founding member of the California Federation of Teachers. Jones retired from acting in 1976, and reclaimed a private life. She died in Los Angeles County in 2017 at the age of 84.

The Surfside Swindle

Season 2, Episode 20

Broadcast on ABC-TV on February 5, 1962
Directed by George Waggner
Written by Robert Vincent Wright
Producer: Joel Rogosin
Supervising Producer: Howie Horwitz
Executive Producer: William T. Orr

<u>Cast</u>:

Troy Donahue	Sandy Winfield II
Van Williams	Ken Madison
Diane McBain	Daphne Dutton
Gerald Mohr	Dawson Wells
Lisa Montell	Nancy Dinato
Ernest Sarracino	Garibaldi Dinato
Richard Crane	Lt. Gene Plehn
Dabbs Greer	Finney Tate
Collette Lyons	Mrs. Myers

<u>Credits</u>:

Cinematography by Robert Hoffman
Film Editing by John Whitney
Art Direction by Howard Campbell
Set Decoration by William L. Kuehl
Makeup Supervisor: Gordon Bau
Hairstylist: Jean Burt Reilly
Assistant Director: C. Carter Gibson
Sound: Samuel F. Goode
Theme Music Composers: Mack David and Jerry Livingston

Music Editor: Charles Paley
60 minutes/ Black and White
Production Company: Warner Bros. Television
Filmed at Warner Bros. Studios on Stages 20 and 24

Notes on the case:

Garibaldi Dinato is taken advantage of by a swindler when he pays the con man a year's rent in advance to lease the Surfside 6 houseboat, not knowing the houseboat is occupied and not available for rent. He plans to convert it into a floating Pizza Parlor. The Surfside detectives search for the crook to retrieve Dinato's money. Their investigation reveals an elaborate web of blackmail, extortion and murder.

Gerald Mohr played the role of Dawson Wells. Mohr was born in Manhattan on June 11, 1914. While recovering from an appendectomy in a hospital, another patient who was a radio broadcaster, was impressed with Mohr's voice, and encouraged him to consider radio work. He was hired by a radio station and became a junior on-air reporter. In the mid-1930s, he joined Orson Welles' Mercury Theatre. During the next 20 years, he played more than 500 radio roles including *Jungle Jim, The Adventures of Philip Marlowe, The Lone Wolf, The New Adventures of Nero Wolfe, The Whistler, Damon Runyon Theater, Our Miss Brooks*, and *The Shadow of Fu Manchu*. He made his screen debut in 1939. His early films include *Charlie Chan at Treasure Island, The Sea Hawk, The Monster and the Girl, The Lady Has Plans, Woman of the Year, Murder in Times Square, King of the Cowboys, The Desert Song*, and the serial, *Jungle Girl*. He served three years in the U.S. Army during World War II. His post-war films include *Gilda, Son of Ali Baba, The Eddie Cantor Story, Terror in the Haunted House, Guns Girls and Gangsters, The Angry Red Planet*, and *Funny Girl*. He played the role of Michael Lanyard/The Lone Wolf in *The Notorious Lone Wolf* (1946), *The Lone Wolf in Mexico* (1947), and *The Lone Wolf in London* (1947). Mohr guest-starred in more than 100 television shows including *Perry Mason, Lost in Space, The Lucy Show, I Love Lucy, Rawhide, How to Marry a Millionaire*, and most of the Warner Brothers' productions including *77 Sunset Strip, Maverick, The Alaskans, Lawman, Cheyenne, Bronco*, and *Sugarfoot*. After completing work on a pilot in Stockholm, Sweden, Mohr suffered a heart attack and died there on November 9, 1968. Mohr was 54 years old. He was survived by his second wife, script supervisor Mai Dietrich, and one son.

Lisa Montell played the role of Nancy Dinato. Montell was born on July 5, 1933 in Warsaw, Poland. Her family escaped Europe in the early days of World War II, and moved to New York. She studied at the newly opened High School of the Performing Arts, but her family moved to Florida where she finished school before moving to Peru. She began performing in English-speaking theater and was discovered by Hollywood producer Dick Welding who put her in her first film *Daughter of the Sun God*. The film was completed in 1953, but not released in America until 1962. When her father died, the family moved to Hollywood so Montell could establish a career in the movie business. Her career was short-lived. She first appeared on screen in the 1955 film *Escape to Burma*. She was typecast as an exotic pinup girl, and made a series of "B" films including *Jump into Hell*, *Pearl of the South Pacific*, *World Without End*, *Gaby*, *Naked Paradise*, *Tomahawk Trail*, *Ten Thousand Bedrooms*, *The Lone Ranger and the Lost City of Gold*, *She Gods of Shark Reef*, and *The Long Rope*. Her several television appearances include *The Gene Autry Show*, *The Millionaire*, *Broken Arrow*, *Colt .45*, *Mike Hammer*, *Sugarfoot*, *Cheyenne*, *77 Sunset Strip*, and *Maverick*. In 1957, she married actor David Janti, and the couple had a daughter two years later. In 1956, she joined the Bha'i Faith. Unhappy with the roles she was being offered, Montell quit Hollywood in 1962. Since that time, she has been a spiritual exponent of the Bha'i Faith, and has worked as a social development advocate for decades.

Dabbs Greer played the role of Finney Tate. Greer was born in Fairview, Missouri on April 2, 1917. He moved to California in 1943, and was an administrator, acting instructor, and performer at the Pasadena Playhouse. He made his credited screen debut in the 1949 film *Reign of Terror*. His more than 100 films include *House of Wax*, *Affair with a Stranger*, *Half a Hero*,

Van, Diane, Troy, and Ernest Sarrachino.

Riot in Cell Block 11, Seven Angry Men, Invasion of the Body Snatchers, Hot Rod Girl, The Vampire, My Man Godfrey, Baby Face Nelson, It! The Terror from Beyond Space, I Want to Live!, Roustabout, Shenandoah, The Cheyenne Social Club, Pacific Heights, and *The Green Mile.* Between 1950 and 2003, Greer played more than 600 roles on television shows including *Adventures of Superman, Lassie, Alfred Hitchcock Presents, Gunsmoke, Perry Mason, Wagon Train, Bonanza, The Dick Van Dyke Show, The Outer Limits, Hank, The Rookies, In the Heat of the Night, Roseanne, Ally McBeal, Diagnosis: Murder, Maybe It's Me,* and *Lizzie McGuire.* He played the recurring roles of Rev. Henry Novotny in *Picket Fences* (1992-1996) and Reverend Alden in *Little House on the Prairie* (1974-1983). He retired in 2003. Dabbs Greer died of heart disease and kidney failure on April 28, 2007 in Pasadena, California at the age of 90. Greer was a confirmed bachelor.

Who Is Sylvia?

Season 2, Episode 21

Broadcast on ABC-TV on February 12, 1962.
Written by Lee Loeb
Executive Producer: William T. Orr

Cast:

Troy Donahue	Sandy Winfield II
Lee Patterson	Dave Thorne
Van Williams	Ken Madison
Diane McBain	Daphne Dutton
Margarita Sierra	Cha Cha O'Brien
E.J. Endre	Manager
Jack Cassidy	Val Morton
Vana Leslie	Gloria
Joan Marshall	Mildred Haynes
Karen Steele	Sylvia Morton
Karl Swenson	Charlie Haynes
Sandra Warner	Irene

Credits:

Cinematography by Ralph Woolsey
Film Editing by John Joyce
Art Direction by Howard Campbell
Set Decoration by Ralph S. Hurst
Makeup Supervisor: Gordon Bau
Hairstylist: Jean Burt Reilly
Assistant Director: Richard L'Estrange
Sound: Robert B. Lee
Theme Music Composers: Mack David and Jerry Livingston

Music Editor: Robert Phillips
60 minutes/ Black and White
Production Company: Warner Bros. Television
Filmed at Warner Bros. Studios on Stages 20 and 24
Margarita Sierra sang "The Cha Cha Twist" in this episode. It was released as a single by Warner Brothers Records, but did not make the Billboard pop chart. The cast, with the exception of Dave, joined Cha Cha dancing the twist.

Notes on the case:

Bathing suit manufacturer Val Morton hires Dave to find his business-partner wife, Sylvia, who seemingly walked off the job and disappeared. Morton warns Dave that his wife is mentally unstable, and actually threatened his life. Dave finds Sylvia, but she refuses to return to her husband and business, and runs off again. When Val Morton is murdered, Lt. Plehn issues a warrant for Sylvia's arrest, and ignores some important information about other possible suspects that Dave and Ken have discovered.

Jack Cassidy played the role of Val Morton. Cassidy was born in Queens, New York on March 5, 1927. He made his Broadway debut in 1943 in *Something for the Boys*. Cassidy appeared in 19 Broadway productions including *South Pacific*, *Wish You Were Here*, *The Beggar's Opera*, *She Loves Me*, *Maggie Flynn*, and *Murder Among Friends*. He starred in national touring companies of *Gyspy*, *Mary Mary*, *Camelot*, and *Wait Until Dark*. His dozens of television guest-starring roles include appearances on *The Lucy Show*, *The Alfred Hitchcock Hour*, *Love, American Style*, *Columbo*, *Night Gallery*, *McCloud*, *The Mary Tyler Moore Show*, and he starred in the TV movie, *The Andersonville Trial*.

Vana Leslie and Jack Cassidy.

Cassidy starred as Oscar North in the 1967-68 series *He & She*. He made his movie debut in the 1961 film *Look in Any Window*. His other films include *The Chapman Report*, *The Cockeyed Cowboys of Calico County*, *Bunny O'Hare*, *The Eiger Sanction*, *W.C. Fields and Me*, and *The Private Files of J. Edgar Hoover*. Cassidy was nominated for two Emmy Awards, four Tony Awards, with one win, and he won a Grammy

Award. He married actress Evelyn Ward in 1948. They had a son, singer/ actor David Cassidy. The couple divorced in 1956, and that same year he married actress/singer Shirley Jones. They have three sons, actors Shaun, Ryan, and Patrick Cassidy. They divorced in 1975. Cassidy suffered bipolar disorder, and alcoholism. He was also bisexual, and had many same-sex affairs, including a relationship with Cole Porter. In the early morning hours of December 12, 1976, after a night of heavy drinking, Cassidy passed out on the couch in his West Hollywood apartment. A burning cigarette ignited the couch. The apartment caught fire, and he burned to death in the blaze. Jack Cassidy was 49 years-old.

Karl Swenson played the role of Charlie Haynes. Swenson was born in Brooklyn on July 23, 1908. He abandoned pre-medical studies to pursue acting, and first appeared on Broadway in 1931. During the next 13 years, he appeared in nine Broadway productions including *The Man Who Had All the Luck*, *A Highland Fling*, and *One Sunday Afternoon*. Beginning in the 1930s and through the 1950s, Swenson was a constant presence on radio, performing in many dramas including *Cavalcade of America*, *Joe Palooka*, *The March of Time*, *The Mercury Theatre on the Air*, *Mrs. Miniver*, *The Adventures of Father Brown*, and *Mr. Chameleon*, among others. His better known feature films include *No Name on the Bullet*, *The Hanging Tree*, *Ice Palace*, *The Gallant Hours*, *North to Alaska*, *Judgment at Nuremberg*, *Walk on the Wild Side*, *Lonely Are the Brave*, *The Birds*, *The Prize*, *Major Dundee*, *The Sons of Katie Elder*, *The Cincinnati Kid*, and *Vanishing Point*. He provided the voice of Lord Merlin in the Disney animated classic *The Sword in the Stone*. Swenson was adept at drama and comedy and played many roles on television shows including *Lassie*, *Perry Mason*, *Hogan's Heroes*, *Bonanza*, *Maverick*, *Leave It to Beaver*, *Colt .45*, *River Boat*, *The Rebel*, *Bachelor Father*, *The Alfred Hitchcock Hour*, *Daktari*, *Dr. Kildare*, *Tarzan*, and *The Odd Couple*. Many fans remember him for playing the role of Lars Hanson from 1974 until 1978 on *Little House on the Prairie*. Days after filming his final episode of *Little House on the Prairie* (in which his character Lars Hansen dies), Swenson was visiting relatives when he suffered a fatal heart attack in Torrington, Connecticut on October 8, 1978 at the age of 70. He was survived by his wife of 27 years, actress Joan Tompkins, and four children from his first marriage.

Find Leroy Burdette

Season 2, Episode 22

Broadcast on ABC-TV on February 19, 1962
Directed by Robert Douglas
Written by Jack Jacobs and John O'Dea
Producer: Joel Rogosin
Supervising Producer: Howie Horwitz
Executive Producer: William T. Orr

Cast:

Van Williams	Ken Madison
Lee Patterson	Dave Thorne
Diane McBain	Daphne Dutton
Margarita Sierra	Cha Cha O'Brien
Susan Seaforth Hayes	Aimee Tucker
Nancy Valentine	Wilma Argus
Richard Crane	Lt. Glen Plehn
Noah Keen	Monte Argus
Herb Vigran	Al
Fred Graham	Hank
Fred Villani	Ziggy
Chuck Hicks	Hank's Partner

Credits:

Cinematography by Harold E. Stine
Film Editing by Noel L. Scott
Art Direction by Howard Campbell
Set Decoration by William L. Kuehl
Makeup Supervisor: Gordon Bau
Hairstylist: Jean Burt Reilly

Assistant Director: Bernard McEveety
Sound: Thomas Ashton
Theme Music Composers: Mack David and Jerry Livingston
Music Editor: Joe Inge
60 minutes/ Black and White
Production Company: Warner Bros. Television
Filmed at Warner Bros. Studios on Stages 20 and 24
Previous footage of Margarita Sierra singing "Baby Face" (first seen in Season 2, Episode 10 "The Old School Tie") was used in this episode.

Notes on the case:

Aimee Tucker, a "simple country girl" from South Carolina, arrives at the Surfside houseboat as Ken is about to go fishing. She convinces him to find her missing boyfriend, Leroy Burdette, who had promised to marry her. Ken learns that the missing man has mob ties, and is somehow involved with the recent murder of a gangster. Daphne and Cha Cha take it upon themselves to work on Aimee's "rough edges" and improve her wardrobe to make her more appealing should Burdette return. At the same time, Lt. Plehn tries to establish a case on the murdered mobster.

Nancy Valentine played the role of Wilma Argus. Valentine was born in Queens, New York on January 21, 1928. She was a Conover Model, and was discovered in 1946 by Howard Hughes at the El Morocco nightclub in Hollywood. Hughes signed her to a film contract. She first appeared on screen in bit roles in 1950. Fans may remember her from the 1952 film *The Black Castle*. She played a few minor roles during the 1950s, and worked for Warner Brothers in the early 1960s. Her final onscreen appearance was in 1973. Her career was mostly forgettable, but her personal life was far more intriguing. In 1949, she married Sri Jaggaddipandra Bhup Bahandar Narayan, the maharajah of Cooch Behar. They met in a Hollywood shoe store. The marriage was annulled in 1951 because the Indian government refused to recognize the marriage and her status as the maharani. She had been married and divorced once before. Valentine returned to California in 1951. She joined the Self-Realization Fellowship and spent three years living at the group's Los Angeles compound. In 1956, Valentine married millionaire businessman Ted Tillinghast III, but the couple divorced one year later. Nancy Valentine died at her Malibu home on July 31, 2017. She was 89 years old.

Noah Keen played the role of Monte Argus. Keen was born in Cincinnati, Ohio on October 10, 1920. He earned a Purple Heart as a bombardier in the U.S. Army Air Force during World War II. After graduating from the

University of Cincinnati, he moved to New York and found work at NBC. He made his screen debut in the 1957 film *A Face in the Crowd*. Until his retirement in 2006, Keen played character roles in more than 100 television shows including *Perry Mason, The Virginian, The Mod Squad, The Waltons, The Rockford Files, Naked City, Arrest and Trial, The F.B.I., The Doris Day Show, Cagney and Lacey, Charlie's Angels*, and *Ironside*. For his final role, he played the part of Johnny Cakes in *The Sopranos*. He is best remembered by fans for his two guest-starring appearances on *The Twilight Zone*. His feature films include *Gable and Lombard, Battle for the Planet of the Apes*, and *Disorganized Crime*. Noah Keen died in Harlem on March 24, 2019 at the age of 98. He was survived by his third wife, four children, and several grandchildren.

Many a Slip

Season 2, Episode 23

Broadcast on ABC-TV on February 26, 1962
Directed by Gunther von Fritsch
Teleplay by Gloria Elmore from a story by Gloria Elmore and Richard
    Lipscomb
Producer: Joel Rogosin
Supervising Producer: Howie Horwitz
Executive Producer: William T. Orr

Cast:

Troy Donahue	Sandy Winfield II
Van Williams	Ken Madison
Diane McBain	Daphne Dutton
Margarita Sierra	Cha Cha O'Brien
Kathryn Hays	Joy Allen
Cathy Downs	Mavis Fenton
Ed Kemmer	Bobby Edwards
Whit Bissell	Hank Fenton
John Hubbard	Guy Fox
Richard Crane	Lt. Gene Plehn
Anna Lee Carroll	Julie Fox
Barnaby Hale	Griff Hunter
Darlene Lucht	Alaskan Model

Credits:

Cinematography by Ralph Woolsey
Film Editing by James T. Heckert
Art Direction by Howard Campbell

Set Decoration by William L. Kuehl
Makeup Supervisor: Gordon Bau
Hairstylist: Jean Burt Reilly
Assistant Director: Russell Llewellyn
Sound: Dean Thomas
Theme Music Composers: Mack David and Jerry Livingston
Music Editor: Ted Sebern
60 minutes/ Black and White
Production Company: Warner Bros. Television
Filmed at Warner Bros. Studios on Stages 20 and 24
Margarita Sierra sang "Make Love with a Guitar" in this episode.

Notes on the case:

Lingerie designer Bobby Edwards plans a fashion show to feature some of his latest designs. He brings in his old friend, Griff Hunter, to stage the event. Hunter, a notorious womanizer, finds himself surrounded by beautiful women from his past, and, he hopes, new women to entertain. When he displays a special interest in one of Edwards' favorite models, Joy Allen, the men's friendship is put to the test. Suddenly, Hunter disappears. Sandy is hired to find the missing man, and unravels romantic double crosses, and a murder. He sends Daphne undercover as a lingerie model to see what she can learn.

Barnaby Hale played the role of Griff Hunter. Hale was born on January 1, 1927 in New York City. He made his television acting debut in 1960 on the science-fiction drama *Men into Space*. His television credits include *Not for Hire*, *Sea Hunt*, *The Asphalt Jungle*, *Shannon*, *The Detectives*, *Rawhide*, *The Untouchables*, *The Gallant Men*, and *The Lieutenant*. He had small roles in several feature films including *The Hook*, *A Ticklish Affair*, *Viva Las Vegas*, *Advance to the Rear*, and *Zebra in the Kitchen*. He is perhaps best known for co-starring in *The Twilight Zone* in the memorable 1963 episode, "He's Alive." Rod Serling wrote the episode which examined a neo-Nazi movement in a large American city. Serling considered this episode, which also starred Dennis Hopper and Paul Mazursky, to be the most important of the series. Barnaby Hale required an emergency surgery, but died of surgical complications on November 5, 1964 in Los Angeles. He was 37 years old.

Kathryn Hays played the role of Joy Allen. Hays was born on July 26, 1933 in Princeton, Illinois. She made her television debut in 1962 in a guest-starring role on *Hawaiian Eye*. Her numerous television credits include *Naked City*, *Wide Country*, *Dr. Kildare*, *Route 66*, *The Nurses*, *Mr. Novak*, *The Alfred Hitchcock Hour*, *The Man from U.N.C.L.E.*, *Run for Your Life*, *Star Trek*, *Here*

Come the Brides, and *Night Gallery*. She starred as Elizabeth Reynolds in the series *The Road West* (1966-67). She appeared on the daytime drama *Guiding Light*, and played the role of Kim Sullivan Hughes on *As the World Turns* from 1972 until the final episode broadcast on September 17, 2010. Hays' several films include *Ladybug Ladybug, Ride Beyond Vengeance, Counterpoint*, and *Yuma*. Her second husband was actor Glenn Ford. Kathryn Hays retired to her hometown in 2010.

Cathy Downs played the role of Mavis Fenton. Downs was born in Port Jefferson, New York on March 3, 1926. She worked as a model and cover girl, and went to Hollywood when she was picked by a talent scout for 20th Century-Fox in 1944. She made her screen debut playing the bit role of Miss Cream Puff in the 1945 film *Diamond Horseshoe*. That same year she played the role of Miss Mascara in *The Dolly Sisters*. Her numerous films include *My Darling Clementine, For You I Die, The Noose Hangs High, The Dark Corner, The Sundowners, The Flaming Urge, Kentucky Rifle, The Phantom from 10,000 Leagues, The She Creature, The Amazing Colossal Man*, and *Missile to the Moon*. Downs' few television roles include appearances on *The Millionaire, Perry Mason, Rawhide, The Lone Ranger, The Life of Riley, The Whistler*, and *Bat Masterson*. She married actor Joe Kirkwood, Jr. in 1949. Kirkwood played the role of Joe Palooka in 11 films during the 1950s, and in the 1954-55 television series *The Joe Palooka Story*. Downs co-starred with her husband in the 1951 film *Joe Palooka in Triple Cross*, and played the role of Ann Howe in the series *The Joe Palooka Story* (1954-55). Downs and Kirkwood were divorced in 1955. She remarried in 1956, and divorced again in 1963. Downs retired from acting in 1965. She struggled financially for many years. Her former husband, Kirkwood, tried to help her, but she died of cancer on December 8, 1976 in Los Angeles. She was 50 years old.

Whit Bissell played the role of Hank Fenton. Bissell was born in New York City on October 25, 1909. He studied drama and English at the University of North Carolina. His Broadway appearances include *The Star-Wagon* (1937), *The American Way* (1939), *Two on an Island* (1940), and *Café Crown* (1942). He served in the U.S. Army Air Force during World War II. Bissell made his screen debut in the 1943 film *Holy Matrimony*. His more than 100 films include *The Horn Blows at Midnight, Another Part of the Forest, Anna Lucasta, Tales of Robin Hood, Creature from the Black Lagoon, Invasion of the Body Snatchers, Gunfight at the O.K. Corral, I Was a Teenage Werewolf, I Was a Teenage Frankenstein, The Defiant Ones, The Time Machine, The Magnificent Seven, Birdman of Alcatraz, Spencer's Mountain, Hud, Airport*, and *Soylent Green*. Bissell's many television appearances include *The Lone Ranger, Peyton Place, Perry Mason, The Rifleman, Lawman, 77 Sunset Strip*,

Star Trek, *The Outer Limits*, *The Man From U.N.C.L.E.*, and *Hogan's Heroes*. He played the recurring roles of Bert Loomis in *Bachelor Father* (1958-60), and Lt. Gen. Kirk in *The Time Tunnel* (1966-67). Bissell retired in 1984. He was married three times, and had four children, including his stepson, child actor Brian Forster. Whit Bissell died of Parkinson's disease on March 5, 1996 at the Motion Picture Country Home in Woodland Hills, California at the age of 86.

The Green Beret

Season 2, Episode 24

Broadcast on ABC-TV on March 5, 1962
Directed by Paul Landres
Written by Charles B. Smith
Producer: Joel Rogosin
Supervising Producer: Howie Horwitz
Executive Producer: William T. Orr

Cast:

Lee Patterson	Dave Thorne
Van Williams	Ken Madison
Troy Donahue	Sandy Winfield II
Diane McBain	Daphne Duttton
Margarita Sierra	Cha Cha O'Brien
Adam Williams	Henry Gifford
Bart Burns	Mike Reagan
Richard Benedict	Mst. Sgt. Steve Belka
Rayford Barnes	Carl Hinbest
Bert Remsen	Sgt. Owen Crawford
Brad Weston	Sgt. Charlie Lightfoot
Ray Montgomery	Richards
Toni Gerry	Alice Mercer
Elaine Martone	Marian Scott
Kenneth MacDonald	Major Croton
James Cavanaugh	Colonel Morgan

Credits:

Cinematography by J. Peverell Marley
Film Editing by Leo H. Shreve

Art Direction by Howard Campbell
Set Decoration by William L. Kuehl
Makeup Supervisor: Gordon Bau
Hairstylist: Jean Burt Reilly
Assistant Director: Fred Scheld
Sound: B.F. Ryan and Earl Snyder
Theme Music Composers: Mack David and Jerry Livingston
Music Editor: Norman Bennett
60 minutes/ Black and White
Production Company: Warner Bros. Television
Filmed at Warner Bros. Studios on Stages20 and 24
Previous footage of Margarita Sierra singing "Bei Mir Bist Du Schon" (first
seen in Season 2, Episode 12 "Prescription for Panic") was used in this episode.

Notes on the case:

Dave is temporarily reactivated by the Army because of his expertise in gue-
rilla warfare to help train a Special Forces team. The Army Intelligence Unit is
surveilling an enemy agent. They know she has a contact within the unit that
Dave is training. Dave must discover the agent who has infiltrated his unit,
and prevent a simulated attack on a nuclear power facility from becoming
real.

Adam Williams played the
role of Henry Gifford. Williams
was born in New York City on
November 26, 1922. He earned a
Navy Cross for his service as a U.S.
Navy pilot during World War II.
He first appeared on screen in
the 1951 film *Queen for a Day*.
His other films include *Flying
Leathernecks, Without Warning!,
The Big Heat, The Proud and the
Profane, The Space Children, Fear
Strikes Out, North by Northwest,
The Last Sunset,* and *The Horse
in the Gray Flannel Suit*. He
guest-starred in many televi-
sion dramas until his retirement
in 1978 including *Perry Mason,
The Twilight Zone, The Rifleman,
Bonanza, Lawman, The Islanders,*

Adam Williams, Richard Benedict,
and Lee.

Have Gun – Will Travel, The Americans, The Asphalt Jungle, and the 1976 television movie *Helter Skelter.* He was married to actress Marilee Phelps from 1949 until 1971. The couple had three children. Adam Williams died in Los Angeles of lymphoma on December 4, 2006 at the age of 84.

Bert Remsen played the role of Sgt. Owen Crawford. Remsen was born in Glen Cove, New York on February 25, 1925. He attended Ithaca College before serving in the U.S. Navy during World War II. He was aboard the destroyer USS Laffey during the Battle of Okinawa. Remsen was injured during the sustained attack against the ship. After working with summer stock theater companies for nearly a decade, he made his television debut in 1952 on *Suspense.* His many television credits include *Maverick, Perry Mason, Thriller, Wanted: Dead or Alive, Rawhide, Alfred Hitchcock Presents, The Outer Limits,* and *Route 66.* He had recurring roles on *Dallas, Gibbsville,* and he played the role of Mario the cook on *It's a Living.* In 1964, he broke his back on the television set of *No Time for Sergeants.* He was unable to act for several years, and worked as a casting director during his recovery. When he returned to acting, he walked with the aid of a cane. He was a favorite of director Robert Altman, and played character roles in *Brewster McCloud,*

Lee.

McCabe & Mrs. Miller, Thieves Like Us, California Split, Nashville, Buffalo Bill and the Indians, and *A Wedding.* Remsen made dozens of other feature films including *Fuzz, Baby Blue Marine, The Sting II, Places in the Heart, Eye of the Tiger,* and *Miss Firecracker,* among many others. Remsen's first wife was actress Katherine MacGregor, who played the role of Mrs. Oleson on *Little House on the Prairie.* He married his second wife, actress and casting director Barbara Dodd in 1959. Bert Remsen died at his Sherman Oaks, California home on April 22, 1999 at the age of 74. He was survived by his wife of 40 years, his two daughters: actress Kerry Remsen and casting agent Ann Remsen Manners, and his brother, actor Guy Remsen.

Brad Weston played the role of Sgt. Charlie Lightfoot. Weston was born in Clarkdale, Arizona on March 5, 1928. He first appeared on television in 1958, and appeared in many television dramas including *The Deputy, Wanted: Dead or Alive, Lawman, Sugarfoot, Maverick, The Rifleman, Alfred Hitchcock Presents, Have Gun - Will Travel, Laramie, Cheyenne, 77 Sunset Strip, Star Trek,* and *The Virginian.* His feature films include *Stagecoach, Rough Night in Jericho, Barquero, Hot Lead and Cold Feet,* and *Kill the Golden Goose.* On June 25, 1980, his daughter, stuntwoman Heidi Von Beltz, was paralyzed after an on-set accident during the making of *Cannonball Run.* She was confined to a wheelchair for the rest of her life. Weston retired from acting to help care for his daughter. Patricia Campbell, his wife of 43 years, died in 1997. Brad Weston committed suicide in Los Angeles in 1999. He was survived by his daughter.

Vendetta Arms

Season 2, Episode 25

Broadcast on ABC-TV on March 12, 1962
Directed by Robert Sparr
Written by Sonya Roberts
Producer: Joel Rogosin
Supervising Producer: Howie Hortwitz
Executive Producer: William T. Orr

Cast:

Van Williams	Ken Madison
Lee Patterson	Dave Thorne
Diane McBain	Daphne Dutton
Dennis Hopper	Trask
Robert H. Harris	Max Mishkin
John Marley	Willy Pergola
James Flavin	Albert Sparks
Richard Crane	Lt. Gene Plehn
Ralf Harolde	Durgan
Jackson Halliday	Garber
William Woodson	Travers

Credits:

Cinematography by J. Peverell Marley
Film Editing by Herm Freedman
Art Direction by Howard Campbell
Set Decoration by William L. Kuehl
Makeup Supervisor: Gordon Bau
Hairstylist: Jean Burt Reilly
Assistant Director: Russell Llewellyn

Sound: Robert B. Lee
Theme Music Composers: Mack David and Jerry Livingston
Music Editor: Lou Gordon
60 minutes/ Black and White
Production Company: Warner Bros. Television
Filmed at Warner Bros. Studios on Stages 20 and 24

Notes from the case:

On an outing, Daphne spots a peculiar looking house. Curiosity gets the best of her and she decides to take a look inside. The house is occupied by five old men – retired crooks – who decide she should be a new permanent resident. A young thug named Trask is also staying there. He is responsible for nearby thefts, and threatens everyone in the house. And he takes a frightening interest in Daphne. Ken and Dave investigate a series of petty thefts, and follow the trail to the house where Daphne is being held.

Dennis Hopper played the role of Trask. Hopper was born on May 17, 1936 in Dodge City, Kansas. He began his on-screen acting career in 1954. During his tumultuous six-decade long career, he guest-starred on numerous television shows including *The Twilight Zone, Bonanza, Combat!, The Time Tunnel, 24, Flatland, E-Ring,* and *Crash*, but his greatest successes were feature films. His more than 100 films include *Rebel Without a Cause, Giant, Gunfight at the O.K. Corral, The Sons of Katie Elder, Cool Hand Luke, The Trip, True Grit, Hang 'Em High, Apocalypse Now, Blue Velvet, River's Edge, Easy Rider, Waterworld, Colors, Speed,* and *True Romance*. Hopper was nominated for two Academy Awards. He was also a talented photographer. He displayed his work in many galleries, and published collections of his photographs. Hopper was married five times. His wives were actresses Brooke Hayward, Michelle Phillips, Daria Halprin, Katherine LaNasa, and Victoria Duffy. Dennis Hopper died at his home in Venice Beach, California of prostate cancer on May 29, 2010 at the age of 74. At the time of his death, there was an ugly, ongoing, and very public divorce action against his fifth wife, Victoria Duffy, who he accused of robbing art worth millions of dollars from his home. His three adult children, including actors Ruthana Hopper and Henry Lee Hopper, sued for their share of his estimable estate.

Robert H. Harris played the role of Max Mishkin. Harris was born in Manhattan on July 15, 1911. He worked at the Yiddish Art Theater when he was young, and made his Broadway debut in 1937 in *Schoolhouse on the Lot*. Harris's first love was the stage, and he starred in numerous Broadway productions including *Brooklyn U.S.A .*(1941-42), *Look Ma I'm Dancin'* (1948), *King Richard III* (1949), *Foxy* (1964), *Minor Miracle* (1965), *Xmas in Las Vegas* (1965), and *Zelda* (1969). He made his film debut in the 1948 movie

The Naked City. His other films include *Bundle of Joy*, *The Big Caper*, *The Invisible Boy*, *Peyton Place*, *The George Raft Story*, *How to Make a Monster*, *Nightmare in Chicago*, *Valley of the Dolls*, *How Awful About Allan*, and *The Man in the Glass Booth*. Harris starred as Jake Goldberg in the television series *The Goldbergs* (1953-54). His many television appearances include *Alfred Hitchcock Presents*, *The Court of Last Resort*, *Perry Mason*, *Voyage to the Bottom of the Sea*, *Gunsmoke*, *The Man from U.N.C.L.E.*, *The Untouchables*, *Suspense*, *Climax!*, *Bonanza*, *77 Sunset Strip*, *Ben Casey*, *Rawhide*, and *Barnaby Jones*. He retired in 1977. Robert H. Harris died in Los Angeles on November 30, 1981 at the age of 70. He was survived by his second wife of 38 years, actress Viola Harris.

John Marley played the role of Willie Pergola. Marley was born on October 17, 1907 in New York City. He served in the U.S. Army Signal Corps during World War II, and made his screen debut in the 1947 film *Kiss of Death*. His dozens of films include *The Naked City*, *Ma and Pa Kettle Go to Town*, *The Joe Louis Story*, *I Want to Live!*, *Cat Ballou*, *Faces*, *The Godfather*, *Blade*, *Hooper*, and *Tribute*. He was nominated for an Academy Award and a Golden Globe Award for his performance in the 1970 film *Love Story*. Marley appeared in seven Broadway plays including *An Enemy of the People* (1950-51), *Sing Till Tomorrow* (1953-54), and *Compulsion* (1957-58). His many television credits include *The Untouchables*, *The Outer Limits*, *The Alfred Hitchcock Hour*, *The Twilight Zone*, *The Wild, Wild West*, *The Name of the Game*, and *Hawaii-Five-O*. He married his first wife, actress Stanja Lowe, in 1951. The couple had three children, including actor Ben Marley, before divorcing in 1971. John Marley died in Los Angeles on May 22, 1984 from complications following heart surgery. He was 76 years old, and survived by his second wife and four children.

James Flavin played the role of Albert Sparks. Flavin was born in Portland, Maine on May 14, 1906. He graduated from the United States Military Academy, and became interested in acting when he joined a summer stock company in Maine. His stock work led him to New York, and ultimately to Hollywood in 1932. He starred in the Universal film serial *The Airmail Mystery*. His career as a leading man never materialized, but he played small and supporting roles in more than 300 films until his retirement in 1971, including *Test Pilot*, *Alexander's Ragtime Band*, *You Can't Take it with You*, *The Grapes of Wrath*, *The Long Voyage Home*, *Hold Back the Dawn*, *Yankee Doodle Dandy*, *Heaven Can Wait*, *Anchors Away*, *Mildred Pierce*, and *Mister Roberts*. He guest-starred in more than 100 television shows, and played the recurring role of stable-owner Slattery on *Mister Ed* (1961-65), and co-starred in the Warner series *The Roaring 20's* from 1960 until 1962. Flavin made his Broadway debut in the revival of *The Front Page* (1969-70). James Flavin suffered heart failure and died in Los Angeles on April 23, 1976 at the age of 69.

He was survived by his wife of 44 years, actress Lucile Browne. Browne died two weeks after her husband's death.

Ralf Harolde played the role of Durgan. Harolde was born on May 17, 1899 in Pittsburgh, Pennsylvania. His work as a young man with a stock company was interrupted when he served with the U.S. Marine Corps near the end of World War I. He returned to work on stage, and was cast in a Pacific Coast tour of *The Front Page*. He made his screen debut in the 1920 film *Headin' Home*. Harolde was typecast as a villain or gangster, and appeared in 100 films during his career. Some of his better known films include *Night Nurse, I'm No Angel, Jimmy the Gent, Baby Take a Bow, Million Dollar Baby, A Tale of Two Cities, Song and Dance Man, The Sea Wolf, Murder My Sweet*, and *The Phantom Speaks*. He appeared in several movie serials including *Gang Busters* (1942), *Secret Service in Darkest Africa* (1943), and *Captain America* (1943). In the mid-1930s, Harolde had a relationship with actor Monroe Owsley. They were involved in a car accident which resulted in the death of Owsley, who suffered a heart attack and died on June 7, 1937. Harolde battled alcoholism, and in June, 1938, he was arrested for kidnapping a six-year old boy from a Hollywood school yard and taking him to a soda fountain for an ice cream. Police were summoned, and although kidnap charges were ultimately dropped, Harolde was still arrested for outstanding traffic violations. He did not appear again on screen for two years. Shortly before his retirement in 1963, he appeared on a few television shows including *The Deputy, Miami Undercover*, and *Mike Hammer*. He had three short-lived marriages. Ralf Harolde died of pneumonia on November 1, 1974 in Los Angeles.

Dennis Hopper and Diane.

A Piece of Tommy Minor

Season 2, Episode 26

Broadcast on ABC-TV on March 19, 1962
Directed by Richard Benedict
Teleplay by John O'Dea from a story by John O'Dea and Ric Hardman
Producer: Joel Rogosin
Supervising Producer: Howie Horwitz
Executive Producer: William T. Orr

Cast:

Troy Donahue	Sandy Winfield II
Diane McBain	Daphne Dutton
Lee Philips	Eddie Groves
Tom Drake	Al Dickens
Kenny Roberts	Tommy Minor
Ann McCrea	Lola Scott
Pegeen Rose	Lucille Dickens
Paul Dubov	Vic Tatum
Penny Santon	Momma
Richard Crane	Lt. Gene Plehn
Murray Kamelhar	Cato
Frankie Ortega	Himself (as Frankie Ortega Trio)
Walter Sage	Drummer
Carl Fredrick Tandberg	Bass Player

Credits:

Cinematography by Floyd Crosby
Film Editing by Byron Chudnow
Art Direction by Howard Campbell
Set Decoration by Hoyle Barrett

Makeup Supervisor: Gordon Bau
Hairstylist: Jean Burt Reilly
Assistant Director: Fred Scheld
Sound: B. F. Ryan
Theme Music Composers: Mack David and Jerry Livingston
Music Editor: Robert Phillips
60 minutes/ Black and White
Production Company: Warner Bros. Television
Filmed at Warner Bros Studios on Stages 20 and 24
Kenny Roberts sang "Bye Bye Blackbird" and "You and the Night and the Music" in this episode.

Notes from the case:

Vic Tatum, a gambling kingpin, owns a gambling boat anchored outside territorial limits. Singer Tommy Minor is deeply in debt to Tatum. Minor's manager is approached by Tatum who offers to forgive the singer's gambling debts for controlling interest in his career. The manager hires Sandy to look into the problem. Sandy is able to wipe out the debt, but Tatum is determined to wrest control of the singer's business. Minor's family is jockeying for money, including his brother-in-law who falls for a Tatum scheme and forces Tommy to sign a contract with the gangster. To make sure Tommy stays in line, Tatum frames him for killing his brother-in-law.

Paul Dubov played the role of Vic Tatum. Dubov was born in Chicago on October 10, 1918. He made his screen debut in the 1938 film *Little Tough Guy*. His numerous films include *Cyrano de Bergerac, I, the Jury, Day the World Ended, The She Creature, Voodoo Woman, The Purple Gang, The Underwater City, Irma la Douce,* and *Shock Corridor*. His many television acting credits include *Perry Mason, Hawaiian Eye, That Girl, Make Room for Daddy, Bonanza, Zorro, The Ann Sothern Show, The Untouchables,* and *Burke's Law*. He retired from acting in 1976. In 1963, he married writer Gwen Bagni. Together they created the television series *Honey West*. His writing credits include *The Green Hornet*, and multiple episodes of *Burke's Law, Honey West, Mod Squad,* and *Eight is Enough*. He wrote the screenplay for the movie *With Six You Get Eggroll*. Dobov and his wife were nominated for an Emmy Award for writing an episode of *Backstairs at the White House*. Paul Dubov died of cancer on September 20, 1979 in Encino, California. He was 60 years old, and survived by his wife.

Kenny Roberts played the role of Tommy Minor. Roberts was born on December 31, 1941 in Modesto, California. His short-lived acting career consisted of appearing in the 1955 film *Six Bridges to Cross*, and guest-starring roles in several television shows including *The Aquanauts, Ripcord,* and

Death Valley Days. His appearance in this episode of *Surfside 6* marked the end of his acting career.

Lee Philips played the role of Eddie Groves. Philips was born on January 10, 1927 in New York City. He appeared on Broadway in *Mademoiselle Colombe* (1954) and *Middle of the Night* (1956-57). He first appeared on television in 1952. Philips' television acting credits include *Naked City, Alfred Hitchcock Presents, 77 Sunset Strip, The Untouchables, The Defenders, Ripcord, Route 66, The Twilight Zone, Perry Mason, I Spy, The Ghost and Mrs. Muir*, and *The Waltons*. He starred as Ellery Queen in the 1959 series *The Further Adventures of Ellery Queen*. Philips played the role of Michael Rossi in the 1957 film *Peyton Place*. His other films include *The Hunters, Middle of the Night, Tess of Storm Country, Violent Midnight*, and *The Lollipop Cover*. He retired from acting in 1975. Philips began directing for television in 1963. For the next 32 years he directed more than 75 television episodes, including numerous episodes of *The Dick Van Dyke Show, Peyton Place, The Andy Griffith Show, The Ghost and Mrs. Muir, Room 222, The Doris Day Show*, and *The Waltons*. He was married and divorced twice. His first wife was actress Jean Allison. Lee Philips died at his Brentwood home on March 3, 1999 of Progressive Supranuclear Palsy (PSP). He was 72 years old, and survived by his two children.

Tom Drake played the role of Al Dickens. Drake was born on August 5, 1918 in Brooklyn, New York. He graduated from the Mercersburg Academy in Pennsylvania. A heart murmur excused him from service during World War II. Drake made his Broadway debut in the 1938 play *Run Sheep Run*. His starring role in the 1942 Broadway hit *Janie* earned him a contract with MGM Studios. He had uncredited roles in a couple of films, but his first credited film role was in the 1940 hit *The Howards of Virginia*. His other films include *Two Girls and a Sailor, The White Cliffs of Dover, Maisie Goes to Reno, Marriage is a Private Affair, Mrs. Parkington, Courage of Lassie, I'll Be Yours, Words and Music, Mr. Belvedere Goes to College, Raintree County, The Sandpiper*, and *The Singing Nun*. He is perhaps best remembered for playing the role of John Truett in the 1944 classic *Meet Me in St. Louis*. His later television appearances include *Climax!, Lux Video Theatre, Perry Mason, The Alfred Hitchcock Hour, The Wild, Wild West, The Green Hornet, Marcus Welby, M.D., Hawaiian Eye, 77 Sunset Strip*, and *Bourbon Street Beat*. He retired in 1978. Tom Drake was gay. He was deeply closeted during his life. His one marriage in 1945, arranged by MGM Studio bosses, lasted less than a year. He battled alcoholism for most of his life. Tom Drake died in Torrance, California of lung cancer on August 11, 1982 at the age of 64.

Portrait of Nicole

Season 2, Episode 27

Broadcast on ABC-TV on March 26, 1962
Directed by Otto Lang
Written by Glenn P Wolfe and Sol Stein
Producer: Joel Rogosin
Supervising Producer: Howie Horwitz
Executive Producer: William T. Orr

Cast:

Lee Patterson	Dave Thorne
Troy Donahue	Sandy Winfield II
Van Williams	Ken Madison
Diane McBain	Daphne Dutton
Roxanne Arlen	Nicole Johnson I
Francine York	Nicole Johnson II
Richard Crane	Lt. Gene Plehn
Kathryn Givney	Mrs. Wellman
Laurie Mitchell	Gloria Claire
Ken Swofford	Garth
Don C. Harvey	George Crane
Peggy McCay	Nicole Crane
Mike Road	Paul Burnett

Credits:

Cinematography by Frank G. Carson
Film Editing by Robert L. Wolfe
Art Direction by Howard Campbell
Set Decoration by John P. Austin
Makeup Supervisor: Gordon Bau

Hairstylist: Jean Burt Reilly
Assistant Director: Victor Vallejo
Sound: Ross Owen
Theme Music Composers: Mack David and Jerry Livingston
Music Editor: Joe Inge
60 minutes/ Black and White
Production Company: Warner Bros. Television
Filmed at Warner Bros. Studios on Stages 20 and 24

Notes on the case:

A racketeer dies and leaves his fortune to a former girlfriend named Nicole
Johnson. But Nicole Johnson cannot be located by the insurance company
which subsequently hires Ken, Dave, and Sandy to locate the missing heiress.
The real mystery begins when the three detectives each locate three different
Nicoles. And each one matches the description of the missing woman.

Francine York played the role of Nicole Johnson #2. York was born in
Aurora, Minnesota on August 26, 1936. She worked as a model, and in the
1950s, she was a showgirl at the famed Moulin Rouge nightclub in Hollywood.
She studied acting with Jeff Corey, and made her television debut in 1959 on
the drama *Rescue 8*. York's many television credits include *It Takes a Thief*,
The Courtship of Eddie's Father,
My Favorite Martian, *Death
Valley Days*, *Burke's Law*, *Perry
Mason*, *Lost in Space*, *Green
Acres*, *Batman*, *Route 66*, *Gomer
Pyle U.S.M.C.*, *Bewitched*, *Hot
in Cleveland*, and *The Mindy
Project*, among others. She also
appeared on the daytime dramas
All My Children, *One Life to Live*,
and *Santa Barbara*. Her feature
films include *The Sergeant Was
a Lady*, *It's Only Money*, *Secret
File: Hollywood*, *Bedtime Story*,

Troy with Francine York.

The Nutty Professor, *The Disorderly Orderly*, *The Patsy*, *Cracking Up*, *The
Family Jewels*, *Tickle Me*, *Space Probe Taurus*, *Curse of the Swamp Creature*,
Mutiny in Outer Space, *Welcome Home Soldier Boys*, *The Family Man*, and
the cult classic *The Doll Squad*. Francine York died in Van Nuys, California
of cancer on January 6, 2017. She was 80 years old.

Ken Swofford played the role of Garth. Swofford was born on July 25,
1933 in Du Quoin, Illinois. He graduated Southern Illinois University with

a Bachelor Degree in Theater in 1959. He began his acting career in summer stock theater, where he met and married actress Barbee Biggs in 1958. Swofford made his acting debut on screen in 1962 in this episode of *Surfside*. His feature films include *Captain Newman M.D.*, *Father Goose*, *Bless the Beasts and the Children*, *The Andromeda Strain*, *Skyjacked*, *The Domino Principle*, *S.O.B.*, *Annie*, *Black Roses*, *Thelma & Louise*, *The Taking of Beverly Hills*, and *Cops 'n Robbers*. Swofford's more than 100 television appearances include *Gunsmoke*, *Here Come the Brides*, *Police Story*, *Mission: Impossible*, *The Rockford Files*, *Dynasty*, *Fame*, *The A-Team*, *Murder She Wrote*, *Ellery Queen*, *Remington Steele*, *Falcon Crest*, *Highway to Heaven*, *Matlock*, *Baywatch*, and *Diagnosis: Murder*. Swofford was convicted of felony drunk driving in 1989, and sentenced to two and a half years in prison. He resumed his career upon his release. He formerly retired in 1995, but performed voice-over roles until shortly before his death. Ken Swofford died in Pacific Grove, California on November 1, 2018 at the age of 85. He was survived by his wife of 60 years, and five children.

"I became friends with Francine years after this episode," Diane recalled. "I was doing a book signing in Hollywood for my memoir, *Famous Enough*, and Francine attended, and re-introduced herself afterwards. She had read my book, and told me she had experienced many of the tougher things I went through working in Hollywood. We had some good laughs, and we stayed in touch. We each won Life Achievement Awards at the 50th Annual Cinecon Convention in Hollywood in 2014. We had dinner together at the banquet, and shared stories and some great belly laughs. At the reception before the ceremony, we were standing at the bar to get a glass of wine. Someone came up to Francine and congratulated her for winning the award. She was gracious, then turned to me and said, "And it's about fucking time!" And it was. For both of us. She was terrific, and a ball of positive energy. I spoke at her memorial service at the Egyptian Theater in Hollywood."

Elegy for a Bookkeeper

Season 2, Episode 28

Broadcast on ABC-TV on April 2, 1962
Directed by Paul Landres
Written by Herman Groves
Producer: Joel Rogosin
Supervising Producer: Howie Horwitz
Executive Producer: William T. Orr

Cast:

Van Williams	Ken Madison
Lee Patterson	Dave Thorne
Diane McBain	Daphne Dutton
Margarita Sierra	Cha Cha O'Brien
Arch Johnson	Emery Stark
Alex Gerry	Bernie Witt
Ross Elliot	Frank Eliot
Richard Crane	Lt. Gene Plehn
Les Hellman	Rondo
Charles Irving	Richard Weldon
Robert Bice	Charlie Coates
Charles Seel	Max Carson
Shirley Knight	Jan Coates
Robert Glenn	Sgt. Woodley

Credits:

Cinematography by Robert Tobey
Film Editing by George R. Rohrs
Art Direction by Howard Campbell
Set Decoration by William L. Kuehl

Makeup Supervisor: Gordon Bau
Hairstylist: Jean Burt Reilly
Assistant Director: Bernard McEveety
Sound: Robert B. Lee
Theme Music Composers: Mack David and Jerry Livingston
Music Editor: Sam E. Levin
60 minutes/Black and White
Production Company: Warner Bros. Television
Filmed at Warner Bros. Studios on Stages 20 and 24
Margarita Sierra sang "Looking for a Boy" and "I Only Have Eyes for You" in this episode.

Notes on the case:

On the day before he is set to be released from prison, bookkeeper Charlie Coates dies mysteriously. Coates is Ken's former client, and he intended to provide evidence to the detective about the mob boss responsible for his imprisonment. Coates' daughter, Jan, agrees to help Ken and Dave investigate the situation. Firstly, the detectives must convince everyone that Coates is still alive. And, secondly, they pretend to have split up over a disagreement with Jan.

Robert Bice played the role of Charlie Coates. Bice was born in Dallas, Texas on March 14, 1914. Typically cast as a "tough guy," Bice played small or supporting roles in more than 250 films and television dramas. He made his screen debut in the 1943 movie *The Ghost and the Guest*. His other films include *Dragon Seed, Thirty Seconds Over Tokyo, The Mysterious Mr. Valentine, The Bachelor and the Bobby-Soxer, Tales of Robin Hood, Captive Women, Tarzan and the She-Devil, The Wild One, The Snow Creature, Jailhouse Rock*, and *It! The Terror from Beyond Space*. The actor's many television credits include *The Lone Ranger, The Cisco Kid, I Love Lucy, M Squad, Fury, Peter Gunn, Bat Masterson, Rawhide, The Rifleman, Wagon Train, Daniel Boone*, and *Death Valley Days*. Robert Bice died in Los Angeles on January 8, 1968 at the age of 53. He was married to actress Andre Stuart.

Arch Johnson played the role of Emery Stark. Johnson was born on March 14, 1922 in Minneapolis, Minnesota. He attended the University of Pennsylvania, and first appeared on stage at the Plays and Players Theatre in Philadelphia in the world premiere of *Stalag 17*. He studied two years at the Neighborhood Playhouse School of the Theatre in New York, and made his Broadway debut in the 1955 production *The Terrible Swift Sword*. His other Broadway credits include *Saint Joan* (1956-57), *The Happiest Millionaire* (1956-57), and the original production of *West Side Story* (1957-59). Johnson reprised his role in the 1980 Broadway revival of *West Side Story*. He made his screen debut in the 1953 movie *Niagara*. His other film appearances include *Garden of Eden, Somebody Up There Likes Me, G.I. Blues, The Liberation of L.B. Jones, The Cheyenne Social Club, The Sting, Walking Tall, Rafferty and the Gold Dust Twins*, and *The Buddy Holly Story*. Johnson's numerous television credits include *Bat Masterson, Gunsmoke, The Twilight Zone, Bonanza, The Virginian, The Munsters, The Monkees, Bewitched, Perry Mason, Mr. Novak*, and *Daniel Boone*. He played recurring roles in the television series *The Asphalt Jungle* (1961), *It's Always Jan* (1955-56), *Peter Loves Mary* (1960-61), and *Camp Runamuck* (1965-66). Arch Johnson retired in 1990. He died of cancer in Snow Hill, Maryland on October 9, 1997 at the age of 75. He was survived by his fifth wife of two years, and five children.

The Money Game

Season 2, Episode 29

Broadcast on ABC-TV on April 9, 1962
Directed by George Waggner
Teleplay by Frederick Brady and Gloria Elmore from a story by Frederick Brady
Producer: Joel Rogosin
Supervising Producer: Howie Horwitz
Executive Producer: William T. Orr

Cast:

Troy Donahue	Sandy Winfield II
Van Williams	Ken Madison
Diane McBain	Daphne Dutton
Margarita Sierra	Cha Cha O'Brien
Gerald Mohr	Hermes Doratis
Nico Minardos	Prince Karan
Roxane Berard	Princess Cassida
Christopher Dark	General Hakim
Charles Lane	Cyrus Radford
Margo Moore	Margo
Bobby Gilbert	Gambler
Mike Lally	Bartender
Harold Mille	Gambler
Murray Pollack	Club Patron
Paul Power	Club Patron
Cosmo Sardo	Maitre d'
Dick Tufeld	Announcer

Credits:

Cinematography by Harold E. Stine
Film Editing by George R. Rohrs
Art Direction by Howard Campbell
Set Decoration by Hoyle Barrett
Makeup Supervisor: Gordon Bau
Hairstylist: Jean Burt Reilly
Assistant Director: Richard Maybery
Sound: B.F. Ryan
Theme Music Composer: Mack David and Jerry Livingston
Music Editor: John Allyn Jr.
60 minutes/ Black and White
Production Company: Warner Bros. Television
Filmed at Warner Bros. Studios on Stages 20 and 24
Previous footage of Margarita Sierra singing "You Must Have Been a Beautiful Baby" (first seen in Season 2, Episode 1 "Count Seven!") was used in this episode.

Notes on the case:

Conniving oilman Cyrus Radford hires Sandy and Ken to set up a meeting with Prince Akran, whose tiny Middle Eastern country is drowning in oil. Radford wants to buy the oil rights from Akran. But another rival for the "black gold," Hermes Doratis, is also after the valuable rights and uses the Prince's sister to influence her brother. The rivals will stop at nothing, including killing Prince Akran.

Nico Minardos played the role of Prince Akran. Minardos was born in Athens, Greece on February 15, 1930. He emigrated to the United States in the early1950s, and became naturalized in 1960. He first appeared on screen in the 1952 film *Monkey Business*. His other films include *The Egyptian, Desert Sands, The Ten Commandments, Istanbul, Ghost Drive, Holiday for Lovers, Twelve Hours to Kill, It Happened in Athens, Cannon for Cordoba,* and *Assault on Agathon*. His many television credits include *The Thin Man, Maverick, Whirlybirds, Sugarfoot, Adventures in Paradise, The Rebel, Route 66, Naked City, The Twilight Zone, 77 Sunset Strip, Hawaiian Eye, Burke's Law, Daktari, The Flying Nun, Mod Squad, Ironside,* and *The A-Team*. Minardos' personal life was more dramatic than any film he appeared in. He romanced and for a short time lived with Marilyn Monroe in the early 1950s, and with Juliet Prowse in the early 1960s. On September 28, 1966, he was filming an episode of the series *Off to See the Wizard* on location in Peru. He was riding in a canoe with actor Eric Fleming, when they overturned in the Huallaga River. Minardos survived, but Eric Fleming was swept away in the rapids and drowned. In 1986, Minardos was caught in an F.B.I. sting on charges of conspiracy to illegally ship arms to Iran with the assistance of a business associate, Saudi arms dealer Adnan Khashoggi. The indictment was eventually dismissed, but the incident ended his career. He filed bankruptcy, sold his Beverly Hills home, and moved to Florida. He bought a yacht and sailed across the Atlantic Ocean with his son to Greece. Minardos lived in Southern Florida until 2009. He suffered a stroke, and was moved to the Motion Picture Country Home in Woodland Hills, California, where he died on August 27, 2011, at the age of 81. He was survived by his second wife of 46 years, and his son and daughter.

Charles Lane played the role of Cyrus Radford. Lane was born in San Francisco on January 26, 1905. His father was an insurance executive instrumental in rebuilding San Francisco after the 1906 earthquake. Lane began acting at the Pasadena Playhouse in 1929. He made his screen debut in 1930. Lane quickly became one of Hollywood's most popular and beloved supporting actors, usually playing mean and miserly old men. His more than 250 feature films include *42nd Street, Gold Diggers of 1933, Mr. Deeds Goes to Town, In Old Chicago, You Can't Take It with You, Blondie, Golden Boy, Mr. Smith Goes to Washington, The Cat and the Canary, Buck Benny Rides Again, I Wake Up Screaming, Tarzan's New York Adventure, Arsenic and Old Lace, It's a Wonderful Life, The Farmer's Daughter, It Happened on Fifth Avenue, Mighty Joe Young, The Music Man,* and *It's a Mad, Mad, Mad, Mad World.* He played the role of Dr. Prouty in *Ellery Queen, Master Detective* (1940), *Ellery Queen's Penthouse Mystery* (1941), and *Ellery Queen and the Perfect Crime* (1941). Lane appeared in more than 100 television shows including *I Love Lucy, The Lucy Show, The Lucy-Desi Comedy Hour, The Real McCoy's, Perry Mason, Dennis the Menace, Mister Ed, Petticoat Junction, The Beverly Hillbillies, The Munsters, Nanny and the Professor, Soap,* and *Little House on the Prairie.* Lane married Ruth Covell in 1931. The couple had two children. Ruth died in 2002. In 2006, he narrated the short film *The Night Before Christmas,* which was his final performance. Charles Lane died of natural causes at his Brentwood home on July 9, 2007 at the age of 102. He was survived by his daughter, and son Tom, who was with him when he died.

Roxane Berard played the role of Princess Cassida. Berard was born in Belgium on January 21, 1933. Her family fled the Nazis, and moved to France, then Sprain, then Portugal, and eventually to America in 1945. She studied at the High School of Music and Art in New York City, and at the High School for the Performing Arts. She made her television debut in 1958. Her numerous television credits include *Bracken's World, Get Smart, Perry Mason, The Dick Van Dyke Show, Zorro, Father Knows Best, The Many Loves of Dobie Gillis, Gunsmoke, The Untouchables,* and *The Tab Hunter Show.* For a short time, she worked under contract to Warner Brothers, and appeared in many of the studio's television productions including *Maverick, Colt. 45, 77 Sunset Strip, Bronco,* and *Bourbon Street Beat.* She had small roles in a few films including *Harlow* and *Mirage.* Berard retired in 1970. She was married and divorced twice, and had three sons. She raised horses, and managed a "tack" shop. Later, she owned ladies' boutiques in San Diego North County. She took up painting in her later life, and was a San Diego based mural painter. Roxane Berard died at the age of 86 on December 31, 2019. She was survived by her three sons.

Margo Moore played the role of Margo. She was born in Chicago on April 29, 1931. Moore contracted polio when she was 13, but recovered after spending two years in a hip-to-shoulder cast. She worked as a model and cover girl with the Ford Modeling Agency, and appeared in numerous television commercials. She made her acting debut in the 1959 film *Hound-Dog Man.* Her other films include *Wake Me When It's Over, The George Raft Story, Bachelor Flat,* and *Who's Been Sleeping in My Bed?.* Moore made her television debut on this episode of *Surfside.* Her other television appearances include *Perry Mason* and *Run for Your Life.* She retired from acting to raise her son from her first marriage, and pursue business interests. In the 1970s, she owned a photography gallery in San Francisco. In the 1980s, she moved back to New York City and managed "The Chocolate Garden," a candy shop in midtown. She was also the corporate events manager for *Working Women* magazine. In 1982, she married a New York City policeman. The couple retired in rural Pennsylvania and opened The Toy Robot and Pig Museum in Stoudtburg Village in Adamstown. Margo Moore died from breast cancer in Greenville, South Carolina on December 16, 2000. Moore was 69 years old, and survived by her husband and son.

Troy and Margo Moore.

Irish Pride

Season 2, Episode 30

Broadcast on ABC-TV on April 16, 1962
Directed by Sidney Salkow
Written by Ed Waters
Executive Producer: William T. Orr

Cast:

Troy Donahue	Sandy Winfield II
Van Williams	Ken Madison
Lee Patterson	Dave Thorne
Margarita Sierra	Cha Cha O'Brien
Sheldon Allman	Schubert
Richard Crane	Lt. Gene Plehn
Terence De Marney	Patrick "Tobe" Tobin
Robert Glenn	Sgt. Woodley
Malachy McCourt	Dan O'Brien
Harold Peary	R. K. Mountain

Credits:

Makeup Supervisor: Gordon Bau
Hairstylist: Jean Burt Reilly
Theme Music Composers: Mack David and Jerry Livingston
60 minutes/ Black and White
Production Company: Warner Bros. Television
Filmed at Warner Bros. Studios on Stages 20 and 24
Margarita Sierra, Lee Patterson and Van Williams sang "When Irish Eyes Are Smiling" in this episode.

Notes on the case:

Dan O'Brien, Cha Cha's Irish cousin, arrives in Miami for a visit. His friend Patrick Tobin supposedly arrived a couple of weeks earlier with O'Brien's savings, which he promised to invest, but he and the money are missing. When Tobin turns up murdered, O'Brien is the prime suspect. Cha Cha teams up with the Surfside detectives to find out what really happened, and who is responsible.

Malachy McCourt played the role of Dan O'Brien. McCourt was born in New York City on September 20, 1931. He made his television debut in 1959. His television appearances include *The F.B.I.*, *Cosby*, and *Oz*. He played recurring roles on the daytime dramas *Ryan's Hope*, *Search for Tomorrow*, and *One Life to Live*. From 1992 until 2009, he played the role of Father Clarence for an annual Christmas-time guest appearance on *All My Children*. He played small and supporting roles in many films including *The Molly Maguires*, *The Brink's Job*, *The Orphan*, *Brewster's Millions*, *The Field*, *Reversal of Fortune*, *The Bonfire of the Vanities*, *The Devil's Own*, *Ash Wednesday*, *The Guru*, *Nick and Nicky*, and *The Fitzgerald Family Christmas*. He has worked on radio, and in regional theater. McCourt's older brother was acclaimed novelist Frank McCourt. McCourt is a respected author in his own right, penning *A Monk Swimming* and *Singing My Him Song*. Many New Yorkers remember him for his bar, Malachy's, a favorite hangout for actors on Third Avenue in Manhattan.

Terence De Marney played the role of "Tobe" Tobin. De Marney was born on March 1, 1908 in London, England. He began his long acting career on stage in London. He toured in *The Last of Mrs. Cheyney*, *The Lady of the Camellias*, *Journey's End*, *Romeo and Juliet*, *'Tis Pity She's a Whore*, *Ten Little Indians*, and *Trilby*. He starred in the radio dramas *Count of Monte Cristo* and *The Saint*. De Marney made his screen debut in the 1931 film *The Eternal Feminine*. His many films include *The Unholy Quest*, *The Mystery of the Mary Celeste*, *The Silver Chalice*, *The Virgin Queen*, *The Ten Commandments*, *Pharaoh's Curse*, *Spartacus*, *Midnight Lace*, *Die Monster Die!*, *The Hand of Night*, *The Strange Affair*, and *All Neat in Black Stockings*. He co-wrote and starred in the 1949 film *No Way Back*. His numerous television appearances

Lee, Troy, and Van.

include *Shirley Temple's Storybook, Bonanza, Bourbon Street Beat, Wagon Train, Peter Gunn, Thriller, Sugarfoot, Adventures in Paradise, Maverick, Doctor Who,* and *The Twilight Zone.* He had many theatrical director credits, and wrote several plays including *Wanted for Murder, The Whispering Gallery, The Crime of Margaret Foley,* and *Search.* Terence De Marney died on May 25, 1971 when he fell in front of an oncoming underground train in London. He was 63 years old. De Marney was predeceased by his wife of 20 years, actress Beryl Measor, in 1965. He was survived by his brother, actor Derrick De Marney.

Green Bay Riddle

Season 2, Episode 31

Broadcast on ABC-TV on April 23, 1962
Directed by Jeffrey Hayden
Teleplay by Herbert Purdom from a story by Whitman Chambers
Producer: Joel Rogosin
Supervising Producer: Howie Horwitz
Executive Producer: William T. Orr

Cast:

Van Williams	Ken Madison
Lisa Gaye	Henri Wakeman
Kathie Browne	Peggy Allen
Simon Scott	Chris Nordheim
Lee Farr	Charles Allen
Frank Ferguson	Sheriff Boyd
Barney Phillips	Murphy
Harvey Korman	Prosecutor
Donald May	Richie Linden

Credits:

Cinematography by Robert Tobey
Film Editing by Byron Chudnow
Art Direction by Howard Campbell
Set Decoration by William L. Kuehl
Makeup Supervisor: Gordon Bau
Hairstylist: Jean Burt Reilly
Assistant Director: Chuck Hansen
Sound: Eugene Irvine
Theme Music Composers: Mack David and Jerry Livingston

Music Editor: John Allyn Jr.
60 minutes/ Black and White
Production Company: Warner Bros. Television
Filmed at Warner Bros. Studios on Stages 20 and 24

Notes on the case:

Charles Allen stands accused of murdering his father-in-law, although the victim's body has not been found. He is acquitted of the crime, but many in the victim's upscale community of Green Bay, including his own brother-in-law, Richie Linden, consider him guilty. Allen's wife, Peggy, hires Ken to investigate the crime and determine who is really responsible, and what really happened to her father.

Lee Farr played the role of Charles Allen. Farr was born in New York City on April 10, 1927. He enlisted in the U.S. Navy upon graduating from high school. He later received a Bachelor Degree in Geophysics from Penn State University. He worked as a geologist before beginning his acting career in 1957. Farr's feature films include *The True Story of Lynn Stuart, Thundering Jets, Tarawa Beachhead, Lone Texan,* and *Gunfighters of Abilene.* His television credits include *M Squad, The Millionaire, Whirlybirds, Lawman, Wanted: Dead or Alive, Trackdown, Have Gun – Will Travel, Lancer, The Rifleman, Laramie, Lassie, Perry Mason, Bonanza, The Invaders,* and *The Rookies.* He played the role of Lt. James Conway in the series *The Detectives* (1959-60). He married actress Felicia Farr in 1949. The couple had one daughter before divorcing in 1955. Lee Farr retired in 1978. He died at his home in Woodland Hills, California from cancer on March 23, 2017 at the age of 89. He was survived by his daughter.

Donald May played the role of Richie Linden. May was born in Chicago, Illinois on February 22, 1927. In 1948, he worked in summer stock theater in Maine, New York, and Vermont. He joined the U.S. Navy in 1951, and became an ensign and a gunnery officer on a destroyer. He was discharged in 1955, and made his screen debut in the 1956 film *The Wrong Man.* His other films include *The Crowded Sky, A Tiger Walks, Kisses for My President,* and *Follow Me, Boys!* He starred in the role of Cadet Charles Thompson in the drama series *The West Point Story* (1956-57). May was a contract player at Warner Brothers, and appeared in most of the studio's television productions including *Sugarfoot, Cheyenne, 77 Sunset Strip, Hawaiian Eye,* and *Colt .45.* He played the role of Pat Garrison in the series *The Roaring 20's* (1960-62). His later television appearances include *Combat!, The F.B.I., Barnaby Jones, Fantasy Island, Falcon Crest,* and *L.A. Law.* Fans remember him for his appearances on several daytime dramas including *As the World Turns, All My Children,* and *One Life to Live.* He played the role of Grant

Wheeler in *Texas* (1981-82), and played the role of Adam Drake on *The Edge of Night* from 1967 until 1976. May's second wife is actress Carla Borelli. He has two sons from his first marriage, actors Christopher May and Douglas May. Donald May retired in 1993.

Kathie Browne played the role of Peggy Allen. Browne was born on September 19, 1930 in San Luis Obispo, California. She attended Los Angeles City College, and was discovered when she starred in a Los Angeles production of *Cat on a Hot Tin Roof*. In 1955, she first appeared on television in *Big Town*. Her many television guest-starring appearances include *Perry Mason*, *Bonanza*, *Gunsmoke*, *Wagon Train*, *Tombstone Territory*, *Rawhide*, *My Favorite Martian*, *Get Smart*, *The Wild, Wild West*, *Ironside*, *The Rockford Files*, *The Big Valley*, *Banacek*, and *Kolchak: The Night Stalker*. Browne's feature films include *Murder by Contract*, *City of Fear*, *The Underwater City*, *Brainstorm*, *Man's Favorite Sport?*, *The Brass Bottle*, and *Happy Mother's Day, Love George*. She retired in 1980 after playing her final role on an episode of *The Love Boat*. She married actor Darren McGavin in 1969. She was a long-term breast cancer survivor. Kathie Browne died on April 8, 2003 in Beverly Hills. She was 72 years old, and survived by McGavin, her husband of 34 years.

Harvey Korman played the role of the prosecutor. Korman was born in Chicago on February 15, 1927. After serving in the U.S. Navy during World War II, he studied at the Goodman School of Drama at the Art Institute of Chicago. He worked in summer theater for several seasons before making his television debut in 1960 on *The Donna Reed Show*. His more than 200 television appearances include *Dr. Kildare*, *The Detectives*, *Perry Mason*, *Route 66*, *Dennis the Menace*, *Hazel*, *Gidget*, *The Lucy Show*, *The Jack Benny Program*, *The Munsters*, *F-Troop*, *The Wild, Wild West*, *The Danny Kaye Show*, and *The Love Boat* among many others. He starred in his namesake series, *The Harvey Korman Show*, from 1977 until 1978, and starred in the series, *Mama's Family*, from 1983 until 1984. His many films include *Living Venus*, *Gypsy*, *Lord Love A Duck*, *The Last of the Secret Agents?*, *Don't Just Stand There*, *The April Fools*, *Huckleberry Finn*, *Herbie Goes Bananas*, *Radioland Murders*, *Dracula: Dead and Loving It*, *Alice in Wonderland*, and *Curse of the Pink Panther*. He also appeared in the modern comedy classic films, *Blazing Saddles* (1974) and *High Anxiety* (1977). His voice-over work includes many cartoons, animated films, and video games. Korman is best known for his appearances on *The Carol Burnett Show* (1967-77), which earned him seven Emmy Award nominations with six wins, and a Golden Globe Award. Harvey Korman died at UCLA Medical Center on May 29, 2008. He was 81 years old, and survived by his second wife of 26 years, and four children.

Love Song for a Deadly Redhead

Season 2, Episode 32

Broadcast on ABC-TV on April 30, 1962
Directed by Richard Benedict
Written by Dean Riesner
Producer: Joel Rogosin
Supervising Producer: Howie Horwitz
Executive Producer: William T. Orr

Cast:

Troy Donahue	Sandy Winfield II
Lee Patterson	Dave Thorne
Van Williams	Ken Madison
Diane McBain	Daphne Dutton
Margarita Sierra	Cha Cha O'Brien
Bobby Troup	Dooley Baker
Shary Marshall	Carol McKee
John Kellogg	Larry Dermott
Richard Crane	Lt. Gene Plehn
Tom Cound	Clarke Tinsley
Grace Lee Whitney	Bernice
Clegg Hoyt	Ozzie Rupert
Roger Smith	Jeff Spencer
Edd Byrnes	Kookie

Credits:

Cinematography by Harold E. Stine
Film Editing by Byron Chudnow
Art Direction by Howard Campbell
Set Decoration by Hoyle Barrett

Makeup Supervisor: Gordon Bau
Hairstylist: Jean Burt Reilly
Assistant Director: Claude Binyon Jr.
Sound: B. F. Ryan
Theme Music Composers: Mack David and Jerry Livingston
Music Editor: Joe Inge
60 minutes/ Black and White
Production Company: Warner Bros. Television
Filmed at Warner Bros. Studios on Stages 20 and 24
Margarita Sierra sang "Sometimes I'm Happy" in this episode.

Notes on the case:

This "cross-over" episode introduced to Miami Beach the characters of Jeff
Spencer and Kookie from the Warner series *77 Sunset Strip*. Spencer comes
to Miami Beach to investigate a threatening note left for a lounge singer. A
beautiful redhead, Carol McKee, meets up with Spencer and invites him back
to her home. While there, he blacks out. When he regains consciousness, he
finds the dead body of McKee's jealous husband. Kookie arrives and joins
Sandy, Ken and Dave as they try to prove Spencer's innocence.

Shary Marshall played the role of Carol McKee. Marshall was born on
March 29, 1935 in Monmouth, Oregon. She was a model and beauty con-
testant, and made her television debut in 1958. Her numerous television
appearances include *Hennesey*, *77 Sunset Strip*, *Perry Mason*, *Hawaiian Eye*,
Dr. Kildare, *The Fugitive*, *Gunsmoke*, *Burke's Law*, *Wendy and Me*, *The Outer
Limits*, and *The Beverly Hillbillies*. Her films include *Gidget*, *The Ladies Man*,
Panic in Year Zero!, *Your Cheatin' Heart*, *Taffy and the Jungle Hunter*, *Tell
Me in the Sunlight*, and *The Street is My Beat*. In June 1966, Marshall and her
boyfriend, heavyweight boxer Eddie Machen, were arrested for public intoxi-
cation after a fight at an all-night Los Angeles restaurant. Her relationship
with the Black athlete was very scandalous at that time, and the embarrassing incident ended her acting career. In 1970, she married realtor Armand
Santilli, and the couple had one daughter. Santilli died in 2013. Marshall
moved to her daughter's home in Laguna Hills, California where she suffered
a fatal stroke on May 31, 2014. Shary Marshall was 79 years old.

Bobby Troup played the role of Dooley Baker. Troup was born on
October 18, 1918 in Harrisburg, Pennsylvania. He made his screen debut in the
1950 movie *Duchess of Idaho*. His other feature films include *Mr. Imperium*,
Bop Girl Goes Calypso, *The High Cost of Loving*, *The Five Pennies*, *The Gene
Krupa Story*, *First to Fight*, *Banning*, and *M*A*S*H**. His numerous television
appearances include *Rawhide*, *Acapulco*, *Perry Mason*, *77 Sunset Strip*, *The
Big Valley*, *Dragnet*, *Mannix*, *Adam 12*, *The Name of the Game*, *McMillan*

and Wife, Fantasy Island, and *Simon & Simon.* Fans remember him for playing the role of Dr. Joseph Early on *Emergency!* from 1972 until 1978. Troup's first love was music. He was a jazz pianist, singer, and songwriter. His musical compositions include "Daddy," "Take Me Away from Jacksonville," "Snootie Little Cutie," and "The Girl Can't Help It." His most popular song was "Route 66." Beginning in 1942, he served in the U.S. Marine Corps. He was one of two dozen White officers to direct recruit training at Montford Point, the depot for the first Black Marines. In 1943, Troup became the recreation officer, and helped build a recreation hall, basketball courts, an outdoor boxing ring, and a miniature golf course. While stationed at Montford Point, he organized the first African-American band of U.S. Marines. Troup married his second wife, singer Julie London, in 1959. She recorded with her husband, and co-starred with him on the series *Emergency!* Bobby Troup suffered a heart attack and died in Sherman Oaks, California on February 7, 1999 at the age of 80. He was survived by his wife of 40 years, and five children.

John Kellogg played the role of Larry McDermott. Kellogg was born in Hollywood, California on June 3, 1916. He worked in New England theater stock companies, and toured in the long-running service comedy *Brother Rat* until he was called to serve during World War II. Kellogg made his screen debut in the 1940 film *High School.* He played small roles in several films, including *Young Tom Edison, The Monster and the Girl, To Be or Not To Be, The Pride of the Yankees, Thirty Seconds Over Tokyo,* and *A Walk in the Sun.* In 1946, Kellogg signed a contract with Columbia Pictures. His later films include *The Strange Love of Martha Ivers, Out of the Past, Twelve O'Clock High, The Greatest Show on Earth, Rancho Notorious, Gorilla at Large,* and *Edge of the City.* Kellogg's many television credits include *Adventures of Superman, Tightrope, Decoy, Rawhide, The Alfred Hitchcock Hour, Bonanza, Gunsmoke, The Virginian, Alias Smith and Jones, St. Elsewhere,* and *Wiseguy.* He played the role of Jack Chandler on the soap opera *Peyton Place* from 1966 until 1967. John Kellogg died of Alzheimer's disease on February 22, 2000 in Los Angeles at the age of 83.

Roger Smith played the role of Jeff Spencer. Smith was born on December 18, 1932 in South Gate, California. He grew up in Nogales, Arizona, and studied at the University of Arizona at Tucson on a football scholarship. Smith served in the Naval Reserve in Honolulu, Hawaii. He was encouraged to pursue a Hollywood career after a chance meeting with actor James Cagney. He signed a contract with Columbia Pictures in 1957. His early films include *Man of a Thousand Faces, Operation Mad Ball, No Time to Be Young,* and *Crash Landing.* Smith moved to Warner Brothers in 1958. He appeared in the films *Auntie Mame, Never Steal Anything Small,* and *For Those Who Think Young.* His television credits include *Father Knows Best, Sheriff of Cochise, West Point, Wagon Train, Sugarfoot, 77 Sunset Strip,* and *Kraft Suspense Theater.*

He played the role of Jeff Spencer in *77 Sunset Strip* (1958-1962). In 1959, he recorded an LP album on Warner Bros. Records titled *Beach Romance*. He left *77 Sunset Strip* in 1962 after suffering a blood clot on his brain. He recovered from surgery, and returned to star as Lt. Douglas Roberts in the series, *Mister Roberts* (1965-66). Smith married actress Victoria Shaw in 1956. The couple had three children, and divorced in 1965. He married actress Ann-Margret in 1967. He retired from acting to manage her career, and produce her television specials. His writing credits include "The Chase" episode of *Surfside 6*, seven *77 Sunset Strip* episodes, an episode of *Mister Roberts*, and the feature films *The First Time* and *C.C. & Company*. In 1980, he was diagnosed with myasthenia gravis. He went into remission in 1985, but was then diagnosed with Parkinson's disease. Roger Smith died in Sherman Oaks of myasthenia gravis on June 4, 2017 at the age of 84. He was survived by his wife of 50 years, Ann-Margret, and his three children.

Edd Byrnes played the role of Kookie. Byrnes was born on July 30, 1932 in New York City. He was employed as an artist's model when he began working in summer stock theater in New England. He made his screen debut in the 1957 film *Reform School Girl*. That same year, he signed a contract with Warner Bros. Studio. His Warner films include *Darby's Rangers*, *Marjorie Morningstar*, *Life Begins at 17*, and *Up Periscope*. He appeared in a few Warner television programs including *Lawman*, *Cheyenne*, *Colt .45*, and *Hawaiian Eye*, but is best remembered for playing the role of Kookie in the hit series, *77 Sunset Strip*, from 1958 until 1963. He was unhappy with his studio contract, and bought himself out in 1963. He continued to work in theater, television, and in a few films, but he never achieved the level of stardom he desired. Some of his better television credits include *The Alfred Hitchcock Hour*, *Burke's Law*, *Love American Style*, *Fantasy Island*, *The Love Boat*, and *Murder She Wrote*. His later films include *Wicked, Wicked*, *Grease*, *Back to the Beach*, and *Troop Beverly Hills*. He worked frequently in summer stock and dinner theater in his later years. He retired in 1999. Byrnes was married to actress Asa Maynor from 1962 until 1971. The couple had one

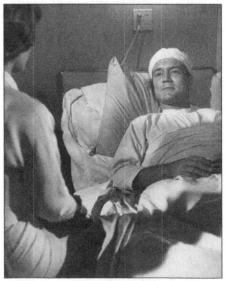

Shary Marshall and Roger Smith.

son, Logan Byrnes, a California television news anchor. Edd Byrnes died of natural causes at his Santa Monica home on January 8, 2020, at the age of 87.

"I worked with Edd a couple of times," Diane McBain recalled. "I couldn't stand him. He was impossible. So full of himself. And he thought he could land any woman he wanted, even while he was married. I was in that awful film, *Wicked, Wicked,* and in 1968 I did a summer stock tour of *Star Spangled Girl* with him and the wonderful Carleton Carpenter in New England. Edd was just the kind of man I didn't like. The self-righteous, smug expression on his face made me want to smack him every time I saw him. He struggled to learn his lines, and he was never prepared. Thank goodness Carleton was there with us. He was delightful. Edd decided he wanted to seduce me when the tour started, but he had a better chance of getting Carleton, who's gay, into bed. And once I rejected him, he was a pouty, petulant, nasty boy for the rest of the summer.

Dead Heat

Season 2, Episode 33

Broadcast on ABC-TV on May 7, 1962
Directed by Michael O'Herlihy
Written by Jerry Thomas
Producer: Joel Rogosin
Supervising Producer: Howie Horwitz
Executive Producer: William T. Orr

Cast:

Lee Patterson	Dave Thorne
Van Williams	Ken Madison
Diane McBain	Daphne Dutton
Jeanne Cooper	Della Bogart
Warren Stevens	Sebastian
Stacy Harris	Buck Lavery
Richard Crane	Lt. Gene Plehn
Harp McGuire	Barney Bogart
Walter Mathews	Morty Karlin
Melora Conway	Peggy
Saul Gorss	Receptionist
Cynthia Lynn	Miss Knox
Robert Glenn	Sgt. Woodley
Duck Tufield	Announcer

Credits:

Cinematography by Louis Jennings
Film Editing by Elbert K. Hollingsworth
Art Direction by Howard Campbell
Set Decoration by William L. Kuehl

Makeup Supervisor: Gordon Bau
Hairstylist: Jean Burt Reilly
Assistant Director: Fred Scheld
Sound: Thomas Ashton
Theme Music Composers: Mack David and Jerry Livingston
Music Editor: Donald Harris
60 minutes/ Black and White
Production Company: Warner Bros. Television
Filmed at Warner Bros. Studios on Stages 20 and 24

Notes on the case:

Mob bookkeeper Barney Bogart is serving a prison sentence. Someone from the underworld is threatening his wife, Della. They believe she knows where her husband hid the loot from his last robbery. Bogart reaches out and hires Dave to protect his wife – even though it was Dave who helped put him in prison three years earlier.

Harp McGuire played the role of Barney Bogart. McGuire was born on November 1, 1921 in Obion, Tennessee. He earned the rank of Sergeant in the U.S. Marine Corps and was awarded the Navy Cross for his service during World War II. He was a successful actor on Australian radio in the later 1940s and early 1950s. He is best remembered for the NBC radio serial *Night Beat*, and for hosting the radio horror anthology *The Clock* (1955-56). McGuire made his screen debut in the 1955 film *Captain Thunderbolt*. His other films include *On the Beach, Inherit the Wind, Cage of Evil, The Walking Target, Moon Pilot*, and *Incident in an Alley*. His television credits include *Bronco, Colt .45, Men into Space, Manhunt, The Twilight Zone, Alfred Hitchcock Presents, Outlaws, The Tall Man, Perry Mason, Gunsmoke, Leave it to Beaver*, and *Tales of the Wells Fargo*. Harp McGuire suffered from coronary sclerosis and died in Los Angeles on October 21, 1966 at the age of 45.

Warren Stevens played the role of Sebastian. Stevens was born in Clarks Summit, Pennsylvania on November 2, 1919. He served in the U.S. Army Air Force as a pilot during World War II. He was a founding member of the Actor's Studio, and made his acting debut in the 1947 Broadway production of *The Life of Galileo*. During the next three years, he appeared in four other Broadway shows including *Detective Story*. He first appeared on television in 1948 on *Actor's Studio*. His more than 150 television appearances include *Suspense, Studio One, Alfred Hitchcock Presents, Climax!, Hawaiian Eye, The Twilight Zone, Bracken's World, Return to Peyton Place, The Richard Boone Show, The Outer Limits, The Man from U.N.C.L.E., The Time Tunnel, ER, The Return of Captain Nemo, Voyage to the Bottom of the Sea, Star Trek, M*A*S*H*, and *Quincy, M.E.*, among others. Stevens many films include *Phone Call from* *a Stranger, O. Henry's Full House, Gorilla at Large, The Barefoot Contessa, Forbidden Planet, No Name on the Bullet, Madame X, Madigan, The Sweet Ride,* and *Stroker Ace.* Warren Stevens died of lung disease on March 27, 2012 at his Sherman Oaks, California home. He was 92 years old, and survived by his second wife of 42 years, actress Barbara French, and three children.

Stacy Harris played the role of Buck Lavery. Harris was born on July 26, 1918 in Big Timber, Quebec, Canada. He was an Army pilot who was injured in a plane wreck in 1937. Due to his injury, he couldn't serve during World War II, but he drove an ambulance with the American Field Service, and worked as a dispatch rider with the French Foreign Legion. For a short time after the war, he worked as a newspaper reporter. He made his acting debut on Broadway in the 1945 production *A Sound of Hunting.* He was a popular radio actor in the 1940s. His radio credits include *This is Your F.B.I., Dragnet, Pete Kelly's Blues, The Adventures of Superman, The Strange Romance of Evelyn Winters, Confession,* and *Pepper Young's Family.* His many television appearances include *Dragnet, Bonanza, Adam-12, Emergency!, Whirlybirds, Perry Mason, The Virginian, The Rebel,* and *Death Valley Days.* Harris made his film debut in the 1950 movie *Appointment with Danger.* His numerous films include *The Great Sioux Uprising, Good Day for a Hanging, Four for the Morgue, It's a Mad, Mad, Mad, Mad World, An American Dream, Bloody Mama,* and *The Wife Swappers.* Stacy Harris suffered a heart attack and died in Los Angeles on March 13, 1973. He was 54 years old.

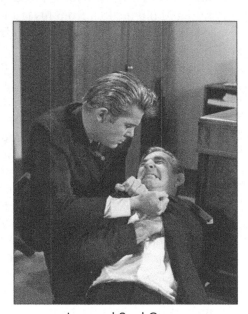

Lee and Saul Gorss.

Squeeze Play

Season 2, Episode 34

Broadcast on ABC-TV on May 14, 1962
Directed by Robert Sparr
Written by Ken Pettus
Producer: Joel Rogosin
Supervising Producer: Howie Horwitz
Executive Producer: William T. Orr

<u>Cast:</u>

Van Williams	Ken Madison
Lee Patterson	Dave Thorne
Margarita Sierra	Cha Cha O'Brien
Andrea King	Martha Wilder
Laraine Stephens	Lydia Wilder
Ted de Corsia	Sam Tustin
Richard Crane	Lt. Gene Plehn
Hal Bokar	Lew Grimes
Virginia Stefan	Nora Tustin
Jack De Mave	Lloyd Preston
Peter Breck	Harry Sturgis

<u>Credits:</u>

Cinematography by Bert Glennon
Film Editing by John Hall
Art Direction by Howard Campbell
Set Decoration by John P. Austin
Makeup Supervisor: Gordon Bau
Hairstylist: Jean Burt Reilly
Assistant Director: Chuck Hansen

Sound: Samuel F. Goode
Theme Music Composers: Mack David and Jerry Livingston
Music Editor: Sam E. Levin
60 minutes/ Black and White
Production Company: Warner Bros. Television
Filmed at Warner Bros. Studios on Stages 20 and 24
Margarita Sierra sang "Pretty Baby" in this episode.

Notes on the case:

Lydia Wilder is smitten with her mother's handsome, younger boyfriend, Lloyd Preston. When she discovers that her mother has given him a large amount of money, she becomes suspicious of his intentions, and hires Ken to do some background checking. But Preston, a known con man, turns up murdered, which complicates Ken's investigation because both his client and her mother confess to the crime.

Laraine Stephens played the role of Lydia Wilder. Stephens was born in Oakland, California on July 24, 1941. She studied music at Los Angeles City College and U.C.L.A., and performed in operas before making her television debut in 1961 on *Leave It to Beaver*. Her dozens of television credits include *The Many Loves of Dobie Gillis, Tarzan, Nanny and the Professor, The Mod Squad, Police Woman, Hawaii Five-O, The Love Boat*, and *Fantasy Island*. Stephens' many made-for-television movies include *The Screaming Woman, Adventures of Nick Carter, The Girl on the Late Late Show*, and *Scruples*. Her feature films include *None but the Brave, 40 Guns to Apache Pass, Hellfighters*, and *The Thousand Plane Raid*. Stephens was married to Emmy winning television producer David Gerber from 1970 until his death in 2010. They owned and operated Laraine Wines and Gerber Vineyards.

Andrea King played the role of Martha Wilder. King was born in Paris, France on February 1, 1919. When she was two months old, her mother moved her to America, where they lived with her maternal grandmother. She attended the Edgewood School in Greenwich, Connecticut where she developed an interest in acting. She appeared on Broadway in *Growing Pains* (1933) and *Fly Away Home* (1935). She signed a contract with Warner Brothers,

Andrea King.

and made her screen debut in the 1940 film *Mr. Skeffington*. Her many films include *The Very Thought of You, Hollywood Canteen, The Beast with Five Fingers, My Wild Irish Rose, Mr. Peabody and the Mermaid, Nightmare Alley, The Lemon Drop Kid, Red Planet Mars, Silent Fear, The Man I Love, Ride the Pink Horse, Outlaw Queen, Darby's Rangers, Dial 1119, The World in His Arms, Band of Angels, Southside 1-1000, The Linguini Incident,* and *Inevitable Grace*. King appeared in most of the Warner television productions including *Cheyenne, The Alaskans, Hawaiian Eye, Maverick,* and *77 Sunset Strip*. King also guest-starred on *Perry Mason, Murder She Wrote, Mike Hammer, The Donna Reed Show,* and *Family Affair*. She retired in 1994. She was married to lawyer Nat Willis from 1940 until his death in 1970. Andrea King died at the age of 84 on April 22, 2003 at the Motion Picture Country Home in Woodland Hills, California.

Jack De Mave played the role of Lloyd Preston. De Mave was born on December 8, 1935 in Jersey City, New Jersey. He is the son of 1920s boxing champion, Jack De Mave, Sr. He worked extensively off-Broadway, and starred in many regional and touring theatrical productions. De Mave made his television debut in 1962, in this episode of *Surfside 6*. His numerous television appearances include *Lassie, The Fugitive, F-Troop, Wagon Train, The Mary Tyler Moore Show, The Doris Day Show, Marcus Welby, M.D.,* and *Ellery Queen*. He also appeared on the daytime dramas *Days of Our Lives, General Hospital,* and *Loving*. He co-starred with Bette Davis in the TV movie *Hello Mother, Goodbye*. His films include *Blindfold,* and *The Man Without a Face*. He married model and film production assistant, Camille Smith, in 1963. Their fifty-year marriage ended with Camille's death in 2013.

Andrea King.

A Private Eye for Beauty

Season 2, Episode 35

Broadcast on ABC-TV on May 21, 1962
Directed by Irving J. Moore
Teleplay by Gloria Elmore and Robert Vincent Wright from a story by
 Leonard Brown and Robert Vincent Wright
Producer: Joel Rogosin
Supervising Producer: Howie Horwitz
Executive Producer: William T. Orr

Cast:

Troy Donahue	Sandy Winfield II
Van Williams	Ken Madison
Lee Patterson	Dave Thorne
Diane McBain	Daphne Dutton
Margarita Sierra	Cha Cha O'Brien
Dawn Wells	Consuela Hernandez
Miguel Angel Landa	Roberto Ybarra
Elaine Devry	Denise
Jerry Oddo	Carlos
Elizabeth Harrower	Mrs. Newcomb
Roger Carroll	M.C.
Ulla Stromstedt	Miss Scandia
John Dehner	Francisco Hernandez

Credits:

Cinematography by Ralph Woolsey
Film Editing by Robert L. Wolfe
Art Direction by Howard Campbell
Set Decoration by William L. Kuehl

Makeup Supervisor: Gordon Bau
Hairstylist: Jean Burt Reilly
Assistant Director: C. Carter Gibson
Sound: Ross Owen
Theme Music Composers: Mack David and Jerry Livingston
Music Editor: Erma E. Levin
60 minutes/Black and White
Production Company: Warner Bros. Television
Filmed at Warner Bros. Studios on Stages 20 and 24, and on location in Miami Beach, Florida
Previous footage of Margarita Sierra singing "Lover Come Back to Me" (first seen in Season 2, Episode 17 "Separate Checks") was used in this episode.

Notes on the case:

Diplomat Francisco Hernandez is in Miami, he says, to chaperone his niece, Consuela, who is representing their Latin-American country in the Miss Universe beauty pageant. He hires Sandy and Ken to keep the young woman away from her boyfriend. But Consuela is an unwitting distraction while Hernandez plots to overthrow her home country.

On June 28, 1961, the *Los Angeles Times* reported that Warner Bros. made arrangements to film scenes for this episode at the upcoming annual Miss Universe Beauty Pageant in Miami Beach. The production company used the pageant and events centering around the actual selection of Miss Universe as background for the show. On July 13, Troy Donahue served as a judge selecting Miss USA, prior to the Miss Universe contest. Warner Bros. offered a screen test to the girl chosen Miss Universe, 1961.

Miguel Angel Landa played the role of Roberto Ybarra. Landa was born on November 4, 1936 in Caracas, Venezuela. He performed as a sketch artist, stand-up comedian, and television host in his native Venezuela before making his American television debut in 1956. He was under contract to Warner Brothers for a couple of years, and guest-starred in most of the studio's television productions. He also appeared on *The Doris Day Show*, *The Name of the Game*, *Mannix*, *The Flying Nun*, *Marcus Welby, M.D.*, *The High Chaparral*, *The Mothers-in-Law*, *The Beverly Hillbillies*, and *Zorro*. In 1973, he returned to Venezuela, and has worked consistently on Venezuelan television. He is best known for hosting the popular sketch comedy series, *Bienvenidos*.

Masquerade

Season 2, Episode 36

Broadcast on ABC-TV on May 28, 1962
Directed by Paul Landres
Teleplay by Anthony Spinner and Erna Lazarus from a story by Erna Lazarus
Producer: Joel Rogosin
Supervising Producer: Howie Horwitz
Executive Producer: William T. Orr

Cast:

Lee Patterson	Dave Thorne
Eva Norde	Margo Hafner
Charles H. Radilak	Carl Hafner
Robert Dowdell	Eric Hirsh
Willard Sage	Manheim
Richard Crane	Lt. Gene Plehn
Ernest Sarracino	Luigi
Larry J. Blake	Ed Williamson
Ralph Manza	Martinelli
Bill Couch	Mack
Billy Curtis	Tippy, the circus midget
Robert Glenn	Sgt. Woodley

Credits:

Cinematography by Jacques R. Marquette
Film Editing by John Whitney
Art Direction by Howard Campbell
Set Decoration by Alfred Kegerris
Makeup Supervisor: Gordon Bau
Hairstylist: Jean Burt Reilly

Assistant Director: Samuel Schneider
Sound: B. F. Ryan
Theme Music Composers: Mack David and Jerry Livingston
Music Editor: Ted Sebern
60 minutes/ Black and White
Production Company: Warner Bros. Television
Filmed at Warner Bros. Studios on Stages 20 and 24

Notes on the case:

Dressed as a clown, Dave goes undercover at a circus to investigate an accident during a show that resulted in a groom being trampled to death by a horse. The horrible incident has caused tension among the European members of the circus cast. Dave discovers that an avowed Nazi is among the troupe of performers. And apparently the Nazi is still fighting World War II.

Eva Norde played the role of Margo Hafner. Norde was born in Sweden. She first appeared on American television in 1961 in the recurring role of Helga on *The Real McCoys*. She also appeared on *Hawaiian Eye* and *The Dick Powell Theater*. In 1963, she sued Steve Allen for $200,000 when he revealed her address and phone number on his program. She claimed she was forced to move, and lost job opportunities as a result of the incident. Norde returned to Sweden in 1964. In her later years, she worked as a studio manager for Swedish television.

Lee and Peggy Ward.

Charles Radilac played the role of Carl Hafner. Radilac was born in Czechoslovakia on January 26, 1909. He began his American acting career in 1952, and guest-starred in numerous television dramas and comedies including *Sugarfoot*, *Hogan's Heroes*, *Outlaws*, *Adventures in Paradise*, *Route 66*, *Dr. Kildare*, *77 Sunset Strip*, *The Wild, Wild West*, and *It Takes a Thief*. He had small roles in several feature films including *The Rise and Fall of Legs Diamond*, *Hitler*, *36 Hours*, *Genghis Khan*, and *Ship of Fools*. He retired in 1969. Charles Radilac died on July 19, 1972 in Inglewood, California. He was 63 years old.

Robert Dowdell played the role of Erick Hirsch. Dowdell was born in Park Ridge, Illinois on March 10, 1932. He attended Wesleyan University, and served in the U.S. Army Corps of Engineers. After his discharge from the service, he took an interest in acting, and made his Broadway debut in the 1956 play *Time Limit!* He also appeared on Broadway in *The Lovers*, and *Love Me Little*. He first appeared on television in a *Studio One* production in 1956. His many television appearances include *Land of the Giants, Adam-12, McMillan & Wife, Hart to Hart, V, Dynasty, Hotel,* and *Hunter.* He starred as Cody Bristol in the 1962-63 series *Stoney Burke,* and Lt. Comdr. Chip Morton in the 1964-68 series *Voyage to the Bottom of the Sea.* His several films include *The Initiation, Assassination,* and *Wicked Stepmother.* Dowdell was married to actress Sheila Connolly from 1965 until 1979. He died on January 23, 2018 in Coldwater, Michigan. Robert Dowdell was 85 years old.

Billy Curtis played the role of Tippy, the Circus Midget. Curtis was born on June 27, 1909 in Springfield, Massachusetts. His fifty-year career in show business began with his appearance in the 1932 film *Tarzan the Ape Man.* His dozens of films include *The Terror of Tiny Town, The Wizard of Oz, Meet John Doe, Saboteur, Ghost Catchers, Buck Privates Come Home, Pygmy Island, Superman and the Mole Men, Gorilla at Large, 3 Ring Circus, The Court Jester, The Thing from Another World, The Incredible Shrinking Man, Planet of the Apes, High Plains Drifter, Hello Dolly!, Little Cigars,* and *Eating Raoul.* Curtis starred in the 1934 Broadway musical *Anything Goes,* and returned to Broadway in 1940 to appear in *Every Man for Himself.* He played guest-starring roles in many television shows including *Gunsmoke, Batman, Star Trek,* and *Gilligan's Island,* among many others. Billy Curtis

Billy Curtis, Larry Blake, Lisa Mitchell, Eva Norde, and Lee.

died of a heart attack in Dayton, Nevada on November 9, 1988. He was 79 years old, and survived by his wife of 40 years, two children, and nine grandchildren.

Willard Sage played the role of Manheim. Sage was born on August 13, 1922 in London, Ontario, Canada. He studied architecture with Frank Lloyd Wright before pursuing a career in show business. Sage made his television debut in 1951, and guest-starred in dozens of programs including *Colt .45, Maverick, Perry Mason, My Three Sons, Star Trek, The Outer Limits, Gunsmoke, Ben Casey, Death Valley Days, Room 222, Land of the Giants, Hogan's Heroes,* and *Banacek.* His numerous films include *It's a Dog's Life, The Tender Trap, Somebody Up There Likes Me, The Great Imposter, That Touch of Mink, Colossus: The Forbin Project, Scream, Evelyn, Scream,* and *Dirty Little Billy.* Sage died in Sherman Oaks, California on March 17, 1974 at the age of 51.

Pawn's Gambit

Season 2, Episode 37

Broadcast on ABC-TV on June 4, 1962
Directed by Jeffrey Hayden
Written by Herman Groves
Producer: Joel Rogosin
Supervising Producer: Howie Horwitz
Executive Producer: William T. Orr

Cast:

Troy Donahue	Sandy Windfield II
Lee Patterson	Dave Thorne
Van Williams	Ken Madison
Diane McBain	Daphne Dutton
Margarita Sierra	Cha Cha O'Brien
Kathie Browne	Jennifer Carson
Otto Waldis	Darius Frimmel
Richard Crane	Lt. Gene Plehn
Lucy Prentis	Martha Denker
Michael St. Angel	Father Damon
Howard McLeod	Sgt. Bellows
Nolan Leary	John Brecker

Credits:

Cinematography by Louis Jennings
Film Editing by George R. Rohrs
Art Direction by Howard Campbell
Set Decoration by Hoyle Barrett
Makeup Supervisor: Gordon Bau
Hairstylist: Jean Burt Reilly

Assistant Director: Gene Anderson Jr.
Sound: Howard Fogetti
Theme Music Composers: Mack David and Jerry Livingston
Music Editor: Donald Harris
60 minutes/ Black and White
Production Company: Warner Bros. Television
Filmed at Warner Bros. Studios on Stages 20 and 24
Margarita Sierra sang "Zing Went the Strings of My Heart" in this episode.

Notes on the case:

An art dealer named John Brecker contacts Sandy and asks him to come to his shop to discuss a job he is afraid to talk about on the telephone. When Sandy arrives at the shop, he finds Brecker's dead body. While Sandy begins his investigation, Dave and Lt. Plehn follow up on a young woman who was mugged on the other side of town. They soon realize that both cases are related, and a smuggling ring is behind Brecker's murder. "This was the last episode that all five of us would appear together on," Diane recalled.

Otto Waldis played the role of Darius Frimmel. Waldis was born in Vienna, Austria on May 20, 1901. He pursued a theatrical career in Austria and Germany. He made his film debut in the 1931 classic thriller *M*. He and his wife fled Austria in 1940, and settled for a time in Birmingham, Alabama, where he worked as a professional photographer. His many films include *The Exile, Berlin Express, Love Happy, Bagdad, Bird of Paradise, Sincerely Yours, Artists and Models, Desert Sands, Judgment at Nuremberg*, and the 1958 classic science fiction film *Attack of the 50 Foot Woman*. His dozens of television appearances include *My Little Margie, Adventures of Superman, Lassie, Maverick, Alfred Hitchcock Presents, Perry Mason, Hogan's Heroes, Mannix*, and *Gomer Pyle, U.S.M.C.* Otto Waldis died of a heart attack on March 25, 1974 in Los Angeles. He was 72 years old. He was survived by his wife of 38 years, who died several months later.

Michael St. Angel played the role of Father Damon. St. Angel was born in Rockford, Illinois on October 9, 1916. He attended Beloit College in Wisconsin, majoring in drama, and transferred to St. Ambrose College in Iowa where he became a drama teacher. When he left his teaching job, he worked in summer stock and traveled around the country. He made his Broadway debut in 1942 in *The Cat Screams*, and then appeared in the hit Broadway comedy *Janie*. In 1943, he signed a contract with RKO Pictures. He made his film debut in the 1943 movie *Gangway for Tomorrow*. His early films include *The Falcon Out West, Seven Days Ashore, Marine Raiders, Bride by Mistake, What a Blonde*, and *The Brighton Strangler*. In 1945, he married actress/singer/dancer Marjorie Holliday. St. Angel's film career declined and he played small roles in a couple of dozen movies including *First Yank into Tokyo*, *The Truth About Murder*, *Easy Living*, *Flying Leathernecks*, *The Pace That Thrills*, and *The French Line*. He was dropped by RKO in 1953. His later films include *Whatever Happened to Baby Jane?*, *4 For Texas*, and *Dead Heat on a Merry-Go-Round*. He appeared in only a handful of television productions. For a time, he worked for Howard Hughes at his TWA office. He later functioned as a personal assistant to columnist Walter Winchell. In the 1970s, St. Angel opened Michael's Los Feliz, a popular restaurant in Los Angeles. He retired from acting in 1974. Michael St. Angel died on January13, 1984 at the Motion Picture Country Home in Woodland Hills. He was survived by his one son. His wife pre-deceased him in 1969.

The Neutral Corner

Season 2, Episode 38

Broadcast on ABC-TV on June 11, 1962
Directed by Jeffrey Hayden
Teleplay by William Bruckner from a story by William Bruckner and Leonard Brown
Producer: Joel Rogosin
Supervising Producer: Howie Horwitz
Executive Producer: William T. Orr

Cast:

Van Williams	Ken Madison
Allyson Ames	Lydia Macklin
Grace Lee Whitney	Wendy Peters
Alan Carney	Harry Crofty
Douglas Dick	Weston
Steve Gravers	Nicky Match
Steven Marlo	Lundy
Chad Everett	Bongo Macklin

Credits:

Cinematography by Robert Tobey
Film Editing by John Hall
Art Direction by Howard Campbell
Set Decoration by William Stevens
Makeup Supervisor: Gordon Bau
Hairstylist: Jean Burt Reilly
Assistant Director: Samuel Schneider
Sound: Frank McWhorter
Theme Music Composers: Mack David and Jerry Livingston

Music Editor: Erma E. Levin
60 minutes/ Black and White
Production Company: Warner Bros. Television
Filmed at Warner Bros. Studios on Stages 20 and 24

Notes on the case:

Champion boxer Bongo Macklin has retired from professional boxing. But the man who holds the boxer's contract, a racketeer named Nicky Match, wants him to fight again. Macklin escapes injury from a couple of questionable "accidents," including a bomb that was placed on the Surfside houseboat during a party there for the champ. Ken is hired to protect Macklin and discovers several suspects who would hurt him including Match, a bitter sports writer, and the boxer's own ex-wife.

Steve Gravers played the role of Nicky Match. Gravers was born on April 8, 1922 in New York City. He studied at the Actor's Studio, and made his Broadway debut in 1956 in *Hatful of Rain*. He made his television debut in 1950. He guest-starred in dozens of television dramas including *Mike Hammer, Peter Gunn, Mackenzie's Raiders, The Detectives, The Untouchables, Dr. Kildare, Combat, I Spy, Columbo*, and *Ironside*. His feature films include *Al Capone, Hell Bent for Leather, Operation Eichmann*, and *40 Pounds of Trouble*. Steve Gravers died of lung cancer on August 22, 1978 in Studio City, California. He was 56 years old, and survived by his fourth wife.

Allyson Ames played the role of Lydia Macklin. Ames was born in Dallas, Texas on August 24, 1937. She made her acting debut in 1961. Her films include *The Phantom Planet, Incubus, The Collector*, and *The Man in the Glass Booth*. Her numerous guest-starring roles on television include *Maverick, Hawaiian Eye, The Virginian, Stoney Burke, 77 Sunset Strip, Saints and Sinners, The Outer Limits, Burke's Law, Checkmate, Perry Mason*, and *Honey West*. She retired in 1975. Allyson Ames died of emphysema on November 3, 1999 in Los Angeles. She was married and divorced four times, and was survived by her four children.

Chad Everett and Van.

House on Boca Key

Season 2, Episode 39

Broadcast on ABC-TV on June 18, 1962
Directed by Robert Sparr
Written by Herman Groves
Producer: Joel Rogosin
Supervising Producer: Howie Horwitz
Executive Producer: William T. Orr

Cast:

Troy Donahue	Sandy Winfield II
Van Williams	Ken Madison
Diane McBain	Daphne Dutton
Richard Crane	Lt. Gene Plehn
Patricia Blair	Allison Haley
Alan Baxter	Lou Triplett
George Petrie	Ernie Wexler
E. J. Andre	Captain Willisett
Jack Easton Jr.	Tommy Martin
Ahna Capri	Anna
Harry Holcombe	Charles Martin
Jackson Halliday	Tollinger
Frank Richards	Bartender
Margarita Sierra	Cha Cha O'Brien

Credits:

Cinematography by Harold E. Stine
Film Editing by Milt Kleinberg
Art Direction by Howard Campbell
Set Decoration by Hoyle Barrett

Makeup Supervisor: Gordon Bau
Hairstylist: Jean Burt Reilly
Assistant Director: William Kissell
Sound: Everett A. Hughes
Theme Music Composers: Mack David and Jerry Livingston
Music Editor: Sam E. Levin
60 minutes/ Black and White
Production Company: Warner Bros. Television
Filmed at Warner Bros. Studios on Stages 20 and 24
Margarita Sierra sang "Pretty Baby" in this episode.

Notes on the case:

Tommy Martin, a drug store delivery boy, borrows a jacket from Sandy to wear to his prom. When he leaves the houseboat, he's mistaken for Sandy, and shot. While Martin recovers, Sandy drops in on a bookie/informant named Ernie, and asks if he's heard anything about the shooting. He sends Sandy to talk with a former showgirl named Allison Haley who was once married to a gangster named Triplett. She tells Sandy that it has something to do with an insurance claim for a man named Paul Gregory that Sandy has been working on, but she warns him to drop his investigation, or he will be killed. Before she can say anything else, she disappears. And when Ernie calls with more information, he's gunned down in a phone booth. Sandy's investigation takes him to the tiny Boca Key.

Jack Easton Jr. played the role of Tommy Martin. Easton was born in Los Angeles on March 12, 1943. He made his television debut in 1959 at the age of 16. Before retiring from acting in 1964, he guest-starred on numerous shows including *Wagon Train, The Virginian, My Three Sons, Bonanza, Alfred Hitchcock Presents*, and *Petticoat Junction*.

Patricia Blair played the role of Allison Haley. Blair was born in Fort Worth, Texas on January 15, 1933. She made her television acting debut in 1953. She appeared in several films including *Jump into Hell, The Black Sleep, City of Fear*, and *Cage of Evil*. Blair guest-starred in numerous television shows including *Perry Mason, The Bob Cummings Show, The Virginian*, and *My Three Sons*. She is best remembered for playing the role of Lou Mallory on *The Rifleman* (1962-63) and the role of Rebecca Boone on *Daniel Boone* from 1964 until 1970. She retired in 1979, and produced trade shows in New York and New Jersey. Patricia Blair died at her home in North Wildwood, New Jersey of breast cancer on September 9, 2013. She was 80 years old.

Midnight for Prince Charming

Season 2, Episode 40, Series Finale

Broadcast on ABC-TV on June 25, 1962
Directed by George Waggner
Written by Ken Pettus
Producer: Joel Rogosin
Supervising Producer: Howie Horwitz
Executive Producer: William T. Orr

Cast:

Van Williams	Ken Madison
Diane McBain	Daphne Dutton
Jo Morrow	Laura Jarrett
R. G. Armstrong	Paul Wyatt
Richard Crane	Lt. Gene Plehn
Richard Benedict	Harry Noonan
Howard McLeod	Detective Bellows
George Cisar	Cable
Joseph Forte	Manager
Mike Road	Dave Jarrett
Margarita Sierra	Cha Cha O'Brien

Credits:

Cinematography by Bert Glennon
Film Editing by Stefan Arnsten
Art Direction by Howard Campbell
Set Decoration by John P. Austin
Makeup Supervisor: Gordon Bau
Hairstylist: Jean Burt Reilly
Assistant Director: Richard Maybery

Sound: Stanley Jones
Theme Music Composers: David Mack and Jerry Livingston
Music Editor: Charles Paley
60 minutes/ Black and White
Production Company: Warner Bros. Television
Filmed at Warner Bros. Studios on Stages 20 and 24
Previous footage of Margarita Sierra singing "Zing! Went the Strings of My Heart" (first seen in Season 2, Episode 37 "Pawn's Gambit") was used in this final episode.

Notes on the case:

Dave and Laura Jarrett are a husband and wife con artist team. Dave Jarrett hires Ken to follow his wife who he claims is cheating on him. The man he accuses her of cheating with is actually the couple's next intended victim. Ken refuses to take the case because the man, Paul Wyatt, is an old friend. When racketeer Harry Noonan forces his way into the scam, he's murdered. Wyatt, a lonely widower, reluctantly admits to Ken that he fell for a young woman who is really a grifter. So Ken takes up the case. *Surfside 6* sputtered to a close with this final episode. Troy Donahue and Lee Patterson did not appear in the final show.

Jo Morrow played the role of Laura Jarrett. Morrow was born in Cuero, Texas on November 1, 1939. She won the title Miss Pasadena in 1958, and a film contract with 20th Century-Fox that same year. She moved to Columbia Pictures a year later. Her feature films include *Gidget, Our Man in Havana, The 3 Worlds of Gulliver, Sunday in New York*, and *Blume in Love*. She may best be remembered for her role in the cult classic horror film *13 Ghosts*. Morrow guest-starred in numerous television dramas including *77 Sunset Strip, Lawman, Maverick, Laramie, Mission: Impossible*, and *Hawaiian Eye* at Warner Brothers. In 1963, she married television producer Jack Barnett. Their first child, a daughter, was born deaf, and Morrow stepped back from acting to care for the child. She took a few roles in the 1970s, but formerly retired from acting in 1976.

R.G. Armstrong played the role of Paul Wyatt. Armstrong was born on April 7, 1917 in Pleasant Grove, Alabama. He studied acting at the University of North Carolina at Chapel Hill, and, after graduating, he attended the Actors Studio in New York. He made his Broadway debut in the 1955 hit drama *Cat on a Hot Tin Roof*. His other Broadway credits include *The Miracle Worker* in 1960. He first appeared on film in *Garden of Eden* in 1954. During the next 40 years, he appeared in dozens of films including *From Hell to Texas, The Fugitive Kind, Ride the High Country, Major Dundee, El Dorado, The Great*

White Hope, Heaven Can Wait, Reds, Dick Tracy, and *The Time Machine,* among others. Armstrong guest-starred in many Western-themed television series including *Have Gun – Will Travel, The Californians, The Tall Man, Riverboat, The Rifleman, The Big Valley, Bonanza, Maverick, Gunsmoke, Rawhide, Wagon Train,* and *Bat Masterson.* He retired from acting in 2005 due to oncoming blindness. R.G. Armstrong died at his Studio City home on July 27, 2012 at the age of 95. He was survived by his four children.

NOTES ON THE END

"In my case," Diane McBain recalled, "I was already working on my next assignment at the studio before the final episode of *Surfside 6* aired. The press asked me if I missed the show. I had no time to think about it, really, it was part of my everyday work at Warner Bros., but I can't say that I missed the show. I never meant to sound ungrateful, but I didn't want to do the show in the first place. I did miss some of the people I had worked with for a couple of years, and become friends with, but the job? No. I didn't miss that. We had a wonderful crew, but I continued to work with them on other projects at the studio. We were all indentured. I wanted better work, and I was afraid that my time on the series hurt me more than helped me. Troy felt the same disappointment. I don't read reviews as a rule, and never paid attention to what the press had to say about *Surfside*. But I know that the show was not a favorite of television journalists, although there was an enormous fan base until the very end."

Television critics dismissed the show before the first episode ever aired. In April, 1960, *Surfside 6* was the announced replacement for *Bourbon Street Beat*. The *Washington Post* described it as like "replacing a violin with a fiddle."

On May 17, 1961, in the midst of Season One, Cecil Smith, writing for the *Los Angeles Times*, called the show "inept." Nevertheless, fan mail poured into the studio mail room.

There were numerous contributing factors that lead to the demise of *Surfside 6*. Production in Hollywood was stymied during the 1960 writer's strike. William T. Orr, the chief of the Warner Bros. Television department, would not be deterred by a strike, and soldiered on by re-purposing existing scripts from previous studio produced series. A number of Warner's detective shows were seemingly carbon copies of one another – several young leads pursuing justice and fun at the same time. The only difference was the setting. Programs were set in New Orleans, Miami Beach, Hawaii, and Los Angeles. During the strike, the names were changed, but the same scripts were used by one show, and then another.

Orr was a successful businessman. He entered the studio into a ground-breaking production/distribution deal with ABC-TV at a time when television was beginning to edge into the movie-going market. For nearly a decade, he was the credited Executive Producer of twenty popular series. In the early 1960s, he had nine hit programs in prime time simultaneously.

Juggling ten different television episodes produced every week was overwhelming for Orr, who had a reputation for being a "control freak." Before long, short cuts and cost-cutting measures affected the quality of the programs. The second season of *Surfside 6* was a victim of fatal budget cuts. Scripts were recycled from other series. Production values were gutted, and the finished shows looked a bit haphazard to the audience, and more importantly to the critics. Many of the actors were bored, and some, including Troy Donahue, did little more than phone in their lines. The music budget was cut by more than half, and many of Margarita Sierra's musical performances were simply edited into a show from previous broadcasts. "I think we all lost interest in it," Diane said, "including the studio. Troy was at the point where he actually resented working on the show. We were doing the same thing over and over again. And when people lose interest in what they're doing, they don't do a very good job any longer.

"The revolving door of directors was mind-numbing for the cast. Near the end, they didn't seem to care about what they were doing either. The parade of guest-stars continued, but the show became nothing more than a launching pad for young actors that the studio considered as potential contract players. Van and I were in the final episode together. And we had a good time. There was a sense of relief and some glee on set, and that was the first time in a long time."

Writer Don Page refused to let the series rest in peace. On August 26, 1962, he took a parting swipe at the cancelled program in his column, "Camera Angles" in *TV Times*. "Parting is such sweet sorrow," he wrote. "Farewell. Follow the sun, you burned a lot of viewers. Sayonara, *Surfside 6*, you were ridiculous!" Mr. Page may have been done with the show, but the fans certainly weren't. His office was inundated with letters chastising him for being so callous and dismissive. Days later, in his column titled "A Critic's Opinions Make Him Unloved" he wrote, "in the August 26 issue of our Sunday magazine, *TV Times*, this writer authored a little feature which kissed off, so to speak, a number of television shows that the networks are eliminating for the fall season. Among them were such shows as *Surfside 6*."

The departing detective series, he added, had been no threat to *Playhouse 90*, or even the *Mickey Mouse Club*! The editor of the *Los Angeles Times* received thousands of letters from distraught fans, mostly young girls between the ages of 12 and 15. Young fans perhaps, but they jumped to the defense of the show, and especially Troy Donahue, who had become one the biggest stars at Warner Bros. by the time the program ended. "They are extremely upset that *Surfside 6* was satirized in the Sunday article," Page wrote. 'You better watch what you say about our favorite program, you lousy creep' writes a sweet little thing from Arlington, Virginia, a Troy Donahue fan. *Surfside 6*, without a doubt, was one of TV's weakest shows. For the most part, it was poorly written and not exactly endorsed by the Actors Studio. But the teenagers loved it to the point of distraction. If you criticize it, you'd better be careful."

"THE CLOWN (Death Is a Clown)"

Teleplay by Lee Leob. Story by Dick Lederer

DAY

FADE IN

EXT. FONTAINEBLEAU HOTEL FULL SHOT

CUT TO:

EXT. SURFSIDE 6 HOUSEBOAT FULL SHOT

CUT TO:

EXT. INDIAN CREEK

SANDY races the jet boat at the side of the dock to Surfside 6.

INT. SURFSIDE 6

KEN finishes putting the proper roll in his sport shirt. DAVE appears from the back room when suddenly there is a loud bump, which jars them. It is Sandy's boat, hitting the Surfside.

TWO SHOT KEN and DAVE

> KEN
>
> Not again!

> DAVE
>
> Don't complain. We're lucky he didn't land in here.

They EXIT Surfside.

SANDY EXITS jet boat and begins to tie it up.

EXT. SURSIDE 6

KEN and DAVE emerge from houseboat and are joined by SANDY, who ENTERS from the dock

DAVE

When are you going to learn to handle that jet?

SANDY

Battered nose gives her character. My skis are in dry dock. I'm taking off for the Palm Beach races, mind if I borrow yours? Thanks.

SANDY moves to enter the houseboat intending to take them away.

KEN (to DAVE)

You believe him?

DAVE

Little shy. He'll get over it.

KEN EXITS.

DAVE looks after him, shrugs, smiles and starts walking out of scene toward Collins Avenue.

EXT. COLLINS AVENUE

DAVE crosses Collins Avenue toward the Hotel Fontainebleau.

EXT. ENTRANCE OF THE HOTEL

DAVE enters the hotel.

INT. THE BOOM BOOM ROOM

A combo is playing a "Cha Cha rhythm." It is early cocktail time, and although the room is fairly empty, there are a few couples dancing. CHA CHA and her STUDENT, an older man in his sixties, are in the center of the dancing group.

CLOSE UP. CHA CHA and STUDENT

She marks time, speaking low-voiced.

CHA CHA

Boom boom…cha cha cha. Boom boom…cha cha cha.

He executes the step, and grins. Gaining confidence, he dances on with creaking bone abandon.

CLOSE UP. CARLOS

As Cha Cha and the student pass. CARLOS, thirtyish, a rugged-looking Latin; there is a distinguishing rash discoloration or burn type mark along the right side of his face at the jaw line. He is standing at the edge of the bar, and is obviously drunk. He peers after Cha Cha lecherously.

CLOSER SHOT. CHA CHA and STUDENT

CHA CHA (to her student)
You do beautiful, Mister Hudson.

STUDENT
My boom boom's all right. It's the cha cha cha that throws me.

CHA CHA
You gonna be fine, Mister Hudson.

STUDENT (proud of himself)
Wait'll I take my wife to the Rotarian dance back in Lancaster.
Their eyes'll pop. Boom boom…cha cha cha.

The music stops. They start off the floor. Remembering, Cha Cha digs into her purse and hands a few of her advertising flyers to the student.

CHA CHA
You tell your friends about Cha Cha, please?
He glances at the paper.

STUDENT
I sure will, Miss O'Brien…Will their eyes pop!
He stuffs the flyers into his pocket, boom-booming and cha cha cha-ing as he EXITS. Cha Cha grins and EXITS to her studio.
CLOSE SHOT. CARLOS
He downs his drink, and follows Cha Cha.
INT. CHA CHA'S STUDIO
As Cha Cha ENTERS, turns to close the door, Carlos appears in the doorway. He is obviously drunk.

CARLOS
Senorita. I would like to take a lesson. We dance together, yes?

CHA CHA
We dance together, no. It is time to close.

CARLOS
You stay open for Carlos.

CHA CHA (firmly)

I'm sorry. No more lessons today.

She moves to close the door.

CARLOS (blocking the door)

I got dollars. Plenty dollars.

He grabs her, and kicks the door closed.

FULL SHOT. CHA CHA and CARLOS

Holding her tightly, he has her partly lifted off the floor, dances in circles with her.

CHA CHA

Let me go!

CARLOS

Carlos is a good dancer. I teach you a few things, maybe!

EXT. BOOM BOOM ROOM

DAVE comes down the stairs and is about to ENTER the Boom Boom Room when he pauses momentarily, his attention taken by something off screen.

INT. DANCE STUDIO

Carlos, still mauling Cha Cha, swings her around in his embrace.

CHA CHA

Let me go, do you hear! Let me go!

Carlos is all over her, giving her a very bad time. Suddenly, the door opens. Dave ENTERS and, seeing the problem, quickly collars Carlos and spins him around. As he does so –

DAVE

May I cut in?

Carlos glares at Dave furiously and takes a vicious swing. Dave ducks, spins Carlos, who staggers back against the wall.

CLOSE SHOT. CARLOS

His face turns ugly and menacing. He pulls a knife, and comes at Dave.

ANOTHER ANGLE

as Carlos advances toward Dave.

CHA CHA

Dave! Look out!

Dave turns in time to ward off Carlos' knife-thrust and, with an adroit application of jujitsu, disarms him and tosses him in a heap in the corner.

CHA CHA (impressed)

You pretty strong, Dave.

DAVE

Our friend is pretty drunk.

Dave crosses the room and reaches down to take a wallet out of Carlos' pocket. As he glances at it –

CLOSE SHOT. DAVE

reading from identification card in wallet.

DAVE

Carlos Manzanares, care of Correro Estate,
Bay Shore Drive, Miami Beach.

ANOTHER ANGLE

CHA CHA (reacting)

Correro! He is a terrible man!

DAVE

His friends aren't too attractive, either.

Dave puts the wallet back, and starts to gather up Carlos to lift him.

CHA CHA

What are you going to do?

DAVE

Deliver him to Senor Correro. I've always wanted to meet a dictator.

As he sets Carlos on his unsteady feet, Carlos vaguely comes to, and we –
DISSOLVE TO:
INT. CORRERO DEN. CLOSE SHOT

Carlos' knife drops on desk. CAMERA PULLS BACK TO REVEAL it is on the desk of Senor Correro in his den in a palatial estate. Present in the room are CORRERO, strong, virile looking, with a certain sense of dignity, and SENOR SILVA, fortyish, soft-spoken, bespectacled South American. Dave is standing across the desk from Correro.

DAVE

Here's one of his toys. Apparently he's under the impression that working for you gives him the right to throw his weight around.

CORRERO

I'll correct that impression at once, Mr. Thorne. And thank you for bringing it to my attention. (turns to Silva) Find where Carlos got the money. He did not save it from a chauffeur's pay.

SILVA

Yes, Presidente.

CORRERO (continuing to speak to Dave)

This must have been an unpleasant experience, Mr. Thorne. I would like to make it up to you.

He reaches for his pen and checkbook.

DAVE (stopping him)

That won't be necessary.

Dave starts out. Correro calls after him.

CORRERO

Mister Thorne…wait!

Whatever Correro has to say to Dave is interrupted as a little boy runs, crying, INTO the room and embraces Correro. RICARDO CORRERO is an attractive eight-year old. Dave stands near the door.

RICARDO (in Spanish)

Papa, papa!...I want to play with other children! Nurse won't let me!

CORRERO (in Spanish, comfortingly)

Senora Gonzalez knows what's best for you. You must listen to her.

The NURSE, a middle-aged, plain-looking woman, ENTERS to retrieve the boy, stops when she sees Ricardo is with his father. The child, seeing her, huddles to Correro, crying anew

                    RICARDO (in Spanish)
I don't want to be with her. I don't like her. I want to go home.
                  I want to see my friends.
        Correro lifts the boy and kisses him tenderly.

                    CORRERO (in Spanish)
      I know, Ricardo. Soon, you will have friends here.
He crosses the room with Ricardo to the nurse. He puts him down.

                    CORRERO (continuing)
                  Try to make him happy.
She nods understandingly, and EXITS with Ricardo, who is still terribly
unhappy.

ANOTHER ANGLE. GROUP

                    SILVA (quietly)
                  She does her best.

                    CORRERO (heavily)
            It is not her fault. The boy is lonely.
Both men, immersed in the boy's problem, have forgotten Dave is present.
Without understanding the language, Dave has a pretty good idea of what
has transpired between father and son. He steps to Correro.

                    DAVE
              You asked me to wait?
CLOSE SHOT. CORRERO
He eyes Dave – an idea dawning.

                    CORRERO
                    Yes.
MED.SHOT GROUP

                    CORRERO (to Silva)
Find where Carlos got the money. He did not save it from a chauffeur's pay.

                    SILVA (in agreement)
                  It will be done.

Silva EXITS.

CLOSE UP of Correro and Dave. Correro peers at Dave, appraisingly, comes to a decision.

CORRERO

Mister Thorne, I will pay you a thousand dollars for an afternoon's work.

DAVE (leery)

What kind of work?

CORRERO

I would like you to arrange a party for my son's birthday, next Saturday.

DAVE

Children's gatherings are a little out of my line.

CORRERO

There will be strangers coming here. Caterers, entertainers – people who might harm me – even Ricardo. You would screen them carefully – protect us.

It is a strange request, and Dave ponders it. He has no desire to work for Correro and is about to say so. Correro senses this, and, before Dave can refuse, he tries to make Dave understand his feelings.

CORRERO

My son has been torn from his friends at home, because of me. He has been denied friendships here.

(strongly)

I ruled my country in a way that I thought right. I made enemies. But I do not want the child to suffer. You saw him. He is lonely, deeply unhappy. All I want is the opportunity for him to make friends. To laugh again.

Dave can't help but put aside his feelings for Correro, the Dictator. He can remember Ricardo's tearful face.

CORRERO

I do not ask for myself – but for Ricardo.

DAVE

What time next Saturday?

CORRERO (relieved)

You name it, Mister Thorne. Mister Silva will help in any way possible.

DAVE

I'll be in touch.

CORRERO (sincerely)

Thank you.

Dave nods, EXITS.

DISSOLVE TO:

EXT. SURFSIDE. MED. SHOT DAY

MOUSIE, precariously balancing a large carton, comes to the gangplank of the houseboat, looks backward, out of breath.

MED. FULL SHOT. P.O.V. (STOCK)

The dizzying traffic before the Hotel Fontainebleau.

MED. CLOSE SHOT. MOUSIE

Mousie sighs with relief, continues to Surfside entrance. But carefully.

INT. SURFSIDE LIVING ROOM. MED. SHOT DAY

Dave is checking a list, sitting at the bar. Silva, seated next to him, is having a drink. Ken is on the phone.

KEN (into the phone)

It's very kind of you to take the trouble...Yes, I'll wait.

Dave, seeing Mousie approach outside, hastens to the door, opens it. Mousie ENTERS, carrying the carton. This is the first time he has crossed the street without mishap – considers this a moment of victory.

MOUSIE (beaming)

I made it!

He steps further into the room, trips, and the carton falls, littering the floor with party paraphernalia. Mousie EXITS in embarrassed confusion. Dave and Silva LAUGHING, put the party hats into the carton.

KEN (into the phone)

We'll pick them up at one o'clock, Saturday. Goodbye.

He HANGS UP, moves to Dave and Silva as they finish picking up.

KEN (continuing)

It's okay with the orphanage. We've got eleven little cherubs. They ought to have a ball.

SILVA

Mr. Correro will be delighted.

There is a KNOCK on the door – BOOM-BOOM CHA CHA CHA. All turn as CHA CHA ENTERS. She leaves the door open. Cha Cha is more than normally excited.

CHA CHA

When you hear what I am going to tell you,
you will kiss me on both cheeks!

DAVE

Mr. Silva, this is Cha Cha O'Brien.

Silva nods politely. Cha Cha nods and rattles on.

CHA CHA

I find him. A wonderful man. Children love him. So funny.
Big star. Magnifico. We going to have such fun!

DAVE (amused)

Slow up. Who is it?

CHA CHA

Tataaa!

(gestures to the open door)

The one and only Pepe, the Clown!

All turn to look O.S.

MED. SHOT DOOR

A hand comes around the door sill and around its fingers is the face of a puppet.

PUPPET (Frightened little voice)

Hey, Pepe…lots of people in here.

PEPE'S VOICE (O.S.)

Well, speak up. Tell them how glad you are to have been invited
to the party.

PUPPET

You speak up.

Pepe's head comes around the corner. We see a pleasant, mild-mannered
man. He is a fine performer and likable.

PEPE (to puppet)

Tell them about me.

PUPPET

Do you want me to tell them that you are the world's most famous clown?
That you have appeared in fifty countries? For royalty! The most beloved
clown of them all?

PEPE

That would be nice.

PUPPET

Nice, but a little conceited don't you think?

PEPE (embarrassed)

Yes, perhaps you're right.

PUPPET

Shall we join the others?

PEPE

Yes.

In the background ELAINA, Pepe's wife, comes to the doorway. She is
American. A quiet, nice-looking woman, about thirty-five years younger
than her husband. Pepe takes her arm and they move into the room.

ANOTHER ANGLE GROUP

CHA CHA
This is my friend, Pepe, and his wife, Elaina.
(excitedly)
The children will have the best clown in the world.
Dave, Ken and Cha Cha converge on Pepe.

GROUP (appreciatively)
Thanks, Pepe! The kids'll love you! Welcome aboard!

SILVA (approaching Pepe)
I am Senor Silva.
(They shake hands.)
My personal thanks, senor.

PEPE (slight accent, modestly)
What is a clown for, but to make children happy?
(introducing Elaina to Silva)
This is Elaina, my wife.
Silva acknowledges the introduction. The others greet her warmly.

PEPE
What time is the party?

KEN
Two o'clock. Plenty of time to get back to the hotel for your show.

DAVE
You'll make it a great day for Correro's boy.
CLOSE SHOT ELAINA
Stunned, horrified.

ELAINA (blurting)
Correro?
WIDER ANGLE GROUP
The group turns to her in wonderment. Pepe takes his wife by the hand.

PEPE

I must get back. The rehearsal is waiting.

DAVE

See you Saturday.

Pepe and Elaina EXIT.

EXT. SURFSIDE MED. SHOT

Pepe and Elaina walk to the sidewalk. Elaina abruptly stops Pepe.

ELAINA (urgently)

You can't! Not for Correro!

PEPE (grimly)

I must, Elaina. Come.

They continue across the street.

DISSOLVE TO:

EXT. CORRERO HOUSE

CAMERA is POINTING DOWN on a patch of lawn. A BOUNCING BALL comes across, and CAMERA PANS with it to the feet of MR. CORRERO. He picks the ball up, as O.S. we HEAR the CHILDREN'S VOICES calling to him to throw the ball. He throws the ball O.S. and EXITS.

EXT. CORRERO GROUNDS. MED. FULL SHOT DAY

The BALL BOUNCES into the scene and TWO CHILDREN race after it. CAMERA PANS UP to show the children's party is in progress. They are all seated around a gaily festooned table, eating. Mousie and a couple of other waiters are serving. Dave, Cha Cha, and Elaina are in attendance, passing out party hats.

CLOSE SHOT. RICARDO

Elaina comes to him, places one of the hats on his head. He ROARS with LAUGHTER, is having the time of his life.

ANOTHER ANGLE. MOUSIE

pulls up a chair and helps feed one of the smaller guests – gets the ice cream in his lap.

CLOSE ON DAVE AND CORRERO

watching, amused. The Houseman comes to Correro, whispers something to him. Correro leaves.

DISSOLVE TO:

EXT. PATIO. MED. CLOSE SHOT PEPE THE CLOWN

performing particularly for Ricardo. His little guests are seated in a semi-circle of chairs. Pepe wears a distinctive costume, completely unrecognizable because of the makeup. The children adore his antics.

OTHER ANGLES. DAVE, CHA CHA, MOUSIE

watching. They are as delighted as the children are.

MED. SHOT PEPE

HOLD ON his performance as long as it is of interest.

DISSOLVE TO:

MED. SHOT

The chairs have been cleared away and the piñata is in progress. There is a hanging papier mache burro suspended from a tree branch. Several children take their turn swatting it with a broomstick. When it comes to Ricardo's chance, the piñata breaks and rains down its treasures of candies, balloons, toys, etc. The squealing children rush for the gifts, hold them up victoriously, shouting their glee.

DISSOLVE TO:

EXT. PATIO MED. SHOT

The children are now playing "Pin the Tail on the Donkey." The "Donkey" is a large placard attached to a tree trunk. One of the children is blindfolded and twirled around by Cha Cha, then pushed in the general direction of his target.

ANOTHER ANGLE

The CHILD wanders one way then in the other, is given directions by SHOUTS of his party friends.

CLOSER ANGLE THE CHILD

moving closer to the "Donkey." Dave is standing close by. The SHOUTS of the kids CRESCENDO, as the little boy pins the "Donkey" on the head. At the moment of contact, there is a woman's SHRILL SCREAM of horror. Dave looks off, runs toward the sound.

INT. CORRERO STUDY CLOSE SHOT NURSE

Looking down horrified, screaming. CAMERA PANS to Dave as he ENTERS through the patio door, hurriedly. He stops dead at what he sees O.S. Silva follows him in. Both look off, and down.

MED. SHOT. P.O.V. CORRERO

lying face down. There is a widening blood stain across his back. A knife is on the floor beside him.

ANOTHER ANGLE

Distracted, Silva steps to the body, leans down, sobs his grief. Dave crosses to the desk phone, dials.

DAVE (into the phone)

Give me Lt. Snediger in homicide.

DISSOLVE TO:

INT. HALL. MED. SHOT

Cha Cha, Mousie, Dave, the Waiters, Silva, and the Correro servants, are seated and standing around the wall. A DETECTIVE is at the exit door to the grounds. LT. SNEDIGAR paces before the group. Seemingly easygoing and relaxed, he is, nevertheless, an intelligent, experienced cop. He is in his late thirties. Snedigar notes something in a little black book, and walks to the Guard (seen earlier at the front gate.) Cha Cha crosses to intercept Snedigar.

CHA CHA

Please, Mr. Policeman, can I go? I'll be late for my show.

SNEDIGAR

Patience is a virtue, Senorita.

CHA CHA

What's that mean?

SNEDIGAR

Stay.

He continues to walk to the Guard.

CLOSER ANGLE

SNEDIGAR (to Guard)

You were at the gate all afternoon?

GUARD

Yes, sir.

SNEDIGAR (gesturing to the group)

You let all these people in?

The Guard glances around the room, before answering.

GUARD

Yes, sir.

SNEDIGAR

The clown is the only one who left?

GUARD

That's right.

SNEDIGAR

You're sure?

GUARD (stubborn)

Nobody else.

Lieutenant Snedigar steps to Silva, the CAMERA PANNING with him. Silva is white-faced, grief stricken.

SNEDIGAR

The iron door in the south wall is the only other exit?

SILVA

Yes, I told you. But it is always locked.

Snedigar nods, notes something on the pad.

WIDER ANGLE

Snedigar addresses the group.

SNEDIGAR

You can go now. Leave your names and addresses with Detective Walsh. Don't leave town. We'll be calling on you.

Relieved, the group moves to the door. Snedigar walks to Dave, who is seated at the edge of the desk.

TWO SHOT. SNEDIGAR AND DAVE

SNEDIGAR (touch of sarcasm)

Swell party, wasn't it?

DAVE

Just dandy.

SNEDIGAR

They tell me you arranged it…Didn't know you were a Correro lover.

DAVE (nettled)

I did it for the kid, Snedigar. Look, Snedigar, there are a dozen others who could have used that knife.

SNEDIGAR

I'll check them out.

DAVE

I've known Pepe for a long time. He wouldn't hurt a fly.

SNEDIGAR

Maybe his feeling about a fly is different from his feeling about a snake.

(afterthought)

I only hope Correro's money racket died with him.

DAVE

Come again?

SNEDIGAR

Correro swiped a fortune in pesetas before they ran him out of South America. His gorillas are peddling them at discount rates.

(shaking head)

This is a joke. The guy who killed Correro ought to get a medal, and I've got to give him a hot foot.

Snedigar moves to the door of Correro's study, turns back to Dave to needle him.

SNEDIGAR

Davey, with all the guys gunning for him, Correro should have hired him- self some protection.

Grinning, Snedigar EXITS. Dave glares after him, burning.

INT. CORRERO STUDY. MED. SHOT

The body, still face down on the floor, is being examined by one of the police lab men. Another is dusting for fingerprints. The lab man studies the dead man's hand as Snedigar ENTERS. Noticing something on the hand he calls to Snedigar.

LAB MAN (to Snedigar)

Lieutentant. Give a look.

CLOSE ANGLE

Sneidar lifts the hand to see – examines it. What he sees is darned important to him. He rises thoughtfully, comes to a quick decision. CAMERA ANGLE WIDENS, as he walks to the other technician.

SNEDIGAR

Call headquarters. Tell them to pick up Pepe Alvarez.

The Technician hurries to the phone.

DISSOLVE TO:

EXT. MUNICIPAL BUILDING COURTHOUSE. DAY   ESTABLISHING SHOT

EXT. MUNICIPAL BUILDING COURTHOUSE. DAY

Dave drives INTO SCENE. He parks the convertible, gets out and places a coin in the parking meter. He moves off to the Courthouse.

DISSOLVE TO:

INT. JAIL. MED. SHOT   PANNING

The JAILER leads Dave to Pepe's cell, and opens the door. Dave ENTERS.

CLOSER ANGLE   PEPE AND DAVE

Seated disconsolately on a cot, Pepe rises hopefully. The jailer locks the door behind them, EXITS.

PEPE

Mr. Thorne, I'm happy that you have come to see me.

DAVE

I spoke to the desk sergeant on the way down. You're booked
for murder, Pepe.

PEPE (urgently)

I didn't kill him. I told the Lieutenant the truth. He didn't believe me.

DAVE

Supposing you tell me…Everything that happened after you performed for
the kids.

PEPE (flatly)

Mr. Thorne. I didn't perform. I never got to the party.

DAVE (reacting)

You were there. I saw you!

PEPE

No! I never left my apartment. My wife left early to help Cha Cha with the decorations. A little later the doorbell rang. I answered it. There was someone outside. I can't tell you what he looked like. It was all so quick.

TIGHT TWO SHOT

Pepe presses his hand across his forehead. The action of a man with an aching head. Dave seats himself beside Pepe.

DAVE

What happened?

PEPE

I was hit with something. That's all I know. When I woke up, I was in the closet, my hands and legs tied – a gag in my mouth.

DAVE

Who released you?

PEPE

No one. I finally worked some of the knots loose and untied myself.

DAVE

Why didn't you report it to the police?

PEPE

I was going to. Before I had a chance, they walked in.

Dave lights a cigarette, reflecting. He rises, examines the bump on Pepe's head.

DAVE

You took a hard one.

Pepe nods, looks at Dave searchingly. It's terribly important to him that Dave believes his story. Dave crosses to the bars and calls out to the jailer.

DAVE

Ready to go now!

ANOTHER ANGLE

Pepe goes to Dave as the jailer APPEARS and goes to the door.

PEPE

It's the truth, Mr. Thorne. I swear it. I was not at the party. You must believe me!

DAVE

I believe you, Pepe.

He pats Pepe on the shoulder reassuringly, and EXITS. The jailer clanks the door shut. Pepe peers after Dave hopefully.

DISSOLVE TO:

INT. LIEUTENANT SNEDIGAR'S OFFICE. CLOSE SHOT SNEDIGAR

His feet are on his desk, and he is leaning far back in the chair.

SNEDIGAR

Crazy story…real crazy…

CAMERA ANGLE WIDENS TO INCLUDE Dave who is at the window.

DAVE

He has a real crazy bump on his head.

SNEDIGAR (lifting his feet off the desk)

I felt the bump. He could have hung it on himself.

DAVE

I doubt it.

(musing)

If Pepe wasn't at the party, somebody else could have impersonated him.

SNEDIGAR

Could have, but didn't. His wife would have spotted a phony in a minute.

Dave can't help but react. He hadn't suspected that Snedigar had gone this far.

SNEDIGAR

Cops work for a living. I talked to her a half hour ago. Convinced?

DAVE (slowly)

I think he's telling the truth.

Snedigar rises, goes to a filing cabinet and takes a paper from the top of it.

SNEDIGAR (handing Dave the paper)

Here's the lab report. Grease paint found on fingers of the dead man. A clown's grease paint.

DAVE (glances at the report and puts it on the desk)

You've got everything. Everything but the motive.

SNEDIGAR

Pepe is Correro's countryman. Everybody down there hated his guts.

DAVE

Pretty thin motive.

SNEDIGAR (confidently)

Okay, I'll find a better one before he goes to trial.

DISSOLVE TO:

INT. FONTAINEBLEAU HOTEL LOBBY. MED. SHOT NIGHT

Dave crosses the lobby. He pauses at the newsstand, picks up a paper.

CLOSER ANGLE SHOOTING OVER DAVE'S SHOULDER

The NEWSPAPER HEADLINE READS:

"D.A. CLAIMS CLOWN IS KILLER

Alleged Killer Arrested

Clown Taken Into Custody"

ANOTHER ANGLE

Dave folds the newspaper, throws a coin on the newsstand desk, continues on, THE CAMERA PANNING. He stops short at a billboard on an easel. Across the top of it is printed:

LE RONDE ROOM Presents

The Clown Prince PEPE!

There are several pictures of Pepe in clown attire in various poses. One of the pictures has been torn from its place. Dave touches the vacant spot, thoughtfully. An attendant appears and carries off the easel. Dave peers after him, then enters the Boom Boom Room.

WIPE TO:

INT. BOOM BOOM ROOM. MED.CLOSE SHOT CHA CHA NIGHT

She sings a Latin rhythm song. We HOLD on her as long as the number is of interest – then her attention is drawn off.

MED. SHOT AT TABLES

Dave, carrying the newspaper, goes to Ken's table and slumps into a chair.

KEN

Anything new?

Dave tosses the newspaper to Ken, who reads the front page.

MED. SHOT. CHA CHA

She finishes her song. She takes her bows and MOVES OFF TOWARD Ken and Dave.

MED. CLOSE SHOT ANGLE DAVE AND KEN

Cha Cha ENTERS, pulls up a chair beside Dave.

CHA CHA (urgently)

You see Pepe?

Dave nods.

> CHA CHA (continuing)
>
> You help him?

> DAVE
>
> I'm going to try.

> CHA CHA
>
> Well, don't sit! Do something!

> DAVE (placating)
>
> Cha Cha, I'm thinking.

> CHA CHA
>
> Think later! Do something now!

> DAVE
>
> Yes, ma'am.
>
> (to Ken)
>
> Is the publicity office open?

Ken nods.

> DAVE
>
> Good. I want to look at some pictures.

He rises and EXITS. Cha Cha throws her hands up in desperation.

> CHA CHA
>
> How you like that? Pepe's in jail and he goes to look at pictures!

DISSOLVE TO:

EXT. FONTAINEBLEAU HOTEL POOL. DAY

ESTABLISHING. A GIRL dives in the pool; others are swimming. Gaily colored umbrellas, etc.

MED. CLOSE SHOT ELAINA AT FORMAL GARDENS. (PROCESS)

She is waiting at a table in the restaurant near the Formal Gardens of the Fontainebleau. She smiles, as Dave ENTERS scene.

MED. CLOSE ANGEL DAVE

Meets Elaina.

> DAVE (a beat)

One thing puzzles me, Mrs. Alvarez. You've seen your husband perform many times before. How is it that you didn't detect the impersonator?

> ELAINA

It didn't enter my mind that it wasn't Pepe. He – whoever he was – wore a costume exactly like Pepe's. I was busy with the children.

> DAVE

Why did he leave the party without you?

> ELAINA

It was arranged. Pepe had to get back for his early show.

CLOSE TWO SHOT

Dave takes out a facsimile of one of the pictures seen earlier on the billboard. He shows it to her.

> DAVE

If someone had one of these – could Pepe's makeup be copied?

> ELAINA

I…I think so.

> DAVE

What about his costume? Was it the kind a person could rent?

> ELAINA

Oh, no. Pepe spent years perfecting it. It was his trademark.

DAVE

Does he have more than one?

ELAINA

I thought of that, Mr. Thorne. It was the first thing I looked for when I went home. His spare outfit is still in the closet.

DAVE

Who makes these costumes for him?

ELAINA

Since we came to Miami it's been Dickinson and Company.
Right off Collins and Sixteenth

Dave gets up, and starts to go.

DAVE

Thanks. I'll keep in touch with you.

Dave EXITS.

DISSOLVE TO:

INT. DICKINSON'S COSTUME SHOP. CLOSE SHOT DICKINSON

A florid, somewhat straight-laced man in his late forties. He is wounded.

DICKINSON (tautly)

…if I made that outfit for anyone else, I would be betraying a trust.
Highly unethical.

CAMERA ANGLE WIDENS

Dave is standing before a counter opposite Dickinson. The counter separates them. There are a couple of dummies dressed in rental costumes – a devil, an Indian, a Victorian dress. Others kinds of costumes are folded on the counter.

DAVE

Would it be possible for anyone else to make Pepe's outfit?

DICKINSON

Not unless he had the pattern.

DAVE

Do you have it?

DICKINSON

Of course. I've tailored Pepe's costumes for several years.

A LITTLE MAN, an elderly Italian, wearing a tailor's apron, ENTERS in the background, picks up the costumes from the counter and EXITS.

DAVE

Could I see it?

DICKINSON (stiffly)

I'm afraid not. Not without Pepe's permission.

DAVE (sharply)

I'm not in the costume business, Mr. Dickinson. Pepe's in trouble. I want to help him. I want to be sure you've still got that pattern.

Undecided for a moment, Dickinson relents. He EXITS into a little alcove where the Little Man sits sewing. As Dickinson goes to a file looking for the pattern, Dave's eyes take in the room, and then his eyes wander down to the floor where something attracts his attention. The floor is littered with scattered pieces of material. He casually reaches down, picks up a piece of material, looks at it and rolls it into a ball in the palm of his hand.

MED SHOT. DICKINSON

Dickinson ENTERS with patterns. He places them on the counter.

DICKINSON

Not that it will make much sense to you, but this is the pants – the vest – the oversized coat – and here is his name on each of the pieces.

DAVE

How long since you've used that pattern?

DICKINSON

It's been over a year since I made a costume for Pepe.

Dave nods.

DISSOLVE TO:

EXT. STREET. (PROCESS) NEAR PIER 5

The Little Man, seen in the preceding sequence, is seen sitting on a bench eating his lunch. CAMERA PULLS BACK as Dave ENTERS from F.G. and sits beside him.

ANOTHER ANGLE LITTLE MAN

DAVE

There was another Pepe costume, wasn't there?

LITTLE MAN (anxious to leave)

I don't know anything about it.

He starts away. Dave grasps him by the arm, takes the small piece of material and holds it up to the Little Man.

DAVE

This look familiar?

LITTLE MAN (nervously)

I told you – I don't know anything.

He would like to get away, but Dave blocks him.

DAVE

Got any kids?

LITTLE MAN (surprised)

I have two fine grandchildren.

DAVE

How old are they?

LITTLE MAN

Joey's five and Lucia's three-and-a-half.

DAVE (selling)

I bet they like Pepe.

LITTLE MAN

Sure they do. What kids don't?

DAVE

You could give them all a break, if you tell me the truth.

Dave stares at the Little Man, questioningly. The Little Man is nervous. He's had a battle with himself – is still having it.

LITTLE MAN (blurting)

Dickinson was lying. I made a Pepe costume. It was a rush job. Had to work practically all Friday night.

DAVE (alert)

Who was it for?

LITTLE MAN

I don't know. It was shipped out by messenger service.

DAVE

Know which one?

LITTLE MAN

I'll check and call you later. Got a telephone?

Dave takes out his wallet, hands him a card and a bill.

DAVE

Buy something for Joey and Lucia.

The Little Man takes the card, refuses the money.

LITTLE MAN

I didn't tell you for money. Pepe's a great guy. The kids would miss him.

He EXITS. Dave watches him go, appreciating the little guy's honesty. He drives OFF.

DISSOLVE TO:

EXT. MIAMI BEACH. PIER 5 (STOCK)

Establishing boats, general activity, etc.

MED. SHOT. DAVE (STOCK)

Drives up in car and EXITS. Walks along the pier, looking for someone. He locates his party O.S. Walks on.

MED. CLOSE SHOT. LT. SNEDIGAR (PROCESS)

Just turning away from a man wearing a nautical cap, as Dave ENTERS scene.

DAVE

Ever think of staying in your office.

SNEDIGAR

Just arranging a little fishing trip. I get Sunday's off, you know. What's on your mind?

DAVE

Pepe.

SNEDIGAR (grimacing)

Go away.

DAVE (squats beside him)

Dickinson and Company made one of those clown outfits, delivered it early Saturday morning.

SNEDIGAR

To whom?

DAVE

The murderer.

SNEDIGAR

How do you know it wasn't delivered to the clown?

DAVE (patiently)

Snedigar, Pepe's got two outfits. He's still got the two.

SNEDIGAR

Who told you?

DAVE

His wife.

SNEDIGAR (feigned weariness)

An unimpeachable source, huh? Look, I've got two suits my wife doesn't even know about. And she's a cop.

DAVE

Still chirping murder without a motive?

He starts away. Dave knows he can't convince Snedigar.

SNEDIGAR

We got the motive, Davey. The jury won't be out five minutes.

Dave comes back, listens hard.

SNEDIGAR (continuing)

Pepe had another wife once – Maria a perfect doll. Another guy wanted her and she walked out with him. Real Pagliacci stuff. One guess who the other guy was…

DAVE (a beat)

Correro?

SNEDIGAR

We got a real good police department down here.

DISSOLVE TO:

INT. VISITORS' ROOM AT JAIL. TWO SHOT DAY

Pepe is sitting across the table from Dave, a wire screen between them. Pepe nervously fingers the little hand puppet.

PEPE

Maria was very young, and very beautiful. We were happy…shared dreams together…Correro was very imposing…the uniform and the swagger stick. He pursued her with flowers and jewels. She was overwhelmed – lost. She left me for Correro. When I tried to see her I was arrested and thrown out of the country.

(rising – throwing the hand puppet to the floor)

It's true I hated Correro. I wanted to kill him…I was going back for just that reason, when I learned of her death.

DAVE (a beat)

But Silva must have told Correro you were going to entertain. Why didn't he stop you from coming?

PEPE

Silva and Correro never knew me as Pepe, the Clown.

DAVE (leveling)

Why did you go there?

PEPE

I wanted to see the boy…I wanted to see Ricardo.

DAVE

Why were you so interested in Correro's son?

PEPE

He is not Correro's son, Mr. Thorne…he is mine.

PAN DOWN TO:

CLOSE SHOT. PUPPET

It wears a forlorn, grieving expression.

DISSOLVE TO:

EXT. MIAMI BEACH STREET. CLOSE SHOT DAY

A DOOR marked:

ACME MESSENGER SERVICE

Instant Deliveries

THE CAMERA HOLDS ON DOOR long enough to read sign, and Dave EXITS from interior and goes out F.G.

INT. CAB OF ACME DELIVERY TRUCK (PROCESS)

WILLY, a sixteen-year-old, and another messenger, are playing gin rummy in the cab of the truck. Both wear the uniform of the Acme Service. Dave ENTERS through F.G.

DAVE

Which one is Willy?

Willy, gripped by the game, plays a card before answering.

WILLY

Me.

DAVE

I'd like to ask you a couple of questions.

WILLY

Just a sec…

DAVE

Can't wait.

He sits between the boys on top of the cards.

WILLY (protesting)

Aww…I'm hooked for sixty cents.

DAVE

You delivered a package for Dickinson Costumes?

WILLY

That's right. Saturday, early delivery.

DAVE

Where did you deliver it?

WILLY

One of them beach hotels.

DAVE

Which one?

Willy is nettled…wants to play cards. He takes a clipboard from behind the cab, flips a few pages.

WILLY (locating delivery)

The Fontainebleau.

DAVE (let down)

You sure?

WILLY (indicating file)

Look for yourself…Mister, you're holding up the game.

DAVE

Did you deliver it to the desk?

WILLY

Naw…to a guy who was waiting downstairs in the arcade.

DAVE (hopefully)

Remember what he looked like?

WILLY

Kinda' short, dark hair –

(shrugging)

Just a guy… Do you mind?

Dave rises, frowning. Standing a little behind Willy, he glances at Willy's cards as Willy rearranges them.

DAVE

Nothing special you can tell me about him?

WILLY

He gave me a buck tip.

Dave hands him a couple of bills.

DAVE

Here's two…

WILLY (without thinking)

He had kind of a rash – or a burn – on the side of his face…

(touches right side of his face)

…along the jaw line.

DAVE (gesturing)

With sideburns down to here?

WILLY (indicating)

Sideburns down to here.

Dave starts out, turns:

DAVE

Willy, you've got gin.

Willy glances at his hand, reacting. He lays down his cards.

WILLY

Yeah! Gin!

Dave EXITS.

DISSOLVE TO:

EXT. CORRERO HOUSE. MED. SHOT DAY

Silva, Bodyguard, Houseman, Nurse and Ricardo (in black dress with mourning arm bands), EXIT house, waiting for funeral limousine. Dave drives his car up, holding it near the limousine, as all but Silva embark.

CLOSER ANGLE. DAVE AND SILVA DAY

Dave takes Silva's arm.

> DAVE (low voice)
>
> Mister Silva?

> SILVA
>
> It was nice of you to come, Mister Thorne. Will you ride to the cemetery with us?

> DAVE
>
> No, thank you.
>
> (beat)
>
> I'd like some information.

> SILVA
>
> Please…not now. Perhaps when I return.

> DAVE
>
> This can't wait. I've got to find Carlos.

> SILVA (getting it over with)
>
> Carlos was dismissed the day you told us about him.

> DAVE
>
> Do you know where he is now?

Silva shakes his head.

> SILVA
>
> I understand he left by ship for South America.

> DAVE
>
> When?

> SILVA
>
> Last Friday.

DAVE

I don't think he did, Mister Silva. He was here on Saturday. He went to that party dressed as a clown.

SILVA (reacting)

You are sure?

DAVE

I know he ordered the costume.

SILVA (grimly)

Then you must find him, Mister Thorne.

Dave nods, EXITS quietly.

DISSOLVE TO:

EXT. SURFSIDE 6 DECK MED. SHOT NIGHT

Cha Cha storms across the pier and bursts into the living room.

INT. SURFSIDE 6 LIVING ROOM MED. SHOT NIGHT

Dave is working at his desk and Mousie is gathering up some dishes to return to his tray. Cha Cha charges up to Dave, spouting dialogue as she does:

CHA CHA

Ahhh! Pepe sits in jail...and you sit behind your desk!

Cha Cha walks over to the door and gestures.

CHA CHA (continuing)

One thing Cha Cha knows for sure. He will not come through the door looking for you!

At this point, Ken ENTERS. Cha Cha's outstretched fingers almost poke him in the eye. Dave goes to Ken.

DAVE

Well?

KEN

Carlos booked passage on the SS MARU, but according to the main office, he never went aboard. He's probably still in town.

CHA CHA (to Dave)

Then we must find him. Cha Cha will help.

Dave takes a sheaf of bills from his pocket.

DAVE

You'll all help. You too, Mousie.

He gives several of the bills to Cha Cha and repeats the action with Mousie and Ken. They are all bewildered.

MOUSIE

What's this for?

DAVE

We're in the market to buy pesetas.

MOUSIE

What do we need with fruit?

CHA CHA (explaining)

Pesetas is dinero!

MOUSIE

Dinero?

CHA CHA (gestures with fingers)

Monies! Monies!

DAVE

Snedigar says they're still peddling pesetas around town.
Carlos is too dollar happy to give up a good thing.

CHA CHA

Smart man. What can I do?

DAVE

You're leaving the country.

CHA CHA (reacting)

Me? Oh no! That's one thing I won't! Cha Cha likes it here!

DAVE

South American Airlines handles all flights to Bueno Puenta. Get a ticket for tomorrow night's flight. Ask the clerk about buying pesetas. If he doesn't sell them, maybe he'll tell you somebody who will.

(urging her to the door)

Scoot. Get to their office before it closes.

ANOTHER ANGLE

MOUSIE

What do I do?

DAVE

You cover the nightclubs, and late spots.

MOUSIE (holds up the dough)

I'm a big tipper. What'll I use for the tabs?

DAVE

Sign 'em.

Mousie nods in agreement…does a late take…and we

DISSOLVE TO:

EXT. YACHT. (STOCK) SANDY

Sandy is stretched out on one of the back cushions, enjoying the luxuries of easy living. The phone RINGS. Sandy interrupts the phone in mid-ring.

SANDY (on phone)

Hello, Dave. Love to help, but can't. Sorry, old pal, the ski finals are tomorrow and I'm in training.

CLOSE SHOT. DAVE

DAVE (into phone)

Okay, Sandy. See you soon.

He hangs up. Starts out.

CLOSE SHOT

A GORGEOUS DOLL ENTERS opposite Sandy. He pulls her into his arms.

> SANDY (with a smile)
>
> Let's get back to training…

As they kiss.

DISSOLVE:

INT. TRAVEL AGENCY. (PROCESS) NIGHT

There is a sign on one wall which reads:

LINEAS SUR AMERICANAS

FLY TO SOUTH AMERICA

Cha Cha ENTERS SCENE and walks quickly to the counter.

> CLERK
>
> What can I do for you?

> CHA CHA
>
> A ticket to Bueno Puente.
>
> (waving arms)
>
> I fly!

Cha Cha opens her purse and places Dave's bills on the counter.

> CLERK
>
> When do you wish to leave?

> CHA CHA
>
> Tomorrow night.

> CLERK
>
> We have a flight at ten-forty
>
> (writing)
>
> Name?

CHA CHA

Cha Cha O'Brien

CLERK

That's an odd name.

CHA CHA

My mother was Spanish, and my father was Swiss.

CLERK (reacts)

Your telephone number, please?

CHA CHA

It won't do any good. I leave tomorrow.

CLERK (primly)

I need it in case there will be a delay.

CHA CHA

Oh. Beach 42080

The Clerk continues making out the ticket. She moves closer.

CHA CHA (continuing; persuasively)

You know maybe where I can buy pesetas?

CLERK

Any bank, Miss. Or you may purchase them when you arrive.

CHA CHA

I hear some people sell them cheap.

CLERK (stiffly)

I'm sorry, I can't help you.

The Clerk hands Cha Cha the ticket. He takes her money, turns to make change. Cha Cha frowns disappointedly.

DISSOLVE TO:

A SERIES OF SHOTS. THE HUNT. (STOCK) NIGHT

Intended to show Miami at night. The night spots, the beach clubs, etc.

DISSOLVE TO:

EXT. NIGHT CLUB.   NIGHT

Ken ENTERS a classy joint.

INT. CLUB. MED.SHOT. CORNER NIGHT

JAZZ MUSIC blasting over. Ken has the HEAD WAITER button-holed and questions him. We do not hear the dialogue. The head waiter shakes his head.

DISSOLVE TO:

EXT. STREET. NEWSTAND.   NIGHT

Dave questions the newsboy, who gestures in the negative.

DISSOLVE:

EXT. BACKSTAGE DAVE. (STOCK)

Pretty girls, in abbreviated costumes, come down a staircase. Others rush madly for the stage, O.S.

CLOSE SHOT INDISCERNABLE B.G. GOPHER

He questions a statuesque show girl, a couple of heads taller than he is. BLASTING MUSIC from O.S. He stands on tip-toe to repeat his questions. She says, "No."

INT. NIGHTCLUB AT HATCHECK BOOTH CLOSE SHOT NIGHT

A scantily-dressed, brassy brunette talks into the CAMERA. Latin music is HEARD O.S. The brunette is strictly American. She looks him over appraisingly, decides he's okay.

BRUNETTE

I'll have to make a call.

She holds out her hand, and Dave puts a bill in it. It isn't enough and she waits. Dave hands her another bill. The brunette is satisfied with the loot, and EXITS INTO the checkroom. Dave, now hopeful, peers after her.

CLOSE SHOT BRUNETTE

The brunette picks up a phone: dials.

BRUNETTE

Hello? This is Georgia. I've got a customer for you...pesetas...a thousand, maybe more...he'll be waiting.

She hangs up and EXITS.

INT. NIGHTCLUB HATCHECK BOOTH. CLOSE SHOT

Dave straightens as the brunette re-appears.

BRUNETTE

He won't be long. Wait at the back entrance.

Dave EXITS.

INT. ALLEY

Lit only by a shaft of light from an open door of the nightclub. MUSIC from a wicked samba OVER. Dave peers up and down the alley – waiting. He leans against the door, puffing a cigarette.

MED. SHOT. SHOOTING DOWN ALLEY

A figure – not recognizable – turns into it. He peers off to Dave to get a better look at his customer.

MED. SHOT P.O.V. DAVE

Smoking. The MUSIC CRESCENDOS.

CLOSE SHOT. DAVE

Impatiently, he flicks the cigarette away. Then, he steps forward to heel it out. The SOUND of a squeaky shoe, and Dave turns. An arm, holding a sap, brings it forcibly down across Dave's head. Dave falls. The attacker's feet move INTO SCENE beside him. Dave struggles to lift himself. The music STOPS. Dave collapses, out cold. The feet EXIT.

DISSOLVE TO:

INT. BOOM BOOM ROOM. DAY

Cha Cha is rehearsing a number – first 16 bars. Suddenly one of the musicians in the orchestra HITS A CLINKER. Cha Cha reacts to this, goes into a short tirade to the orchestra; and is interrupted as a bartender motions her over to the phone. She crosses to answer the phone.

CHA CHA (on the telephone)

Hello? Yes, this is Miss O'Brien. No…

(remembering quickly)

I mean yes, yes. I go to Bueno Puente tonight. Who is this?

INT. TRAVEL OFFICE CLOSE SHOT CARLOS

CARLOS

I hear you are interested in buying pesetas. I have some for sale.

ANOTHER ANGLE

To INCLUDE the Clerk, seen earlier. Carlos winks at him.

CARLOS

Meet me in front of the restaurant at 315 King Terrace.

CLOSE SHOT CHA CHA

CHA CHA

Just a minute.

Excited, she rummages around in her purse for a pencil and paper, then picks up the phone.

CHA CHA

215 Keene Terrace?

315 Keene Terrace…

INT. TRAVEL OFFICE CLOSE SHOT CARLOS

CARLOS

No, no senorita. Not Keene – KING. K-I-N-G, King, like El Rey.

INT. BOOM BOOM ROOM CLOSE SHOT CHA CHA

CHA CHA (on phone)

315 Keeng, like El Rey. Very good. A half hour? I will hurry.

Cha Cha hangs up.

DISSOLVE TO:

INT. SURFSIDE 6 LIVING ROOM. MED. SHOT   DAY

Ken ENTERS, closing the door behind him. He is low, dispirited. Dave ENTERS from the bedroom. He is in his shirt-sleeves, and holds an ice bag on his head.

> DAVE
>
> Get anything?

> KEN
>
> That checkroom girl clammed up, says she never heard of you...doesn't know anything about pesetas, telephone numbers – nothing. And she's scared stiff.

> DAVE
>
> It was worth a try.

The men turn at the SOUND of Cha Cha's VOICE. The door opens and she BURSTS IN. She rushes to Dave.

> CHA CHA (excitedly)
>
> He called me, Dave, he called me! He says he has pesetas to sell.

> DAVE
>
> Did he have an accent?

> CHA CHA
>
> Si, just like Carlos'.

> DAVE (alert)
>
> Did you get his address?

> CHA CHA
>
> 315 El Rey Terrace.

> KEN
>
> El Rey?

Dave takes Ken by the arm, urges him to the door.

DAVE

I've got a street map in the car.

Cha Cha hurries after them.

CHA CHA

He says he waits thirty minutes. Now you have only twenty!

DAVE

We'll be there.

(pecking her cheek)

Book me for a whole course of Cha Cha lessons.

Dave and Ken EXIT in a hurry. Cha Cha is pleased with the kiss. She opens her handbag to take out a cigarette. As she does so, she sees the flyer on which she has written Carlos' address.

CLOSE SHOT. INSERT CHA CHA'S FLYER

"CHA CHA WITH CHA CHA O'BRIEN

HOTEL FOUNTAINEBLEAU

MIAMI BEACH, FLORIDA

MED. CHOSE SHOT CHA CHA

CHA CHA (reading)

315 King Terrace.

Abruptly, realizing she gave Dave the wrong address, she is horrified.

CHA CHA

I told him El Rey!

She rushes to the door…opens it, looking for Dave's car, realizing it's useless to call them back. Her eyes follow the car as it disappears into traffic O.S. She pauses, wondering what to do, then hurries OFF.

DISSOLVE TO:

MED. CLOSE SHOT   STREET SIGN HANGING FROM A LAMP POST

It reads:

KING TERRACE

CAMERA PANS DOWN AND ACROSS to pick up Carlos, standing in front of a small restaurant. He glances at his watch, waits.

ANOTHER ANGLE

PANNING from Carlos to Cha Cha's car coming to a halt a short distance down the block.

CLOSER ANGLE. CHA CHA

waiting until she is unobserved, she quickly steps out of the car and walks INTO a cigar store.

INT. CIGAR STORE CORNER AT THE TELEPHONE BOOTH

She quickly DROPS a COIN into the box and DIALS. We hear a steady BUZZ of ringing. She peers out the window toward Carlos, worriedly, hoping Dave will pick up the phone.

INT. SURFSIDE 6 LIVINGROOM.

The room is empty. The Telephone is RINGING.

INT. CIGAR STORE CLOSE SHOT CHA CHA

Concerned, she hangs up and moves to the window to watch Carlos, O.S.

WIPE TO:

EXT. STREET. MED. CLOSE SHOT STREET SIGN

which reads:

EL REY TERRACE

The CAMERA PANS DOWN TO PICK UP Dave and Ken driving to CAMERA. Dave brakes the car. Ken and Dave look OFF.

CLOSE SHOT P.O.V.

A large, empty lot…a whole block in area.

CLOSE SHOT DAVE AND KEN

exchange glances. Dave turns the wheel and heads back to Surfside.

MED. CLOSE SHOT CARLOS

Restive, he glances at his watch again. He's waited long enough. He peers up and down the street for someone who might be Miss O'Brien. Then, with a frown of annoyance, he walks to his flashy convertible and gets in.

MED. CLOSE SHOT CIGAR STORE.

Cha Cha is flattened against the doorway. She sees that Carlos is about to leave.

MED. LONG SHOT P.O.V.

Carlos starts the motor and eases the car from the curb.

MED. SHOT AT CIGAR STORE.

Cha Cha hurries to her car. She DRIVES OFF.

DISSOLVE TO:

EXT. HACIENDA MOTEL MED. FULL SHOT DAY

Carlos drives his convertible to the entrance, disembarks and EXITS.

ANOTHER ANGLE CHA CHA.

Cha Cha's car comes to a halt, some distance behind. There is a break SQUEAK.

MED. CLOSE SHOT CARLOS.

walking. In the b.g. is an office lettered: "MANAGER." Carlos turns at the SOUND, looks off.

MED. CLOSE SHOT CHA CHA IN CAR.

She turns away quickly. She doesn't want to be recognized by Carlos.

MED. CLOSE SHOT CARLOS

He walks to the room numbered "17." Finds the door open.

ENTERS

MED. CLOSE SHOT CHA CHA

disembarks. She looks around for a telephone. She hurries to the manager's office.

INT. MANAGER'S OFFICE

A cubicle containing a small counter, a key rack and mail boxes. The MANAGER, a normally ill-tempered woman, in her mid-fifties, comes around the desk with a load of towels and soap – almost collides into Cha Cha.

CHA CHA

You have telephone, please?

The manager points to a wall pay telephone.

MANAGER

Right there.

Cha Cha hurriedly goes through her purse, looking for the proper change. The manager has started through the door. Cha Cha calls after her.

CHA CHA

You maybe have change for a dollar?

The manager returns, places the towels on the counter, goes behind it to make change.

MANAGER

They said I'd be a motel manager.

(frustrated)

I'm a housemaid, gardener, bellboy. Now I'm a banker!

CHA CHA (taking it straight)

Very good business – banking.

The manager bangs cash register. She gives Cha Cha a dirty look, then gives her the change. Picks up the towels and EXITS. Cha Cha places a coin in the wall telephone and dials.

INT. SURFSIDE 6 CLOSE SHOT ON TELEPHONE

It RINGS. The CAMERA PULLS BACK to REVEAL the empty room.

INT. MANAGER'S OFFICE CLOSE SHOT CHA CHA

She bites her lip, waiting…hoping for an answer.

CHA CHA (frustrated)

You stupid phone! Say something! Say something!

INT. SURFSIDE 6 DAVE AND KEN

HEARING the telephone, they hurry IN. Dave picks up the receiver.

DAVE

Hello? Cha Cha…where are you?

INT. MANAGER'S OFFICE CLOSE SHOT CHA CHA

CHA CHA

I am sorry, Dave, I give you bad address. But I go to right one. It is Carlos! I followed him. Hacienda Motel. Room seventeen.

MED. CLOSE SHOT DAVE AT TELEPHONE

Ken hovers near him.

DAVE (repeating)

Hacienda Motel. Room seventeen.

(warningly)

Stay out of sight. I'll be there in ten minutes.

CLOSE SHOT CHA CHA

CHA CHA (into phone)

You got no worry. I'm a good detective. He didn't even see me…

Abruptly, a pair of hands grab her and wrench her from the phone. Cha Cha SCREAMS.

INT. SURFSIDE 6 CLOSE SHOT DAVE AND KEN

Dave and Ken have heard the scream.

DAVE (into the phone, worried)

Cha Cha!

No answer from Cha Cha. Dave replaces the receiver, disappears INTO the bedroom. He RE-ENTERS, carrying a gun. He puts it in his back pocket and EXITS with KEN.

DISSOLVE TO:

EXT. HACIENDA MOTEL MED. FULL SHOT DAVE AND KEN

Dave drives up, parks his car directly behind Cha Cha's. They disembark, and moving quickly, go to Cha Cha's car, peer inside.

CLOSER ANGLE. THE CAR. DAVE AND KEN.

The car is empty. They exchange meaningful glances and continue to the motel.

ANOTHER ANGLE DAVE AND KEN

pass the manager's office, looking for Room Number "17." Dave takes out his gun, tries the door. Finding it open, he pushes it in with a CRASH. Dave and Ken ENTER.

INT. MOTEL.

A rumpled bed, a bureau, a worn shirt flung carelessly over a chair, a couple of valises in a corner. Dave carefully opens the closet, peers inside, closes it. He moves to the bathroom door, opens it. Dave reacts at what he sees. Ken comes up behind him. They exchange glances, look OFF.

MED. SHOT PORTION OF BATHROOM

HANGING LEGS in the F.G. Dave and Ken at the door.

> DAVE (looking up)
>
> Carlos…

ANOTHER ANGLE

He closes the bathroom door, glances once again around the room. There is a sheet of paper on the bed with writing on it. Dave picks it up, reads it. He grunts, hands the letter to Ken. As Ken reads it, Dave does a rapid search of the room.

CLOSE SHOT DAVE

At the bureau, opening the drawers. In the bottom one he finds the clown's costume. He holds it up for Ken. Ken looks into the drawer, leans down, picks up a small sheaf of bank notes.

> KEN
>
> Pesetas…

Dave nods thoughtfully, puts them into his pocket.

> KEN (continuing – waving letter)
>
> You believe this!?

DAVE (shaking head)

Do you?

Ken agrees with Dave. He replaces the letter on the bed. They start out.

EXT. HACIENDA MOTEL MED. CLOSE AT MANAGER'S OFFICE

The lady manager stuffs a pile of soiled linen into a laundry bag, at the entrance. Ken and Dave ENTER SCENE behind her.

DAVE

Pardon me....

She straightens, rubbing her aching back.

MANAGER

Laundry! The next thing they'll be asking me to wash it!

(tired)

What is it?

KEN

We're looking for a small, dark-haired girl. Wearing a light blue dress...

MANAGER

What about her?

DAVE (insistent)

Have you seen her?

MANAGER

She was using the phone about fifteen minutes ago.

She jerks her finger to the entrance of the office. The men move toward the office door.

MANAGER (continuing, calling)

If she did something wrong, she ain't even registered.

Without turning back, Dave and Ken ENTER the office.

INT. MOTEL OFFICE

The phone is off the hook and hanging. Dave takes the receiver and hands it to Ken.

DAVE

Call the police. Tell them to put out a call for Cha Cha.

Ken digs for change as Dave EXITS.

DISSOLVE TO:

EXT. CORRERO HOUSE AT GATE MED. FULL SHOT

Dave slows the car to a halt. The Gateman questions him, and waves him on.

EXT. CORRERO HOUSE MED. SHOT DAVE

parking his car, he disembarks and starts to the entrance.

INT. BEDROOM MED. SHOT CHA CHA

Small, it contains a bed, a chiffonier, and a rickety straight-back chair. There is a single, round, louvered window placed high on the wall.

Cha Cha has lifted the chair onto the soft bed and climbs it to get at the window. The chair creaks as she puts her weight on it, as she pulls herself up on the sill. In this precarious position she looks out and down.

MED. LONG SHOT P.O.V.

Dave heads to the entrance.

INT. BEDROOM MED. CLOSE SHOT

Cha Cha shoves open the louvered window – is about to call out when the chair falls. She finds herself hanging by her fingers. She lets herself down to the bed, frustrated.

INT. HALL MED. SHOT

Dave ENTERS. The Houseman and Bodyguard carry a trunk and place it near the door. It is significant to Dave that Silva and the group are leaving.

DAVE (to Houseman)

Is Mister Silva around?

INT. HALL CLOSE SHOT

Silva APPEARS in b.g. He is calm, self-possessed. He greets Dave as a friend.

SILVA

Ah, Mister Thorne. Nice of you to visit.

DAVE

Moving someplace?

SILVA (with a gesture)

This is rather expensive for a man of my means. We're looking for smaller quarters, closer to the city.

(indicating outside)

May I serve you a drink?

He EXITS INTO the patio. Dave follows, eyeing him thoughtfully.

EXT. PATIO MED. CLOSE SHOT

Silva goes to a portable bar, takes out glasses, etc.

SILVA

What would you like?

DAVE

Nothing, thanks. Dropped around to tell you we finally located Carlos.

SILVA (making drink)

Good. Where is he?

DAVE

In a motel. Dead.

SILVA (stunned)

Dead!?

DAVE

Suicide. He left a note saying he killed Correro. We found the clown costume in a bureau drawer.

SILVA (uncomprehending)

A life for a life, Mr. Thorne. I'm glad it's finished.

DAVE

It isn't. Carlos was selling pesetas all round town. Pesetas you stole from your country.

(throwing peseta notes on the table)

Here's a few he didn't get rid of.

He looks at Silva accusingly.

SILVA (completely self-possessed)

You are accusing me?

Dave does not allow Silva's coolness to faze him. He moves closer to the older man, as Silva completes making his drink.

DAVE (relentlessly)

I got a call from Cha Cha who followed Carlos to his motel. I arrived a short time later. During that short time, Cha Cha had disappeared. Carlos wrote a letter to the police, made a noose, hanged himself. You think he could do all this alone? Or did he have help? Your help?

SILVA (easily)

My help? I don't know what you're talking about.

Silva sees a movement in the bushes. Dave is unaware of it

DAVE

I think you do. And I intend to prove it.

INT. BEDROOM MED. SHOT

Cha Cha has again rigged the chair on the bed, and she pulls herself up on the louver sill. Trying to keep her balance, she pushes open the window a little. She peers out, and down.

MED. LONG SHOT P.O.V. PATIO

Dave and Silva, talking. At the bushes, not seen by the men, is the Bodyguard listening to the conversation. He has a gun in his hand.

INT. BEDROOM CLOSE SHOT CHA CHA

About to scream for help, she realizes that it would endanger Dave. She quickly steps down from the chair, wonders what she can do to attract Dave's attention. Struck with a thought, she opens her handbag, takes out one of her flyers, and quickly makes a little airplane of it. Stepping onto the bed, and then onto the chair, she pulls herself up to the sill and throws the airplane out and down. The sudden motion throws her off balance. The chair splinters and breaks as she falls onto the bed.

MED. SHOT FOLLOWING FLIGHT OF PAPER AIRPLANE

It is caught in a draft of wind. Tossing about, it turns back to the building and falls on a ledge – immediately above Dave and Silva on the patio.

EXT. PATIO. CLOSE SHOT AIRPLANE

It quivers in a puff of air and then lies still on the ledge. The CAMERA PANS DOWN to Dave and Silva. Silva carries his drink to the table and seats himself. He appears thoughtful, as if digesting the import of Dave's accusation.

DAVE

You said Carlos had left the country on Friday. And yet he was here in this house the next day in a clown's costume. You knew he was here, Silva. You told him to be here.

SILVA

I told you what I thought was the truth, Mr. Thorne. I can well understand your suspicions of me, but I know nothing of what you say. I would suggest you inform the police. They…

Dave begins to be nettled by Silva's calmness.

DAVE (interrupting)

I'll tell the police. When you're in prison, Silva, try hanging yourself from a ceiling pipe without something to climb on. A chair or a table…

Dave leans on the table with both hands, speaks almost directly into Silva's face.

DAVE (continuing)

It would have been more convincing if you had left something for Carlos to jump from.

SILVA (smoothly)

You're quite right, assuming I had anything to do with it. Now, if you don't mind –

Frustrated, Dave straightens, peers at Silva, trying to control himself.

MED. CLOSE SHOT AIRPLANE ON LEDGE

A puff of wind moves the little paper airplane closer to the edge of the ledge. It hesitates, and then tumbles off.

WIDER ANGLE AIRPLANE

The airplane falls to the ground behind Dave. Dave is unaware of it. He starts to move away. His foot squashes the airplane flat.

CLOSE SHOT

The CAMERA ZOOMS DOWN to the flyer, which reads:

"LEARN TO CHA CHA WITH CHA CHA O'BRIEN

HOTEL FONTAINEBLEAU

MIAMI BEACH, FLORIDA"

ANOTHER ANGLE DAVE

turns back to Silva.

> DAVE
>
> When the police question you, you'd better have an answer for this one. Where did Carlos get the pesetas he was peddling?

He turns again, is about to start out, when he spies the paper on the ground. Dave picks it up.

CLOSE SHOT SILVA

reacting. A frown of apprehension crosses his face.

CLOSE SHOT BODYGUARD AT THE BUSHES

He has seen above action and he looks up at the building to the bedroom. He moves closer to the bushes, holding his gun ready.

MED. CLOSE SHOT DAVE AND SILVA

Dave returns to the table where Silva sits, tosses the paper to Silva – draws his gun.

> DAVE
>
> Where is she, Silva?

MED. CLOSE SHOT AT BUSHES

A gun comes between the foliage and aims at Dave. The SOUND of a brittle twig breaking.

ANOTHER ANGLE DAVE

Hearing the sound, Dave swirls. He sees the gun, drops, pushing upwards on the table, overturning it on Silva.

CLOSE SHOT SILVA

falling. His head hits a rock and he is knocked out cold.

MED. SHOT BUSHES

The Houseman barely discernable. He FIRES off at Dave.

ANOTHER ANGLE

Dave is using the table as a shield. The bullet pings into the metal near Dave's head. Dave returns the fire.

ANOTHER ANGLE

The Houseman, clutching at his chest, falls GROANING through the bushes to the ground.

ANOTHER ANGLE

Dave rises, moves to Silva, peers down at him. Abruptly, the Bodyguard jumps him from the rear. Dave's gun falls. There is a knock-down-drag-out fight between the much heavier bodyguard and Dave. Dave looks as if he's going to take a licking.

DISSOLVE TO:

INT. BEDROOM MED. CLOSE SHOT CHA CHA

fashions another paper airplane and slides it through a small crack at the top of the window. It is the old-fashioned high window, and Cha Cha is standing on her toes to reach it. She jumps down, begins to make another airplane. She hears footsteps coming down the hall. Frightened, she dives for the nearest hiding place – crawls under the bed.

CLOSE SHOT CHA CHA

peers to the door, swallows.

MED. SHOT P.O.V. OF THE DOOR

The SOUND of the lock being turned. The door opens, and FEET move across the room toward the bed.

CLOSE SHOT CHA CHA

CHA CHA

You leave alone! Don't touch me! I tell the police everything!

MED. CLOSE SHOT P.O.V.

THE FEET are now at the bed, and a hand reaches under it. Cha Cha scrambles away.

CHA CHA

Go away! I'll scream!

DAVE'S VOICE

It's all right now, Cha Cha. You're safe.

MED. CLOSE SHOT DAVE

showing signs of the fight, tries to smile through a cracked lip. Cha Cha peeks her head from under the bed to make sure she's been hearing right.

CHA CHA

Dave!

She crawls from under the bed, throws her arms around him.

CHA CHA (continuing)

You saved me! You smart man!

Dave holds out her flyer, grins.

DAVE

You smart girl!

CHA CHA

One thing Cha Cha knows for sure. It pays to advertise!

She takes the flyer, gives it a light kiss, then gives Dave a thank you kiss, as we...

DISSOLVE TO:

INT. BOOM BOOM ROOM   MED. CLOSE SHOT

The music combo we saw in the first sequence is beating out a CHA CHA RHYTHM.

MED. CLOSE SHOT CHA CHA

is giving Lieutenant Snedigar a dancing lesson. She marks the time.

CHA CHA

Boom – boom – Cha – Cha – Cha…

Boom – boom – Cha – Cha – Cha …

Snedigar is awkward, flounders. The MUSIC comes to the finish of the number and stops. Snedigar drops his arms. He feels silly.

SNEDIGAR (frustrated)

It's no use. I'll never make it.

CHA CHA

Leave everything to Cha Cha. You doing fine for a cop.

She leads him OFF toward the table.

INT. ENTRANCE OF THE BOOM BOOM ROOM

MED. CLOSE SHOT KEN AND DAVE

They ENTER the Boom Boom Room, look off and grin.

P.O.V. SNEDIGAR

dancing with Cha Cha

FULL SHOT

Ken and Dave ENTER to Snedigar and Cha Cha.

KEN

I've got to be honest, Snedigar – as a dancer you are a great fisherman.

CHA CHA

Don't be such a smart one. He'll learn.

SNEDIGAR (meaningfully to Dave)

I can learn – even from amateurs like you.

(offering hand)

So I made a mistake.

Dave shakes hands with him.

DAVE (lightly)

I remember once, when I made a mistake myself. How's Pepe?

CHA CHA

Look!

She points O.S. The group looks off.

MED. SHOT P.O.V.

Elaina, Ricardo and Pepe are seated at one of the tables. Ricardo is devouring an enormous ice cream sundae. Pepe and Elaina watch him adoringly.

MED. CLOSE SHOT CHA CHA

rises, reaches for Dave's hand.

CHA CHA

Come. Let's go over. We'll make a party for them.

KEN (shakes his head)

Nothing like a happy ending.

The music begins again.

DAVE (taking Cha Cha into his arms)

Now…shall we show the Lieutenant how the dance should really be done?

Dave, gathering her into his arms, dances with her, very expertly.

CLOSE SHOT SNEDIGAR

He rubs his cheek, impressed.

MED. CLOSE SHOT CHA CHA AND DAVE

As they cha-cha their way through a group of dancers, we –

FADE OUT

THE END

From the desk of Daphne Dutton Winfield

August 22, 2021

A lot of folks have wondered whatever became of all of us. It's hard to believe our story began more than sixty years ago. As I write this, I'm looking out from my 15th floor penthouse in Miami Beach at the Surfside houseboat still docked below. It's looking a little worse for wear, but aren't we all?

When the detective agency closed, many of us went in opposite directions. Kenny returned to his native Texas. He settled down, and married his old high school sweetheart. He opened his own private detective agency in Austin, specializing in insurance fraud. Kenny and his wife had two sons. One became an FBI agent. His younger son became a defense attorney, and later a Texas politician. We stayed in touch by phone, and he was Sandy's best man when Sandy and I got married. Sadly, that was the last time we saw each other, although we spoke now and then on the phone until his death.

Dave was a sailor at heart. He moved back to his native British Columbia. After a couple of frustrating years of self-proclaimed "dry dock," he bought a 200-foot sailboat, and began a journey that would eventually take him around the world, and back. In Cambodia, he met a lovely woman. The two fell in love, and married. They had one son who became a travel agent. Dave's travels brought him back to Miami Beach several times. It was always wonderful to see him again. On his last visit, he decided to sell the Surfside houseboat. He bought out Kenny years earlier. It was untouched for many years. I had paid for a caretaker to watch over it during Dave's prolonged absences. I always thought he'd be back to settle in Miami one day. I just couldn't see anyone else owning the houseboat, so I bought it. Dave died in Jamaica. I'm sure he died a happy man doing just what he wanted to do.

Sandy was hit hard when the agency closed. He was from a wealthy family, and he had unlimited monetary assets at his disposal, but he told me he felt lost. Working with the boys on cases, although he was so often distracted by pretty girls, had finally given him some purpose in life. He surrendered to alcohol, and harder drugs, for a time. When he finally hit bottom and accepted his problem with addiction, I helped him find a proper healing facility. I even attended AA meetings with him when he was released. It didn't surprise any of our friends, but it did surprise Sandy and me when we fell in love and got married. We had a good marriage, and had a beautiful daughter who became a successful actress.

Sandy and I pooled our family fortunes and became real estate developers in southern Florida. Miami Beach, though, was always our home. We also created a charitable entity called the "Dutton/Winfield Foundation," benefitting substance abuse, hunger, and homeless causes. Like our dear friends, Kenny and Dave, Sandy died too young. I miss them terribly, but it's better to accept reality than be traumatized by it.

Our daughter lives in Los Angeles, but her two sons, Chris and Kyle, live here in Miami Beach. Kyle is a model. Chris certainly could be, but, bless him, it's too much work for him. I love them dearly. Kenny's beautiful granddaughter, Cassie, lives here, too. She has been living on my old yacht, docked next to the Surfside houseboat. She works in cyber-security. And Dave's grandson, Davey, who inherited his grandfather's love of the sea, settled in Miami Beach, and lives on the houseboat. And, yes, I'm still standing after all these years. All the grandkids are about the same age, and they get along like typical loving and battling siblings. I see their dads in all their eyes. They all help me with various projects. I'm so thankful to have them around me. I don't have just two grandkids, I have four.

Not long ago, Davey discovered several boxes of closed and unresolved cases from the Surfside detectives shoved in a corner of a closet on the houseboat. We've had many happy and sad moments perusing the files. After so long, it feels right, and the kids are getting to know their grandparents as they never knew them. I'm filling them in on details and answering their questions as best as I can remember. They're all quite interested in what we did so long ago, and seem intrigued at the prospects. Who knows? Maybe Surfside 6 will be up and running again.

And that's Hollywood, my dears. The only place where we can write our own endings.

Love, Daphne

Acknowledgements and Thanks

Thank you to Diane McBain who made her archives of interviews, photographs, and scripts available to me during my research for this book. And thank you Diane for your great memories and stories about *Surfside 6*. Thank you to the gracious Daphne Dutton. Who would have thought so many years after watching her on *Surfside 6* that I'd become friends with Ms. Dutton!

Grateful acknowledgement is made to the Beverly Hills Public Library, the Los Angeles Central Library, and the Academy of Motion Picture Arts and Sciences Library, and the wonderful librarians who have always accommodated my many requests. Support your local library – a dependable and free source of truthful information.

Thanks to Ben Ohmart who has been so receptive to my projects. We have an excellent working relationship, and I'm thankful. Special thanks to my long-time manager, Larry Robins, who didn't live to see this book to fruition. He loved the idea behind this project, and was always very encouraging and enthusiastic. He was a decent, honest, and reliable man who is profoundly missed. And another shout out to my long-time editor, Jeri Coates. She is no longer able to work, but I am forever grateful to her for her encouragement and help through the years. I had the best cheerleading team ever!

About the Author

Daphne Dutton with the author.

Michael Gregg Michaud is the author of the critically acclaimed, best-selling, Lambda Book Award nominated *Sal Mineo, A Biography* (Random House/Crown Archetype, 2010). The biography was a pick of the month in *Los Angeles Magazine* and by *Turner Classic Movies*, appeared on Leonard Maltin's recommended holiday list in December 2010, and was later adapted for the screen as a feature film, *Sal*, by James Franco. Michaud is the co-author with actress Diane McBain of *Famous Enough, A Hollywood Memoir* (BearManor Media, 2014). He wrote the *Classic Images* 2017 Best Book of the Year, and two-time 2018 Next Generation Indie Book Award nominated biography *Alan Sues, A Funny Man* (BearManor Media, 2016). He edited and annotated *Mae West Between the Covers* (BearManor Media, 2018), which was nominated for the 2019 Next Generation Indie Book Award for Best Anthology, and wrote *Mae West: Broadcast Muse* (BearManor Media, 2019), which was nominated for the 2021 Next Generation Indie Book Award for Humor/Comedy. Michaud also edited and annotated *Marlene Dietrich Between the Covers* (BearManor Media, 2020). He writes about Hollywood, and has contributed to numerous books about show business and the arts. He updated and edited actress Tippi Hedren's book, *The Cats of Shambala* (Shambala Press, 1992), and contributed to actress Linda Blair's book *Going Vegan* (SHA, Inc., 2001).

Michaud appears in the 2012 *Biography Channel* documentary *Hollywood's Most Notorious Crimes* (Sharp Entertainment) and in the 2019 feature length documentary film *Steven Arnold: Heavenly Bodies*. He is also a contributor to the 2020 *PBS American Masters* feature documentary *Mae West-Dirty Blonde*.

Michaud supports numerous animal rights charitable organizations. He worked with the Roar Foundation for twelve years, and is a founding director of Linda Blair's WorldheartFoundation. He was also a consultant to the Museum of California Design, Inc. for more than a decade, and was a contributing editor of Museum of California Design publications including *The Clay Canvases of Tyrus Wong* (2004), and *California's Designing Women 1896 – 1986* (2013).

Made in the USA
Las Vegas, NV
12 December 2023

82592142R00233